1991

W9-CMN-476

Two Sisters for Social Justice

Two Sisters for Social Justice

A BIOGRAPHY OF
GRACE AND EDITH ABBOTT

LELA B. COSTIN

University of Illinois Press
URBANA AND CHICAGO

Publication of this work was supported in part by a grant from the Campus Research Board, University of Illinois at Urbana-Champaign.

This book is printed on acid-free paper.

LIBRARY OF CONGRESS CATALOGING IN PUBLICATION DATA

Costin, Lela B.
  Two sisters for social justice.

  Bibliography: p.
  Includes index.
    1. Abbott, Grace, 1878–1939.   2. Abbott, Ed-
ith,   1876–1957.   3. Social   reformers—United
States—Biography.   4. Social   workers—United
States—Biography.   5. Feminists—United
States—Biography.   6. Social   justice.   7. United
States. Children's Bureau. I. Title.
HV27.C67   1983   361'.922 [B]   82-21790
ISBN 0-252-01013-2

CONTENTS

PREFACE

AMONG THE MANY PERSONS attracted to Jane Addams's Hull-House in the first decade of the twentieth century were Grace and Edith Abbott. They had grown up in the 1880s and 1890s in a small prairie town on the plains of Nebraska in a distinctive way of life, one that has since vanished from our society. Hull-House and Chicago provided a setting in which the Abbott sisters could find a creative solution to the restrictive status of women, meet their strong personal needs for work and achievement, launch their careers, and contribute to social reform.

Between the Progressive era and the enactment of social reforms in the 1930s, Grace Abbott was a leader among organized women and a highly influential avant-garde public administrator, best remembered for her dynamic direction of the U.S. Children's Bureau during its "glory days." Edith Abbott, in turn, became a towering figure as a "social investigator," a dauntless advocate for the development of a humane system of social welfare, and the chief architect of a pacesetting model of education for the newly developing profession of social work. However, the span of the Abbott sisters' professional interests and social reform activities was far broader than is reflected in such a summary statement of their achievements.

Before their careers ended the Abbott sisters had turned their energies and keen minds to a wide range of social, political, and legal issues—woman suffrage, the rights of women in industry, the evils of child labor, the international traffic in women for purposes of prostitution, the immigrant "problem," tenement housing, delinquency, prison reform, the peace movement, the right of women to safety in child-bearing. The Abbotts played a major role in turning "charity work" into a new profession and, when the Great Depression swept the country, the Abbott sisters became strong advocates of the old and the new poor and used their wide influence to help gain adequate measures of emergency relief and lasting programs of social security.

Although Grace and Edith Abbott began their careers out of Hull-House and felt strong affection for Jane Addams (indeed they became part of the Hull-House inner circle of influence), each was significantly different from her. From a study of women reformers, Jill Conway identified two clearly distinct types of American women, both of whom were feminists and social critics in the late nineteenth and early twentieth centuries. The first type Conway called the "sage" or "prophetess," who saw her role of agent for social change as growing out of the unique qualities with which it was believed the feminine temperament was endowed. The sage or prophetess claimed access to hidden wisdom by virtue of feminine insight and intuition. Jane Addams represented the best example of this model of feminist as Victorian sage to be found in American culture during her active public career from 1889 to 1935.[1]

The Abbott sisters were of the second type of social reformer—the professional expert who took on the role of social engineer and in doing so challenged the prevailing image of woman in a way that the prophetess did not. The woman as expert was a problem-solver who sought an understanding of the entire social system and a specialized competence to deal with it. She made no claim to expertise simply by virtue of being female or possessing special insights common to her sex. Julia Lathrop, a close associate of the Abbott sisters, in responding to comments of a sentimental nature about the role of women, expressed the distinction: "I do not believe that solely because we are women we shall necessarily have any more light or inspiration on the Board [of Charities] than the men have. I have a suspicion that the common dust out of which men and women were made enjoyed no spiritual transmutation when it passed through Adam's rib. . . . I am sure that we do not monopolize any of the finer qualities of human nature. . . . The power of tenderness and sympathy and adaptation are those that belong to choice individuals, and not to man or woman as such."[2]

What Conway found interesting about the two types of women reformers was that "the sage had great resonance for American popular culture." Such women became great public figures, culture heroines, in contrast to the woman as expert, who did not capture the popular imagination in the same way or remain widely known beyond her generation as a model of feminine excellence. A dominant motive in my undertaking this study was to help correct that imbalance.[3] More specifically, I wanted to document the character and the achievements of notable women who have been lost in history. I was concerned that today's students of social welfare often emerge from formal study into a demanding involvement with troubled individuals, families, and communities with little or no awareness that others in the past have confronted equally difficult social problems—often ones remarkably similar to those of today. Without the support of extended experiences that a study of history and of illustrious figures of the past can provide, contemporary social welfare professionals and concerned citizens risk a kind of rootlessness and parochial thinking. At the same time, because this volume is a biography, there are limits to the scope of historical background that can be presented. Nevertheless, the record of the lives of Grace and Edith Abbott illuminates various facets and events of the social history of their times.

Why Edith and Grace Abbott, and not some other early and insufficiently recognized social feminists, became the focus for my study undoubtedly relates to some intriguing impressions about the Abbotts that had lain dormant in my mind. Lines of thought had been seeded by a few articles in the *Social Service Review*, in which persons who had associations with some of the dynamic women at Hull-House recorded their remembrances of Julia Lathrop, Florence Kelley, Sophonisba P. Breckinridge, and the Abbott sisters. Edith Abbott's own sensitive expression of "A Sister's Memories" hinted at lines for inquiry into the Abbott sisters' lives and work that could not be forever ignored. A review of the seminal writings of the Abbott sisters left no doubt about their grasp of social problems and their contributions to rational solutions. In addition, a certain fascination with the personalities of Grace and Edith Abbott seemed still to exist in certain quarters, reflected in an almost endless supply of stories about their activities, behaviors, and eccentricities, told with humor and affection and suggesting a developing legend. It seemed that each of the Abbott sisters had in a curiously impressive and lasting way touched the lives of those who came into the orbit of her active world.

"A Sister's Memories" forecast the possibility of a fuller documentation of the Abbott sisters' childhood and pioneer background, of the influence of their father's pride and faith in the undeveloped western plains, of convictions acquired from a Quaker heritage, and of the lasting influences that stemmed from a lively and intellectually stimulating home. It seemed clearly evident that "our western heritage," a concept that appears repeatedly in Edith Abbott's speeches and writing, went beyond the aggregate of the Abbott sisters' childhood and adolescent experiences. However the particular meaning that attached to that reference remained to be discovered. In addition, "A Sister's Memories" gave no hint of the answer to an intriguing question: What circumstances led Edith and Grace Abbott to leave Nebraska? What decisive events had occurred between the end of their pioneer childhood and their arrival at Hull-House some fifteen years later? Pursuing this line of inquiry led to the unfolding of the Abbott sisters' late adolescent and early adult years during the devastating drought on the Great Plains in the early 1890s. It yielded a chronicle of Grace Abbott's experience as a frontier town school teacher in Broken Bow, Nebraska, the genesis of Edith Abbott's drive toward self-support and financial independence from male relatives, and the origins of the Abbott sisters' intense level of industry throughout their lives.

The Abbott sisters had learned from their mother the lessons of woman suffrage and pacifism. Their experience at Hull-House early in their careers and the associations it offered with others in the women's movement provided the means for testing the convictions acquired in childhood: Edith Abbott in the suffrage demonstrations in England in 1907 and Grace Abbott as a member of the Hull-House delegation to the International Congress of Women for Peace at The Hague in 1915. During all their long careers the Abbott sisters remained particularly concerned for women of the working classes, who, they said, found opportunity very much as their grandmothers had left it. They believed that intellectually the case for equality for women was won in 1869 with John Stuart Mill's *The Subjection of Women*, but that the long, painful triumph over prejudice and indifference had not yet been attained. Consequently, in the early twentieth century Grace and Edith Abbott worked for and defended the need for protective legislation for low-income working women, holding that interests of business and professional women who sought an equal rights amendment in the 1920s and 1930s were not the same as the needs of the wage-earning woman. Like many other social feminists, they believed that without the support of organized labor and a guarantee of fair wages and hours legislation throughout industry the principle of legal equality would not actually bring equality to those women who had the lowest level of skills and the greatest vulnerability to industrial exploitation.

Another important line of inquiry has been to document the influences that stemmed from Edith Abbott's experience during a year of study in England in 1906–7. Therein lay strong and lasting reinforcement to her commitment to the idea of "the scientific spirit applied to human purposes." Unfolding the record of her English experiences showed her struggle to come closer to the individual poor person behind the statistics of her early research and her effort to reconcile two competing and opposing strains of thought about the problems of the unemployed casual laborer—the Fabian position and the doctrine of the Charity Organization Society.

Much has been written about the second great wave of immigration that brought millions of persons to the United States from the countries of southern and eastern Europe. In a national political climate in which the new immigrant bore the brunt of society's antagonisms, the Chicago Immigrants' Protective League was formed in 1907. Grace Abbott became its director, and the immigrant's effective advocate. The record of the Abbott sisters' years is replete with evidence of their liberal position on the "immigration problem." Uncovering this evidence led to an acquaintance with the young immigrant girls from Italy, Poland, and Russia, with the sturdy men from Bulgaria who fell victim to the market for casual laborers, with the foreign-born who encountered injustice in the courts, the immigrants banks, and the private employment offices, and with the other new citizens who enriched the national life of America. Grace Abbott's unusual journey into the Balkan states in 1911 to study "immigration at the source," her rational and compassionate service on a League of Nations committee in behalf of women caught in an international traffic in prostitution, Edith Abbott's presentation of the facts about the relationship between crime and the foreign-born—all this and more deserved more widespread dissemination and appreciation.

Even a tentative reading of some of the writings of Grace and Edith Abbott suggested common goals and a partnership of ideas and action. Yet remaining to be documented were the different personality traits and particular competencies that made possible an enormously effective division of labor. Edith Abbott was the scholar, Grace the sister who took the initiative in translating knowledge into action. Yet the boundaries of their separate roles were flexible and their influence and stimulation reciprocal. Certain leading ideas run throughout the published writing of each sister, sometimes making it appear to be one work. Nor is it always possible to define clearly which sister originated the many ideas and undertakings in their partnership. Both were far ahead of their times in conceptualizing social programs to reduce the hazards of life. Each was assertive, sometimes dominating. Yet each was distinctly different from the other in certain personality characteristics.

Edith Abbott had been the somewhat favored child at home, shyer and more fearful than Grace. A former childhood friend remembered her as "the gentle Edie of our playhouse days."[4] In the course of her long career and her fight to advance social justice, Edith Abbott lost all vestiges of fearfulness and she usually hid the sensitivity in her personality behind a veil of austerity and brusqueness. "The gentle Edie" seemed lost in the long years of the past. Grace Abbott had been the more harum-scarum, daring, and unpredictable child. As an adult she once referred to herself as the family "ugly duckling." It was she who learned how to negotiate herself through official Washington, to interpret unwelcome facts to congressmen and gain support for her proposals, to function effectively within the urbanity common to international government meetings, and, as the U.S. government's chief delegate at such meetings, to preside with sophisticated formality over the social affairs that accompanied such appointments.

A major part of my inquiry has been into the record of Grace Abbott's years with the Children's Bureau (1917–34), that remarkable experiment in national advocacy for children and families. Many issues of social justice were thrust forward for attention, and to them Grace Abbott turned her rare style of public administration. She conceptualized and demonstrated an original method of federal-state collaboration in the administration of the first child-labor law, and of the Sheppard-Towner legislation for maternal and infant welfare. The record also made apparent her remarkable ability to build and maintain coalitions among a diversity of constituencies of organized women. She was a significant leader in an extraordinary early twentieth-century network of feminist reformers, bound together through friendship and commitment to advancing social justice. Within that network, in addition to the Abbott sisters, were Florence Kelley, Julia Lathrop, Josephine Goldmark, Sophonisba Breckinridge, Alice Hamilton, M.D., Carrie Chapman Catt, Rose Schneiderman, Harriet Taylor Upton, Emily Balch, Josephine Roche, Margaret Dreier Robins, Cornelia Pinchot, and others.

An especially intriguing question left from a reading of "A Sister's Memories" was why the record of the 1930 White House Conference on Child Health and Protection was "too full of bitter memories" for Edith Abbott to write about, and what events had produced this aversion. Pursuing an answer led to a richness of understanding on numerous counts. These involved startling findings from Children's Bureau investigations about death of women in childbirth; the careful timing of Julia Lathrop's resignation as chief of the Children's Bureau to facilitate the appointment of Grace Abbott as her successor; the passage of maternity and infancy legislation (the Sheppard-Towner Act); the scurrilous opposition and sexist ridicule of Grace Abbott and other women reformers which persisted on the part of "professional patriots," the Public Health Service, and the American Medical Association; and the underlying essential philosophical differences between the Public Health Service and the founders of the Children's Bureau that intensified the question of the nature and needs of childhood and the proper domain for child health services. An analysis of the White House conference also revealed the human drama that emerged in administering the Sheppard-Towner Act when Grace Abbott and her staff reached out to women all over the country—in the inner cities, the rural ranch lands of the west, and the mountain homes of Appalachia—to women who wanted to learn about their bodies, attain control over their reproductive functions, and find safety in childbirth for themselves and their infants. The antagonism that President Hoover felt for Grace Abbott became understandable with evidence of her growing political influence, and the dramatic confrontations at the White House conference between her constituency of organized women and the male physicians who controlled the conference. Out of it all was left a legacy of gains and losses for the women's movement.

The final years of the Abbott sisters' partnership occurred in the 1930s. The desperate suffering of millions of people brought the Abbotts into the fight for federal intervention into the unprecedented national crisis. A study of their careers during this period led to an examination of the Hoover administration policies and the passionate outrage which Edith Abbott expressed at his continued disclaimer of a national emergency. Her enormous contribution to defining the profession of social work and shaping the development of a public welfare system is documented. So are the reasons for the Abbott sisters' ambivalence toward Harry Hopkins and the Federal Emergency Relief Administration. Their writings, speeches, and congressional testimony show them to have been challenging advocates for a sound and just system of social security and for fair and just legislation for adult and child workers. All this and more filled their years in the 1930s.

During the course of their childhood and early adult years, the Abbott sisters accepted for themselves special goals held for them by their parents, goals not common for girls or young women growing up in the late nineteenth century. As their careers advanced, Grace and Edith Abbott demonstrated qualities often found in creative individuals who became distinguished in their endeavors—an ability to grasp the global nature of problems, to see patterns and connect divergent ideas, a readiness to challenge existing assumptions and to take risks to advance the causes to which they were committed.

In a review of the changing status of women Grace Abbott once wrote: "Some women and some men wonder why change in the position of women has been desired. Repeatedly they ask: 'Why should anyone choose the "strenuous life," seek a part in the struggle to end the injustice and ugliness of our modern life?' They are the lotus-eaters who prefer to live in a gray twilight in which there is neither victory nor defeat. It is impossible for them to understand, that to have had a part in the struggle, to have done what one could, is in itself the reward of effort and the comfort in defeat."[5] These words reflect the guiding force that led Grace and Edith Abbott to persist in their search for social justice.

Acknowledgments are due to many persons who have given me direct help in this project and sustained the kind of interest that has enabled me to complete it.

I wish to express appreciation to the late Mark P. Hale, who, as director of the School of Social Work, University of Illinois, encouraged me to pursue my ideas for study and to apply for financial support. I extend my appreciation as well to the Trustees of the Woods Charitable Fund, and especially to the late Frank H. Woods, for responding to my ideas and plan of investigation and for being willing to provide a generous grant of money that made possible travel to various sources of information. I am also very grateful to the University of Illinois for providing that essential component for research—time—by furnishing "seed money" from the Research Board in the early stages of the research, and by a sabbatical leave, a semester's appointment to the Center for Advanced Study, and a year's leave for Faculty Study in a Second Discipline.

An important consultant was James Brown IV, who listened to my proposal for studying the Abbotts, recognized its worth, and by his interest helped to make financial support possible.

I particularly want to thank Charlotte Abbott for her sensitive generosity in allowing me to enter into her family, which she did by numerous conversations and by giving me access to early family correspondence and other archival materials that were still in her possession. She graciously allowed me ample time to use these before contributing them to the Regenstein Library of the University of Chicago, to be added to the already established Abbott Papers there. From the perspective of her intimate relationship with each of her aunts, she may disagree with some of my interpretations. Yet at no time has she placed obstacles in the path of my independent research.

I wish to thank Edna Hughes, who was on the staff of the Children's Bureau when I began my investigation. From the beginning of the project to its completion, she maintained an enthusiastic interest and was a gold mine of information about means of locating former bureau staff members who could be helpful to me.

Oral histories and less formal interviews with individuals who had worked with and remembered one or both of the Abbott sisters have provided special insights. For these I express appreciation to Martha M. Eliot, M.D., Katharine Lenroot, Dorothy Bradbury, Elisabeth

Shirley Enochs, Ella Oppenheimer, M.D., Judge Fay Bentley, Robert Hutchins, Walter Friedlander, Wilma Walker, Mary Macdonald, Lilian Ripple, Helen Harris Perlman, Bernece K. Simon, Frank Bane, Virgil Hampton, Marguerite Wooley, Ollie Randall, Clara Beyer, Phyllis Osburn, Arlien Johnson, and Ethel Verry.

I also wish to thank colleagues who have maintained an interest in my study, especially Nancy Weinberg and Mary Lee Spence, who read the manuscript in various revisions and who provided valuable insights. I am indebted to Jeannette Ingram, who typed numerous drafts of chapters, always in continuing good humor and with interest in its content.

Most particularly I thank Professor Clarke A. Chambers. From the time I went to the Social Welfare History Archives Center at the University of Minnesota to pursue certain lines of inquiry about the Abbotts, he maintained a continuing professional interest in my study, and the kind of infusion of ideas that enable one to push further the boundaries of inquiry and knowledge.

Two Sisters for Social Justice

> *Grace and I always agreed that our most cherished memo-*
> *ries were those of our prairie childhood. We were born in*
> *one of the oldest Nebraska towns, not far from the once*
> *famous Overland Trail, and this western town and state*
> *were always home. . . . The old frontier, of course, com-*
> *pletely vanished with our childhood—vanished like the*
> *beautiful herd of antelope that my father used to see from*
> *the door of his first law office—antelope grazing on the buf-*
> *falo grass of the plains. But our memories of those early*
> *days always remained very clear.*[1]   — EDITH ABBOTT

CHAPTER I

Western Heritage

Even before the little Nebraska town where Grace and Edith Abbott were to grow up was given a name, the "grand island" between two channels of the Platte River was well known. As the Union Pacific Railroad pursued its westward thrust across the plains, it was the custom of its engineers to name towns along its developing tracks after familiar places on the Oregon Trail, a route that the railroad largely paralleled through Nebraska. The engineers made a plat of the first survey of the little town 157 miles west of Omaha, reserved one block on the north side of the railroad and marked it "Court House Square"; thus they fixed the location of the future county seat of Hall County, and named the town "Grand Island."[2]

Grace and Edith Abbott's father, Othman Ali Abbott, first came to Nebraska in 1867 with his brother, Marcus Riley. When they reached Grand Island, they found that the government had issued an order halting all overland civilian travel westward and corralling emigrants' wagons because of Indian hostilities. Othman Abbott looked over Grand Island and decided to establish his law practice there. His brother homesteaded land on the Wood River.

The Nebraska Territory had become a state in the Union shortly before, but Grand Island was sparsely settled—only a half dozen small houses, a general store, restaurant, billiard hall, and saloon. In all of Hall County there were fewer than one thousand persons.[3] Stage lines were still being used on the old Overland Trail, not more than a mile south of what was to become the location for the Abbott children's first home. In Hall County the Overland Trail was also called "the Oregon Trail," as well as "the Mormon Trail," since all three routes were identical as they followed along the Wood River. By the time Grace and

3

Edith Abbott were born, the great westward movement of wagon trains had stopped on the Overland Trail. But people in Grand Island still recalled the Prairie Schooners—the "Conquering Chariots of the West," and pride reflected in their stories was passed on to listening children.

Othman Abbott was a veteran of the Civil War, like many other Nebraska settlers. Even before he had been finally mustered out of the Ninth Illinois Calvary as a first lieutenant, he had resolved to take up the practice of law. Following his discharge from service he completed two years of reading law with an Illinois attorney and was admitted to the bar in Illinois. Law was to become Othman Abbott's chief interest in life for the next half century.

The Abbott children's mother, Elizabeth Griffin Abbott (or Lizzie as she was always called) was born on January 20, 1845, in a log house in Franklin Township in DeKalb County, Illinois. Her parents, James Griffin and Emeline Gardner Griffin, had emigrated to Illinois in the late 1830s with other members of their close Quaker families from the Genesee Valley in New York. The Gardner and the Griffin families were ardent abolitionists and worked for the Underground Railroad in their part of Illinois.

Throughout her life, Lizzie Abbott believed deeply in the worth of formal learning; education was one of the special goals she held for her daughters. She began college at an early Universalist institution, Lombard College in Galesburg, Illinois. But the loss of her only brother, along with four other Gardner/Griffin sons, in the Civil War had left her mother more alone than ever, so Lizzie transferred to a closer school, Rockford Female Seminary, later named Rockford College. She entered there some eleven years earlier than did Jane Addams, whose Hull-House associates Grace and Edith Abbott were to become.

Upon her graduation in 1868, Lizzie Griffin became a teacher as she had set out to do, and at the time of her marriage in 1873 she was a respected high school principal in West Liberty, Iowa.[4] The courtship of Othman Abbott and Elizabeth Griffin had moved at a considered pace. Othman was now over thirty and Lizzie twenty-eight. Each was independent and not eager to rush into a marriage unless it would provide support for shared beliefs and principles as well as some separation of identity. Somewhat guardedly, Othman Abbott described their courtship in these words: "I had become lonesome in the prairie wilderness of Nebraska. I wrote her occasionally, and in the winter of 1870, she gave me permission to visit, and when I left we were engaged to be married."[5]

4

The marriage (in late winter of 1873) produced four children: Othman A. Jr., September 14, 1874; Edith, September 26, 1876; Grace, November 17, 1878; and Arthur Griffin, March 10, 1880.

Othman Abbott was born on September 19, 1842, in Hatley in the Province of Lower Canada, now Quebec, where his Tory grandparents had moved before the close of the eighteenth century. Later, when some difficulty arose in relation to the British government wanting an oath of allegiance to the Crown, their son Abiel Abbott (Othman's father) and his brothers decided to move their families to the rich and undeveloped land of southern Wisconsin and northern Illinois. Othman Abbott was a boy of about eight years then.

Abiel Abbott bought a farm in Kingston Township, DeKalb County, Illinois, about ten miles from Belvidere. It was here that Othman Abbott grew up and attended the same high school as Elizabeth Griffin. Edith and Grace Abbott were influenced in their own developing attitudes and behavior by the stories their father told them of his boyhood. Highly significant in his memory of his school life were the debating societies held in the schoolhouses at which both young and old discussed a range of important subjects of the day—temperance, the Indian policy of the government, slavery, and homestead laws.

Abiel Abbott, a "Black Republican," supported Lincoln for president as a "step in the right direction." Othman Abbott accepted his father's views on slavery. He told his daughters that their grandfather was an "out and out anti-slavery man. . . . It was a part of his religion, so to speak, that slavery was a national sin, a relic of barbarism." However, unlike the family to which his future daughter-in-law belonged, Abiel Abbott believed William Lloyd Garrison and John Brown were using wrong methods to end slavery and he did not approve of the Underground Railroad.

Concern for the oppressed was part of Lizzie Griffin Abbott's legacy to her daughters. During their childhood there were still many Indians in their part of the plains. Although most of them lived on reservations, they could be seen in Grand Island coming and going through the streets. Lizzie Abbott had earnest convictions about the injustices they had suffered and Grace and Edith listened to her stories about how the Indians had always followed "the sorrowful trail" and how every road they had traveled had been a road of injustice.

One of the clearest teachings in Grace and Edith Abbott's childhood home had to do with women's rights and the message came from both their parents. The Abbott sisters sometimes said as adults that they had been born believing in women's rights, and they were, in fact, very young when Lizzie Abbott would say to them, "I was always a suffragist, and even if you are little girls, you can be suffragists too because it is right and just."

Susan B. Anthony traveled out to Nebraska in 1882 to speak at a large public meeting in Grand Island. She stayed overnight in the Abbott home and since there was no "guest room" in the Abbott's first small house, it was encumbent upon Grace or Edith to share a bed with her (as they were called upon to do for others of their mother's suffrage speakers). On this occasion it was six-year-old Edith who later could claim the honor of having "helped the cause" by sharing her bed with the famous Susan B. Anthony. At the time she was at a loss to appreciate her mother saying to others, "Poor Miss Anthony, that was the best we could do for her."

In the richness of many of their childhood experiences, "play-things" were scarce in Grace and Edith Abbott's childhood. Edith was to recall: "We lived in a world that was made for work, and even as children we knew that our world did not play very much . . . , we understood that there were reasons for taking a serious view of life's responsibilities."

Family vacations were rare on the plains. To children, "vacation" meant a time when school was not in session, and to Edith, who always liked school, sometimes the summer seemed endless. Long after the buffalo had gone from the plains, the young Abbott sisters and brothers used to pick up buffalo horns which could be polished to a rich ebony. They worked industriously with sandpaper, but never could decide what to do with the horns after they were polished. They came to suspect their father of encouraging a harmless occupation during the long hot days of summer.

Some nights in the early fall, after the hot, dry month of August had turned the buffalo grass to brown crisp and the prairie was a vast stretch of dry grassland, the children sat on the porch roof and watched the prairie fire creeping along the horizon, distant and dramatic. Driven by the fierce wind, the fire soon became a line of high, dangerous, and spreading flames. The children had seen the "fire guards" or "fire breaks" around prairie homes—narrow plowed strips that formed a protective boundary around the house and barn. Edith, more vulnerable to childhood fears than Grace, worried (not without reason) that their little town might be caught up in one of the wild conflagrations of fire.

The front porch roof was a refuge on many summer evenings when everything was hot and breathless in the bedrooms under the sloping roof. Grace always wanted to see a hummingbird moth that was supposed to appear at dusk on the porch vines, posing the threat that she

6

would fall off the edge in her excitement. The children might be allowed to take a quilt out—perhaps to sleep for a while where it seemed one could look up and almost feel the sky bright with stars. They would try to find the Big Dipper and the Little Dipper. Sometimes their father would join them and help them find other constellations. As a boy Othman Abbott had been interested in the stars and his father had given him a book with maps of the heavens which he pored over and eventually brought to his Nebraska home.[6] His knowledge and ease in relation to the vastness of the heavens, to peals of thunder and streaks of vivid lightning, impressed his daughters and extended to them a kind of freedom of mind denied to many children.

Othman Jr. was sometimes objectionably bossy with his younger sisters and brother, leading them to band together with Grace as the articulate one in defense of their rights. Once when Edith cried because of some offense of her older brother, her grandmother was almost scornful. "Grace doesn't let him do that to her. What is thee afraid of? Little Grace knows how to fight for her rights."

After Grace Abbott's death, Edith Abbott wrote a touching and nostalgic tribute in which she described Grace as she then remembered her from early childhood:

> There was always infinite variety with Grace as a companion. Her resources were endless—and always unexpected. She was not able to run faster or farther than my brothers, although she often challenged them so vigorously that she made us all expect to see her "come out first." But she always knew how to find the thickest cat-tails and the longest bulrushes in the old prairie slough. She knew where the violets were earliest, largest, and thickest in the spring, where the prairie flowers could be found in the endless monotony of the buffalo grass in the summer, and where the wild grapes grew in a hidden thicket near the river. She was more amusing than the rest of us: full of undreamed-of-possibilities and wonderful stories; could ride or drive the fastest horse; could think of the strangest places to go; could meet with the most unforeseen adventures and come home safe and sound and always with a very humorous and completely disarming account of her wanderings beyond bounds.[7]

There were some other diversions for the "poor benighted prairie children" as Lizzie Abbott fondly called them sometimes. Grace and Edith took considerable interest in the local revival meetings of the fundamentalist sectarian groups. Attending the revivals held in a large tent and observing the rather large-scale conversions and baptisms was something different to do. Lizzie Abbott didn't altogether approve their attending, but their grandmother would say, "What harm in it?" Medicine shows were another occasional form of amusement in the uneventful life of the town. Occasionally a circus came to Grand Island, a one-ring, rather tawdry affair, and the children soon observed that the circus posters were better than the dingy reality. Still, it provided novelty.

Church suppers and ice-cream socials provided diversion as well. Othman and Lizzie Abbott were not church members, but Lizzie Abbott wanted the children to feel they belonged in some way to everything in the community so she participated in church activities to a limited extent. Othman Abbott went to no church; instead he worked regularly in his office on Sunday mornings. He was greatly interested in Darwin's *Origin of Species* and the writings of Robert Ingersoll. He frequently expressed impatience at what he called "cant and hypocrisy" and was outspoken about men whom he claimed went to church because it was "good business" or "good politics."

Lizzie Abbott let her children know that while the Abbott family members were free to hold their own religious views, other people also had that right. She would not tolerate attitudes of superiority or self-righteousness on the part of her children toward those with whom they did not agree. In their small town and for their times, the Abbotts were quite nonconformist. It was taken for granted that the ways of the Abbotts could be expected to be different. Lizzie Griffin Abbott did not mind that. She and her family had faced disapproval in abolition days, but she said, "A great cause was at stake then."

School was important in the childhood lives of Grace and Edith Abbott. The Abbott parents expected their children to enjoy school and succeed there, and it was where other children were to be found. Children usually entered school at age five, but differences between individual children were accepted with few rules. When Othman Jr., the oldest, went proudly off to school, Edith continued to be so unhappy and tearful at being left behind that her mother arranged with one of the teachers to let Edith come at age three on an informal basis. Later Grace, also before age five, made a claim to be allowed to go to school and the same teacher consented.

As an adult Edith Abbott recalled that children at school were attracted to Grace as a leader whether she was twanging a new "Jew's Harp," or being a cowboy with a lariat, or teaching them the engaging words of a new song. Other children were interested in what Grace was going to do next. She could think of new and interesting games. She was different, and not always predictable. Her teachers were often a little bewildered by her honesty and sudden gay remarks that led to a harmless but disconcerting excitement among the children. Once when her remarks had kept the other children laughing, a teacher said, "Grace, I don't know what to do with you. I'll have to talk to your mother." "But mother doesn't know what to do with me, either," Grace answered openly, "and sometimes I don't know what to do with myself."

Grand Island had been first settled by German immigrant farmers and persons of German origin were substantial citizens in the town. The German language was taught in the upper grades of elementary school and, in addition, Lizzie Abbott insisted that all her children should study German even earlier from a teacher she engaged privately.

Music, unlike literature, was not a particular interest of the Abbott parents. But Lizzie Abbott thought perhaps she and her husband had missed something which their children ought to have. So each one was given piano lessons and urged to practice on the Chickering piano in their home. Edith, always eager to please her parents, pursued her task more diligently than the others and acquired considerable skill by the time she was an adolescent.

Without doubt, the greater part of Grace and Edith's early academic education took place at home. Edith Abbott was to write that most of it came from three black walnut bookcases—Lizzie Griffin Abbott's small bookcase-secretary which she had had at Rockford Female Seminary and had brought to Nebraska filled with her favorite books; a large bookcase that had come out with the wedding furniture purchased in Chicago; and another which was brought home from Othman Abbott's first law office.

Book buying and sharing was a family habit carried out often at the sacrifice of other household expenditures. When presents were exchanged, Lizzie Abbott regarded a book, and occasionally a set of books, as clearly the most suitable gift. But these were expected to be the "best books," old and new, and not "just stories to amuse people." Consequently, the Abbotts had few children's books, as such. *The Old Curiosity Shop* was a substitute, as were *Aesop's Fables*, *Arabian Nights*, Andersen's and Grimm's fairy tales, *Robinson Crusoe*, and *Gulliver's Travels*. Grace and Edith shared a great enthusiasm for two books which came to them outside the usual pattern of aquisition—*Toby Tyler or Ten Weeks with a Circus* and *Huckleberry Finn*. A teacher gave *Toby Tyler* to Grace, and their mother bought *Huckleberry Finn* at the door to help a fellow townsman who had had hard luck and was selling books to friends and neighbors. Grace read *Huckleberry Finn* aloud to her grandmother; and while she and Edith yearned for *Tom Sawyer*, it was not until the public library was established years later that they had the longed-for chance to read it.

Othman and Lizzie Abbott subscribed to magazines which included *The Century, North American Review*, and *Harper's Weekly*. The children pored over the cartoons by Thomas Nast in the latter. Edith was to remember that "when *Harper's Weekly* was supporting the Mugwumps and the Democratic ticket, father swore very loudly and said he would stop his subscription; but we children were so full of indignation over our prospective deprivation that father said if *Harper's Weekly* interested the children he guessed it was all right."

Othman Abbott's law practice was another rich source of information and influence in the development of Grace and Edith Abbott. His office during the long course of his practice was impressive to his children with its handsome black walnut furniture and bookcases built all around the walls. Their father discussed his practice at home, and no one could fail to grasp the excitement and satisfaction it held for him. His early practice dealt largely with the work of the United States Land Office, which he and other early settlers had helped bring to Grand Island in 1869.

When Grace and Edith Abbott were adults, they sometimes said that the county courthouse of their childhood had been their substitute for movies. It was built on the edge of the prairie where the town was expected to grow and was surrounded by a wood fence with stiles at the corners to keep cattle out of the open square around it. Their father used to encourage Grace and Edith to come to the courthouse to watch and listen from the balcony when there was part of a case he thought they might understand. During a trial he might look up and wave when his daughters arrived, and some of the other lawyers might wave too or even come up to "speak to the Abbott girls." It was an exciting world and Grace always went home sure she wanted to be a lawyer.

In the same room where Grace and Edith hung over the balcony to watch court proceedings, political meetings were sometimes held. Grace came home one day and reported that she had stayed on at a political meeting in order to hear William Jennings Bryan. She said that he was a great orator; everyone had stood and cheered him after his speech; and, looking at her father, she said that she had wanted to cheer him too. "Nonsense! You have too much sense to be taken in by a windbag, Grace," was her father's not unexpected reply.

The Abbott sisters remembered when the Populist party began to create critical political interest. A staunch Republican, Othman Abbott had little use for what he called "demagogues" or, as he described them, "men who do not want to work themselves and do not want anyone else to work," or "men who haven't the courage to take a dose of hard times and who think someone has always got to make them comfortable and keep them out of debt." Lizzie Abbott thought too that the Populists were misleading the farmers. Othman Abbott went with Grace and Edith to hear William Jennings Bryan when he came through Grand Island in his battle of 1896. On the way home, he tried to explain to his daughters that they "had been listening to a great demagogue." But Edith and Grace were by then nineteen and seventeen years old and had begun to decide that some of their father's theories were wrong and to disagree with some of his strongly held points of view. But they maintained in their later adult life that their father had belonged to the best of the old "rugged individualists"—those with indomitable spirit and ability to go on working when everything seemed hopeless. They said that his influence had helped them become able to take controversial stands during their own careers and yet understand the point of view and the good intentions of many of the men and women who opposed them.

In addition to his expanding law practice Othman Abbott became connected with business enterprises such as the Grand Island Improvement Company, a new city street-car system, and a bank for which he served as a director.[8] On the expectation that his business interests and law practice would continue to expand, he and Lizzie Abbott in 1884 built a large and expensive Victorian home across from the courthouse square.

Changes came in the family composition when Emeline Griffin, the Abbott family's beloved and trusted "counselor-grandmother," died in 1887. Then in 1890 Othman and Lizzie Abbott assumed an additional responsibility when they undertook to finish rearing two children of Othman's deceased sister; a thirteen-year-old girl, Sabre, and a boy of six years, Thomas.

Lizzie Abbott had long wanted Edith and Grace to have more educational opportunities than their small-town schools offered, perhaps by sending them to her own old school, Rockford College, which still had a college preparatory department. But Illinois seemed far away from Nebraska in those days. So she looked into the educational program of an Episcopalian diocesan boarding school in Omaha. The Abbott parents' decision was that Edith should enroll there and that Grace would do the same two years later.

In September, 1889, when she was not quite thirteen years old, Edith in her own words, "was sent away alone," which she felt as a sharp breaking of home ties. She was later to write: "I should not like again to relive any period as completely unhappy as the first lonely months at boarding school. The teachers at the new school were undoubtedly better than those in the schools at home in those days. But I lost the wonderful teaching that we got from mother and father and the educational values of the family group." Homesickness in varying degrees was a part of Edith Abbott's life thereafter.

Edith Abbott's letters to her family, those after she had made the hardest part of her adjustment to being away from home, portray a normal and quite young adolescent girl for her times. The program was demanding and to Grace, in Edith's mind still comfortably situated at home, she complained, "U pity me Grace. Latin is the worst stuff I have ever laid eyes on in my life." There were the all-important close-knit groups among the girls and sometimes school-girl pranks—"putting sedlitz powders in some of the girls' chambers and some prickly stuff out of a pine pillow in Miss Davenport's bed"—which led Edith to write with satisfaction, "Just think of the risks we took." Her letters also show how earnestly she was trying to please her parents and teachers and conceal her anxiety about changes at home and her father's increasing money problems.[9]

Edith completed her high school work at Brownell Hall and graduated in 1893. She won the Gold Scholarship medal and at Commencement played a piano solo, Schumann's *Abendmusik*. Her valedictory essay was on "Some Characteristics of American Literature."[10]

Over Nebraska "hard times" became a reality and the cruel decade of the 1890s was bringing disappointments and sometimes despair. Edith's boarding school fees had become increasingly difficult to pay in view of Othman Abbott's growing business difficulties and the plan to have Grace follow Edith to Brownell Hall had been abandoned. Othman Jr. left the University of Nebraska and found work in a grocery store. Arthur was doing hard summer work in the beet fields.

While the Abbott sisters never lived on a farm, like everyone else in a prairie town they knew that the life of the community depended on the farmer's successes or failures. An ever-present dread was the specter of drought, which seemed to appear in cycles. Over the country as a whole the period of 1886–90 had been marked by good crops and profitable prices for agricultural products. Those favorable conditions had been accompanied by a prosperous growth among manufacturing interests and a steady extension of credit operations by banks. But in 1890 in the vast farmlands of the Midwest the drought-stricken farmers' forewarnings of a complete crop failure were realized.

In Nebraska the crops were little or no better in 1891 and again in 1892 and not sufficient to permit farmers to pay the debts incurred by the ravages of the 1890 crop failure or to meet mortgage payments. The year 1893 was another grievous one of disaster with only half a crop or less. Unresolved apprehensions in the country and abroad about the ability of the United States to maintain the gold standard of payments persisted. The breakdown of the stock market marked the beginning of widespread financial disaster across the whole country. Othman Abbott was far from alone among those who found themselves with a crushing burden of debt contracted during the the relatively flush times of the 1880s. The most prominent feature of the crisis during the summer of 1893 was the long series of bank failures. One bank which failed in Nebraska was the Citizens National Bank of Grand Island, of which Othman Abbott was a director, stockholder, and attorney.[11]

Other business enterprises and institutions of which Othman A. Abbott had been an officer or director "wound up affairs," "discontinued," or "failed." He was obliged to sell a downtown building and then a farm. Almost everything that could be sold was sold. Lizzie Abbott's legacy from her mother and her Aunt Lydia Gardner had been invested in Othman's bank and was lost. The fine home, built when the future looked so bright, was kept simply because it wasn't salable. It was necessary to mortgage the house at a fraction of its original worth, an encumbrance which became an agonizing burden before it was finally paid off. Othman Abbott was deeply hurt by the failure of his bank and felt keenly the grave consequences suffered by his family, old friends, and neighbors. He refused to go into bankruptcy and, at great cost to himself and his family, worked many years to pay off his indebtedness.[12]

Lizzie Abbott was so determined that her daughters should have every possible opportunity for learning and new experience that, in spite of the stringent times, she carried out her early and carefully developed plan to have Edith and Grace visit the World's Fair in Chicago in the summer of 1893 following Edith's graduation from Brownell Hall. As an attorney for the Burlington Railroad, Othman Abbott could get passes for his daughters to travel to Chicago and their mother arranged for them to stay with people she knew. So Grace and Edith embarked on their slight resources for Chicago. "Whether the trip was worth what it cost mother in savings and planning in those hard times I do not know," Edith wrote later, "but it was almost our last reasonably carefree outing for a long period of years." Significantly, what Edith remembered especially from the trip was not the great World's Fair, but that on that site she and Grace had seen for the first time the beginnings of the University of Chicago.

It was of course not possible for Edith to go away to college as she wished. The only way to earn money seemed to be to teach, so, although she was still only sixteen, she obtained a position in the city schools at a salary of $15.00 a month and the responsibility to teach an assortment of classes—algebra, geometry, English, history, and Latin.

Grace and Arthur were still in high school and Grace was in some of Edith's classes. At night Grace helped Edith all she could in her preparation for the next day's teaching. Many of the students were bigger and older than Edith and she felt her responsibilities keenly. In recalling the first days of that job, she expressed some of the awesome demand upon her and the intrusion into her girlhood that it represented by saying that when she began "it took as much energy to keep from crying as it would have to run a steam engine."[13] She found some compensation just being home again and away from the narrow boarding school restrictions. And the evening's work of studying with the specific objective of teaching the material the next day or the next gave her a definite and continuing goal and perhaps eased the burden of the harsh times in contrast to those who had no work and no routine to hold to. Then too, the knowledge that the Abbotts were having a hard time financially and were trying to weather the storm with integrity generated a supportive kind of small-town regard for them.

The beginning of a burning hot summer in 1894 signaled that the drought was not broken and there would be another total crop failure. Despair settled on the Great Plains. Pastures were bare and horses and cattle were without food; they could not be expected to go through another winter. Some farmers shot their stock hogs to keep them from starving. To Edith the dying trees were the most dramatic symbol of the disaster. She found the dry sunbaked earth holding the gaunt frames of dead trees a strangely moving sight. Yet nothing could diminish awareness of the terrible plight of people. Merchants could no longer carry the debts of farmers' families. Men and boys on farms were without shoes as they did their outdoor work, and as the ground grew cold and frozen they had only improvised "gunny sacks" for boots. The entire state was almost in the grip of famine. Farmers could not pay interest on their mortgages nor could land be sold at any price.[14]

Despite the hard times, the Abbott family members carried on. Ottie went into Othman Abbott's law office to begin reading law. Along with her teaching, Edith began taking correspondence courses at the University of Nebraska, and Grace, after graduating from the Grand Island High School in 1895, enrolled in a new small college established in Grand Island by the Baptist church. Arthur began college there two years later. At home there were still family discussions, stimulating arguments, and new political interests.

William Jennings Bryan with his magnetic personality and his political positions that were such anathema to Othman Abbott provided fuel for some of these discussions. By taking on the coinage issues of Populist thinking, Bryan captured the Democratic party in Nebraska in 1894 and did the same thing nationally in 1896. Bryan's nomination for the presidency created great excitement in Nebraska. His defeat of McKinley in Nebraska brought Nebraska's electoral votes into the Democratic column for the first time in history. Also for the first time in the history of Nebraska politics, the Republican party lost all the state offices. Othman Abbott campaigned over Nebraska for "sound money" and against "sixteen to one." Edith studied the economic questions related to money, and the history of bimetallism. She made her first political speech during the 1896 campaign.

The Abbotts, however, including Edith and Grace, never embraced the agrarian myth that was so important in Populist ideology.[15] The Abbott sisters' rejection of Populism was for more reasons than their father's Republican rugged individualism. Although they lived in a small western town, the Abbotts were never intellectually isolated. They read widely and used their keen intelligence to debate progressive issues. They were aware of the effect of the international market on the agrarian crisis in both Europe and America and that the silver issue was an inadequate panacea. They did not regard the cities as alien or unfriendly territory. They were, in fact, attracted by the intellectual complexity of the city. They lived among farmers and knew them well and saw no reason to invest the farmer with special virtues, more able than others to speak for democracy or to carry on the traditions of the old pioneer ideals. They saw and deplored the way cheap land had invited careless cultivation; they had no illusion that the farmer was attached to his land for its own sake and not to the money value of the land. They lived through the hot searing winds, the grasshoppers, and sandstorms and they saw poor farm families whose homes were dugouts, none of which lent support to the agrarian myth. And even though the Abbotts were always proud of their own pioneer background, they were never nativist in their thinking. Edith Abbott's concept of "our western heritage" was different, focusing chiefly on the notion of opportunity, career, and challenge, and qualities that enabled people on the Great Plains to tolerate hardship, to persevere, and to overcome great difficulties.

Nevertheless, the Populist movement was being debated during the years when the Abbott sisters' childhood had come to an end and sober responsibilities were placed upon them. They could respond positively to the current of protest and criticism, to the Populist attempts to do something about the problems created by industrialism, to the insistence that the federal government had some responsibility for the common weal. The Populist debate reinforced their interest in the oppressed and in political and economic reform and extended the groundwork for their eventual identification with Progressivism when it appropriated many of the Populist issues in modified form.

By the summer of 1897, there were some cheering signs that the terrible depression was passing. Rains came again to Nebraska, agricultural prices began to improve, and unemployment declined. The period of intense stress seemed to be ending. However, the Abbotts were far from recovered financially, and Othman Abbott was still struggling to lift himself from his burden of debt. They were that summer a household of eight, mostly adults: the two parents; Ottie, now twenty-two; Edith, twenty; Grace, eighteen; Arthur, seventeen; and two cousins, Sabre, nineteen; and Tommy, thirteen. That year Edith began attending summer sessions at the University of Nebraska in Lincoln and with her correspondence credits accumulating a substantial part of a college program. Without Edith's companionship it was a lonely summer for Grace. She pursued her study of Virgil, tutored two young children each afternoon in reading and arithmetic, and took on many of the arduous cleaning and cooking tasks in the busy Abbott home.

For the most part life that summer was unexciting and seemed to hold no inspiring purpose. Grace and Edith continued on their path of education but not without romantic fantasies of a different life. Communication in letters from family members to Edith tended to be a recital of events, with underlying feelings glossed over, only occasionally breaking through, as when Othman Abbott had to ask his daughter for the money she had been saving to go full-time to college. It was Lizzie Abbott who wrote: "My dear Edith, I want you or rather Papa does to let him have your money for a little while . . . I hope he will be able to put back a good deal of it in the bank for you before you come home. My dear it is very hard for me to write this to you but there seems no other way. . . . I have shed some tears over this and papa told me how much he hated to ask you for money. He has said you were having the house painted because he said he owed and people would think he ought to pay before he painted the house. . . . You will always know Edith how much you have done for us all."[16]

For all the ways in which Edith and Grace Abbott were alike, each was very different from the other. Their individual traits had been apparent when they were children. Edith was highly sensitive and somewhat fearful; she was anxious for parental approval, tended to cling to home, and loved learning and scholarship. Books were a treasure to her. Grace in turn was more adventuresome and self-confident, more able to question and oppose her parents. Learning to her was highly important but she did not invest it with the "preciousness" that Edith was inclined to; to Grace, learning was to find an answer on which to act.

A study of short stories which each wrote in the long years of the depression of the 1890s and as the sober pace of life stretched into the early 1900s illustrates their different temperaments. Grace's short stories were portrayals of dramatic behaviors, romantic actions, and bold characters. Edith's stories, with their literary phrases of beauty and introspective qualities, were more artistic, often in a somber mood. The themes were frequently of nature and prairie hardships, the virtues of hard work, sacrifice, and endurance. The characters were pioneer women, Indian women, worthy sons, or young unhappy children.[17]

In June of 1898 Grace Abbott completed her college work and obtained a teaching position in the high school of Broken Bow, the county seat of Custer County. Its population was only a little over a thousand persons. There were two brick schoolhouses and six churches.[18]

In the small towns of the Midwest of those times, teachers had few rights and many duties. They were expected to provide a decorous model of behavior, avoid frivolous activities such as dancing, take an active interest in all of the affairs of the town but not introduce alien influences, maintain strict discipline in the classrooms, work uncomplainingly for long hours, put up with less than comfortable living arrangements, and attend church regularly. In addition, their "contract" was tenuous; parents felt free to complain, board members exercised surveillance over teachers, and it was not uncommon for teachers to be dismissed within the school year.

When Grace Abbott arrived in Broken Bow teaching conditions were not exceptional. She was very anxious to succeed. She liked teaching and her ability and drive were readily apparent. The very small town with its constraints was never satisfying to Grace Abbott, however. Although the people were friendly and interested in her, she missed others to talk to about the concerns that were most important to her. There were few amenities, no lyceum series or public library, only a small WCTU reading room. Living styles were far plainer than in Grand Island. She fulfilled the requirement of church attendance for the most part with a detached observation but as the year went on it became irksome. She missed her home with its warmth and challenging discussions and books and magazines to read. But she threw herself into her teaching with enthusiasm and an intent to excel. She taught seven classes a day—plane and solid geometry, algebra, Caesar, German, rhetoric, and English literature. She handled make-up classes after school and even agreed to instruct two of her fellow teachers in German. Occasionally her frustration with her situation showed in letters home, as when she wrote that she had not even heard how the election went: "Out here on Piety Hill we never talk of such things."[19]

Grace Abbott's determination to do well at her job, show that she could succeed under difficult circumstances, as Edith had, and save some money tempered her impatience with the arbitrary restrictions of the school board. But she was restive for more satisfying experiences and ready to try to find a route to them by enrolling for some graduate work at the University of Nebraska the next summer. She felt she had been too long in her parents' home and needed experiences away; these were not to come about for another seven years however.

In February Grace had contracted a severe cold, which hung on and reduced her strength. Then Broken Bow was plagued by a typhoid epidemic. Grace contracted the disease and was very seriously ill. Her mother came to Broken Bow to help care for her in the makeshift hospital to which she had been moved. Lizzie Abbott's letters to her husband and family at home convey the acute anxiety with which the family lived until Grace began slowly to improve.[20] Othman Abbott then went to Broken Bow to arrange to bring Grace home for convalescence.

Grace apparently felt a strong sense of failure at being required to give up her teaching and go home. Many years later when Grace Abbott was chief of the Children's Bureau a woman who had taught with her at Broken Bow heard her speak on the radio and wrote her. Grace replied, "Of course I remember you and the old days in Broken Bow. I can never forget it for it was my first job and my first work away from home, and I felt when I came down with typhoid fever that spring as though I had failed completely and utterly."[21]

Grace convalesced at home all spring and summer. By fall she was strong enough to work again. Edith took her small savings and with a loan from the bank enrolled at the University of Nebraska to complete her college work. Grace was hired in her place in the Grand Island High School.

At the University of Nebraska Edith Abbott was singled out by her instructors for personal attention and sometimes was invited to their homes where she met interesting people. It was in such ways that she came to know Willa Cather, who had graduated several years earlier. Louise Pound, a sister of Roscoe Pound, had begun to take an interest in Edith during the summer sessions when Edith was her English student.[22]

Edith Abbott wrote the senior class play (for the times, a daring spoof of faculty) and she was admitted to Phi Beta Kappa. Her friends encouraged her to wear the key. Reflecting the distaste of ostentation which was to become so characteristic of her, she wrote Grace: "I don't like to swell around with my PBK pin but this week I wore it and the comments elicited were worthwhile . . . I hated it the first time."[23]

Not only was Edith an excellent student, she was physically attractive—tall and slender with crowns of gold blonde hair, brown eyes, and fine regular features. Her expression was usually serious, but her smile when it came lighted her face and made the observer conscious of her beauty. The latter part of her senior year was marked by the rituals of graduation and by the national convention of Delta Gamma sorority, which Edith's chapter hosted.[24] The convention enabled her to meet college women from other parts of the country and to play an active role in the ceremonies, rituals, and business meetings. Edith Abbott had never particularly enjoyed social events, and often dreaded them, nor did she ever again welcome them throughout the rest of her life. But her letters to Grace written in her last days of college reflect a light-heartedness and youthful pleasure that had not shown itself since she left Brownell Hall and accepted the duty that the painful 1890s thrust upon her.

Edith obtained a teaching position in the Lincoln schools in the fall of 1901 and stayed there two years. In the interval between terms she attended summer school at the University of Chicago where she attracted the interest of professors, including Thorstein Veblen, all of whom recognized her potentiality and encouraged her to continue.[25] When they offered her as inducement the likelihood of a small fellowship, she replied that she would have to return to Nebraska and discuss it with her father, which she did. Othman Abbott, although not yet free of debt, stood firm in his support of his daughter's ambition and said that she must go and if necessary he would find a way to borrow the money to make it possible. So in the fall of 1903 Edith left Nebraska for full-time study at the University of Chicago.

Grace, in the meantime, continued in the routine of teaching and living at home except for the academic year 1902–3 when she did graduate work at the University of Nebraska. Little information survives about her experiences that year (which was Edith's last year of teaching in the Lincoln public schools). She took courses in history and philosophy and a law course taught by Roscoe Pound. She joined the same sorority as Edith had. One of her friends was Ruth Bryan, daughter of William Jennings Bryan. Their friendship was still alive during the Washington years when Grace was chief of the Children's Bureau and Ruth was a congresswoman from Florida. Grace Abbott once told about some of their Nebraska experiences together in amateur theatricals. In one play Ruth Bryan was the leading lady and Grace Abbott was the English butler. It had been difficult to assemble a wardrobe but

Grace finally made her appearance arrayed in some clothing borrowed from the "Great Commoner" himself. The coat and hat, though many times too big for her, evoked great applause.[26]

In her Grand Island teaching post Grace Abbott made vigorous demands upon students which she tempered with enthusiasm and true interest in them. She met the additional expectations for extracurricular activities—coaching a girls' basketball team and directing plays. She took an interest in local and state political questions and helped her mother in her civic endeavors. During this period Lizzie Abbott experienced many days of fatigue and depression in the aftermath of the crisis and hard years of struggle which the 1890s had brought. Grace recognized her mother's condition and gave her attention and support. In addition, by signing his note she gave her brother Arthur financial backing for a loan to attend law school at the University of Chicago between 1905 and 1907.[27]

But these years of teaching in Grand Island and living at home were difficult in many ways for Grace Abbott. She had recognized her need for larger experiences even while she was in Broken Bow, and the additional years at home did not begin to use fully her potentiality for growth and leadership. Her future was by no means clear and she seemed to be marking time. As a young, attractive, and dynamic woman in an approved vocation, undoubtedly she could have married while she lived in Grand Island. She was for her times remarkably free of constraints in relation to men. Even though she was more intelligent than many, she had an easy ability to talk to men and to enjoy her association with them. She once told her niece about a vacation she spent in Colorado in the summer of 1904 with a group of young men and women of her own age, acquaintances from her summer term at the University of Nebraska perhaps. They went without the usual chaperons and camped at the foot of Pike's Peak. A photograph which survives shows Grace with two other women and a man, each one vital and attractive, posing to acclaim their victory in reaching the top of Pike's Peak.[28]

Yet Grace speculated about the role of women by writing in her notebook: "What occupations are now sanctioned for a married woman—art? music? Those that keep her in the home. Many that take her out of the home so long as she doesn't make any money at them."[29] In 1906 Grace attended summer school at the University of Chicago and then returned to Grand Island to teach another year before leaving for Chicago and full-time study.

The character that Grace and Edith evidenced came in no small measure from their parents. In the finest sense of the term, as one observer noted, the senior Abbotts were "aristocrats of the prairie."[30] During the long years of their life together, Othman and Elizabeth Griffin Abbott held in common basic values that never wavered. They believed in the rights of the individual—to think one's own thoughts, speak one's own mind, to act independently and in nonconforming ways as long as the rights of others were not abridged or the sensibilities of others unnecessarily flaunted. They were each unequivocally opposed to slavery when this was a perilously divisive issue in this country. They shared a conviction that not only men but women had rights and these should be equal, that the potential capabilities of women were as important as were men's. They believed that the human mind could solve great problems and if properly trained could enhance life for all people and that men and women had a responsibility to nurture and use that highest gift. Neither was religious in the sense of being a "believer," and they eschewed formal religious organizations. But each was loving, humanitarian, compassionate to those who had met misfortune, and willing to share, whether the need be money, their home, or their counsel.

Against the steady background of these shared values, Othman and Lizzie Abbott demonstrated a willingness to differ with each other on how these values were to be acted on from day to day. They never agreed upon the question of prohibition as a means of regulating the sale and use of liquor and differed openly on it before their children. To each the Civil War had been necessary, but each drew from the experience different views about the role and responsibility of the South and instructed their children according to their separate conclusions. Thoughtful discussion and lively debate were a part of each day in the Abbott family. Argumentiveness was not seen as a negative characteristic; indeed, it was encouraged and positively reinforced, and in the process the parents showed their children how it was possible to differ in debate and still share common values and goals. As Edith Abbott observed, "There was never anything small or mean about either mother or father."

Each of the Abbott parents played a highly significant role in the development of the two sisters, Grace and Edith. They identified with their mother's concern for the oppressed, with her interest in progressive ideas and social reform, her pacifist beliefs, and her commitment to equal rights for women. Her capacity for practical compromise and strategic conciliation was certainly not lost on them. Lizzie Abbott was as determined in relation to her beliefs as was her husband. She held special goals for her daughters and clearly intended to offer them opportunities that in their times were not commonly provided for the girls of a family.

Othman Abbott, in turn, demonstrated for his daughters a vigor and love of new experiences, a fearlessness in the face of challenge, a readiness to express his feelings freely and openly while still retaining a capacity for detached observation. From his sharing of his legal experiences, his daughters learned much about reasoned and orderly thinking, about action strategies and the nature of planned attack.

The relationship between their parents maintained a balance and reliability in the Abbott sisters' lively and intellectually stimulating environment. The Abbott family life was not always easy. In a home where "speaking out" was encouraged, tensions were sometimes high. Nevertheless, in their home, Othman and Lizzie Abbott were equals. They treated each other with love and respect, even when they openly differed with each other. They saw their children as individuals and accorded them respect as well, their daughters no less than their sons. Grace and Edith Abbott were given freedom and encouragement to be themselves, to go freely about their small town, to question, to think, to express their opinions openly at home and away from home, and to attempt any worthy endeavor even against adversities.

By the time Edith and then Grace Abbott left Nebraska for new opportunities in Chicago, each in all likelihood was intent on pursuing a career rather than marriage, a decision that was a product of parental influences, societal norms and conditions that circumscribed women's choices of life roles, and unanticipated effects of the economic hardships of the 1890s.

The kinds of behaviors their parents reinforced must have influenced Grace and Edith Abbott to remain single. Those favored behaviors were ones not usually considered important among families where a primary aim was for the daughters to marry—qualities such as assertiveness, intelligent inquiry, initiative, independence, and honest outspokenness. For even though they were expected by both parents to look good, to treat others with courtesy and respect, and, as they grew up, "to dress according to their position," in their childhood and adolescence domestic tasks and the feminine niceties such as flirting or standing back to permit boys to appear superior were not particularly valued.

Lizzie Abbott wanted more than she had had for her daughters—perhaps wanted opportunities for them to achieve what she had been denied by her times and by marriage, even by a happy and successful marriage. And as young adults, faced with the new demands of the hard times of the 1890s, Edith and Grace Abbott drew closer to their mother, partly out of a responsibility to give her emotional support and partly out of an early identification with her. Even in those hard times

Lizzie Abbott maintained her civic interest and activities at a level impressive and unusual for her day and she consistently provided a model for her own generation of women.[31]

If either Grace and Edith Abbott were to marry, then, each must have realized that she would have to find a man who would respect her intelligence and competency, her potentiality, and her desire and need for achievement in her own right. In the small towns and cities of the Great Plains, as elsewhere in the society of the early 1900s, these qualities were not representative of the expectations held by most men who were eligible for marriage. And if such a man were found, marriage in times when reliable methods of contraception were not easily available was likely to result in some unplanned number of children. Furthermore, a woman faced formidable barriers in combining marriage and child-rearing with any kind of career, barriers that most often were defeating. Even as late as the third and fourth decades of the twentieth century, employed married women in public jobs were expected in slow economic times to resign their positions to make way for an unemployed man; many women chose to keep their marriages secret rather than risk loss of their occupations.

Additional and special conditions restricted Edith Abbott's early male-female experiences and had they been different she might have thought more openly of marriage. At less than seventeen years of age, just out of a girls' high school, she began to teach students her own age and older; thus she was denied the normal opportunities for late adolescent male-female friendships and dating patterns. She had always been more shy than Grace, more immersed in achieving academic superiority at a level that for many boys and young men was restraining. With the beginning of her public school teaching, her days and evenings were filled with demanding work and she felt a heavy and very adult responsibility to succeed, to become independent, and to help her parents. During those important young years she had little time or energy for the idea of marriage—it was a choice she could hardly afford to contemplate.

Grace Abbott, because she enjoyed men in a way Edith did not, may have had greater conflict about not marrying during her Grand Island days. But her desire for leadership and for contributing to society was very strong, so she made her choice. If she had once wanted marriage, it was not a disappointment she carried through life. In her middle age, at a time when one of her staff members faced difficulties in her work because of her husband's lack of full acceptance of her career, Grace could say naturally and convincingly to another colleague that she was glad she hadn't married, faced as she was with the exacting demands and responsibilities of her position of leadership among women all over the country.

When they first went to Chicago, both Edith and Grace Abbott wanted to do something important and useful. But what that was to be would depend upon circumstances and opportunities yet to be presented to them. Even with their heritage of values in relation to women's rights, concern for the oppressed, and interest in progressive ideas, it is very unlikely that they then conceived of their future as "social investigators" or "reformers." They were still Republican-oriented in politics; they had been reared in a staunchly Republican home and had scarcely been outside their Republican-controlled state. No evidence indicates that either yet had any particular awareness of or attraction to Jane Addams and Hull-House.

For Edith Abbott it was a straightforward love of learning and an overwhelming need for greater knowledge that propelled her to the University of Chicago. For Grace Abbott it was boredom and awareness of her own potentiality and the lack of opportunity at home. Years later when she was being considered for appointment to the president's cabinet, she answered a newspaper reporter's questions thus: "I always was happy in Nebraska, but there isn't much opportunity for a girl in a small city, and it seemed inevitable that I leave. A boy can come home from college, begin the practice of his profession, and advance rapidly in his home town. But when a girl comes back, what can she do? She can teach, but after she's done that she finds that she has reached the top, that there is nothing more for her."[32]

Much more awaited each of the Abbott sisters as they entered the new and exciting world of the University of Chicago and Hull-House. But much, too, had come from the childhood years on the prairie and the economic troubles of their adolescence. Out of those demanding times Grace and Edith Abbott gradually crystallized the elements of what Edith Abbott always after referred to as "our western heritage," a concept which appears over and over in her writing and speeches throughout her long career. To Edith Abbott, "our western heritage" meant tenacity when one believes in a cause, a sense of fair play, steadfastness of purpose, a belief in the strenuous life, and the pioneers' genius for work. It meant fortitude, sturdiness of conviction, and a great courage that inspired not only the Abbott sisters but many others whose lives they touched during the course of their careers.

Although the Abbott sisters lived most of their adult lives in Chicago and the nation's capital, and their careers took them to cities all over the country and into Europe, Grace and Edith Abbott were usually re-

ferred to as "the Abbott sisters of Nebraska." Prairie life was distinctive; its impact was profound. Another Nebraska woman of the same
generation described it this way: "We were talking about what it is like
to spend one's childhood in little towns like these, buried in wheat and
corn, under stimulating extremes of climate; burning summers when
the world lies green and billowy beneath a brilliant sky, when one is
fairly stifled in vegetation, in the colour and smell of strong weeds and
heavy harvests; blustery winters with little snow, when the whole
country is stripped bare and grey as sheet-iron. We agreed that no one
who has not grown up in a little prairie town could know anything
about it. It was a kind of freemasonry, we said."[33]

Today we are faced with the pre-eminent fact that if civilization is to survive we must cultivate the science of human relationships, the ability of all people, of all kinds, to live together and work together, in the same world, at peace.[1]

— FRANKLIN D. ROOSEVELT

CHAPTER 2

The Scientific Spirit and Human Purposes

EDITH ABBOTT was the first of the sisters to seek wider opportunity outside of Nebraska. She began doctoral study in economics at the University of Chicago in the fall of 1903, leading her into new experiences and relationships in this country and in England which gave a lasting shape to the course of her career. The most significant influences came from two sources: Sophonisba P. Breckinridge, who became her long-time academic colleague and intimate friend; and Beatrice and Sidney Webb, who inspired her to master the craft of a social investigator and the facts and issues in the long debate about poor-law reform. The Breckinridge and Webb influences, while very different in surface ways, each demonstrated for Edith Abbott the essence of the scientific spirit applied to human purposes, a principle upon which she built her long career.

Edith Abbott did not make a random choice of an institution for her graduate study. She had seen the beginning of the great midwestern university when she was only sixteen, before the long years of hardship, sacrifice, and deferred expectations had closed in around her. She had not forgotten it. Then, too, the distance between Nebraska and Chicago seemed endurable with the sweeping tracks of the Union Pacific Railroad stretching between. A factor not least important to the Abbott sisters: the University of Chicago was a coeducational institution.

The decade from 1890 to 1900 had brought an unprecedented growth in the number of coeducational colleges and universitites in the central and western states. One which moved swiftly into the ranks of the foremost educational institutions was the University of Chicago. The Abbott sisters saw coeducation as part of the western heritage and promise which had captured their childhood loyalties and ideals. It was linked for them to the democratic goal of offering equal educational opportunity so far as possible to every individual. In addition, they distrusted the quality of instruction in women's colleges compared to that given in men's colleges.

However, even in coeducational universitites the distribution of women and men in curricula and in courses was still sex-bound. Women had substantially appropriated English literature classes and had largely invaded history, the modern languages, and classical studies. But men had things almost to themselves in mathematics, geology, and biology, as well as in philosophy and social sciences, which furnished the transition to the exact sciences and to law and medicine. Except for courses prescribed for every academic degree, the distribution of women was closely similar to that found in women's colleges.[2]

By registering almost exclusively in courses in economics, political science, and law, Edith Abbott, and Grace Abbott when she followed to the University of Chicago, invaded the male precincts, as Grace had done earlier at the University of Nebraska when she enrolled in a law course taught by Roscoe Pound. Neither sister was yet directly identified with social work and each ignored the opportunity to study subjects that were the traditional concern of social workers. They apparently did not attend lecture courses designed as preparation for "philanthropy and social work" given by future co-workers Graham Taylor and Jane Addams in the Extension division.[3]

Among the graduate courses in which each of the Abbott sisters did enroll were ones taught by Sophonisba P. Breckinridge, and thus began a significant personal and professional association that lasted the rest of their lives. This friendship and collegial relationship was especially significant in the careers of Edith Abbott and Sophonisba Breckinridge ("Nisba" to her close friends and associates). Although they were vastly different in personal characteristics, for the next four decades they worked so closely together that it is often impossible to separate their particular contributions in their joint endeavors of social investigation and public policy analysis. Nisba Breckinridge played a significant part as well in helping to launch Grace Abbott's career in Chicago.

When Edith Abbott first came to the University of Chicago, Nisba Breckinridge was an assistant professor in Marian Talbot's Department of Household Administration. Breckinridge had impressive credentials: she had earned a doctorate in political science and economics, and another in jurisprudence, in each instance the first woman at the University of Chicago to do so. She later recalled her early acquaintance with

Edith Abbott, who was among the students who took courses on the legal and economic position of women: "I said something about the way in which women had carried the work of the world while men were doing the fighting and hunting. 'Do you mean to say?' she asked. 'I thought I did,' I replied. 'I must look into that,' she replied. And her 'looking into that' resulted in her [book] Women in Industry."[4]

Upon receiving her doctorate in economics in 1905,[5] Edith Abbott accepted a two-part job in Boston—a Women's Trade Union League secretaryship and a research assignment by the American Economic Association. Nisba Breckinridge, a charter member of the Chicago Women's Trade Union League, had been influential in securing the position for Edith and accompanied her to Boston early in September to complete the negotiations. Nisba was particularly interested in seeing that Carroll D. Wright, economist and statistician and longtime U.S. commissioner of labor, allowed Edith to take on a substantial and significant piece of research.[6]

The Women's Trade Union League had been organized in the fall of 1903 during the American Federation of Labor convention in Boston. The development of the new organization has been viewed as an "example of the pro-labor attitude of . . . [settlement house] social workers, and illustrates the cooperation that existed between some reformers and some labor leaders in the progressive era."[7] The basic aim was to help secure improved conditions of work for women—shorter hours, just pay, and better working conditions—by organizing women wage earners into trade unions. At the beginning of the twentieth century there were few women's trade unions, and the working woman was usually a kind of perpetual apprentice, barely tolerated by most men in the labor movement. To give service to the cause of women, the new league undertook to bring together not only women actively working in the trades but certain others of the leisure or professional class—those suffragists who saw the success of women in the industrial struggle tied to success in getting the vote. The new organization fitted into the women's movement as an integral part; the league served as a women's movement within the labor movement and as labor's advocate within the women's movement. Mary Morton Kehew, with whom Edith Abbott was to work, was a longtime friend of the Boston labor movement and had been named the new organization's first president.[8]

Edith Abbott decided to live at Dennison House, a social settlement long active in the labor movement, and as soon as she was settled, she wrote her sister Grace about Boston, her new duties, and her apprehensions. The latter were in two directions: that labor union leaders would find her too conservative, and at the same time that her father would worry that she was departing too far from his political beliefs.

Dear Sister,

It was good to get Mamma's letters and yours. Tell the boys to write and tell Papa I haven't gone over to the Trade Unionists in any such way that he can forget he has a "tall girl" though she is abroad in "Bosting town". . . .
Definitely my work for the League is something like this—Mrs. Kehew wants the League (which means the sec'y) to be *the* authority on labor questions and conditions in Boston particularly as regards women's work. I am expected to meet labor committees, arrange meetings for those interested in the work, be ready to speak at women's clubs and so forth, help organize women in different trades, investigate sanitary conditions or anything that comes along in that line. I am afraid I am too conservative for the Labor people. I shall get on alright [sic] with Mrs. Kehew and the League but I am very much afraid of the other side of it. . . . I feel as if I were walking on eggs. . . . However I won't do them any harm and shall get a lot of valuable information out of it.[9]

As a part of an industrial history of the United States which the American Economic Association and Carroll Wright were undertaking with funds from the Carnegie Institution, Edith Abbott was given responsibility for the parts on "wages and prices" and "women's work." By Janaury 1906, Edith's competence as a researcher had so impressed persons at the Carnegie Institution that she was offered a full-time position at $100 a month, which she accepted. It gave her an opportunity to resume an investigation of the employment of women as a problem in economic history, which she had become interested in during her first class with Nisba Breckinridge. At that time they had published jointly an analysis of census statistics dealing with the employment of women that showed that the presence of women in mills and factories was by no means a new phenomenon, leading Edith to want to discover just how long and to what extent women had been an industrial factor of importance.[10]

Edith Abbott's position with the Carnegie Institution brought her into contact with other researchers, such as Frances Gardiner Davenport of the Department of Historical Research at the Carnegie Institution, who gave Edith collegial support and reassurance that her subject was worthy of investigation as a neglected chapter in economic history and the status of women. The new position also extended Edith Abbott's experiences into other cities with contrasting problems and people and into the pleasures of exploring a new environment. She derived sweet pleasure from the museums where she saw originals of many pictures she had learned to know from the books of art in her childhood home.[11] She was excited by New York, where she did some preliminary canvassing of sources of data about the cigar factories and garment industry. She wrote Grace that New York was "so big and dazzling [with] its rush and hustle and skyscrapers [that] make me think of Chicago as queer little Boston never did." And she said, "I am getting young again since I withdrew from the Trade Union firing line." In New York she stayed at College Settlement, where her interest was captured by the tenements so very closely built and higher than in Boston, and the Jewish quarter with its "Yiddish signs on all sides and the streets filled all hours of the day and night and the flickering lights from the push cart porches making the whole thing like a show on the stage." But the position she was to take later in relation to the development of social work on the eastern seaboard was forecast when she wrote of "the weak sentimentality" of many of the eastern settlement people, and, as she was leaving for Washington, how she looked forward to "a good tonic" from Frances Davenport's "intellectual robustness" and some rousing political discussions with Joy Webster, a college friend from Lincoln who was living in Washington.[12]

Edith Abbott was invigorated by living and working in the nation's capital. She marveled at the neatness and cleanliness of the city and the springtime's beautiful blossoming, so unlike what she was used to in Nebraska or Chicago. However most of Edith's waking hours (as was to be true for the rest of her life) were spent in pursuing the goals she set for herself in her work. Before the year was out she had completed the major part of the research for her book, *Women in Industry*, part of which was published as a series of articles beginning in 1906 in the *Journal of Political Economy*.[13]

Women in Industry, when completed, was an authoritative historical account of the facts about the presence of women in American industry. Edith had investigated the women agriculturists, tavern keepers, shopkeepers, "spinsters," and weavers in the colonial period; the transition to a modern factory system and the employment of women in the early "manufactories" and in the first cotton mills; the differences in industrial conditions in America and England; the creation of new work when the scarcity and high costs of male labor were met by employing women and children and using machinery specially adapted to their use. She had analyzed official documents of industries employing women as well as census statistics. And she had traced the conditions under which women were employed and the problems of women's wages in selected industries—the cotton industry in the early mill towns, the manufacture of boots and shoes, cigar making, the clothing industry, and printing. She had also won a competition for a Foreign Fellowship of the Association of Collegiate Alumnae, which with some Carnegie funds would take her to England for a year.

By the fall of 1906 Edith Abbott, in London, wrote enthusiastically: "There's no doubt about this being the most fascinating place in the world. *Everything* is interesting."[14] She lived on Torrington Square near the British Museum and off and on stayed at St. Hilda's Settlement in Bethnal Green. Her immediate attention was engaged in the tasks of planning a course of advanced study in statistics, mathematics, economics, history, public finance, municipal government, and sociology from the curricula of the London School of Economics and Political Science.[15]

"Everything" that was interesting included stimulating interactions with highly competent and sometimes noted persons, intensified exposure to socialist thought, the practicalities of London's municipal politics, and the ferment building up within the newly appointed Royal Commission on the Poor Law. In all of these Beatrice and Sidney Webb, Fabian socialists, were central figures.

When Edith Abbott as a student at the London School of Economics came to know the Webbs, they were well along in the extensive research of English local government which they carried out for over thirty years. Beatrice Webb described the division of labor in their partnership by saying, "I am the investigator, and he the executor . . . and we have a wide and varied experience of men and things between us."[16] Edith Abbott was immediately impressed by the Webbs' sense of history, their commitment to painstaking research and factual detail, and their faith that the scientific spirit could and should be applied to human purposes.

One of the courses at the London School of Economics that influenced Edith Abbott most significantly was "Methods of Social Investigation." The course content had been developed by the Webbs together. During the term in which Edith attended, the lectures were given by Sidney Webb. In this particular course his lectures dealt with material and ideas now well established. But in the early 1900s, sociology was a young and incomplete science. He lectured on the various branches of sociology and the place of sociology in the hierarchy of sciences; the need, as a preliminary to the study of society, to understand general scientific culture and the scientific method. He presented the methods of investigation in economics and political science that were common to other sciences—hypothesis, collection of data, verification, experimentation, observation of processes and results, statistical analysis; and those methods peculiar to sociology—the interview, documents, literature, the distinction between firsthand and secondhand literature and their respective uses and values. He lectured as well on the effect of a given social environment on the average man or woman and the possibility of applying knowledge to alter the environment.[17] Edith Abbott later introduced a course in "Social Investigation" as a mainstay in the curriculum of the University of Chicago's School of Social Service Administration.

During the months Edith Abbott was at the school, Beatrice Webb lectured each week, saw students, and talked over their work with them. Direct in manner, quick and clear in speech, often brusque and challenging, she was, like her husband, able to handle thorny questions with candor and without sentiment. She ignored numerous conventions and to many was a daunting figure. As an established social investigator, she presented a model of the professional woman. She treated students like colleagues rather than disciples and they usually found her charming.[18] Given her own personal habits and standards of work, Edith Abbott could only have been enormously impressed. One possession that Edith brought from her year in London was a large photograph of Beatrice Webb, taken by G. Bernard Shaw, with Beatrice Webb's scrawling signature at the bottom to give it additional distinction.

During the time Edith Abbott was in London the Fabian Society was growing at an unprecedented rate. The society and its most prominent members, which included the Webbs, were often in the news. Socialism, as the Fabians presented it, contained concepts and strategies which were compatible with Edith Abbott's character and personality and state of knowledge. Fabian socialism was intellectual, yet practical. It never deviated from outrage against the ever-present suffering of people who live in poverty and squalor. It rested on a moral responsibility of men and women to bring about a better social order through a two-way channel of duty—the state to the individual and the individual to society. Its primary strategy was not revolution; its leaders carefully distinguished themselves from the militants of the day. Research and education were primary aims, not socialism obtained as a result of an outbreak of violence. Fabians sought to permeate all existing parties and organizations and to use the existing governmental machinery to legislate against poverty and other social ills. All of these concepts and strategies Edith Abbott found acceptable and she integrated them firmly into her own agenda for teaching social reform.

The Fabian intent to bring all major industries under the control of a democratic government, however, ran counter to her father's early political instruction and was a more difficult issue for her. Edith and her father carried on a lively correspondence. Othman Abbott was always ready for new experiences, even vicariously. As his daughter began to learn more about the politics of the London County Council, she wrote to him with an indication of interest in some of the Progressive programs. Othman Abbott answered with a trace of sternness not usually found in his letters: "If I were there I would have to vote against you I think . . . I admit, Edith, that I am opposed to governmental interference in private concerns or occupations."[19] In response, Edith's letters reflected the tie to her parents and the homesickness to which she was always vulnerable, and the stress of trying to integrate her new experiences.[20] There was, after all, no consensus in public opinion at the turn of the century between an uncompromising rugged individualism and the concept of government as a social force against the hazards of life.

Beatrice Webb's appointment in 1905 to serve on the Royal Commission on the Poor Law and the Relief of Distress occasioned another far-reaching influence upon Edith Abbott. In England at that time two groups were opposed for different reasons to the existing state of affairs on poor relief—the Fabians and Labour because change was not coming fast enough; and the Local Government Board, supported by the Charity Organization Society, because the principles of the 1834 Royal Commission inquiry were being eroded. The Charity Organization Society, as was true later of its United States counterpart, had a significant influence upon public policy in relation to relief. The COS took the position that poverty was the fault of the individual, resulting from a personal inadequacy, indolence, or vice, and indicated a need for personal reform. It favored private philanthropic efforts over an extension of governmental activity and supported a deterrent Poor Law. When the work of the newly appointed commission began, its members soon allied themselves into support of one or the other of the two opposing factions. "The work and vigor of the Fabian-Labour attack was chiefly carried by the Webbs, for the appointment of Mrs. Webb to the Commission obviously and automatically brought the other member of 'the firm' into the study. The battle soon defined itself as the Webbs against the Poor Law."[21]

The Poor Law that was under attack grew out of the repressive philosophy and principles of the 1834 Royal Commission report aimed at reducing pauperism and the costs of public relief. For over seventy years the Local Government Board had relied upon practices consistent with the concept of "less eligibility" (keeping the relief recipient poorer and in a less desirable condition than the lowest paid laborer). Such a condition was produced by stigmatizing the pauper, taking away his or her freedom through detention in a workhouse, disenfranching him, and offering relief to individuals outside the workhouse only as a temporary exception and at a severely inadequate level.

The Webbs completely rejected the Poor Law in philosophy and methods and sought its abolition. The inquiry of the 1905 commission continued for four years. Beatrice Webb's viewpoint did not prevail, as it was apparent almost from the beginning that it would not. However she produced a minority report that was signed by three other commission members. The Webbs' drive and continuous search for new solutions to the old problems are generally credited with the commission's having delivered a majority report substantially less conservative than it might otherwise have been.

Beatrice Webb's diaries for the period of the Poor Law inquiry show clearly how her responsibilities in relation to it dominated her thoughts, activities, and verbal exchanges with others. The issues and opposing points of view as reported in newspapers and by the Webbs and their supporters were grist for debate around the London School of Economics and among other persons with whom Edith Abbott associated. Her students in future years were to hear her cry to abolish the Poor Law just as Beatrice Webb had recorded her own appeal.[22] They were to study the history of the English Poor Law and draw lessons from it for the American relief system. Edith Abbott was to teach from her convictions about a progressive public welfare system and she was to act out those convictions by sending her best graduates to staff the system at its critical points.

These convictions, however, were not attained without Edith Abbott's having to work through two compelling and opposing strains of thought about the problems of the unemployed casual laborer—the Fabian position and the doctrine of the Charity Organization Society. The latter she encountered face to face through her settlement experiences in London's East End.

The settlement where Edith Abbott chose to spend some time, St. Hilda's, was founded in 1889 to serve as a "civilizing influence." The building that the Ladies Guild had access to was the best in the area—four stories and a basement; it provided accommodations for fifteen residents, classrooms, a large drawing room, and a library, a commodious dining room, kitchen, and office and, "to be thoroughly up to date, . . . a room expressly for the storage of bicycles." The top story was an "oratory," a small chapel for the use of residents.[23]

During the year in which Edith Abbott spent time at St. Hilda's, most of the residents were managers of elementary schools in Shoreditch and Bethnal Green or managers of special schools for mentally and physically defective children.[24] The settlement was "distinctly religious" in character and the expectation that residents would attend religious services was strong.[25] Despite its religious atmosphere, Edith Abbott was comfortable there.

The work of the settlement included district visiting, Sunday-school teaching, charity organization work, country holiday and club management, classes for invalid children—in fact any work which supported or supplemented the work of the local parishes of the Church of England. One resident served as Poor Law Guardian and all were expected to "set an example of simple, sober, unsensational methods." It appeared to be "a very active and well-conducted organisation," according to one of Charles Booth's investigators.[26]

During the time Edith Abbott was at St. Hilda's the settlement was rather heavily engaged in work in connection with the Unemployed Workmen's Act, with residents assisting in the home visiting and investigation of applications for relief.[27] Edith Abbott's work for the settlement, in addition to interviewing unemployed casual laborers in Stepney, was mostly in a Whitechapel Charity Organization Society with its "Skilled Employment Committee" for apprenticing girls into industry.[28]

During Edith Abbott's stay in England, many young intellectuals from Oxford and Cambridge were giving service in settlement houses as an outlet for doubts and uneasy consciences. Edith Abbott's reason for doing so was more directly related to her struggle to reconcile the Fabian view with that of the COS. Through her interviews and home visits from the base of St. Hilda's, she was trying to come closer to the individual poor person behind the facts and statistics of the Webbs. She was testing the notion that, in addition to reform legislation, individual remedies for individual causes of distress would still be required. It is probable too that she was rejecting the element of elitism in Fabianism, which showed itself in an image of an elite offering salvation to a poor and unfortunate population, an attitude vested with a certain self-righteousness that the Abbott sisters' mother had never tolerated in her children.

When Edith Abbott later became a resident of Hull-House, she found Jane Addams's settlement very different from St. Hilda's. The COS philosophy was not there, nor was the Fabian brand of elitism. There was no escape from the necessity to reconcile her conflicting interests and beliefs. In 1914, a little more than six years after the end of her English experiences, swarms of unemployed men marched down Halsted Street or gathered in Bowen Hall at Hull-House to demand jobs. Hull-House residents were face to face with the effects on their neighbors of a significant lag in business and industry. Edith Abbott headed a Hull-House Committee on Relief and, in her own words, "I was then, for a settlement worker, quite a good supporter of C.O.S. doctrine." She regularly attended meetings of the West Side United Charities District Committee and "thought everything could be arranged in an orderly fashion." Edith Abbott urged Jane Addams to set up a plan for "made work" at Hull-House. So Jane Addams secured some funds and arranged with the man in general charge of the buildings to plan house repair work to give a few days' work each week to as many men as possible. Then the work was extended to cleaning the alley and the nearby streets over and over again. Still there were men all about Hull-House clamoring for work. Grace Abbott warned Edith that it would be "like trying to sweep back the tide with a broom." Edith Abbott remembered that it had been "a bewildering experience."[29]

When the majority and minority reports of the Royal Commission on the Poor Law were given to the public, Edith Abbott, by that time settling into a mature perspective from the base of her position in the Chicago School of Civics and Philanthropy, reviewed the progress that had been made in England toward poor-law reform and presented a balanced evaluation of each side of the issue. Her views reflected her respect for COS leaders Octavia Hill, Helen Bosanquet, and C. S. Loch. They also reflected her commitment to the Webbs, their character, competencies, and beliefs. She recorded her regret for the acrimonious spirit reflected in the debate on each side, and noted especially the failure on the part of the Webbs to have made a fair presentation of the case in their new volume, *English Poor Law Policy*. She saluted the theory of the Webbs that "nothing of today can really be understood without its history," but said almost sadly that their new volume "must be a disappointment to those who have learned to respect their fine spirit of scientific investigation."[30]

In England, as had been true when Edith Abbott studied at the University of Chicago, many persons recognized her abilities and were interested in her and her views. She was asked by the editor of the *Independent* to write an account of the English woman suffrage movement. In one evening she turned out a hard-hitting attack on newspapers that had grossly exaggerated their accounts of the behavior of the new militant woman suffrage workers, on the metropolitan police who had caused more disorder than the women demonstrators, and on the English government that had jailed a group of women "long respected for work in a hundred good causes" and now demanding an extension of the franchise. In the days preceding the request to write the article, Edith Abbott had stood in a drizzling rain for more than two hours with a crowd in Hyde Park and listened to the "agitators" present their cause. On another day she had watched a great demonstration in Trafalgar Square by the women workers from the textile mills of Lancashire, Cheshire, and other industrial centers. The strong renewal of her interest in suffrage was clear in her concluding but humble statement: "To one born and bred a believer in woman's suffrage, but long accustomed to regard it apathetically as something which would come only in that long future which holds so much of truth and justice, the past week in London has been one of inspiration and new hope. And in default of the personal possession of the moral courage to serve in a campaign of this sort, it is a pleasure to acknowledge, humbly and gratefully, a deep obligation to those whose service has been great."[31]

In addition to her settlement work and her advanced course at the London School of Economics, Edith Abbott taught a short course at the School of Sociology and Social Economics, founded in 1904 to arrange for the theoretical and practical training of social workers. The school had no direct connection with any university until 1913, when it merged with the London School of Economics. The larger women's settlements, St. Hilda's among them, sent their workers to the school. Hand in hand with the course work went a practical training that usually was combined with residence in a settlement.[32]

During her London stay Edith Abbott occasionally allowed herself some recreation, sometimes to put aside her books in the British Museum Library and go off to Hampstead Heath to walk in the soft English sun or take a Sunday morning excursion on the LCC steamboats down the Thames River. She made two trips to the Continent—to Paris for Christmas on the round trip bargain fare of five dollars, and again in March when she went to Belgium.[33] And she took up smoking cigarettes while she was in England. Perhaps she was emulating Beatrice Webb, who smoked freely. In any case, the time was more than a decade before the end of World War I brought greater freedom to some women, and for a woman to smoke cigarettes publicly was quite unusual. When she returned to Chicago, she found the practice affronted most people and she quit smoking except when she visited Grace Abbott in Washington, D.C. She resumed again in the 1930s.[34]

The two years spent in the eastern part of the United States and in England were significant ones in Edith Abbott's development. Although they were stimulating, not everything about them was easy. She was, for example, not experienced enough then to be fully comfortable in the Boston Trade Union assignment with its demands upon her by union leaders. But it turned out as she had forecast earlier, "I won't do them any harm and shall get a lot of valuable information out of it." And perhaps because in her early life she had occupied a somewhat favored position in the family, she felt that her parents held "special" goals for her, in turn leaving her less free than Grace Abbott always was to be herself and to change as new experiences opened the way. Nevertheless the two years were catalytic ones. She established herself as a researcher and an economist of merit, one who could write clearly and convincingly. She encountered people with characteristics and points of view unlike those with whom she had lived and worked. She lived in several social settlements, saw the poor and the casual laborers of East London, whose problems and living conditions were outside her previous experience. She began to focus on the human being behind the statistics of her early research. She was exposed to a beginning of education and training for social workers closely linked to residency in a social settlement, a school not unlike the School of Civics and Philanthropy in Chicago in which she eventually invested so much. Her course work and the Poor Law controversy laid the basis for her contributions to the development of social work curriculum and compilations of teaching materials used all over the United States. She developed an expertise, unusual in her day, in the development of the Poor Law and social security that enabled her later to speak and write so forcefully on behalf of a sound and progressive system of public welfare. The interest she later took in Chicago city politics and government certainly was to some extent a reflection of the learning she acquired as she studied the workings of the London County Council. In retrospect it seems quite natural that upon her return her research interests turned from a somewhat narrow concern with labor force statistics about the employment of women to broader considerations of the protection of women and children, housing conditions of immigrant families, juvenile delinquency, child labor, and other aspects of people in interaction with their environment.

In April 1907, while Edith Abbott was still in London, she accepted a teaching position for the fall at Wellesley College, a small and elite women's college in Massachusetts. She was to work with Katherine Coman, an economics professor.

During Edith Abbott's new experiences Grace Abbott had been in Grand Island. Life had been less than exceptional although she was constantly busy with teaching, civic endeavors, housekeeping duties, and special attention to her mother. In the summer of 1906, when her brother Arthur returned to Grand Island from law school, Grace Abbott enrolled in the summer session at the University of Chicago, taking courses in political economy, political science, law, and one course with Sophonisba Breckinridge.[35]

In later years as Grace Abbott became nationally and internationally recognized, Edith tended to defer to her and in some ways to be quite dependent upon her. But in the summer of 1906 Edith was still the more experienced sister, and she wrote to Grace with a full measure of sisterly and somewhat sentimental advice as to how to pursue her new opportunities at the University of Chicago, which Edith Abbott loved so much. Her advice was laden with loneliness. She wrote Lizzie Abbott, "I was not homesick tell Grace when she wrote that she was to have my old room at Green Hall for I am homesick all the time anyway. I never expect to be so happy again anywhere as I was my first year at Chicago."[36]

At the end of the summer session Grace Abbott returned to Grand Island for another year of teaching and saving, but with a plan to go back to the University of Chicago a year later for full-time study. She spent part of the summer of 1907 teaching in Broken Bow, probably in a "teachers' institute," and making arrangements for the running of the household after she was to leave for Chicago. Lizzie Abbott had taken a fall that left her lame and she seemed not so well to Grace, who was glad to be going to Chicago where she could "get home almost on a moment's notice" if she needed to.[37] As the years went on and their parents grew older, the Abbott sisters worried about them and made frequent trips to Grand Island, often at considerable hardship in view of their demanding schedules.

By the fall of 1907, Grace Abbott had returned to the University of Chicago. By late October she was well into the development of her thesis for the Master of Philosophy degree in political science, an analysis of the legal position of married women in the United States. Nisba Breckinridge wrote Edith Abbott, "Grace is doing splendid work on her married ladies. She has something of your rapidity in getting over ground which quite takes my breath away."[38] Grace Abbott's interest in married women's legal rights was first stimulated by discussion in her own home. Her choice of topic also reflected her firm commitment to the extension of rights to women in all sectors of society.

To help meet her expenses Grace Abbott accepted a temporary position early in 1908 with the Juvenile Protection Association. The purpose of the association as described by its guiding hand, Louise de Koven Bowen, was "to keep children out of court by removing many of the demoralizing conditions which surrounded them . . . trying to protect children and young people wherever they congregate." The association divided the city into districts, each with "a paid officer whose duty it was to keep children out of disreputable ice cream parlors, candy stores and pool rooms." Grace Abbott's perception of her job, as she wrote her brother Ottie, was that it meant "a sort of police duty in the interests of children. I shall work on the west side and will probably move to Hull-House next week."[39]

As the job was defined it was not the kind of work that satisfied Grace Abbott. She had waited a long time and was ready for an opportunity to play a larger role in the development of program and policies. Nisba Breckinridge wrote Edith, "I saw Grace for a moment yesterday, and I am afraid she is not very happy, but her job is only a six months job, and I cannot think that it will be a wasted time."[40] Nisba Breckinridge was not as disinterested as the tone of her statement might suggest. She was highly impressed with Grace Abbott's analytical mind, her energy and confidence, and she was watching for the right opportunity. That opportunity was the direction of the newly formed Immigrants' Protective League. In very large measure, it was Sophonisba Breckinridge who prepared the way and in the late summer of 1908 launched Grace Abbott in a new career of which her years of creative and effective work on behalf of immigrants were to be a highly significant part.

During these same months Sophonisba Breckinridge and Julia Lathrop were endeavoring to bring Edith Abbott back to Chicago. Nisba Breckinridge had remained in close touch with Edith during her two years in Boston, Washington, D.C., and London and she was in touch with her at Wellesley. She understood Edith Abbott's commitment to coeducation and knew that she was not fully happy at a women's college. She grasped Edith's enlarged perspective and readiness to return to the openness of the Midwest and the ferment of Chicago. An expanded program for Chicago's School of Civics and Philanthropy provided the needed opportunity.[41] By fall, Edith Abbott had joined her sister Grace at Hull-House.

Come and show me another city with lifted head singing so proud to be alive and coarse and strong and cunning.

— CARL SANDBURG[1]

CHAPTER 3

Chicago — New Frontiers

HALSTED STREET and the neglected river wards of Chicago's West Side presented a vigorous challenge to the Abbott sisters. With her incisive mind, her zest for drama and colorful differences among people and places, and her interest in protecting the friendless against injustice, Grace Abbott immersed herself in the teeming immigrant life about her. Her capacity for leadership and her extraordinary ability to organize and administer began rapidly to take form. Edith Abbott said she was so glad to come back to Chicago that she forgot about "the steaming summer heat and the smells in the Hull-House neighborhood—they seemed only part of the welcome contrast between the vigorous activity of Chicago's Halsted Street and the cool aloofness of a New England college for women."[2]

Grace and Edith Abbott spent most of the next ten years together at Hull-House, where they entered into a new and exciting life-style that brought lasting personal and professional friendships. They welcomed the surge of social, political, and legal issues that the Progressive era brought to the forefront of American life. Woman suffrage, the rights of women in industry, the evils of child labor, questions about the "traffic" in women for purposes of prostitution, the problems and the rights of immigrants, tenement housing, delinquency, the peace movement—to all these and more the Abbott sisters turned their energies and their keen minds.

Hull-House and the old West Side were still part of the vast city wilderness when the Abbott sisters went to live there in 1908. The streets were atrocious, rarely cleaned, and either unsurfaced to become summer dust beds and fall bogs of mud or paved with worn-out cedar blocks. Irregularly laid wooden sidewalks held traps for the unwary pedestrian. Horses with odors of rotting stables and filthy alleys seemed to be everywhere. Many of the overcrowded tenements with their dilapidated outhouses and uncollected garbage had once been wooden shacks built before Chicago's Great Fire, later raised up high on a new foundation to permit the addition of extra rooms.[3]

European immigration by 1908 was at high tide. Thousands of foreigners poured into Chicago and its West Side, where their problems were sharply evident to Hull-House residents. Foreign colonies were well established and English was little spoken in the streets and in the shops. Italian colonies bordered Hull-House on two sides and adjoined the largest settlement of Greeks in Chicago. To the north was a Bulgarian colony inhabited mostly by men who had not been able to bring their families to America. To the south was the ghetto. With its competing pushcarts heaped with shoes, old and new clothing, dishes, pots and pans, potatoes, onions, and other food it seemed to the Abbott sisters as picturesque as it seemed unsanitary.

The Greeks were the nearest Hull-House neighbors and many came for clubs and classes. In their colony was the Greek Orthodox Church with a school supervised by the priest in which, Grace Abbott noted, about thirty children were taught "a little English, some Greek, much of the achievements of Hellas, and the obligation that rests on every Greek to rescue Macedonia from the Turks and Bulgarians." Signs on the windows of the stores for two blocks had only Greek characters. By recalling her college study, Grace could identify such businesses as the Cafe Appolyon, the newspaper *The Hellas*, and on Blue Island Avenue the Parthenon Barber Shop. She visited the neighborhood on the night of Good Friday when the shops were draped with purple and black and watched the solemn procession of Greek men chanting hymns and marching down the street with burning candles. It was as though she were no longer in America, she thought, but upon reflection, "this could be no place but America for the procession was headed by eight burly Irish American policemen and along the walks were 'Americans' of Polish, Italian, Russian Jewish, Lithuanian, and Puritan ancestry watching with mingled reverence and curiosity this celebration of Good Friday, while those who marched were homesick and mourning because 'this was not like the Tripolis.'"[4]

Jane Addams and Hull-House were magic words when Grace and Edith Abbott entered upon their new Chicago life together. The house that Jane Addams and Ellen Starr located for their social settlement had been built in 1856 by Charles J. Hull west of the Chicago River in an attempt to have the new home completely outside of the city. The river proved attractive to industry and that moved west as well. Jane Addams had other buildings constructed as the settlement's activities expanded and, by the time the Abbott sisters came, the sprawling complex of thirteen buildings was virtually complete. The Hull-House mansion remained the center of activity.

The second floor held Jane Addams's living quarters and office. Twelve of the women residents, including Grace and Edith Abbott, lived "in the House with Miss Addams" on the third floor that she had added to the original structure. But the rest of the settlement was a maze of adjoining buildings—a girls' residence, a men's residence, apartments for married couples and for additional women residents, a coffee house, an art gallery, a theater, and the all-important residents' dining room. The dining room was important to residents as well as to the Hull-House neighbors who used it in the evenings for clubs or classes.[5]

Men and women who wanted to live at Hull-House and who offered promise of value to the settlement were admitted as vacancies occurred. Living expenses were managed by a House Committee on the plan of a cooperative club. All Hull-House residents took their share of evening door and telephone duty as well as "toting" duty—escorting visitors about the buildings, the neighborhood, and the city. Residents were expected to help out in other ways as a need arose appropriate to their particular talents.[6] For the Abbott sisters sometimes this meant helping Jane Addams with her heavy correspondence. When Grace and Edith first went to Hull-House, Jane Addams did not have a secretary. She would pick up mail each morning, look it over hurriedly at the breakfast table, and distribute letters to be answered to different residents on whom she particularly relied. Of course Jane Addams wrote a great many letters herself but Edith Abbott remembered that, on the whole, a considerable amount of mail was taken care of reasonably well in that informal way.

Certain traits seemed to be characteristic of most individuals who chose to become settlement residents. Grace and Edith Abbott in large measure matched such a profile.[7] They were young: Grace was twenty-nine and Edith thirty-one when they joined the Hull-House group. They were college graduates; Edith had an advanced degree and Grace was completing the requirements for one. Edith had studied abroad and neither had taken courses in social work as such. Like most other settlement residents they were unmarried. In 1908 educated women still faced formidable obstacles to combining marriage with a career of any kind, and settlement living was hard for many married couples to adapt to and in addition offered difficult conditions for rearing children. Florence Kelley was one who had been married and divorced, and she had three children when she first came to Hull-House. However, during her residence there, her children lived most of the time in the home of Mr. and Mrs. Henry Demarest Lloyd in Winnetka.[8]

Like many other settlement residents, the Abbott sisters came from an old-stock American family, were born in the Midwest, and grew up in a moderately well-to-do family. Even after Othman Abbott's serious financial difficulties following the Panic of 1893, the Abbott home still offered more advantages and a higher standard of living than most others in Grand Island. Like most settlement residents, the Abbott sisters had grown up in a pleasant residential neighborhood that left them with no direct experience with the poor of large cities. However, their parents had been actively involved in reform or concerned with aiding the poor and they had inherited a tradition of service. Edith and Grace Abbott quite rationally wanted to use their education to do something useful and important in their changing society and they believed that a settlement met an authentic need. Each was strong, energetic, analytical, and self-confident. Neither could be charged with a psychological or status deficiency or with being alienated from the mainstrean of American life. Each had known stringent "going without" and had deferred her own desires in the hard times of the 1890s. Each had succeeded in exacting daily work not always of her liking and for little pay. They had left Nebraska in search of opportunity and learning. Hull-House and Chicago provided a setting in which they could find a creative solution to the restrictive status of women, meet their strong personal needs for work and achievement, and contribute to social reform. They carried no great weight of guilt for their happy and privileged childhood.

Prior to 1900 settlement workers were likely to have had theological training or to be responding to what they perceived as an opportunity to apply Christian ideas of service to an urban, industrial society. Time eroded the religious impulse and it became less important as a motive for entering settlement work.[9] Even though Jane Addams in the early years of Hull-House had encouraged regular evening devotions and had even led in evening prayers, by the time of the Abbott sisters' arrival she had become an agnostic. She was sometimes charged with being opposed to religion and to many that was equivalent to a commitment to socialism.[10] But the neutral religious atmosphere at Hull-House suited Grace and Edith Abbott. Grace once wrote her mother about having "toted" a visitor through the house who was quite agitated because no religious exercises of any sort were held there. Grace wrote with amusement, "I made the most of her [Jane Addams] being a prominent member of the Ethical Society but that was all I could do."[11]

Certainly the humanitarianism of the Abbott sisters did not spring even in part from religious fervor, although the Quaker teachings of their mother and grandmother were important to them. They were not unlike many graduate students in sociology and political economy and other reformers and writers interested in studying the city and its problems. Yet they were different; they were more determined and more deeply committed to human service and social change than many such students; and they were women.

That Hull-House was a center for social research was part of its attraction to the Abbott sisters. Jane Addams once pointed out that the settlements antedated by three years the first sociology departments in universities and by ten years the establishment of the first foundations for social research.[12] The stream of books and articles written by settlement workers often provided the only information available on various aspects of urban living in the late nineteenth and early twentieth centuries. At the same time, these early settlement investigations were hardly objective, undertaken as they were to prepare the way for reform and often including moral judgments about what had been observed.[13] Still the emphasis at Hull-House on fact-finding about the social conditions residents wanted to change offered Grace and Edith Abbott an opportunity to combine skill in scientific appraisal with empathy for the human condition. Furthermore Grace's capacity for orderly thinking and detached observation and Edith's training and experience in the scientific method of social investigation put them in a position to moderate the tendencies of some of the more impassioned residents.

When the Abbott sisters came, there were then about twenty-five women and twelve men residents and several married couples, all of varying professions and interests—music teachers, artists, club leaders, social workers, lawyers, journalists, physicians, and a few successful businessmen who wanted to work with a social reform group.[14] A residents' table in the coffee house was the setting for spirited discussion over the morning newspapers. "Our political opinions varied widely," Edith Abbott wrote, "and our arguments not infrequently began at the breakfast table; and during the day the various participants in the current controversy seemed to have sharpened their weapons and prepared for the new arguments that were sure to be heard at the dinner table."[15] In the late evening hours, discussion still went on among those who sat around together when the house was officially closed and the neighbors had all gone home, leaving the reception room and parlors to the residents alone. Known since childhood to thrive on controversy, Grace Abbott wrote happily to her parents, "This is the place to get radical opinions."[16]

Yet Francis Hackett, a resident and editor of the *Chicago Evening Post*, was to recall that he could not imagine a diverse community in which there was less division or friction. "We did not behave like business partners trying to round the corners of each other's silences, or like huddled intellectuals, or like rasping literary groups, or even like those theological seminaries and college faculties whose members develop vested interests and are full of gossip and spite. . . . My recollection is one of vivid and colored personalities, that managed in some way to harmonize."[17] Grace and Edith Abbott would surely have agreed with Alice Hamilton, who said that "the life there satisfied every longing— for companionship, for the excitement of new experiences, for constant intellectual stimulation and for the sense of being caught up in a big movement which enlisted my enthusiastic loyalty."[18]

Much of the "big movement" for the Abbott sisters stemmed from the insurgence in American politics that came to be labeled the Progressive movement. They were caught up in it, not only by the enthusiasm for Progressivism at Hull-House, but as a logical extension of their own developing political beliefs. The Progressive thrust had been at work for some time in both political parties and the Abbott sisters had followed its evolution in the Republican party, led by Theodore Roosevelt, and from farther to the left by Senator Robert M. La Follette.

The Progressive movement caught the energetic loyalty of Grace and Edith Abbott in large measure because it offered activist backing for their convictions about woman suffrage. For the Abbotts, securing the franchise was essential if women were to find their own full and individual identities and be able to share equally in the rights and duties of the citizenry. Gains for woman suffrage had been almost nil in the years from 1896 to 1910; some suffragists referred to the period as "the doldrums."[19]

As late as 1908 Theodore Roosevelt, although not openly opposed to woman suffrage, by his own statement was not an enthusiastic advocate of it; for him it was simply not a very important matter.[20] But with the birth of the Progressive party, he was eager for Jane Addams's support and willing to be influenced by her. After all, she was widely regarded in the decade before World War I as America's most famous woman. The Abbott sisters believed that Jane Addams had been primary in persuading Roosevelt to support woman suffrage and accept its inclusion in the party platform. They traced the thrust of her influence to an incident some months before the Progressive party convention. Roosevelt had come to Chicago to speak at a large public meeting to honor naturalized citizens, an affair Grace Abbott as director of the Immigrants' Protective League had organized for the prestigious Union League

Club. Before the hour for his major address, Roosevelt came to Hull-House to speak to people from the West Side neighborhood. Afterwards Grace Abbott rode with him and Jane Addams to the Armory where the larger meeting was held. During the ride, Grace reported later, he asked Jane Addams about woman suffrage; did she think it really important? Jane Addams gave compelling reasons why she thought it was very important and he replied, "Well, that's that; I think you're right, Miss Addams, and if you're for it, I'm for it, and I'll support it."[21] To persuade Jane Addams to enter the arena of national politics, support for woman suffrage was critical. Undoubtedly Theodore Roosevelt appreciated this fact, whether or not his conversion was fully complete by the time he arrived at the speaker's rostrum.

The social and industrial plank of the Progressive party platform along with its position on woman suffrage made it possible for the Abbott sisters to give enthusiastic support in 1912 to the new party and to Theodore Roosevelt. This part of the platform was a direct outgrowth of the work of the National Conference of Charities and Correction between the years 1909 and 1912 through its Committee on Occupational Standards (later termed Committee on Standards of Living and Labor). By the time Jane Addams was elected president of the NCCC in 1909 (the first time in the thirty-six years of the conference's history that a woman had been chosen), the conference was no longer dominated by the thinking and purposes of the early charity organization societies. Settlement workers and charity workers had moved into a fuller measure of cooperation and the conference emphasis was now upon social reform, prevention, and the means to solve society's problems that oppressed the nation's people.[22]

The new Committee on Occupational Standards created during the 1909 conference sessions was chaired by Paul Kellogg, a social reformer and editor of *The Survey*, the most influential social work journal of that day. At the conference, women and men who worked in child labor advocacy groups, consumers' leagues, settlements, charity organization societies, and other parts of the nascent social welfare field undertook to chart a course of industrial action that they could stand for collectively. Although there were trade unionists and representatives of employers' associations among those who developed the standards, most were persons who Paul Kellogg believed were "lumped together generally as social workers."[23]

By the time the conference met in 1912, the committee was ready to present clear-cut standards that they believed "offered the public a new conception of the sphere of governmental concern in industry." The contributors were able and often noted persons. Among them, Grace

Abbott had spoken on the strengths and problems among the immigrants who had been recruited to the American economy and Edith Abbott and Nisba Breckinridge from their expertise on the problems of women in industry.[24]

The standards were based on the conviction that "industry should be subject to certain tests of social efficiency." The document related principles now commonplace but then regarded as daring. They were reflected in the belief that "all industry today is social. The employer has an important stake in it; so has the workman; but the largest stake holder in any industry is the public."[25]

The NCCC platform principles called for a living wage; the regulation of hours of work; standards of sanitation and safety including compensation for injury and prohibition of manufacture of poisonous articles dangerous to the life of workers; the right to a home, safe and sanitary in healthful surroundings, with abolition of home work and tenement manufacture; the regulation of the term of the working life, bounded by a minimum age to protect against child labor and a maximum age to insure the wage earner a time of economic independence from daily toil; and compensation against heavy loss sustained by industrial workers as a result of unavoidable accidents, industrial disease, sickness, unemployment, and old age.[26]

After the conference adjourned, some of the reform-minded social workers undertook to make their standards a part of the presidential campaign. They presented their "Platform of Industrial Minimums" to the Republican party platform committee and saw it promptly rejected. Because Theodore Roosevelt had shown some interest, however, the social-work group met with him to pursue the matter further, and then met with the platform committee of the new Progressive party. As a result, the party's social and industrial plank was adopted almost word for word from the NCCC standards.[27] The Progressive party platform was termed a "Contract with the People," a document of great political significance between the time of the Populist platform in 1892 and the Democratic platforms in the 1930s.

Jane Addams's biographer, Allen F. Davis, has written that "it is impossible to recapture the exuberance, the enthusiasm and the hope that many social reformers felt in the summer and fall of 1912." After years of struggle for social reform, "now a national political leader was listening to their reasoning, a political party was taking their social justice programs seriously."[28] For the Abbott sisters, still in the dawn of their long careers, the future looked bright; they were vital and confident. They attended all the sessions of the Progressive convention, where Jane Addams was a prominent delegate. She asked them, along with

Nisba Breckinridge and a few other Hull-House residents, to join her at the party headquarters hotel to meet some of the other delegates and talk over some of the issues. Especially for Grace Abbott, who relished the workings of the political process, it was an exciting experience.[29] She had already been an interested onlooker at the Republican convention held earlier in Chicago; at that event, when the Taft-Roosevelt struggle was expected to come to a test, she had clung to her seat "despite hunger, fatigue, and heat."[30] Now at the Progressive convention she and Edith listened to Jane Addams emphasize the social justice measures contained in the party platform as she seconded the nomination of Theodore Roosevelt. William Allen White wrote that when Jane Addams rose to give her seconding speech, "the delegates and the scattered spectators in the galleries rose and cheered. Not even the Colonel got much more rousing cheers than Jane Addams."[31] She was, he said, the Progressive party's "prize exhibit" on the speaker's stand. From their gallery seats, Grace and Edith vigorously applauded and sang "Onward Christian Soldiers" with the delegates and spectators. It was a heady time. With satisfaction Grace wrote her mother late that summer, "Things are very busy these days. All the Progressives are here and here means at Hull-House . . . the excitement is communicated!"[32]

The Progressive party achieved significant gains in 1912 in the legislatures of western and middle western states and significantly affected the suffrage movement there. The result was apparent in Illinois, where the Progressives held the balance of power in the legislature. The residents of Hull-House worked tirelessly to support the suffragists' carefully organized campaign. Grace Abbott was among a group of over 300 women "from the ultra fashionable to the somewhat queer" who traveled from Chicago to Springfield by special train to promote the cause of woman suffrage.[33] Because a constitutional amendment was so difficult to achieve in Illinois, the suffrage leaders sponsored an act which, without amending the constitution, would give women the right to vote for all offices for which the constitution did not specify that only male citizens were to be electors. This strategy would allow women to vote, not in state elections but in presidential elections, for all city, county, and township offices, and on public policy questions appearing on the ballot. The bill became law in 1913, making Illinois the third largest state and the first east of the Mississippi River to pass woman suffrage legislation.[34] Grace Abbott joined other celebrants in a Jubilee parade in downtown Chicago. Edith Abbott did not go.[35] She was heavily engaged with research, writing, and teaching, and she tended to find it hard to set aside a piece of work she had embarked on. Moreover, unlike her sister, she did not relish parades, demonstrations, and lobbying. She was as committed to causes, but more comfortable and effective as a social investigator, educator, and interpreter of these causes.

But Edith Abbott did join 10,000 women from all socioeconomic classes in the great Woman's Suffrage parade in 1916. The parade was organized to try to influence the Republican National Convention, then meeting in Chicago, to include a suffrage plank in its platform. It was a day of cold wind and drenching rain. Grace Abbott wanted naturalized women to be well represented and had recruited a large group of them. She marched at the head of the naturalized women and Edith Abbott undertook to help marshal her followers. Some last minute confusion left her staunchly carrying a banner "Lithuanian Women Want the Vote" but disconnected from and searching for the Lithuanian group. It added an amusing touch. More significantly, the driving rain and chill acted to dramatize solidarity on the suffrage question and loyalty to their sisters in nonsuffrage states on the part of Chicago women who had the vote.[36]

Jane Addams often turned to the Abbott sisters to perform tasks related to the drive for woman suffrage. She somewhat rashly accepted speaking engagements many months ahead and frequently found as the time approached that she had other pressing commitments. So she would come up the stairs to the third floor saying, "I need an Abbott to make a suffrage speech." Although she did not "assign" her residents to work, she knew she could safely commit Grace Abbott to a rather extensive engagement on behalf of suffrage. When Nebraska was considering a woman suffrage amendment, Jane Addams (who was on a speaking tour) wrote Grace from Denver, "I promised the Nebraska suffragists that I would urge you to give a week's speaking to the State before election. . . . All quite concerned about the German counties and think that you would be the person to help." She found Grace to be an excellent lobbyist and liked to have her along when she went to Springfield in behalf of some pending legislation.[37]

Nisba Breckinridge was an active member of the National Board of National American Woman Suffrage Association. Together, Edith Abbott and Nisba Breckinridge responded to a request from the Boston Equal Suffrage Association to prepare a reply to a pamphlet, "The Wage Earning Woman and the State," written by an active antisuffragist, Minnie Bronson, who held that where women had the vote they didn't use it to further women's interests. Her pamphlet was being used at many state legislative hearings after suffrage bills had been introduced. Their reply,[38] with an introductory note by Jane Addams, was circulated widely until the federal amendment was passed eight years later.

Anti-suffragists frequently claimed that where women had the vote they had not produced any special reforms or beneficial effect on politics. After the first Chicago election in which women could vote, the *New Republic* carried an observation to the effect that if men had remained away from the polls, the result of the Chicago mayoralty election would have been precisely the same—the election of an "undesirable" Republican candidate; women had been only "obedient copycats of male opinion." Because the women in Illinois had limited suffrage, special ballots were given them and women's and men's votes were counted and recorded separately, making it possible to study the returns and determine if women voted just as men did. Edith Abbott had been making such an analysis when the editorial prompted her to reply. She looked at the vote at the preceding mayoralty primary where it was evident that women had given a substantial plurality of their votes to a "fusion reform candidate" agreed upon by the Merriam Progressives and the reform element in the Republican party. But the men in both parties, who had more votes than women had, had given the nomination to an undesirable Republican and an undesirable Democrat, leaving the women in the regular election to choose between two undesirable candidates.[39]

Edith Abbott continued to analyze the election statistics for two years. She concluded that the woman's vote was a source of strength to the good government forces, that in one ward after another a larger proportion of women than men voted without regard to party affiliation for the candidates recommended by the Municipal Voter's League. Within two years, women added ten "good" aldermen to the Chicago City Council.[40]

But the Abbott sisters were realists; they did not expect that with the winning of the federal suffrage amendment women would vote as a solid block; the vote would not be an instant panacea to the problems in the status of women; their faith and determination to contribute equally to the political process would not compensate fully for their political inexperience. Grace Abbott especially understood why women would not immediately vote in the same proportion as men, that some would get little encouragement to vote by husbands who regarded politics and government as a man's game. She knew too that many immigrant women, even after naturalization, would hesitate to vote because of the strangeness of the balloting process or fear of being embarrassed by their imperfect, even awkward use of English. "The Nineteenth Amendment," she wrote, "provided us with a ticket of admission to the political fair-grounds. But it did not admit us to the races nor to the side shows, nor did it insure us a place on the committee which awards the prizes. The most that can be said is that it made access to all these easier."[41]

When Grace Abbott marched in suffrage parades or spoke before brave groups of women looking for encouragement and guidance in their efforts to gain political equality, she felt a close kinship, even mutual affection. And for her those feelings extended to women who seemed to take no part in the struggle. She once related an incident that took place during the 1912 Republican convention when she had seized a short period of routine business in the proceedings to rush across the street to a restaurant. "Next to me on a stool at the lunch counter was a woman obviously like myself from one of the smaller cities of the middle west. We fell into conversation. She asked me if I came from the convention and told me her husband was State Committeeman and I could see she was proud of the position he held in the State. After a silence she asked me if I was a suffragist and when I replied that I was, she said slowly and with great seriousness, 'Well, so am I, but John doesn't know it,'—and then she added, 'But I am going to tell him some day.'"[42]

Grace Abbott once told a group of women that her interest in suffrage was "as wide and as deep as the subject itself."[43] She was not concerned, as some were, that suffrage would give the "wrong kind of voter" the right to go to the polls, nor did she offer reassurance that native-born women were so much in the majority as to diminish the power of ignorant foreign women. She wanted suffrage for all women citizens. The rights of the married woman had long been one of her concerns. After the Nineteenth Amendment was passed she turned to the pages of *The Survey* to raise before the public a suffrage-related problem—the lack of safeguards of political rights for the naturalized married woman and the American-born citizen married to an alien. Legislation in 1907 provided that an American woman who married a foreigner must take the nationality of her husband. In other words, the husband determined the citizenship of the wife, a practice, Grace Abbott said, that was based on an outgrown theory of the husband's responsibility for the wife. An American woman marrying an alien should be able to retain her own citizenship if she wished, and an alien married woman in the United States, desirous of becoming a citizen, should not have to wait until her husband wanted citizenship for himself and thus be deprived of political rights in her new country. She advocated changes in the naturalization process that would give the married woman a choice independent of her husband; the right to initiate naturalization proceedings; and expanded opportunities for learning English and preparing for citizenship.[44]

Grace Abbott's ability to identify with many kinds of women, to project the empathy she felt, and to enlist their interest was a characteristic that came to be highly significant during her years in the Children's Bureau. It was a key to her ability to build and maintain constituencies in support of the bureau's work.

Hull-House for the Abbott sisters was more than an interesting place to live. It was a setting from which each was required to test the extent to which she had integrated into her own character and personality many of the beliefs and ideals that as a child she had accepted from ancestral models and the strongly held viewpoints of parents. Woman suffrage was one of those beliefs. Even before coming to Hull-House, Edith Abbott had begun this testing when she had watched the demonstrations of militant English women in Trafalgar Square and Hyde Park. She had "learned the arguments" to use at suffrage meetings from her mother, had even substituted for her mother at suffrage meetings in Nebraska. But at Hull-House the goals seemed within reach and the "arguments" she had learned had to be reevaluated; they were suddenly for use in her own time and with her own generation.

Grace Abbott believed in suffrage so deeply that the opportunity for action was one that she could grasp almost intuitively. The women's peace movement that flowed out of the eruption of World War I required something more. As a child, her father's colorful stories of the Civil War had added drama and excitement to many a long evening discussion; she had known also her mother's quiet but unyielding opposition to all war.

Most people in the United States had little warning of the impending war. International peace had been given a benign endorsement by the country's political parties. In spite of her distrust of the Kaiser, Grace Abbott had written her mother in 1909 about her optimism for a peaceful coexistence in the world.[45] Now in the summer of 1914 Europe was plunged into war. The flaming headlines and the reality of war in her own time excited and disturbed her. Grace Abbott's work in the Immigrants' Protective League had made her keenly aware of America's human ties to all the world and given her a conviction that the United States held a unique opportunity to contribute to better international relations.[46] In 1911 she had traveled throughout the countries of Europe that were now being swept along a path of destruction. She had made the trip in an effort to better understand the cultures and communities from which the immigrants came. During that journey she had witnessed the age-long rivalries, hatred, and jealousies combined with militarism in Central Europe. With the outbreak of war she saw daily the economic and emotional effects of the sudden outburst of a world war as they were almost immediately reflected in the Hull-House neighborhood and the lives of the immigrants about her.

Carrie Chapman Catt and Jane Addams jointly called a national conference to which women's groups from all over the country were invited. Several thousand women came to Washington in January 1915 to consider the great tragedy the world war represented to them and to try to unify their efforts for peace. Out of this conference, the Women's Peace party was formed. European women, organized for suffrage and peace, had been waiting for such a signal from women in the powerful and neutral country of America. Within another month, an invitation came to Jane Addams and her new organization to attend an international congress of women pacifists from both neutral and belligerent nations to be held at The Hague, April 28 to May 1, 1915. Jane Addams was asked to preside over the congress. The ambitious plan was launched by a small number of Dutch, Belgian, British, and German women, all of whom were suffrage leaders in their own countries.[47]

At Hull-House interest was keen but considered. Each delegate would have to pay her own expenses. Beyond this, to go would require fortitude, optimism, and an ability to remain unperturbed by the criticism of those who saw the venture as inappropriate and impractical and by the ridicule and hostility that the women's efforts for peace drew from many quarters of American and European life.

The United States delegation as it was eventually formed was made up of forty-seven distinguished women from different professions and social endeavors. The Hull-House delegation, besides Jane Addams, included Grace Abbott, Alice Hamilton, M.D., and Sophonisba Breckinridge.

The established competence of the American delegates did not deter opposition to the international congress. Theodore Roosevelt, strongly against Wilson's policy of neutrality, led off with a vigorous assault that stimulated other criticism. The platform of the international congress, he said, was both "silly and base." He wanted the women to cease their "vague and hysterical demands . . . ," abandon their neutral efforts for peace, and join him in his militarist denouncement of the German invasion of Belgium.[48]

The women delegates sailed from New York on April 13 aboard the *Noordam*, a Dutch-American liner. Grace Abbott wrote her mother before leaving that "I am all fixed for finances without borrowing anything. Did not even have to touch my beloved bond!" She also tried to allay her mother's fears about the trip. "There is always some danger in anything one does . . . whether one merely sits at home or ventures from. Something may happen but the chances are all against."[49] Just before sailing from America, Jane Addams had spoken for many when she stated, "We do not think we can settle the war. We do not think that by raising our hands we can make the armies cease slaughter. We do think it is valuable to state a new point of view. We do think it is fitting that women should meet and take counsel to see what may be done."[50]

The congress delegates numbered 1136, representing twelve nations including all the neutral countries of Europe and 43 delegates from Germany, Hungary, and Austria. Dr. Aletta Jacobs of Holland gave a stirring address in the opening session and clarified the congress's purpose by saying, "Those of us who have convened this Congress . . . have never called it a PEACE CONGRESS, but an International Congress of Women assembled to protest against war, and to suggest steps which may lead to warfare becoming an impossibility."[51]

In some sessions there were as many as two thousand visitors in the galleries and the police, expecting clashes along national lines, were numerous. The interest of visitors continued, but the police gradually withdrew as the congress went on without disturbance. For the most part the deliberations were remarkably free of acrimony. Yet the sessions were not without tension. Emily Balch summed up the atmosphere thus: "Because there were no clashes along national lines, it must not be thought . . . that the Congress was stagnantly placid. . . . The sessions were heavily fraught with emotion, it could not be otherwise. . . . People cared too much for the subject under debate for that to be possible. There were most vigorous differences of opinion over details, and some energetic misunderstandings for which the necessity of translating each speech into two other languages supplied many openings. . . . One's every faculty was on the stretch hour after hour, and we wondered afterwards why we felt so exhausted."[52]

The work of the congress was facilitated by the commitment to similar principles which the delegates shared and which they translated into resolutions.[53] With their new concept of continuous mediation by a conference of neutrals without waiting for an armistice, the delegates were publicly advocating a break with political tradition, one that powerful political leaders were unwilling to consider seriously.

Brave women paid a high price for openly opposing war and engaging in international political activity. They were pursuing a highly unpopular cause by a means unsanctioned by their governments. Jane Addams's efforts for peace cost her tremendous national prestige and led to accusations that she was a dangerous traitor. Not until 1931 was she vindicated by the award of the Nobel Peace Prize. When the war years brought an attack on the principles of academic freedom, Emily Balch found that her appointment at Wellesley College had been summarily terminated after her twenty years of teaching. In 1946, at age seventy-nine, she too was belatedly recognized by the award of the Nobel Peace Prize, the third woman to receive that high honor. When Grace Abbott as chief of the United States Children's Bureau sought to advance federal legislation for women and children, red-baiters and other "professional patriots" charged her with socialism, communism, and disloyalty, which they derived from her association with Jane Addams and other women in the movement for peace. Women delegates from other countries also encountered prejudice and discrimination in varied forms.

The significance of the International Congress of Women was lost sight of in large measure by the sexist ridicule it was subjected to when women attempted to voice their organized opinion in relation to war, the province of men. Yet it is a record of courageous women who made a significant contribution to reconceptualizing society as a global system. In addition they advanced the women's movement by redefining women's roles in relation to peace and world order and by demanding political equality in decisions about war and peace and other aspects of international foreign policy. Despite the threat to the international organization of suffragists that the war brought, the bold demonstration by fully committed women from both belligerent and neutral nations enabled the concept of the solidarity of women to hold fast during those turbulent years.[54]

For Grace Abbott, some of the most meaningful experiences of the congress were those she had following the adjournment. Passenger boats were not moving across the Channel to England so Grace and Nisba Breckinridge used the opportunity to visit some of the Dutch charities, the Amsterdam School of Philanthropy, the immigrant quarters, and art galleries. They took a long motor ride through acres of tulips, a respite from considerations of war. Fruit trees were in blossom and Grace wrote her mother that "all Holland is fragrant." But along with "cunning little villages and canals" they saw bridges that were mined, trenches, barbed wire entanglements, and Dutch soldiers mobilized. Then came the news of the sinking on May 7 of the *Lusitania*, which Grace felt as "a fearful blow," coming as it did with reports of poisoned wells in Africa and the use of gas near Ypres.[55]

Together with Mabel Kittredge and Lucy Biddle Lewis, Grace Abbott and Alice Hamilton arranged a trip into Belgium to see for themselves the effects of war. In Belgium its full impact was immediately apparent, and, in her words, Grace was "suddenly very much older and fearfully depressed." On the train to Brussels they saw the destruction of entire villages, and upon their arrival they began to experience more fully what life was like in an invaded country. Grace Abbott sensed the heavy oppression of the spirit of Belgians whom she met in the streets or shops. In addition, she wrote home, "there is the worst irritating regulation of every kind of thing. The Belgians have settled down to a kind of desperate waiting which is most terrible to see."[56]

Getting out of Belgium was much more difficult than getting in and the four women were never sure until the last minute that they would be allowed to leave. From German officials they endured cold suspicion, repeated humiliating searches, and long delays over trivial matters. To be safely back in Holland was, as Alice Hamilton said, like "escaping from a dark and stifling room into fresh air and sunshine."[57]

Grace Abbott had gone to the international congress not only to demonstrate her commitment to pacifism but also to test it by association and debate with women from other nationalities. Her trip into Belgium brought her sharply into an awareness of the daily despair and suffering of people whose country had been invaded. She saw the war as one between races and cultures and believed that preventing such wars would require a new scheme of attitudes and values. She returned to Chicago more conscious than ever of the interdependence of America and Europe. With the upsurge in the United States of openly expressed nativist prejudices, she felt that America had neglected a precious opportunity to enrich its life by failing to see that, if encouraged to express their own characteristics, the Slavs, the Italians, and other foreign-born groups would give to American life "the color, the gaiety, and the self-expression which Puritanism denied to it and which no reading of Russian literature or attendance on Italian opera can give to the Anglo-American."[58] Her political efforts for peace continued through 1916 when she organized a Conference of Oppressed or Dependent Nationalities held in Washington, D.C. as a final offering to the second convention of the Woman's Peace party. The objective of the conference was to help develop and organize public opinion relative to the rights of people to control their own destinies and determine their own institutions. Grace Abbott and Jane Addams and others at Hull-House believed that that kind of public opinion should grow out of the experiences of the new Americans from the European countries, who could best interpret the problems of their people as these related to international policy.[59]

Grace Abbott recruited participants for the program from each of the American immigrant groups: Irish, Belgian, Serbian, Albanian, Armenian, Syrian, Russian and Romanian Jews, Croatian, Lett, Lithuanian, Pole, Ukranian, Slovak, Bohemian, and Finn. The meetings were not always convivial because the various minority groups proved not to be in easy agreement as they reflected on their individual personal and political experiences. The conference had little impact except upon the participants. Grace concluded, however, that at least it had set out some of the involved problems that were sure to be a legacy of the war.[60]

Grace Abbott remained a pacifist all her life, although during her years of federal public administration she accepted the required restrictions on her political activity. But pacifism and her experiences during World War I continued to hold deep meaning for her. When World War II came and America's direct involvement appeared inevitable, Grace Abbott was very ill and she confided to her sister, Edith, that she felt she could not endure the experience of another world war so sure to hold even new horrors and destruction.[61]

Like many other Progressives, Grace Abbott turned to support for Woodrow Wilson in 1916, although she was deliberate in her decision. Charles Evans Hughes had been endorsed by the Progressive party but only by a narrow margin and as the campaign went on, Hughes seemed to yield to pressure from the right and not to be abreast of Progressive issues. However, Wilson had not supported child labor legislation or woman suffrage in 1914, both of crucial importance to Grace Abbott. But he had favored immigration by his veto of the literacy test and he had appointed Louis Brandeis to the Supreme Court in 1916. By 1916, for various reasons of political necessity and changing political convictions, Wilson moved to support of Progressive measures, including child labor protection. His successful fusion during the campaign of Progressivism with the peace cause and his eventual endorsement of woman suffrage were enough to persuade Grace Abbott to give him her vote.[62]

The circumstances that brought Edith Abbott from Wellesley College back to Chicago, apart from her own interest in returning to the Midwest and to a coeducational institution, can be credited to Sophonisba P. Breckinridge's growing interest in the need to train people for social work. After Nisba Breckinridge began teaching at the University of Chicago she moved into the life of the city in a broader way. She joined the Women's Trade Union League and formed contacts with the Hull-House group.

Chicago's first effort at systematic training for social work began in 1903 under the direction of Graham Taylor in the Institute of Social Science. The training consisted largely of a series of lectures given by various social workers in the community and more notably by Graham

Taylor of the Chicago Commons, Julia C. Lathrop of Hull-House and the State Board of Charities, and Charles Henderson of the University of Chicago. In 1907 the institute began enlarging and reorganizing as a School of Civics and Philanthropy, made possible by a grant from the Russell Sage Foundation, which Julia Lathrop secured with assistance from Nisba Breckinridge. The grant was for the purpose of establishing a social research department. Julia Lathrop was named to direct the new department of social research and to coordinate the research program with Graham Taylor's instructional program. Sophonisba Breckinridge agreed to assist her as fully as she could while retaining her appointment at the University of Chicago.[63]

Early in 1908 Nisba Breckinridge and Julia Lathrop went to Wellesley to persuade Edith Abbott to come to Chicago and serve as assistant director of the social research department. They offered her a beginning salary of $1500 and the opportunity to live at Hull-House. Edith Abbott gladly accepted.[64]

Edith Abbott's Wellesley friends were astonished and Katharine Coman was less than agreeable about it. Their amazement is not hard to understand. She was leaving a college well recognized in academia to go to a vaguely known place called a school of civics and philanthrophy that was not even connected with a college or university and whose financing was tenuous. But Edith Abbott wanted the freedom to work out new methods of social research in a way that would relate closely to the professional interests of social workers and at the same time make social research an integral part of professional education.[65]

At the same time the Chicago School of Civics and Philanthropy was completing its plan to inaugurate a social research department, a similar development was taking place at the Boston School for Social Workers and at the New York School of Philanthropy. The three programs initially began to develop im somewhat different directions but the idea in each was to develop a permanent staff of trained investigators who would form a nucleus of a larger body, some of whose members would change from year to year.[66]

Students of the school were expected to combine classroom instruction and fieldwork; advanced students would engage in social research that could help enrich the curriculum and contribute in practical ways to the solution of social problems in their respective localities. Once selected, students were given unusual opportunities to learn firsthand about the problems of people in a great city, to go into the homes of many families, to see and hear firsthand the strengths of people and the ills which overcame some of them who could not maintain themselves in the rapidly growing industrial society, and to observe and record the processes at work in the community's institutions—the courts, the public schools, the correctional institutions, and the hospitals.

Edith Abbott and Nisba Breckinridge investigated and analyzed many aspects of urban life. Early in their work together was a series of studies of housing conditions in Chicago where families lived in furnished rooms, in the densely populated tenement houses, in the stockyards district, and in south Chicago where people lived in the shadow of the steel mills. Their investigations of urban problems and their interest in ethnic differences made them aware in a new way of the special problems Negroes faced because of racial discrimination. Both immigrants and blacks were the primary occupants of the seriously inadequate dwellings in Chicago. One difference was a more powerful element of discrimination against blacks. Among immigrants, only the poor were confined to inadequate housing; but at any income level blacks found it difficult to acquire a satisfactory place to live. Nowhere in Chicago did these social investigators find more dilapidated and poorer sanitary conditions than in the city wards populated by Negroes. Delinquency rates were highest among black and immigrant children. Among immigrants the delinquency appeared to Abbott and Breckinridge to be caused largely by the conflicts immigrants experienced between the culture and customs in America and those in the country from which they or their parents had emigrated. Black children, on the other hand, were influenced into delinquency by the barriers they experienced through a denial of civil rights and the concomitant loss of opportunities.

To the investigators sent out, directed, and supervised by Edith Abbott and Nisba Breckinridge, even more important than sanitary conditions in housing were the problems of family life under such circumstances and the questions of social planning that such facts highlighted. The serious housing conditions that they had found, deadening to the human spirit, led Abbott and Breckinridge to emphasize that whether it was in a stockyards district or the steel mills area or any of the other neighborhoods studied, the housing problem could not be solved unless those responsible for the great industries upon which people depended for employment and which in turn depended on them for existence came to realize the necessity of altering industrial conditions so that decent standards of family life could be maintained. It was not fair to the workers or the community as a whole, they wrote, that great and powerful industries were allowed to blight the neighborhoods at their gates.[67]

The juvenile court, established in Cook County on July 1, 1899, in large part through the initiative and vision of the Hull-House group, was widely regarded as a great social invention. Edith Abbott and Nisba Breckinridge believed that if the prized new court was to operate effectively, it must be evaluated and facts obtained for its future development. The result was a study of the juvenile court in its relation to the families and homes from which its wards had come. The records of all the delinquency cases handled by the court from the date of its establishment to June 30, 1909, were studied, as was information about what had happened to children before the new court came into being. These data were supplemented by home visits and interviews with parents of all the children brought to the court during the year under study. Again students were thrust into a powerful learning situation as they worked under Edith Abbott's and Nisba Breckinridge's direction to help gather and analyze data and in the process observe the exacting and creative way in which these two women approached social investigation.

The delinquent children before the court were found to be there for related causes, manifested differently among the children. The analysis focused on the child but fixed the "problem" not on the child but on an aspect of his or her social and economic environment. The study had shown the relationships in delinquency between the characteristics of individual children and their families and the characteristics of complex social situations. As Julia Lathrop pointed out in an introduction to the published study, no cure-all had been found, but the searching and subtle relationships in youthful delinquency had been uncovered.[68] The book was of interest not only in this country but in England as well, where one observer called it "a noble book . . . an application of C.O.S. principles to cases of delinquency . . . on such a scale as to be absolutely original."[69]

The lack of effective enforcement of school attendance laws led Edith Abbott and Nisba Breckinridge to study nonattendance problems in the Chicago schools. The results caused them to argue a need for school attendance officers, and they held that these should be social workers (leading to an assignment of the first visiting teachers in Chicago schools), since the reasons for nonattendance were interwoven with the social ills of the community—poverty, lack of adequate adult wage levels, illiteracy, and ill health—conditions that existed in many families but were not known to other agencies in the community, only through contact with the school.[70]

Edith Abbott had a persisting interest in prison reform and studied the deplorable conditions under which alleged offenders were kept in county jails. Her investigation led her to conclude that "the only way to solve the county jail problem is to abolish the county jails" and develop alternative measures.[71]

She also found time to write a perceptive article for the *New Republic*, one that reflected both the Abbott sisters' commitment to union organization and collective bargaining as a means of improving conditions for the poor and their strong interest in the problems of women in industry. The article was about the twelve-week strike of the Chicago garment workers, which was breaking up in the last days of 1915 with few gains for the strikers. She borrowed the phrase "Cheap Clothes and Nasty" from a famous indictment of the early garment industry, and used it as a title. She cited evidence of the justice of the workers' demands—less than a living wage for a full week's work. She hit hard at the refusal of Samuel Gompers and the American Federation of Labor to recognize the Amalgamated Clothing Workers, thus closing the treasury of Chicago unions that might have come to the assistance of the strikers and leaving the poorest and weakest groups of the community to fight the battle alone, many of them women and girls who were making their first sacrifice for the principle of collective bargaining.[72]

Edith Abbott's writing in these Hull-House years continued to reflect her interest in England's poor-law reform, its developing system of social security, and the implications for this country. She was also establishing on a firm basis her convictions about the right direction for social work education, a controversy in which her leadership was to become highly significant.[73]

The work pattern Edith Abbott set for herself was intensely demanding; she seldom allowed herself even a brief vacation without performing some work. She had begun to suffer from frequent severe headaches and her family worried about her pace of work. She was beginning to add to her income by her writing, and, although this was not her primary purpose in undertaking the books and articles which she turned out, she cared about payment for them. Edith Abbott had learned the meaning of money in the 1890s; she once replied to an anti-suffragist with an article entitled "Are Women Business Failures?" and in doing so revealed some of her own deep personal feelings about financial independence. "No self-respecting American woman of the middle classes," she wrote, "is any longer willing to be supported by her masculine relatives."[74]

Although Edith Abbott had moved into the role of a productive scholar at the School of Civics and Philanthropy, the future of the school was unclear. Finances had been a continuing problem as the Russell Sage Foundation began to phase out its funding of social work training schools; the Chicago school received its last annual grant in

1915. By 1916 the situation was most tenuous. Julia Lathrop, by then chief of the U.S. Children's Bureau, contracted with the Chicago school for several studies she wanted carried out and this helped, but the arrangement could not make up completely for the loss of foundation funds. Enrollments had increased, adding sharply to operating costs. Each month tended to become a financial crisis, often necessitating a delay in salary payments to Graham Taylor, Edith Abbott, and Nisba Breckinridge, sometimes for several months running. To attract competent lecturers was becoming more difficult each term.

As the problems worsened, Graham Taylor endeavored to engage the school's trustees in viable financial planning but with little success. In 1918 he offered to resign. The trustees, preoccupied with matters related to World War I, preferred that he stay on. Edith Abbott and Nisba Breckinridge believed that the school was drifting along most precariously.[75]

Financial problems alone did not fully account for Edith Abbott's and Nisba Breckinridge's restlessness, and even despair, about the school's future. They held significantly different views from those of Graham Taylor about the direction social work education should take. Breckinridge and Abbott were convinced that a university was the proper setting for social work education and that such an affiliation would provide important academic and financial advantages. Edith Abbott recorded in a letter to Julia Lathrop that she "heartily agreed" with Felix Frankfurter, who spoke at the 1915 National Conference of Charities and Correction where he had "told the Training Schools that they would never become properly equipped professional schools until they were University Schools."[76] Taylor tended to agree, more or less, that a university affiliation would be beneficial. He had, in fact, as early as 1907, looked into the possibility of a merger of his program with either the University of Illinois or the University of Chicago. The University of Illinois had shown interest and an appropriation bill was introduced into the state legislature but was lost in 1909, at which point Graham Taylor abandoned the search for a university affiliation.[77]

Taylor, Abbott, and Breckinridge also differed about the focus of the curriculum. Taylor saw practical experience in community agencies as the primary component; Abbott and Breckinridge regarded fieldwork as essential, but only to the extent that it embodied carefully planned and supervised learning experiences in selected agencies. Edith Abbott was influenced by Abraham Flexner's ideas about the training of medical students in clinics; she believed social work students should be given just as carefully planned and executed experiences in social agencies.[78] In addition, she and Nisba Breckinridge wanted rigorous academic standards in classroom courses at a level consonant with graduate education in disciplines related to social work as they knew those standards at the University of Chicago. They wanted their students to have access to a better library than the school was able to provide and to selected courses in the social sciences as these were being taught in major universities.[79]

In turn, Graham Taylor seemed to fear that the two women emphasized theory and principles too heavily, with a loss to students in practical ideas. He spoke of the "spirit" of his program as being at serious risk.[80] The conflict forecast a developing issue between proponents of privately sponsored "training" courses and social work "education" within scholarly institutions of higher education.

Nisba Breckinridge reopened the question of university affiliation in 1915 in a report to the school's trustees in which she outlined the advantages both financially and academically and urged that negotiations be attempted. A committee was appointed to consider the question, which in time led to some preliminary discussions with the University of Chicago. But in the face of pressing concerns as World War I drew closer, the matter was dropped.

In the spring of 1920, Graham Taylor, not in the best of health, took a leave of absence and went to California for two months. Nisba Breckinridge was appointed acting president during his absence.[81] At that time, the current year's deficit had not been met, there were no assurances of financial plans for the coming year, and the program for the fall had not been formulated or announced.[82]

In the face of these difficulties, Edith Abbott later explained, Nisba Breckinridge "accidentally" came into a discussion about the school's program with Albion Small, professor and head of the Department of Sociology at the University of Chicago. Nisba emerged encouraged that Professor Small supported the idea that social work education should be a graduate professional program and not an appendage to sociology. Abbott and Breckinridge consulted others, including Jane Addams and Charles Merriam, professor of economics. Merriam was enthusiastic about a merger. Jane Addams favored going along as they were for another year "for the sake of Graham Taylor," a view with which Abbott and Breckinridge did not agree. Jane Addams clearly preferred an independent school, but, in the face of the heavy financial difficulties, reluctantly agreed with Merriam and said Nisba Breckinridge should "at least . . . talk with the President."[83]

Professor Small arranged a meeting with the president of the University of Chicago, and, by the time Graham Taylor returned in June of 1920, negotiations were well under way for the University of Chicago to take over the work of the School of Civics and Philanthropy as a graduate professional course. Nisba Breckinridge and Julius Rosenwald (a chief financial benefactor) carried the major negotiating responsibility for the school with Graham Taylor a reluctant participant following his return. Under the terms, the school through its benefactors would be required to guarantee an annual income of $25,000 for five years.[84]

By August the University of Chicago had officially established the Graduate School of Social Service Administration with A.M. and Ph.D. degrees offered. Having been a lecturer at the University of Chicago since 1914 and having established a sound academic reputation, Edith Abbott was named an Associate Professor of Social Economy. Nisba Breckinridge worked hand in hand with Edith Abbott in the new social work program, but for the time being she kept her affiliation in Marian Talbott's Department of Household Administration and continued to serve as Assistant Dean of Women.[85]

By the time the negotiations were fully complete, most of the constituents of the School of Civics and Philanthropy were satisfied that the merger would mean an enriched curriculum, higher academic standards, and renewed financing, and that the move had probably been arranged at the right time. However, Edith Abbott and Nisba Breckinridge had had to explain and interpret to various individuals and groups and ask for patient understanding until the new program at the University of Chicago could begin to meet its promise for the future of social work education.[86] Julia Lathrop, who had showed concern initially about the plan, responded to a long letter from Edith Abbott with this endorsement: "I fully agree that there is no advantage in postponing the change. I do not see yet just how to cheer up Dr. Taylor but I am sure that delay is not the way. . . . There is much to be said for the success you have achieved in gaining recognition as a graduate school. That is a genuine triumph which will descend into the history of education."[87]

Much of the criticism had come from individuals, particularly those in the eastern social work training schools, who believed that a research-oriented university would not retain a strong fieldwork component in the curriculum.[88] It was in relation to Graham Taylor that Edith Abbott and Nisba Breckinridge received most criticism. His biographer, Louise Wade, wrote that Taylor had returned to Chicago from his leave in "a mellow and contemplative mood," that he had been "jolted" by the developments that had taken place in his absence. He recorded in his diary with some bitterness that the trustees seemed "glad to be relieved of further responsibility. None making any stand to conserve the whole distinctive life and work costing 18 years of sacrificial struggle."[89]

Wade concluded that Nisba Breckinridge and Edith Abbott had tended to discount Taylor's important achievements in establishing and administering an independent training program and had been "tactless in their dealings with the older man."[90] Tactless they probably were. Edith Abbott did not conceal her opinion that Graham Taylor romanticized his "years of sacrifice" for the school[91] and both Abbott and Breckinridge were intolerant of indecisiveness and compromise with academic standards. Furthermore, they felt they had been left with almost insuperable problems when Taylor went to California, and, with the school "on the brink of ruin,"[92] the situation seemed to them to require firm action of a kind that left tact clearly of secondary importance.

An underlying explanation of why Edith Abbott's and Nisba Breckinridge's action was criticized heavily was not doubt about the wisdom of the merger or their lack of tact. It was that two women had daringly challenged a man's leadership and that they did so because they were competent and ambitious, they believed in a yet untested model of social work education, and they were willing to take risks. They were competitive women who showed characteristics like those frequently displayed by men in rivalrous academic or business situations—characteristics that in the male were traditionally applauded and rewarded and in the female considered unexpected and threatening. That the merger represented a considerable degree of "personal victory" for Breckinridge and Abbott generated criticism of them in some quarters.

The transfer of the School of Civics and Philanthropy, in Edith Abbott's view, was "an act of faith on both sides. The University had faith in us when we said we wanted to develop *not* a vocational school but a professional school with a broad educational program and an emphasis on research. We had confidence in the University authorities when we were offered equal status in the University with the professional schools of Law, Divinity, and Medicine."[93] By 1924 the Board of Trustees at the University of Chicago elected to make the work of the School of Social Service Administration a permanent part of the university. Edith Abbott was named dean of the school.

Considering Nisba Breckinridge's longer years with the University of Chicago and the fact that she had been so largely responsible for negotiating the school's entrance into the university, why was Edith Abbott and not Nisba Breckinridge named dean when the school passed its "apprenticeship?" Possibly Nisba's very active and visible role in bringing about the transfer was itself one reason. In such difficult negotiations, even the most able individuals often acquire some enemies. Perhaps her accompanying Jane Addams to The Hague to protest World War I was a factor. Other women delegates certainly encountered hostility for doing so over a period of years. That she had held a pacifist position may have heightened Graham Taylor's personal feelings against her—so his biographer suggested.[94] Perhaps Nisba Breckinridge's close association with Marian Talbott played a part. Many academicians regarded home economics as less rigorous than other disciplines; and however much the university valued Marian Talbott's services as Dean of Women, she was often difficult; those who had differences with her may have made an association to Nisba Breckinridge. Or perhaps Breckinridge genuinely wanted Edith Abbott to have the post. She admired Edith Abbott tremendously and they were very close friends; Nisba may have preferred to continue her close association with Edith without the full responsibility as administrator.

Edith Abbott believed that schools of social work should do more than just respond to personnel needs as social agencies defined them. She saw a larger task—that of developing and defining the social work profession itself. By 1924 Grace Abbott was well established as chief of the Children's Bureau. Edith's new appointment put the two sisters in a position to build on the kind of research collaboration between the federal government and a university that Julia Lathrop had initiated earlier between the Children's Bureau and the School of Civics and Philanthropy. In addition, Grace Abbott's perspective from government in Washington and Edith's from a position of authority at the University of Chicago opened up a singular opportunity to affect the direction of change in the developing social welfare system.

It is said . . . that the quality of recent immigration is undesirable. The time is quite within recent memory when the same thing was said of immigrants who, with their descendants, are now numbered among our best citizens.[1]

— GROVER CLEVELAND

CHAPTER 4

Advocacy and Immigrants

THE RECORD of the years that the Abbott sisters spent at Hull-House is replete with evidence of their liberal position in relation to the "immigration problem." Within the sisters' partnership, Edith Abbott became the immigration scholar and Grace Abbott the creative administrator and advocate for new foreign-born Americans.

A major wave of immigration, which included the foreigners pouring into Chicago when Grace Abbott became director of the Immigrants' Protective League, began around 1880 and aroused much resentment. In 1882 three of every four immigrants came from northern and western Europe. But by the turn of the century more than half were coming from the countries of southern and eastern Europe. The earlier and more easily assimilated immigrants were succeeded by Italians, Slavs, and Jews, substantial numbers of whom were poor, illiterate, and unskilled.

The general prosperity and tolerance of the Progressive era did not extend to the "alien races" who came to America in such numbers. Increasingly the new immigrant bore the brunt of society's antagonisms. Social ills of whatever nature were associated with the recent arrivals. Labor conflict was attributed to the presence of foreigners who worked too cheaply; political corruption was a result of the necessity to capture the immigrant vote; urban congestion, vice, and crime—all were due to the presence of an alien element that resisted assimilation and undermined society's institutions. Underlying the negative attitudes was race prejudice, with lack of acceptance of differences that would not meld easily into the Anglo-Saxon culture. To justify abandoning the ideal of America as a refuge for the oppressed of other nations, the characteristics of the new immigrants were cited and the causes of the conflict ignored. Scapegoating the immigrant was the substitute for reform, and restriction of immigration was espoused as a remedy.

Within such a social and political climate, the Chicago Immigrants' Protective League was formed in 1907. It grew directly out of a committee of the Women's Trade Union League that had become interested in young immigrant women who had come alone to the United States. The committee found quickly that serious problems existed not only among immigrant women and girls but among men as well, and that the types and extent of exploitation were beyond its ability to handle, thus prompting the creation of a new organization. Sophonisba Breckinridge had been a leading force in getting it established and Jane Addams tried to interest her in heading it. But although Nisba Breckinridge gave time to guiding the new organization through the early months, she was not willing to give up her position at the University of Chicago. Jane Addams then suggested that they "find a competent man" to act as Nisba Breckinridge's assistant while she continued to give some time to overseeing the work. Breckinridge rejected the need to search for a competent man since a competent woman was at hand; she proposed Grace Abbott.[2]

When Grace Abbott accepted the position with the Immigrants' Protective League, she had not given up the idea of continuing her graduate study. In 1909 she reduced her work for the league to half time and moved to Beecher Hall (where she served as head resident) so that she could study in the university libraries at night. She taught a course in political science and enrolled in courses in the University of Chicago Law School. But the challenge of the Immigrant's Protective League was more attractive to her than academic life. Her law and political science courses had given her a grasp of fundamental legal principles, government structure and processes, and political organization. Having obtained that base of knowledge, she was eager to use it in a position of administrative leadership. So after six months and the award of her master's degree in political science she went back to Hull-House and devoted herself fully to the administration of the league.[3]

The first president of the Immigrants' Protective League was Judge Julian W. Mack, whose maternal grandfather had been a significant pioneer in the influx of Jews to America in the early nineteenth century.[4] Judge Mack became a staunch friend and supporter of Grace Abbott.[4] Julius Rosenwald, the founder of Sears Roebuck and a noted philanthropist, was a board member of the league from its beginning; he continued to be a board member during all the years of Grace Abbott's tenure. Not only was he generous with gifts of money to the league, he became a strong friend of Grace Abbott, one whose interest in her work and in her as a person followed when she moved into the Children's Bureau.[5] Ernst Freund, a distinguished professor of law at the University of Chicago, was another member of the league board. He remained a friend and consultant to Grace Abbott on the position of the child in law after she went to the Children's Bureau. He continued on the board of the Immigrants' Protective League for twenty-five years, sometimes as president, and his counsel to Grace Abbott on national and state policy in relation to immigration was invaluable.[6]

When Grace Abbott began her work with the Immigrants' Protective League, the organization's purposes were only generally stated in its constitution. It intended to discover and then to counteract those agencies and conditions which led the immigrant into serious problems. The league was prepared to concentrate on situations that were peculiar to the immigrant rather than the native-born American, such as difficulties of admission, exclusion, naturalization, relatives living abroad, and the need to guarantee a safe arrival to the many immigrant women traveling alone. It was ready as well to examine the lack of facilities and services that affected both native-born and immigrant but from which the immigrant suffered more frequently and acutely, for example evening schools, well-administered public employment agencies, and regulated banks. It intended to avoid duplicating already existing services and looked to the established public and voluntary agencies for certain basic services already offered the native-born and now needed by some immigrants—services when an individual was destitute, ill or physically infirm, or orphaned.[7]

The league's concern for immigrants and its approach to helping them was different from that of other social agencies represented in the National Conference of Charities and Correction. The Charity Organization Societies were largely interested in making charitable efforts more efficient. When the charity organization workers dealt with immigrants, it was with the individual case, and the cause of the immigrant's difficulties was believed to be clearly allied to an element of personal fault or inadequacy. The State Boards of Charity were another important force in the national conference. Representatives of these boards were concerned about policies and finances within institutions, and about corruption in their management. Their concern tended to center on the matter of legal settlement and the hazards of having to assume financial responsibility for dependent immigrants from other states or localities. The other large representation in the conference was from the settlement houses. These "social workers" were especially interested in the immigrants about them, in their life-styles and the problems posed by the demands for their acculturation. They were sometimes misguided and patronizing in their efforts to help, but on the whole introduced humane insights into the immigrants' situations and gave much practical help in concrete difficulties.[8]

The Abbott sisters and Nisba Breckinridge perceived immigrants as oppressed and in need of protective services, not because immigrants were personally inadequate and helpless individuals but because they came into an inferior social, economic, and political status upon their arrival in this country. The Abbotts and Breckinridge were interested in facilitating the assimilation of immigrants to the extent necessary for them to secure and keep self-sustaining employment, support their children in their American school life, become citizens with voting and other political rights, and in general gain access to the opportunities they had envisioned when they left their own countries. The Abbotts and Breckinridge valued the individual cultures and customs of the various immigrant groups. Grace Abbott, especially, wanted the newcomers to stamp their contribution to American life with the national individuality they brought from their homeland. All three were alert to the development of immigrants' own self-help charitable institutions, and believed these should be encouraged and expanded. Their aim was characteristic of a social work tenet—to help people to help themselves. At the same time they seldom doubted that they knew the correct solution to many of the immigrants' problems, particularly those requiring a familiarity with governmental organizations and a capacity for utilizing official agencies. In those instances, the Abbotts and Breckinridge believed, immigrants would need the help of organizations like the Immigrants' Protective League.[9]

Grace Abbott, with the support of her board members, intended to provide a broad service to Chicago's foreign newcomers. The professional approach which she evolved was a dynamic and farsighted form of advocacy. Her strategy included two levels of intervention: one, personal and protective services for individual immigrants and families in trouble; the other, use of the courts, governments' regulatory authority, state and municipal agencies, and other influences for social action with the aim of changing conditions creating the problems. She intended to secure the interest and cooperation of civic leaders, voluntary organizations of all kinds, and state legislators, and she proved especially resourceful in doing so.

Grace Abbott assumed it was essential to have a staff who could speak the languages of the people who came to them, not only for those newly arrived but for those who had been in America for several years but were still quite dependent on their native language in any emotionally laden or technical discussion. As a result she recruited and directed a group of bilingual staff—women and men—who had competence in one or more of these languages: Bohemian, Croatian, Italian, Greek, German, Lettish, Lithuanian, Magyar, Norwegian, Polish, Russian, Ruthenian, Slovak, and Yiddish.[10]

The league was confronted with almost overwhelming tasks demanding attention. Its broad charge meant that Grace Abbott had to select from among all the immediate problems those undertakings that after some investigation seemed most promising for improving the immigrants' situations and changing the external conditions that created their difficulties. She dealt with the complexities of the demands by identifying the interrelationship among problems and the characteristics of the larger system of hardships and injustices. Without this analytical approach she might have been submerged into the confusion of the immigrants' many immediate and pressing needs.

Even so, league visitors gave a vast amount of direct service to individuals and families. They supervised the release of thousands of immigrants newly arrived into Chicago's railroad stations and arranged for their delivery to correct addresses of relatives or friends. They provided accommodations for immigrants who were temporarily stranded. They made thousands of visits into the foreign colonies of the city to identify problems and offer help. They traced lost baggage; secured money due immigrants from railroad and steamship companies, employment agents, employers, and bankers; translated papers which immigrants were being urged to sign but could not read; helped make arrangements to bring over the relatives that immigrants had had to leave behind; explained how to begin the process of naturalization and where to go to get assistance in securing work; prepared affidavits for persons whose relatives were detained at Ellis Island or threatened with exclusion from the country; helped distraught newly arrived immigrants find the relatives or friends in Chicago whom they had expected to join but for whom they had a wrong address; they performed many other tasks appropriate to an individual's or family's situation.

Not atypical, although her situation was far simpler than many, was the girl whose first introduction to Chicago was the police station where she had been taken because of an inadequate address for finding the friend who expected her. "She had the name and address of the girl friend who lived in Chicago and had promised to get her work, written in the front of her prayerbook, and she could not understand that it was incorrect. She tearfully insisted on accompanying the Polish visitor of the Immigrants' Protective League on the search for her friend and grew more and more discouraged as one clue after another was tried and failed. Finally the girl said that her friend worked in a bed-spring factory. Starting out anew on this clue, she was found in the third bed-spring factory they visited." One number had been left off the address she so carefully had written in the prayer book.[11]

The most difficult and exacting individual cases that came to the league, particularly those that involved complicated legal questions growing out of the federal immigration laws, Grace Abbott handled herself. In the first months of her new job, she achieved a notable success defending an immigrant threatened with deportation. Edith Abbott described the problem:

> The old imperial Russian government was always reaching out its strong arm to bring back for trial at home the political figures who had started abortive "revolutions." On this occasion the Russian government demanded the arrest and extradition of a hard-working Lithuanian carpenter, a devout Lutheran, who had escaped to America and had been living and working quietly in South Chicago. The man and his friends appealed to the newly organized Immigrants' Protective League and its young director for help. Was this man, whom the Russian government charged with murder and arson, properly subject to extradition or was he a political refugee entitled to asylum in this country? He had been involved in an unsuccessful uprising in a Lithuanian village in which one or more persons had been killed and the village partly destroyed by fire. Grace became convinced that he was a political rebel who had taken part in an attempt to resist a despotic and oppressive government. He was, by all of our laws and all of our traditions, entitled to an asylum in America.[12]

Grace Abbott organized material for the man's defense and presented it before the United States Commissioner of Immigration, who subsequently refused the Russian government's request for extradition. The victory was all the sweeter because the Russian authorities had able male representatives there to present evidence against the alien. It was an event to savor when Grace Abbott came in late to Hull-House and the dining hall to tell Jane Addams and Julia Lathrop and other eager residents about the outcome.

The case of the obscure carpenter did not go unnoticed by those who feared the presence of "anarchists" brought to this country by the tide of immigration. Grace Abbott's successful defense, backed as it was by Jane Addams and other settlement workers, provided an occasion for reactionary newspapers again to attack Hull-House as a center of socialism. Because she was Chicago's most noted settlement worker, Jane Addams was the focus of most of the publicity.[13]

Undertaking to give adequate protection to immigrants as they reached Chicago was one of the demanding responsibilities that Grace Abbott assumed for the league. The government gave supervision to the arrival of immigrants only up to their port of entry into the United States. But on the long overland train journey and upon entrance into the bewildering confusion of the Chicago railway stations, immigrants were left to shift for themselves. Large numbers of them needed special help—those who spoke no English, who were not met by relatives or friends, or who had incorrect or doubtful addresses to go to. When immigrant trains arrived at the station, railroad officials and police steered the distracted foreigners in the direction of private express or cabmen. With their official-looking caps and badges and a stock of foreign phrases, such drivers and their runners could get the attention of the anxious immigrants and herd them into their vehicles. Many immigrants were let out at incorrect addresses, often far from their hoped-for destination; baggage was lost; and overcharging was rampant.

Grace Abbott secured the cooperation of officials of the Chicago and Western Indiana Railroad who furnished the league with a two-story building across the street from the Dearborn Street station. She pressed for better cooperation from the police in getting the foreigners out of the station and across the street where league staff helped put them in touch with friends or relatives or provided overnight accommodations until friends could be located. In 1913, 41,322 persons were brought across.

Grace Abbott attacked the organized opposition of the unscrupulous taxi drivers and express men. Her persistence in the use of friendly agreements, complaints to the Inspector of Vehicles, suspension of licenses, and arrests eventually brought some relief.

In all of this, Grace Abbott sought to demonstrate that official supervision of overland immigrant travel was necessary. She continually pointed out that such problems were beyond the proper authority or financial resources of a voluntary agency and constituted a responsibility that belonged to the federal government. She called attention to the annual head tax collected by the government from each immigrant. In 1913 the tax yielded an income of nearly two million dollars in excess of the total appropriated for immigration service. Grace Abbott believed, as did her board, that this revenue should be regarded as a trust fund and used to assist the immigrant during the difficult period of adjustment to American life. She thought there should be federal immigration stations at interior localities and to that end enlisted the help of influential groups, particularly the Commercial Club of Chicago. Her aim was to bring pressure upon Congress to establish a federal station in Chicago that would take on the responsibility of protecting the immigrant upon arrival.

The combination of demonstrated effective help at the local level, strategic pressure on Congress, and Grace Abbott's testimony to Charles Nagel, secretary of commerce and labor, resulted in the passage of an act in 1913 that placed responsibility for protective services to the arriving immigrant on the United States immigration inspectors, including the placement of inspectors and matrons on the immigrant trains. Various delays on the part of the federal government kept the federal station in Chicago from being opened until World War I had almost brought the massive flow of immigration to an end. But the principle of governmental responsibility for the protection of the arriving immigrant had been established.[14]

Foreign men and women were often the victims of the "immigrant banks," unchartered institutions that flourished on business from the most recently arrived aliens. American banks were usually without clerks who could speak foreign languages; they were generally impatient with immigrants, and the banking hours made it inconvenient or impossible for these newly arrived persons to do their banking there. With no regulation of private banking in Illinois, any man could set himself up as a banker and receive money from alien immigrants for transmission abroad or for safekeeping. These bankers often conducted other businesses as well. Many were also steamship agents (because this offered clients a recognizable link to their mother country). Others were grocery-story owners, barbers, tailors, or saloonkeepers and Grace Abbott was amused to find that one even found it possible to be both banker and plumber.

Not all the immigrant bankers were dishonest or unbusinesslike in their methods. Some acted as spokesmen for their nationality groups and performed many useful services in the foreign colonies. But in substantial numbers unscrupulous ones exploited the foreigner by failing to transmit the money abroad, charging excessive fees, or putting the immigrant's funds to their own personal use. Jane Addams installed a postal substation at Hull-House, partly for the convenience of the neighborhood but also to protect immigrants who wanted to send part of their hard-earned money home to support a family member or to buy a steamship ticket that could bring a wife or parent to this country.

The suffering caused by loss of savings was more than financial; it brought emotional stress as well. Grace Abbott was particularly touched by a seventeen-year-old boy who had given his savings to a banker to send to his mother in Kiev. The money had been collected painfully from the ten dollars a week that he earned in a tin can factory.

Many months passed before he learned that his mother had not received the money. He was overcome with fear that she would think her son had forgotten her.[15] There were many similar cases.

Firm and persistent intervention on the part of the league could sometimes retrieve the newcomer's savings from a dishonest banker, but when prosecution was indicated, it was usually unsuccessful since principal witnesses to the fraud were in another country and the courts would not accept as evidence cables or affidavits sent from outside the United States.

With Ernst Freund's assistance Grace Abbott prepared a report in 1913 for the Illinois Bankers' Association, recommending the regulation of all private banks and the licensing and inspecting of all agents engaged in the foreign exchange business. Her recommendations were accepted by the association's committee in Chicago but the membership of the more conservative statewide association voted against any kind of regulation. Two years later even the failure of a large number of private banks, some whose depositors were chiefly Americans, failed to stir the state legislature to action. Municipal regulation as a temporary expedient was proposed. Grace Abbott testified before the city council in support of the proposed ordinance although she believed that regulation was properly a matter for the state.

Exploitation made possible by the lack of regulation of private banking continued to be a frustrating problem. In her last annual report Grace Abbott called attention to the new banking law passed by the state legislature in 1917 and awaiting ratification at the next general election. The act contained some of the provisions suggested by the league, especially those relating to safeguarding money sent abroad.[16]

Another pitfall for immigrants was the legal system. Many foreigners were arrested, brought before the municipal court, tried, and convicted without ever understanding the charge. Frequently no competent interpreter was present to speak to the immigrant in his or her native language or to translate for the court. Sometimes the police officer who made the arrest or the prosecuting attorney acted as interpreter. Grace Abbott brought these kinds of injustices before the County Bar Association and pressed hard to get qualified interpreters and public defenders appointed. In particularly flagrant cases of an attorney preying upon the poorest immigrants, she appeared before the Bar Association's grievance committee to try to get disbarment. In such instances it was her style to have the facts and the law clearly in mind and then to appear fearless in facing the unscrupulous attorney.[17] Her keen interest in law and the skills she learned early in life from her lawyer father made her relish such encounters.

Her work brought Grace Abbott into contact with many immigrant men and women who were in prison for nonpayment of fines. Many were too poor to have employed a lawyer to defend them and too unskilled in the use of English to have understood the charges against them. Edith Abbott was at that time employed as a statistician for the Chicago City Council Committee on Crime. Using Grace's intimate knowledge of the circumstances of immigrant men and women in trouble with the law and Edith Abbott's research skills, the two undertook, as Edith Abbott phrased it, "to set out the statistics from the House of Correction in a proper way." They found that about four-fifths of all the prisoners were in the House of Correction for nonpayment of fines, most of them poor foreigners.[18] It was one of many examples of the reciprocal nature of the Abbott sisters' work.

Because public employment agencies in Chicago were poorly administered and underfunded, the immigrant was quite dependent on private employment agents. Grace Abbott carried out a study to determine what kinds of work could be obtained through private employment agencies, in what ways the immigrant was exploited, and the changes needed in laws to reduce such exploitation to a minimum. One hundred ten agencies were investigated, all those in the city that made a speciality of placing foreigners.[19] The employment situation was complex for the immigrant man. Because of his ignorance of English he could not work without an interpreter, and interpreters could be profitably employed only when large groups of men worked together. Chicago, Grace Abbott found, was a clearinghouse for the seasonal laborers of the country. The only kind of work offered by 68 percent of the agencies handling immigrant men was at a distance of from one hundred to one thousand miles from Chicago. Groups of men were sent to parts of the country of which they were entirely ignorant, and the work was by its very nature sure to be of short duration—harvesting Dakota crops or Michigan berries or Minnesota ice; working in the oyster beds of Maryland; or building a railroad in Wyoming or Arkansas.

The work was poorly paid and board was expensive and poor in quality. In addition, the men had to try to save for their return rail ticket to Chicago in order to obtain their next job. Even when work was available near the locality where they were when the job ended, they had no means of knowing where the work was. With limited funds and difficulty in speaking English, they were afraid to venture far in search of work. Discouraged and homesick, they did whatever they had to do to get back to their small circle of friends or family in Chicago.

Grace Abbott described concrete cases that had come to the attention of the league. Not atypically, an employment agency had sent a group of Bulgarians to Arkansas to work at building a railroad—fifty-three men and two women (one with a baby) who expected to act as cooks. Each person had paid the Chicago agent fourteen dollars and was promised steady work and at least average daily pay. When they arrived in Arkansas they were told the work was twenty-five miles away. They walked the distance only to have the foreman say he had no work for any such number of men. Eventually he employed fifteen men and the woman unencumbered with the baby. The rest started walking back to Chicago. At the end of the third day the woman was exhausted and the men pooled their money to send her with her baby back to Chicago by train. Then they scattered to try to find work. Two were shot by the police in St. Louis. The rest eventually reached Chicago. With Grace Abbott's help they finally recovered the fourteen-dollar fee each had paid; but in their relief to be back in a familiar part of Chicago they put aside what they had suffered in their long walk from western Arkansas, and did not consider the concept of damages which she presented.[20]

At the mercy of contractors and employment agents and in danger of becoming a homeless wanderer, the American workman did not want such employment. Because the immigrant could do the work and had to have work immediately, he accepted it. But he was commonly exploited by the private employment agent who charged excessive fees for the services rendered, sent him out for work which was not as represented to him in character, permanency, or wages, or sent him to jobs which did not materialize at all, leaving the foreigner many miles from the city labor market.

Such conditions, Grace Abbott concluded, reacted upon the city itself by making Chicago the headquarters of an army of casual laborers who kept down the wages of the regular unskilled workers in the city. Worse, she pointed out, the disappointed seasonal workers became the material out of which a degraded working class was created.

Grace Abbott recommended that the free public employment agencies be reorganized and strengthened and she stated specific changes which should be made in the employment agency statute which would give more protection and right of redress to the immigrant. She organized a series of meetings with influential groups including Chicago's prestigious Union League Club and the Commercial Club and presented the results of her study and the contrast with better practices in some states. As a result of the publicity given her report, she was invited to meet with the secretary of the state Bureau of Labor and the inspector of private agencies in Chicago. A tentative agreement was reached on a bill to be introduced in the state legislature, which Grace

Abbott drafted in consultation with Ernst Freund and lobbied for in the state capital. The bill was passed by the legislature, making it possible for an immigrant to go out of the city to work with a contract in the language he understood and containing a full statement of the kind of work to be done, the wages promised, the terms of transportation, and the probable duration of the work, all of which made remedies for misrepresentation and fraud more available upon his return to Chicago.[21]

The new legislation did not do all that Grace Abbott had advocated. The public agencies were not reorganized then, nor did the new statute end exploitation of casual laborers in the boarding camps of many of the railroad and construction companies. But substantial gains had been made in putting the employment of immigrant men on a sounder basis. Such gains, made in the first year of the Immigrants' Protective League, constituted a significant demonstration of Grace Abbott's uncommon ability, not only in fact-finding and analysis, but in successfully using her findings to garner prompt and influential support for her recommendations.

Grace Abbott's first year accomplishments were realized despite an appendicitis operation in early January. Any surgery was risky then, and she did not have an easy time. When she was able to leave the hospital, Mr. and Mrs. Samuel Dauchy took her to their home to convalesce and to protect her from returning too soon to the demands of the league and the strenuous activity of Hull-House.[22]

During the two months that Grace was away, Edith Abbott not only carried her own work but met Grace's most pressing responsibilities at the league office. And Edith, who deplored financial dependence on masculine relatives, was the one to appeal to their older brother, Othman Jr., for help with medical bills. To benefit her sister Edith could set aside her pride and defensive thrust toward independence.[23]

Grace Abbott's strong interest in working conditions related to her desire to find ways for immigrant women to enter a trade that had a future. It was not possible to live at Hull-House and not be caught up in the trade union movement. For the Abbott sisters the Garment Workers strike of 1910 dramatized a never-to-be-forgotten struggle of an oppressed group of workers that eventually was to result in one of the world's great labor organizations, the Amalgamated Clothing Workers of America.

There were then in Chicago about 45,000 clothing workers, half of whom were women and girls, and three-fourths of whom were recent immigrants, in large measure recruited into the industry because they

79

were uneducated, desperate for work, and could be easily exploited. Trouble started in September when a small group of women walked off work at Hart, Schaffner and Marx; their protests at a reduction of the piece rate for seaming pants from 4¢ to 3¾¢ had gone unheard. The action spread without direct orders from anyone and within seven weeks 40,000 clothing workers were resisting the accumulated injustices.[24]

The strike began in warm weather, but winter came early, increasing the suffering of the hungry workers and their families. Hull-House was a reliable place for sympathetic support. Jane Addams, Ellen Starr, Grace Abbott, and Margaret Dreier Robins of the Women's Trade Union League worked with the United Charities of Chicago to collect funds for food, coal, and clothing for children. Strikers from the Hull-House neighborhood also helped collect funds, often by door-to-door contributions in the poorest quarters. Edith Abbott assigned students from the School of Civics and Philanthropy to interview strikers to learn more about the character of the trade and their grievances. Grace worked on two citizen committees organized to investigate the grievances and to try to find remedies.[25]

The end of the strike came when strikers found they were no longer physically able to keep up the fight. They had been forced into accepting the impossibility of continuing the bitter struggle against hunger and cold. Some gains were made in the Hart, Schaffner and Marx establishment, but, for the most part, the strike was lost. Yet it was not lost completely. As was noted on the pages of *The Survey*, "Even among the 20,000 starved into submission—the word starved is used here in its literal meaning—the gain in spirit and in learning how to stand by one another through a long and bitter struggle will scarcely be lost."[26]

Sidney Hillman, then a young cutter at the Hart, Schaffner and Marx factory, emerged as a labor leader. Later he wrote to Edith Abbott about Grace Abbott's support for the strikers: "She joined our picket line, helped to collect funds for food and shelter, spoke at our meetings, presented our case to the public, and appealed to the city administration to arbitrate the strike." Even more significantly for her future work with child labor, Hillman recalled, she had "recognized the basic issues of the struggle and realized the need for the introduction of orderly industrial-relations machinery in the clothing industry, which had at that time just been making its initial steps and needed support and encouragement. She . . . helped to show that labor disputes are not private encounters between employers and employees but that they are of profound social and economic import and affect the entire community."[27]

From the beginning of her work in Chicago Grace Abbott was interested in understanding the individuality of the different foreign groups who needed the league's help. In her first year of work with the league she published a study of the Greeks, who were populous in the immediate neighborhood of Hull-House. She studied the Bulgarians, too, stimulated by the fact that in April 1908 600 unemployed and starving Bulgarians had marched on city hall to demand work. With the assistance of the demonstration leader, Grace Abbott studied 100 of the men who had marched on city hall. They described to her how the steamship agents had come to their villages and given glowing accounts of the marvelous prosperity in the United States. The agents went to the coffee houses of the village and read letters from the United States which said "unskilled workmen often earned $200 a month; jobs were so abundant that a man after landing only had to choose which one he would take." The Bulgarian peasants talked together and decided to go to "that blessed land," even though they knew nothing of the size of the country and the higher cost of living. To get the fare they sold their cattle or borrowed money with their father's small piece of land as security. Most of the men in Grace Abbott's study had arrived in Chicago in October as winter came on. Inevitably they became part of Chicago's summer army of casual laborers.

Grace Abbott found the Bulgarians to be a strong, sober, quiet, and intelligent people. They had come from a system of compulsory education in Bulgaria and they brought an enthusiasm for learning. They were eager to work. Grace Abbott perceived them as "splendid material for skilled workmen" and she thought "there should be some way by which they could be turned more quickly and with much less suffering into the valuable citizens they are sure to become."[28]

As Grace Abbott continued her work with the Immigrants' Protective League, she began to feel that it was not possible to go on assisting people in adjusting to American conditions without seeing "the problem at its source" and coming to a fuller understanding of the immigrants' "normal home life" as they had known it in their native land. So in the late summer and fall of 1911 she traveled to Europe to visit the countries from which most of the "new" immigrants came to Chicago. The officers of the league granted her a three-months leave of absence to make the journey.[29]

The Abbott sisters went together in late August on the *Teutonic* from Montreal to England. They parted there and Edith stayed on to renew her English friendships and make inquiries into labor conditions and other related matters. With an English friend, Maude Marshall, Edith went into Germany to interview Labour Exchange officials in Stuttgart, Cologne, Nuremberg, and Frankfurt and to observe government housing projects for working people.[30]

How Grace and Edith Abbott financed this trip to Europe is unclear. Possibly they had been able to save for it, but if not they probably borrowed from a bank in Grand Island or from their brother Othman Jr. (who never seemed unwilling to meet their requests but did give his sisters periodic businesslike accounts of their indebtedness and repayments). Once the Abbott sisters had embarked on their careers in Chicago, they were reluctant to let lack of money stop them from any kind of experience that added to their professional development. Edith once told her niece that she borrowed money to go to Europe "to look into things" that she wanted to know about and urged her niece to do likewise. The confidence each of the Abbott sisters had in her own future was impressive.

The fact that in 1911 Grace went by herself into Europe and from one country to another where she could not speak the languages also attests to her special self-confidence and zest for new experiences. Traveling about Europe alone at that time was unusual for a woman. Single women most often traveled with relatives or with another female as a companion and antidote to the loneliness of moving about in a man's world and the frustration of coping with arrangements and language barriers. It is doubtful that Edith Abbott would ever have chosen to make such a trip alone; she found using her incomplete mastery of German in the cities she visited "hard work" and had been a little reluctant at first to take the trip into Germany, even with a friend, because of the anticipated difficulties with language and finding comfortable hotels at reasonable rates. Grace Abbott, however, appeared to go with the utmost confidence even into countries that were little visited by Americans. At the end of her three-months leave her only complaint was that she could not go into Greece as she had planned to do. "The people here think it is not at all safe," she wrote her mother from Budapest. "The war has begun in the Aegean and there is cholera in both armies and the Bubonic Plague in North Africa. I am disappointed and wish now I had come by way of Greece."[31]

The area of Europe where Grace Abbott spent most of her leave was the old Austro-Hungarian empire with its many different unassimilated peoples. Ruthenians, Poles, Magyars, Croatians, Bohemians—all guarded their separate cultures, religions, and national loyalties. Grace studied conditions not only in the important cities of Vienna, Budapest, Fiume, Krakow, Lemberg (or Lvov), and Prague, but she went as well into the remote villages of the rural countryside. She visited labor exchanges, factories, schools, churches, hospitals, prisons, and reform schools for girls and for boys. She went into homes of rich and of poor people; and she went into the fields and the home industries where peasants were at work. Her interest was principally in the regions from which there was the greatest emigration to America; but she sought to learn too about the people who were either too poor or too prosperous to consider leaving.

In all her observations Grace Abbott sought to establish the reasons why people emigrated from their homeland. Most important, she believed, were poverty and class distinctions that kept many people quietly plodding along but sent others to risk everything on possible success in America. The social and economic life, she said, turned many peasants into immigrants "because, as an American would say, the people have no future." The "racial struggle," in Grace Abbott's perception, was an important cause of emigration from Austria-Hungary. In Hungary she heard people express bitterness over the fact that although Hungary had six large cultural and ethnic groups, there was only one official language. But Austria had twelve official languages and yet she witnessed the same or even greater friction among the separate groups. Each wanted its own schools and fiercely resisted any real or imagined governmental effort toward assimilation. Grace Abbott found it puzzling. She wrote her parents, "In Chicago and the U.S. generally the children become American quite with their approval and here they lie awake nights fearing they may lose their Bohemian or Polish characteristics while they sleep. Language seems to make the man here." In her attempts to integrate her perceptions of immigrants in Chicago and their family members and friends still in their native land, Grace Abbott was beginning to realize in a new way what powerful demands the immigrants encountered when they left their villages of Central Europe and entered the teeming industrial growth of Chicago. In an effort to survive, many of their preferences and values had to be discarded for new ones—ones that were not so much "foreign," as they were labeled in America, but were actually "American"—a new form of American behavior with no counterpart in the simpler environment of their native land.[32]

Her visit to Central Europe gave Grace Abbott an admiration for the individuality and strength of the people she met. Upon her return she told her board members: "I felt as I went about in Austria and Hungary and saw so much in the national habits and institutions to admire that we must insist that the Hungarian, Bohemian, Polish or Croatian American is not doing his duty to America unless he makes a Bohemian, Polish, or Hungarian contribution to American life. . . . A great means of enriching our national life is lost if we give those who are coming from the various nations of Europe the impression that we desire to neglect all but the Anglo-Saxon element in our population."[33]

Not all Americans felt as Grace Abbott did about the immigrants' potential enrichment of national life. Exclusionists were not satisfied with attempts to limit admission and sought further means to restrict the new immigration, with the introduction of a literacy test as a chief proposal. President Cleveland vetoed the first bill, passed in 1897, that provided for a test of literacy of all immigrants over sixteen. He called attention to the "radical departure from our national policy" that the provision implied. But the controversy between restrictionists and anti-restrictionists continued. In 1907 Congress appointed a federal commission to carry out a comprehensive inquiry into immigration to the United States. Among its recommendations was the exclusion of those persons unable to read or write in some language. Arguments advanced for a literacy test were varied. The need to reduce the sheer numbers of aliens entering was cited—the country could not look after all who wanted to come in; the influx of unskilled laborers willing to work for the cheapest wages meant depressed wages and lowered standards of living for American workmen. Edward T. Devine, then director of the New York School of Philanthropy, favored a test of literacy because he believed the new immigrant would increase "the relief problem." The immigrants of the twentieth century, he said, bore little resemblance to the colonists of the early days of the Republic.[34]

Senator Henry Cabot Lodge was one of the best-known spokesmen for adopting a literacy test. Such a test, he stated, would scarcely affect people from the United Kingdom or English-speaking Germans, French, or Scandanavians; it would bear most heavily on Italians, Russians, Poles, Hungarians, Greeks, Asiatics—people who were alien to the great body of citizens of the United States. He associated illiteracy as found in these national groups with criminality, juvenile delinquency, slums, pauperism, and the abhorred "birds of passage" who came to the United States and then returned to their native land taking the money earned in America with them. He argued forcefully that the quality of American citizenship was threatened—"nothing less than the possibility of a great and perilous change in the very fabric of our race."[35]

Judge Julian Mack was among the outspoken opponents to a literacy test. At the annual meeting of the Immigrants' Protective League in 1911 he warned against a revival of the "old spirit of Know-nothingism" that had condemned the Irish and the German in the revolutionary times of 1848 and that was now being called forth to condemn the Italian and the Slav and the Russian Jew.[36] Grace Abbott responded to the restrictionists through the pages of *The Survey*. The federal Commission on Immigration had endorsed restriction because of the character of the new immigration and the oversupply of the kind of labor it furnished, so she cited evidence from the commission report itself. Conviction for crime was not more common than among the native-born; new immigrants were rarely found among the victims of alcoholism, were generally not "diseased" nor in the ranks of paupers; their homes were in reasonably good or fair condition; and they sent their children to school in such numbers as to show that the advantages of an education were fully appreciated.

As to the argument that immigrants introduced a lower standard of living by offering their labor cheaply, Grace Abbott pointed out that immigrants never intentionally underbid in the labor market—the desire to raise their standard of living was a major reason for their coming to America. But they often unwittingly accepted wages below the market rate when they were confronted by unscrupulous employers or dishonest employment agents. Protective measures to save immigrants from industrial exploitation seemed more sensible to Grace Abbott than a literacy test to restrict their entry into this country.

As for the claim that the new immigrants as a class come to this country only to accumulate money to take home, Grace Abbott pointed out that the immigrant among the 30 percent of those who returned permanently to their native country "had never been known to take back with him the railroads, canals, and subways he has built, or the great industries that have been developed through his labor." Further, the commission report had indicated that the 30 percent was made up very largely of "victims of disease and industrial accident, the aged, the temperamentally unfit, the widows and children of immigrants who had died here."

Grace Abbott challenged the findings of the commission report that immigration should now be looked upon as an economic problem only. She cited the continued need for a religious asylum, for an escape from landlordism that kept families in poverty, and for a place for the political idealist. She gave examples of the kind of atrocities still committed upon Jews in Russian pogroms and contrasted it with the relatively mild persecution suffered by the Puritans whose courage Americans had been taught to respect. She asked if the commission had not adopted an entirely new standard of "intolerable conditions."[37]

In 1912 Grace Abbott went to Washington to testify before the House Committee on Immigration and Naturalization relative to the further restriction of immigration. Congress subsequently enacted a provision for a literacy test but it was vetoed by President Taft. If Edith

Abbott's record of the event is accepted, then Grace Abbott was an effective witness: "President Taft told our friend Mr. Rosenwald that 'it was Grace Abbott's statement' that had persuaded him to veto the literacy restriction."[38]

The push for restriction continued. Grace Abbott went again to Washington in 1914 to testify at a public hearing held by President Wilson.[39] Again Congress passed restrictive legislation which President Wilson vetoed with a message that the *New Republic* termed "more interesting as an expression of latter-day liberalism than as a contribution to our stock of ideas on the subject of immigration."[40] Congress could not override his veto, but persisted by passing similar legislation in 1917 and this time was able to override Wilson's second veto. A test of literacy for entry of immigrants became law.

Proposals to restrict immigration had always provoked controversy but in 1917 concern for the immigrant was eroded by the nationalism of wartime. Protest against the literacy test was minimal.

The non-English-speaking immigrant girls and young women who came on their own to the United States were of special interest to Grace Abbott; she made them a particular concern of the Immigrants' Protective League. A great stream of them came between 1910 and 1915 — over half a million between the ages of fourteen to twenty-nine. Of these, over 70 percent were less than twenty-one years of age. They came "to make their own way" and to be able to help their parents at home or bring a brother or sister over for new opportunities.[41]

One of Grace Abbott's first efforts at the league was to negotiate with the immigration authorities at the ports of entry so that the names of women and girls who were coming alone from Europe to Chicago would be sent to the league as they began their overland railroad journey. Each one was visited in Chicago as soon as possible after her arrival by a league staff member who spoke her own language. In the period 1910 to 1915 almost 27,000 young women were visited in this way. Almost all wanted advice about work, night school, or a boarding house and many kinds of injustices were uncovered with occasions to give help. The league visitors offered communication with a competent and friendly woman in the bewildering city. In addition, under Grace Abbott's direction her staff systematically collected information to be used in program-planning for the league.

Women were more likely to come to well-established friends and not to be in debt. But girls between fourteen and twenty-one years of age faced formidable problems in their attempts to become self-supporting and self-directing. Usually they arrived owing money to a relative or friend who had paid their passage. Many had no near relatives to rely upon in Chicago. The "friend" whom they joined upon arrival might be someone of a very casual connection. When in their own country they had discussed their wish to come to America, some villager had volunteered that they could stay in Chicago with "my cousin" or "brother" or "friend" until they were settled. In such instances, as soon as the girl found a first job the relative or friend felt no further responsibility for her.

Grace Abbott felt close to these young immigrant women. She had visited the villages of Central Europe where girls now in Chicago had lived in intimate contact with nature. Grace Abbott reported to her board with keen sensitivity to the enormous changes with which young immigrant girls and women had to cope:

> Many of those who come are so young that their work at home had been to watch the sheep and the cattle in the fields or on the mountain slopes from sunrise to sunset. Others worked side by side with the men in the harvest fields or in the factories. Some of them were hod-carriers and toiled up the ladders with the heavy brick of stone which the masons—always men—laid. . . . They were never in any sense regarded as the equals of the men with whom and for whom they toiled. The belief in the inferiority of women was deep rooted. . . . In those districts in which there were no schools, or in others in which the term was very short, or where the number of those allowed to attend was limited, as among the Jews in Russia, illiteracy was much more common among the women then among the men. . . . Most of them are, at first, homesick and disappointed. The streets of the city are not always broad and beautiful, and life not always gay and bright as they had hoped it would be. . . . Sometimes it seems to the peasant girls as if they had exchanged the green fields and woods and the long, quiet winters for a hideous round of noise, heat, and bitter cold.[42]

Overcrowded housing was seen by the league as having drastic social consequences that hindered the immigrant woman in her adjustment to America. Many had left villages that had fewer people than lived on a single street in Chicago, where they were confronted with new demands on the world of space about them. Because more men than women emigrated, the family with whom the girl lived usually had a group of men lodgers as well—partly to help one's compatriots and partly to help supplement low wages and avoid the danger of becoming public charges subject to deportation. The danger, as Grace Abbott stated it, was that such overcrowding meant a lack of privacy and of the restraints which privacy reinforced. Overcrowding, she said, made inevitable a certain familiarity among the occupants and contributed to the breaking down of barriers, particularly after some special excitement—a wedding or other celebration where liquor had been used freely. She believed that too rapid Americanization was a hazard and that a young woman who had left her family, who was expected to learn a new language, who was changing her way of dress and her manners could easily conclude that all of her old-world ideals should be abandoned for some different and less-clear moral code.

In such a situation league visitors usually urged the only immediate alternative, "to change from scrubbing in a restaurant on State Street to scrubbing in the Presbyterian hospital where she would also live." But Grace Abbott recognized that this was not likely to be acceptable. For it meant a lonely kind of job—leaving the foreign district and friends to perform the same hard work in a setting of strange events and stranger food. Grace Abbott wanted more boarding clubs for girls similar to the ones established near the Jewish colony by a group of Chicago's Jewish women.[43]

It did not seem surprising to Grace Abbott that unwed pregnancy occurred among the young immigrant women and that many remained unmarried by the time the baby was born. Their break with old-world ties left them with an ambiguous basis for decisions about people and situations. Some worked at jobs where a man who used the threat of dismissal could exercise control over them by a combination of persuasion and force. A need for affection and even temporary release from ill-paid drudgery led some to become pregnant, sometimes with hopes of marriage, only to be abandoned as "an easy mark" or because of forces in the men's lives over which they had no control. The immigrant girls and women lacked the opportunities for the kind of outdoor recreation they had been used to at home; their new environment offered mostly dance halls at the rear of disreputable saloons. Grace Abbott accepted the fact that girls who had worked long hours in factories or at scrubbing and sometimes in jobs where no one spoke to them all day would want some recreation on Saturday night. She told the board members of the league that she regretted the fact that the women's excessive weariness at the end of the work day kept some from attending night school regularly but that still she was happy to say that many of them did go to dances and nickel shows in spite of their fatigue.[44]

Grace Abbott was concerned with sex outside of marriage not as a sin but because of its likely consequences. The dangers were real. The lack of access to successful birth control methods or abortion except under the most hazardous conditions maximized the woman's vulnerability to unwed pregnancy and the toll that it exacted from her. The stringent reality of the double standard of morality placed the burden of responsibility for an unwed pregnancy directly upon the woman. It was she who felt the shame, even scorn, that society leveled upon her. It was she who was held responsible for the baby and who witnessed the painful effects of the stigma assigned to her child thereafter. She might even face the possibility of deportation. Grace Abbott cited for her board the case of some Russian-Jewish girls who were deported (even though they had been in the United States since they were children) because of their unapproved sexual behavior. Reflecting her strong feelings about the injustice done them, Grace wrote, "Added to the family separation, these girls were ordered returned to a country in which religious prejudice made their outlook the more uncertain. . . . They were sent away from any possible sources of help to live in what was to them, in spite of their background, an alien country. And after these girls had been banished, could any one feel that the country was safer when the men and the conditions responsible for their ruin were left here in the United States—a menace to other girls, both immigrant and American? There is no reason to feel that the moral health of the country will be promoted by special severity in dealing with the immigrant girl who has gone wrong."[45]

Of special concern were immigrant girls who never arrived in Chicago after having started from their port of entry. In the year 1909–10 20 percent of the unaccompanied girls destined for Chicago were unaccounted for at the end of their journey. Even after better procedures had been set up for immigrants' arrival in the Chicago stations, each year as many as 10 percent of the women traveling alone remained unaccounted for. Sometimes it could be established that she had gotten off the train before reaching Chicago, either by mistake or by suggestion or persuasion on the part of a stranger. But in many instances no trace at all could be found of a woman who had a correct address to go to in Chicago and apparently had every intention of going directly to the friends or relatives who were expecting her. Grace Abbott showed more objectivity and restraint than most in her response to the "vice crusade" then current in Chicago and other American cities. She knew that a young girl who failed to arrive at her announced destination could be in a number of places besides a house of prostitution. She believed that a very large number of them eventually safely reached friends and had not needed any special assistance. Yet enough cases came to the league's attention and were found to be "precarious in the extreme" to suggest some real basis for alarm at the number of these "lost immigrant girls."[46]

Prostitution in America had become the focus of a sweeping attack, almost a national mania.[47] To the idea of prostitution, in itself repugnant to many, was added the danger of "white slavery"—an organized traffic in women for high profits. The hysteria of alarmists became the inevitable accompaniment to the concern of the more objective-minded citizens. Sensational stories abounded of innocent girls and unwilling women who were deceived or persuaded by false messages or appeals to come to someone's aid and then were spirited away to a house of prostitution. It was believed that in foreign countries as well as in America young girls and women were sexually attacked and then transported to foreign brothels under the control of large vice syndicates. Young immigrant girls coming to America without their fathers, mothers, brothers, or other relatives to protect them were considered to be in special danger of procurers who watched the arriving ship's gangplank to identify the naive girl by herself who could be tempted away by promises of an easy job, good pay, and fine clothes.

A distinct characteristic of the crusade against prostitution was the assumption that the nation's foreign newcomers were back of the evil, not only by becoming the city's prostitutes but by organizing, supporting, and thriving upon the lucrative traffic of prostitution. The nativist's attacks were directed in large measure toward southern Italians and Austrian, Hungarian, and Russian Jews.

Grace Abbott's analytical way of thinking made her deplore the hysteria that attached itself to the debate about prostitution and white slavery. She was alert to the prejudiced and restrictive thrust of the nativists and clearly understood that although prostitution and immigration were not causal in their relationship, there was a dangerous effort to link them in the public mind. In all her work on behalf of the young immigrant girls, Grace Abbott undertook to interpret their need for protection and opportunity, and to differentiate their presence and problems from the rise of prostitution.

To Grace Abbott the question of traffic in women was a problem of the status of women rather than a problem of vice and immorality. She recognized that some of the fallacies in the movement to stamp out prostitution also lent support to continued suppression of women. One such fallacy was built on the notion of the natural perfection of women and imperfection of men, a belief used to justify the double standard of sexual behavior with its resultant censure of the "fallen" woman. Grace Abbott knew not all females were innocent and not all males were predatory. But she recognized the real handicaps that women faced in society.

She recognized another fallacy used as propaganda to justify a continuing limited view of women's capabilities. That was the notion that by nature women were weak, easily tempted and deceived, and if once "ruined" they necessarily would give up and be docile about entering a house of prostitution. Grace Abbott looked upon the vice crusade as a means to improve the status of women. During the campaign, as prostitutes came to be perceived by the public as victims, they were viewed by some more sympathetically as part of a class of women who had suffered the wrongs of society, wrongs that should be corrected to prevent other women from suffering such degradation.

Another outcome of the attack on prostitution was the extensive involvement of women as leaders. It proved to be another means to improve the status of women and gain recognition of their readiness to contribute to needed social reform. Grace Abbott was one who advocated a variety of liberal reforms as an alternative to "forcible repression" of vice and as a solution to the hazards faced by immigrant women and by many other women in America as well.[48]

In 1921 the League of Nations held a conference out of which came further proposals for international efforts to control the traffic in women and children as well as a recommendation for a permanent advisory committee to the league on the subject. As a body of experts the new advisory committee was to study related developments in the different countries and consider ways to prevent the traffic. At its first meeting in 1922 the new committee recommended that Germany and the United States should be invited to appoint representatives to serve on the committee, even though neither country was a member of the League of Nations. Following approval of this resolution and an invitation accordingly extended to the United States, in late 1922 the secretary of state, with the president's approval, appointed Grace Abbott (by then serving as chief of the Children's Bureau) to represent the United States on the league's advisory committee "in an unofficial and consultative capacity."[49]

On March 4, 1923, Grace Abbott sailed for Europe aboard the *President Harding*. Lillian Wald saw her off in beautiful weather and Florence Kelley wrote Edith Abbott in her inimitable style, "It *is* a new world when this country sends a woman citizen abroad in the interests of the victims of the slavers!"[50]

Grace Abbott was the first American to serve on any committee of the League of Nations and as such her appointment was heartening not only to those who wanted to see women in important posts but also to persons who had been disappointed at America's decision not to join the league and who still hoped that American points of view would be heard through the League of Nations. An announcement of her appointment was made at the dinner meeting of the Women's Pro-League Council in New York. A Harvard law professor who attended wrote Grace Abbott, "They hailed your appointment to the committee as if it were the opening of heaven itself." Harriet Laidlaw of the Pro-League Council wrote that "people really rose to their feet and shouted when the letter from the Department of State was read."[51]

Of the ten committee delegates meeting in Geneva, only three were women—Grace Abbott, Dr. Paulina Luisia, a physician from Uruguay, and Dr. Estrid Hein of Denmark. The Advisory Committee on Traffic in Women and Children moved at a sometimes tortuously slow pace for Grace Abbott. It often appeared that the task of the committee was to defend society against prostitutes, rather than to find means to prevent their exploitation and the infamous "traffic." Grace Abbott had not expected progress to be swift, since any significant gains involved fundamental changes in the position of women. But as the parliamentary procedures crawled along, it became apparent that some of the official representatives wanted only to protect their country's system of regulating prostitution through licensed houses.

Grace Abbott emphasized the need for facts as a basis for the committee's recommendations. The European men on the committee in 1923 were hardly prepared for the American delegate, who was a woman courteous but unimpressed by their aura of authority and able to negotiate herself through the formalities and urbanity common to international governmental meetings. She was not a simple person to deal with. She never went into a formal session without comprehending the agenda in terms of issues and proposals that could be expected to emerge, the positions that would be taken for and against those proposals, and the likely coalitions. Furthermore, she had always managed to interpret informally her own point of view and organize her own nucleus of support before the meeting.

By the second meeting of the committee Grace Abbott was ready to put forward a proposal for a scientific investigation of the facts about prostitution in the various countries and the international traffic. Her object, she said, was to obtain "official and accurate" data regarding the existence and nature of the traffic in women and young girls. She advocated an inquiry among several groups of countries in different parts of the world and in the major cities representative of those known to have different laws, regulations, and forms of legal administration. Much progress in social reform in the United States had grown out of investigations carried on by impartial and experienced experts, she told the delegates. Moreover, people of the world had been given conflicting reports regarding the traffic and they desired to know the truth. She proposed that such an investigation should ascertain whether there was in fact an international traffic in women and girls for purposes of prostitution; if so, between what countries the traffic was being carried on; the methods used in procuring and transporting women and girls; and the effectiveness of national measures undertaken to eliminate the traffic. She said it was "absolutely necessary to secure the facts to refute sensational exaggerations or general denials as to the traffic and . . . of supreme importance to have an intelligent basis for a sound programme for international cooperation for the suppression of the traffic."

Grace Abbott's proposal met some heavy opposition. The French delegate, who had resisted other attempts to learn more about practices that were approved or condoned in his country, argued for asking each country to make its own investigation within its borders. Grace Abbott countered that this was not practical since the necessary facts would relate to the situation inside the country from which the victims were abducted as well as the situation in the country to which they were taken. No single government would be able to investigate conditions within its own territory and within other countries as well. When the proposal was finally voted upon, five countries voted in favor of it; the French delegate, along with the Japanese and Romanian, voted against it.[52]

Before she left the meetings in Geneva, Grace Abbott held out hope that money could be found in America to finance the study that was to be done by a "Special Body of Experts." Upon her return she approached Raymond B. Fosdick in his capacity as an associate in John D. Rockefeller's Bureau of Social Hygiene and proposed that the bureau support the investigation. Fosdick agreed to an amount not to exceed $75,000, with the funds to be forwarded to the League of Nations through Grace Abbott, acting for that purpose as a private citizen. Dr. William F. Snow, a public health administrator with special interest in the field of social hygiene, assumed responsibility for the study of the traffic.[53]

The extensive investigation revealed facts that helped to bring about more effective international agreements. Clearly there was an organized international traffic in women and young girls for purposes of sexual exploitation. The traffic out from Europe was related to the postwar unemployment and the enormous excess of women. By contrast the Latin countries of the Western Hemisphere had both money and a surplus male population. Some of the victims were lured into going abroad with men who later forced them into prostitution. Their plight was little worse, however, than that of the experienced prostitute who could scarcely have foreseen the sort of exploitation and virtual slavery to which she would be subjected upon finding herself illegally in a foreign country, ignorant of the language and without friends.[54]

In 1924 the League of Nations had taken over the work of the International Association for the Protection of Children (formed under Belgian leadership in 1921) and asked the Advisory Committee on Traffic in Women and Children to propose a child welfare program. Grace Abbott viewed the advisory committee's focus on traffic in women and young girls as too narrow for an international program of child welfare. She wanted a child welfare committee separate from the traffic committee, one that would concern itself with broader aspects of children's lives through an emphasis upon a scientific approach to understanding childhood and adolescence and to preventing and ameliorating their problems. She stressed that concern about the traffic, though valid, emphasized an oppressed status of girls and women and was drastically limiting in relation to the needs of children and young persons in more nearly "normal" situations. It was true, she acknowledged, that children were sometimes the victims of prostitution but that this was only a small part of the problems of neglect and delinquency among children. And she recognized that the practice of always linking women and children in any discussion of problems or programs was a reinforcement of traditional attitudes toward women. She told the committee that "women and children are frequently spoken of as though the interests of both could be served by the same measures. The reverse is true. Women and children have both suffered by the assumption that they and their problems should be classed together."[55]

Grace Abbott wanted also to have additional assessors appointed to the committee. Those non-voting but official participants were all European or British. Grace wanted others appointed from other parts of the world—the United States, South America, Asia, and Australia—and from among persons who had specialized knowledge in child welfare. She reminded the committee participants that most of them had been appointed as specialists in the subject of prostitution and traffic in women and that they were considering the problems of children from a narrow standpoint and in so doing injuring the cause of children.

Grace Abbott's memorandum to the committee recommending a program for a separate committee on child welfare caused extensive debate. The British delegate, who had been influential in the committee from its inception, was firmly opposed to a division of the committee into separate assignments. Grace Abbott held just as firmly to the position that if all the problems of children were not kept in view but continued to be made subordinate to the narrower concern of traffic in women, the committee's usefulness would be enormously reduced. In the end her proposal was adopted almost in its entirety and the committee's final report carried this statement: "The advisory committee thinks it right to take the normal child as the basis of its study and to emphasize the constructive side of child welfare as much as the more limited though vital question of protecting the child from adverse influences or wilful exploitation." It was agreed that the committee's existing title gave a misleading impression of the scope of its work; it was changed to the "Advisory Commission for the Protection and Welfare of Children and Young People." The commission was to consist of two committees, the "traffic in women and children committee" and the "child welfare committee." The delegates of the governments represented would sit upon both committees but each committee would have its own separate group of assessors with the appropriate expertise.

The work to be undertaken included a study of the law relating to the protection of life and health in early infancy; law relating to the age of consent to marriage; the repatriation of abandoned delinquent or neglected children; child labor; family allowances; and the effect of the cinematograph on the mental and moral well-being of children. Again Grace Abbott was able to garner financial support for part of the child welfare program from a grant by the American Social Hygiene Association.[56]

Grace Abbott's well-developed and well-executed plan to enlarge the scope of the committee was noted by John Palmer Gavit, an American journalist following league affairs in Geneva. He wrote:

> While the ponderous and much advertised International Conference on Traffic in Arms and Munitions of War was dragging its tortuous and voluble way toward its end in Nothing Much . . . in another part of the great headquarters of the League of Nations . . . fifty-five countries . . . took formal notice of the Little Child. . . .
>
> Grace Abbott felt compunctions about voting on the budget of the Committee, since her government was not contributing a penny to its funds. By the same token, since her relation to the Committee was "consultative" (under the extraordinarily anomalous conditions of American official relationship with the League), she declined election as its vice-president . . . but the new child welfare work goes a long way toward offsetting the attitude which her official position forced her to take. . . . Grace Abbott thought she couldn't properly be vice-president, but she was a whole team of horses on the job![57]

95

The question of why the State Department had instructed the distinguished head of the United States Children's Bureau not to accept the committee vice-chairmanship was raised by Raymond B. Fosdick in a letter to the *New York Times*. If the State Department took the position that a United States official should not hold office on a League of Nations committee, then why had it allowed Dr. Hugh S. Cumming, the surgeon general of the public health service, to serve as vice-chairman of the health committee. The reason, Fosdick said, was that the State Department had no policy at all in relation to the League of Nations and had "blown hot and cold with no pretense of consistency."[58] He did not mention the additional probability of bias about women in high positions.

Serving on the committee was a difficult assignment, as Grace Abbott often discussed with Edith and with Julia Lathrop and Nisba Breckinridge. Day after day participation in the European male atmosphere of *"maisons tolérées"* was wearing. The slow pace and the formal dinners added to fatigue, and the entire experience was made more difficult by the American government's undefined stance in relation to the league. On the one hand Grace Abbott was permitted to participate in the meetings as an official delegate of the United States government without formal instructions as to what resolutions to propose or support. She voted on all issues that came to a vote and had the freedom to make her own decisions as to whether she needed to consult the State Department. At the same time she believed that the "move to make me Vice Chairman with a view of making me Chairman the following year was really done to embarrass the government which was very uncertain what it did or did not want to do" in relation to league activity. In addition "neither Secretary [of Labor] Davis or Secretary Doak were really interested [in the Committee on Traffic in Women and Children] or in favor of cooperation," although, Grace stated, "my impression is that the State Department wants me to go."[59] Attendance was costly in time and further complicated by the expectation that such business should be incidental to other official business if travel authorizations were to be agreed to.

The time of year in which the committee's meetings were held made it difficult for Grace to attend, coming as they did in the spring when a new presidential administration was taking over or when congressional appropriations for the Children's Bureau were in a critical stage of debate. When she was appointed to the committee she had expected to be able to attend every two years at the most, but even that proved impossible. After Julia Lathrop was appointed as an assessor she was freer than Grace to attend and did much of the early work in trying to launch the league's new child welfare program. Although Grace had been appointed to the Advisory Committee on Traffic in Women and Children for a continuing period during her years as chief of the Children's Bureau, she did not attend another session until 1930 and then for a special committee on the traffic in the Far East.

World War I brought the stream of immigrants almost to a halt. In view of the upsurge of nationalism and the likelihood that funds for work with immigrants would be harder to find, Grace Abbott reasoned that her opportunity for constructive work with immigrants was likely to be curtailed, at least for the duration of the war. The Immigrants' Protective League from its beginning had had serious financial problems, and by the end of 1917 even Julius Rosenwald, who had been by far its largest contributor, declined Nisba Breckinridge's usually successful plea for additional contributions on the basis that the amount he had contributed in relation to the total budget always had been out of proportion for any one person.[60] So Grace Abbott accepted Julia Lathrop's pressing invitation that she come to Washington to administer the first federal child labor law. The league granted her a leave of absence.

The years the Abbott sisters spent at Hull-House were seminal ones for them. Certainly Hull-House had a powerful and impressive list of residents, unsurpassed by any other settlement; and Jane Addams had an unusual ability "to create a sense of unity, a sense of purpose among the residents." Edith Abbott stated the reason simply: "We were held together by the sincere and gracious liberalism of Miss Addams."[61] Like most of the Hull-House residents the Abbott sisters held great admiration and affection for Jane Addams. She in turn had been quick to recognize their talents and potential. Grace Abbott especially moved swiftly into an easy relationship of trust with her, partly because Grace was open, confident, and outspoken. Edith Abbott was inclined to be somewhat more deferential toward Miss Addams. Jane Addams heartily respected the good judgment of both sisters and trusted them even on issues where she was personally vulnerable. When she hoped to be elected president of the National Conference of Social Work in 1922 and found herself facing the very disappointing prospect of losing, she conferred of course with Florence Kelley and Julia Lathrop, who with Jane Addams made up "the inner circle" of Hull-House influence, but she delayed her telegram indicating her withdrawal from the race until she had had one from Julia Lathrop saying that "the Abbotts agreed."[62]

The extent of Jane Addams's ever growing confidence in and regard for Grace Abbott can be seen from the fact that sometime before her last illness she had let Grace (and others as well) know that she hoped Grace would become her successor at Hull-House. In 1935, when Jane Addams's death was imminent, Alice Hamilton wrote to Grace in Geneva about the seriousness of the illness, the critical importance of filling Jane Addams's position at Hull-House with the right person, and the qualities that Grace possessed that made her seem a logical choice. She urged her to give positive consideration to becoming the next head resident at Hull-House.[63]

Grace Abbott declined the opportunity to follow Jane Addams at Hull-House. She was pleased to have Jane Addams's trust but by 1935 she had many options from which to choose how she would expend her energy and she had carried heavy responsibilities and had serious illnesses. But the opportunity gave her satisfaction and served as an integrative force to the parts of her outstanding career.

As World War I came closer to the lives of the American people, the Abbott sisters' years together at Hull-House ended. These had been immensely productive years for each, not only in tangible and lasting achievements, but in the shaping and firming of the structure of their lifelong partnership. By the time Grace Abbott went to Washington, the character of that partnership had become clearer. The two sisters' interests coincided, having been developed together through a close association that began in early childhood. Each was keenly intelligent and committed to common values and goals. At the same time their different personality traits and particular competencies made possible an enormously effective division of labor—one reflecting separate roles with flexible boundaries.

Edith Abbott was the scholar—always thirsting to establish the facts and a fuller understanding that would provide a more exact base of knowledge for their common endeavors. Her early investigation into women in industry, child labor, tenement housing, the juvenile court, truancy and school attendance policies—all this and more became part of Grace Abbott's repertoire of knowledge, on which she relied in the arena of social reform and public administration. Grace was the sister who took the initiative in translating that knowledge into action. She could masterfully interpret data to influential groups whose support was essential to the Abbott sisters' goals. As Edith put it, "I could assemble the facts and write a report, but Grace had the gift of applying the proper legislative remedy"—a statement that though accurate reflected Edith's practice in her later years of underplaying her achievements in comparison to those of her younger sister.

In fact, their influence and stimulation were reciprocal, an aspect of their partnership which is apparent from examining their published works on immigration. Certain leading ideas run through each one, making them seem almost one work. These major points of view are ones that Grace Abbott drew out of her daily work with the Immigrants' Protective League and set forth in her annual reports to her board, in her book, *The Immigrant and the Community*, and in her report to the Massachusetts Commission on Immigration.[64] In turn, Edith Abbott was prompted to begin a long period of research that produced two classic volumes on immigration. In *Immigration: Selected Documents and Case Records* and in *Historical Aspects of the Immigration Problem*, she made use of case records (which Grace selected for her from the files of the Immigrants' Protective League) and public documents to which she added her own insightful introductions and interpretations. The result was a sound historical, legal, and philosophic base for the resolution of immigration policy issues that is still of interest today.

Each sister understood and trusted the other implicitly and never made major decisions without consulting the other. Each could accurately predict the other's reaction to a new situation, although when it was politic to do so, either one might convincingly convey the impression that she had "no idea what my sister would say." Each worked tremendously hard, Edith more intensely without the relief that might have spared her serious headaches and other forms of stress. Each had a quick wit, but Edith's often had a biting edge, while Grace's was of the kind that in any discussion cleared the air, cut through any person's self-assumed importance, and brought about a more relaxed perspective on the question at hand—even as she bore in with a reminder of the data and a proposed line of action.

As Grace Abbott prepared to leave for the nation's capital, the sisters' unusual partnership was yet to show the full fruition of their uncommon talents.

*The child labor movement has in every country supplied the
shock troops in the struggle for decent working conditions.*[1]
—GRACE ABBOTT

CHAPTER 5

The Iniquity of the Fathers

JULIA LATHROP, who was responsible for bringing Grace Abbott into
the federal government, was probably a greater influence upon the
younger Abbott sister than was Jane Addams. When the Abbott sisters
arrived at Hull-House in 1908, Julia Lathrop was already there, having
come very soon after its founding in 1889.

In background and convictions Grace Abbott and Julia Lathrop were
much alike. They were quite different in manner, however. Julia Lathrop used persuasion and even cajolery and made her points in a circu-
itous way with frequent expressions of empathy for another's point of
view. Grace Abbott was forthright, sometimes abrupt, immediately direct in her presentation of facts and in her responses to the position of
others. At the same time, each possessed administrative ability reflected in capacity for sound judgments and readiness to make and im-
plement decisions. Each had a sense of humor in daily affairs. More
rare was their quality of "disinterestedness" in relation to the social issues they worked for. Jane Addams noted this quality in Julia Lathrop—"that sort of disinterested virtue which has been designated as
'the refusal to nurse a private destiny.'"[2] Felix Frankfurter described it
in Grace Abbott—"a rare degree of disinterestedness and indifference
to the share of her own ego in the cosmos, and the fruitful humor that
so often goes with real disinterestedness."[3]

Grace Abbott was close to Julia Lathrop from the time she went to
Hull-House until Julia Lathrop died in 1932. Grace had also moved
easily into a position of trust with Jane Addams. With the child labor
movement as a special link, Florence Kelley too came to rely upon
Grace Abbott. Thus it was that Grace Abbott (and inevitably Edith as
the other sister in the partnership) came to enter the Addams-Lathrop-

Kelley inner circle of Hull-House influence which extended over so many years.

When the Children's Bureau was established by Congress in 1912, President Taft appointed Julia Lathrop as chief upon the urging of the National Child Labor Committee, influential in the bureau's creation. Julia Lathrop had wanted Grace Abbott to join the staff of the Children's Bureau prior to the passage of the new child labor legislation, but Abbott was reluctant to leave Chicago. However, diminishing resources for the immigrants' cause and the opportunity to administer the new federal child labor legislation were enough to draw her away. So she moved to Washington, D.C. in April of 1917. In Chicago Nisba Breckinridge wrote in her melancholy style, "We saw Grace Abbott off this morning, gladly and yet, very sadly. Life here is a much more dreary waste without her."[4]

Child labor in America has a history as old as the settlement of the colonies. Although early reformers tended to assume that child labor was a phenomenon of their day, Edith Abbott's investigations revealed that children had been employed in the very earliest of America's factories. It had been a natural consequence of the colonial belief in the virtue of industry and the sin of idleness, even in children. The social reform movement, however, belonged to recent if not contemporary history; it had taken a long time for public opinion to become enlightened enough to take heed of the social sin of child labor.[5] Once it came, the child labor movement held the attention of reformers and their adversaries from the 1880s until the 1930s.[6]

The progressive reform climate of the early twentieth century fostered a new interest in the conditions of child labor. Branches of state and federal government undertook major inquiries using trained investigators. Significant among these was the *Investigation of Woman and Child Wage Earners*, begun in 1907 by the Bureau of Labor Statistics and published in nineteen volumes. Edith Abbott, Sophonisba Breckinridge, and Mary McDowell are credited with developing and launching the idea for this ambitious undertaking. Abbott and Breckinridge's work on the employment of women in industries, begun in 1905, had shown the inadequacy of census data as a means of getting at the causes, conditions, and effects of female labor. The three women agreed that obtaining authoritative information would require a national study, financed by Congress but carried out by experts. Together they launched a movement to obtain congressional authorization and financing for the study.[7] Congress was interested at the time in undertaking an investigation of child labor, and in responding to the pressure for a study of women's employment it linked the interests of women and children into one large study. When completed, the findings had recorded not only the conditions of child labor but also the history of attempts to secure protective legislation, suggesting the need for a federal child labor law.[8]

By the beginning of the twentieth century most of the progressive states had enacted some kind of age and hours legislation as a protection to children against exploitation in certain work situations. However, employers resisted enforcement on the claim that industries in states without child labor legislation had an unfair advantage. As the controversy grew, many of the nation's leaders, supported by the Progressive party in 1912, believed that the evils of child labor could be controlled only by federal legislation. The National Child Labor Committee, organized in 1904 to carry on nationwide investigation of children's employment and to campaign for stronger legislation and better enforcement, had been divided as to the need for federal law-making. Most of the committee's activity had been aimed at reform at the state level. But by 1914 this influential committee joined those who pressed for uniform standards through federal child labor legislation.

In spite of national interest, however, the battle continued to be heavy. As Grace Abbott later observed, from 1890 to the enactment of the first federal child labor law in 1916, public opinion divided as sharply and bitterly over the subject of child labor as it did later over governmental enforcement of the right of workers to organize.[9] Child labor bills were first introduced into Congress in 1906. During the following ten years, other bills were introduced, killed in committee or reported out but not brought to a vote, or passed by only one house of Congress.

Conditions in some southern states, especially North and South Carolina, furnished strong evidence of the need for a federal law. In writing about the period, Grace Abbott recorded that

> the employment of large numbers of young children in the South led to national and even international criticism in the twentieth century. The millowners were riding high in those days, and in the textile states of the South legal standards were low and generally disregarded. . . . Southern manufacturers demanded the same freedom in the exploitation of children that the millowners of England and New England had had a century earlier and denounced the movement for federal legislation as the effort of northern agitators to kill the infant industries of the South. . . . They argued before Congressional committees that the children had to learn to spin when they were young to provide a skilled labor supply and that they were better off in the mills than they had been on the

mountain farms from which they and their parents were brought by the millowners.[10]

When the Democratic party came into power in 1912, the South, because of its strong power base in both houses of Congress, continued to block child labor legislation. But when a new presidential election impended, spokespersons of the social justice forces let President Wilson know that they regarded the pending child labor bill as "the acid test of his progressivism."[11] As a result, child labor legislation (the Keating-Owen bill) was adopted on September 1, 1916, to become operative one year later. In passing the bill Congress had acted under its power to regulate interstate and foreign commerce. The intent was to close these channels to the products of child labor.[12]

The act prohibited the shipment in interstate or foreign commerce of products of a mine or quarry that employed persons less than sixteen years of age, and of a mill, factory, or manufacturing establishment that employed children less than fourteen years of age. In addition, children in these establishments were not allowed to work more than eight hours a day, six days a week, or at night. The act left unprotected the much larger numbers of children working in home industries, in agriculture, and in the street trades, and no conditions were prescribed for employed children's educational level or state of health. Nevertheless, passage of the act signaled the beginning of a new national policy for the protection of children and represented a significant victory for the reformers.

The administration of the law was assigned to the Department of Labor and the secretary in turn delegated the responsibility to the Children's Bureau. Congress appropriated $150,000 for the act's enforcement and necessary preliminary work, making it possible for Julia Lathrop to bring Grace Abbott into the Children's Bureau as director of the newly created Child Labor Division five months before the act took effect.[13] She was clearly Julia Lathrop's choice; however a few weeks after arriving in Washington, to smooth out some rough edges in the appointment process, Grace Abbott reached out to her Chicago network of support. She wrote Edith that "it seems the Child Labor people here and the Government Reference bureau had picked a young lawyer for my job who had had experience in drafting legislation and who worked on the Child Labor Bill and I think they have made it a little uncomfortable for Miss Lathrop. Mr. [Thomas I.] Parkinson—Columbia Law man—who runs the Bureau is still recommending him for something. Mr. Parkinson has great respect for Mr. Freund and I think and Miss Lathrop agrees that if Mr. Freund would write Mr.

Parkinson mentioning my coming and saying what he could in regard to me it would be of some help. If Nisba [Breckinridge] does not object, I wish she would ask Mr. Freund to write him."[14]

The congressional child labor appropriation was too small to allow a large-scale field staff and the other expenses that duplicating state enforcement procedures would entail. Moreover, the framers of the legislation had clearly intended to avoid imposing a burdensome regulatory machinery upon the states. The act had included a clause that left the door open for the Child Labor Division to accept, for purposes of the federal act, a child's employment certificate of age issued by a state labor department if that state could assure a reasonably satisfactory certificating system at standards as high or higher than the federal ones. Clearly how effectively the act's purposes could be attained would depend heavily upon the quality of federal-state cooperation. Abbott and Lathrop worked closely together throughout the life of the first federal child labor law. However, Julia Lathrop gave Grace Abbott full credit for developing and maintaining the basis of cooperation with states upon which the entire administration of the act was founded.[15]

The mode of federal-state relations which Grace Abbott evolved in large part was shaped by a philosophy of childhood and the powerful societal influences upon it. At its founding the Children's Bureau had been directed to consider the problems of children and child life as a whole. Edith Abbott's early studies had shown the links between the exploitation of children in work situations and phenomena such as poverty, illiteracy, school attendance, and children in trouble with the law. Grace Abbott and Julia Lathrop hoped that uniform implementation of child labor legislation would make clearer the need for comprehensive attention to children's welfare. They wanted the federal effort to strengthen the capabilities within the states for planning, legislating, and administering effective and related child welfare programs. In addition, their plan for federal-state cooperation reflected a respect for the initiative and sense of responsibility within the states. As Grace Abbott stated it, they knew that "all wisdom did not reside in Washington; constructive and creative leaders could be found in state and local government." Federal-state cooperation would have to be based on a "genuine working relationship"—one that would use the prior experience of states and build on it.[16]

Abbott and Lathrop were aware of the persistent and organized opposition to the act in southern states and that the constitutionality of the act would be challenged. In addition, Julia Lathrop was concerned about protecting the Children's Bureau, still young and proving itself as a new form of federal social welfare activity. The ability of women in public administration also remained a question in the minds of many. So the approach that Abbott and Lathrop agreed upon was innovative but cautious. Grace Abbott characterized it as a policy of "frankness, of intellectual honesty in discussion and planning, of conference, of recognition of the fundamental importance of the state and local health and welfare agencies."[17] Those were the qualities that she offered in her contacts with state officials, the federal Child Labor Board and its advisory committee, mill owners and manufacturers, the citizen-reformers who had worked so hard for the legislation and whose interest in its administration remained keen, and her own staff. She intended to downplay the public perception of the federal role while maximizing its influence.

Two major tasks demanded her prompt attention: drafting the rules and regulations for carrying out the provisions of the act and determining which states could be designated as in compliance with the federal act and thus permitted to issue their own employment certificates. In order to have the proposed rules and regulations as sound as possible before presenting them to the public for comment, Grace Abbott consulted widely—with Florence Kelley and Owen Lovejoy of the National Child Labor Committee, with Ernst Freund, who had given her wise counsel in relation to the Immigrants' Protective League, with Roscoe Pound and Bernard Flexner. She interpreted the act and listened to mill owners, officers of textile manufacturing associations, and state labor department officials in states where child labor legislation had been resisted. She handled demanding correspondence with a range of persons seeking information or offering suggestions about the act's enforcement.

Strained relations between the National Child Labor Committee and the Children's Bureau complicated Grace Abbott's efforts to obtain consensus on a draft of administrative rules and regulations. The NCLC had been a significant influence in bringing about the creation of the Children's Bureau; thereafter it assumed a paternalistic advisory role. In its earliest years, the bureau was unproved and vulnerable to attacks by hostile congressmen, making it practical for Julia Lathrop to keep the close ties to the NCLC and look to it for special support and protection. However, by 1916 conflicts that had been under the surface began to emerge. Now that the status of the Children's Bureau had been heightened by having an important piece of legislation to administer, Julia Lathrop was eager to move her agency into a clearer identity of its own—one that would free it of any tinge of control by the NCLC and enable her to garner and coordinate support from a wider base.[18]

In addition, personal antagonism between Julia Lathrop and Alexander McKelway, the committee's secretary for its work in the southern states and its Washington lobbyist, had existed from the time of Lathrop's appointment as chief of the bureau. McKelway doubted women's administrative ability and was irritatingly condescending to her. In turn, she held him in poor regard because of his white supremacy views and his belief that the principal cause of child labor was greed of parents for their children's earnings.[19] Grace Abbott may have carried some negative feeling because the committee, or at least McKelway, had favored someone else for her position. In any case, Lathrop and Abbott saw the committee as given to hasty and poorly thought-out action. They usually looked to Florence Kelley, as a member of the committee, to protect the bureau's interests and interpret their point of view to other committee members. Sometimes, however, given Florence Kelley's impassioned style of action, Lathrop and Abbott feared that even she would move too abruptly and further complicate their negotiations.[20]

By the middle of the summer, prior to the September date for beginning to enforce the act, Grace Abbott and the federal board were ready to hold public hearings on proposed rules and regulations. They had met first with employers from across the country, and a few days later with state officials. Differences of opinion existed on whether certificates should be issued to the child or to the employer, whether certificates should be issued for children claiming to be sixteen, and what proofs of age should be accepted.

Abbott and Lathrop's position prevailed in a decision to issue certificates to employers even though some additional expense and administrative difficulty were entailed in the necessity to issue a new certificate each time a child changed employment. However this decision was consistent with the original charge Congress had given the Children's Bureau—"to investigate and report upon all matters pertaining to the welfare of children and child life among all classes of our people." Useful data would be forthcoming about the status of working children: where they were employed and in what numbers; the increase or decrease in the numbers of working children in a particular locality or industry; and the frequency with which children changed employment.

Because of the administrative expense, a compromise was made in deciding not to issue certificates to children claiming to be between sixteen and seventeen years of age, except for employment in the most dangerous sites, mines and quarries.

The nature of documentation of age that could be accepted was controversial. Reliable evidence was the key to successful enforcement of the act. Its availability was limited because birth registration systems in most of the states were incomplete. An official birth certificate provided the best proof of age but alternative forms of evidence would have to be used as well—records of baptism; family-Bible records; and the opinion of a physician as to the age of a given child, supported by a school record and a parent's statement. Manufacturers in the southern states pressed hard for accepting a parent's affidavit by itself, but experience under state child labor administration had shown that this practice was unreliable; too many parents were under compelling pressure to swear that a child was old enough to work in order to add to the meager family income.[21]

While rules and regulations were being developed, Abbott and Lathrop were trying to determine in which states a reasonably satisfactory system could be assured so that state certification of age could be accepted for purposes of the federal act. The states divided roughly into three groups: a small group with child labor standards higher than the federal ones; the majority, where they were the same; and a smaller number with standards lower than the federal requirements. (Eager to minimize the necessity for federal inspectors to come in, a number of states with low standards of protection had amended their legislation during the year between passage and enforcement of the act.) Differences in how effectively standards were applied was a more complicating factor in classifying the states.[22]

Grace Abbott emphasized continuing communication with state departments of labor in order to maintain an optimal level of cooperation. She looked for means to strengthen the local and state basis for enforcement, as when she requested an expression of opinion from directors of state departments of labor as to whether their authority would be reinforced by being named federal inspectors on a dollar a year basis. They voted unanimously that it would, and this policy was then followed in the states designated to issue their own employment certificates.[23] Abbott and Lathrop counted success in terms of improved child labor administration within the states, rather than the number of prosecutions and fines for violations. However, reflecting what they had learned from studying the experience of the Bureau of Chemistry in administering the food and drug law, when prosecution became necessary, they intended that it should be so carefully planned and centralized that a successful outcome could be predicted.[24]

The decision was made to make federal inspections, during the first year, only in those states where the standards were below the federal level or where there was strong opposition to enforcement. The Child Labor Division reserved the right, however, to make inspections in any state at any time, either upon its own initiative or in response to complaints or the request of state officials.[25]

Five states—North Carolina, South Carolina, Georgia, Mississippi, and Virginia—were found to have child labor standards far below the federal requirements. In these states Grace Abbott and her field staff put their major expenditure of time and energy. Abbott and Lathrop proceeded cautiously in recruiting and hiring a staff for the Child Labor Division. Julia Lathrop, always alert to any attempt to "politicize" the Children's Bureau, was determined to avoid patronage appointments, as were being sought by southern textile interests, and to bring staff in through the rules of the Civil Service Commission. Once field agents were hired, Grace Abbott worked closely with them as they went into the five states where federal administration was necessary.

The field agents, and Grace Abbott when she went into the states to troubleshoot or constructively present federal authority, traveled and worked under less than comfortable conditions. Mill villages were frequently isolated and large geographical areas had to be covered. The accelerated activity around military installations in 1917 meant that trains and hotels were crowded. At night her staff wrote Grace Abbott long handwritten reports of the information they were systematically assembling about employers and conditions of work and, particularly, the difficult discretionary judgments they were called upon to make in verifying children's ages. Each of the forms of evidence of a child's age that had been provided for in the regulations posed problems. In the two states with the largest number of working children—North Carolina and South Carolina—birth certificates were available for fewer than one percent of the children who applied for work permits. Records of baptism were almost as unusual. Family Bibles were often a reliable source with a notation of births and deaths carefully entered one at a time over the years; but many Bible records were not authentic, featuring crudely made erasures and obviously changed birth dates. The genuineness of family records was often doubtful. "There were Bibles that bore no date of publication; there were entries . . . so badly written as to be altogether illegible; entries made in many different kinds of writing—'by any neighbor who could write'—and old records which were said to have been copied by these neighbors who could write when the family left the mountains and the old family Bible went to another son or daughter. . . . There were Bibles that were 'back in the mountains' and off the railroad, and the cases were continued from month to month in the belief that, if the record did, in fact, show the child to be fourteen, a means of establishing contact with that isolated mountain home would be found."[26]

Children's insurance policies, taken out by parents to make a decent burial possible in the event of a child's death, often proved unreliable.

When parents' work was slack, policies were allowed to lapse, only to be taken out again, so that it was common to have parents present several lapsed policies with a child's age recorded differently on each, a discrepancy that the mother often blamed on the father—he had taken out the policies and he could never remember his children's birth dates. In many instances a physician's certificate (the least satisfactory proof of age) had to be obtained, and then it often was found to conflict with a school record.

In the day-to-day administration of the child labor act, Grace Abbott was almost inundated by myriad details demanding her attention and the many individual judgments to be made. Yet out of it all a compelling saga of the ills of childhood was emerging. Evidence in all the states, not only in the South, showed a defeating circle of poverty, ignorance, poor physical development, and child labor. Among the white families recruited from the mountain farms into the textile mills, poverty was pervasive. In instance after instance, parents were dependent on the earnings of their twelve- and thirteen-year-old children. More than one-fourth of the children to whom federal employment certificates were issued could not write their names legibly. The illiteracy which the administration of the act exposed was linked to inadequacies in the educational system. In the states in which federal certificates had to be issued, public schools were poorly organized and staffed and opposition to compulsory attendance was strong because it meant education for Negroes. In states with no official system of birth registration, physicians' examinations were relied upon heavily to establish a child's age; these in turn revealed children in serious states of physical health and development characterized by uncorrected physical handicaps, poor nutrition, stunted growth reflected in substandard height and weight, and children who were victims of hookworm, anemia, and other evidences of physical neglect.[27]

The lack of organized health and welfare services compounded the problems. Policies of local relief agencies were restrictive; private philanthropic organizations were not to be found in most communities from which Grace Abbott received protests about the effects of the child labor law. The typical complaint came from a citizen, either genuinely concerned or with industrial interests, who detailed the pitiful conditions in a family where ill or incapacitated parents were dependent on the earnings of their young children, now prohibited from seeking work. Some congressmen and other government officials also asked if exceptions could not be made for members of their constituencies. In reply Grace Abbott could say little except to point out the importance of child labor legislation in breaking the circle of ignorance, poverty, and poor health and the necessity for related gains in public policy which would permit such families to receive publicly supported health and welfare services.[28]

Through it all, the question of the act's constitutionality hung over like a threatening cloud. Immediately after the passage of the legislation, southern cotton manufacturers began to devise a strategy for a court test. "The case will be one of such extraordinary importance," they said, "that the utmost care should be taken in choosing the circumstances and locality of jurisdiction."[29] They chose the North Carolina western federal district court, whose judge was James E. Boyd, well known for his opposition to child labor laws, and a case that clearly illustrated the contrast between the federal and the state statutes.[30] Three days before the law was to go into effect, a United States district attorney in North Carolina was enjoined from enforcing it as a result of a suit brought by Roland H. Dagenhart, a father dependent upon the earnings of two sons, thirteen-year-old John and fifteen-year-old Reuben. Each worked in a cotton mill. If the act was enforced, John would not be eligible to work because of his age, and Reuben would be discharged because he could not be permitted to work the entire eleven hours each day common to North Carolina mills.

The United States government appealed the case. While it was moving toward the Supreme Court, the Child Labor Division continued to issue work certificates. The demand by shippers for guaranties provided a significant incentive for employers to comply with the law. A dealer who shipped a mill's products across state lines was protected against prosecution by a guarantee from the mill owner that the standards of the act had been observed. Shippers continued to demand this guarantee, even to a limited extent in the North Carolina western district, where employers then requested that the Children's Bureau agents come in to issue certificates. Grace Abbott wrote Edith that she was going to South Carolina because "their congressmen want a ruling on whether the grading or sorting and stemming of the tobacco leaves is an agricultural process or not. The guaranty clause of our law is getting in its work—all kinds of wholesalers are requiring guaranties from my southern friends."[31]

Despite the confidence Grace Abbott reflected, in early June with the act having been in force only nine months, the Supreme Court handed down a decision declaring it unconstitutional on the basis that the act was not a legitimate exercise of Congress's power to regulate interstate commerce.[32]

Grace Abbott and Julia Lathrop were not so immediately discouraged by the decision as might have been expected. Grace got off a postcard to her mother saying, "Don't worry about the Supreme Court Decision. We are bearing up."[33] And Julia Lathrop recorded that the decision "at first shock" might seem conclusive but that a careful analysis of it justified the view that it was "not a defeat but only a stimulating setback."[34] Abbott and Lathrop based this curious degree of optimism on certain acknowledgments and assertions in the majority and minority opinions that left the way open to expect a new attempt at federal legislation. The majority justices had acknowledged that there should be limitations upon the right to employ children in mines and factories; they had not questioned the motives of Congress in enacting the legislation, only the use of the interstate commerce clause as the regulatory vehicle. A five to four vote also gave hope, underscored as it was by Justice Holmes's vigorous dissent for the minority with its clear reprimand to the majority justices for their preoccupation with technical questions about the rights of Congress while they ignored the rights of children. "If there is any matter upon which civilized countries have agreed," Justice Holmes wrote, "it is the evil of premature and excessive child labor."

The end of federal regulation and the demand for child labor in a wartime economy sent thousands of children back into the labor market. Reformers saw an imperative need for another attempt at federal legislation. As Julia Lathrop termed it, there should be no aristocracy in the protection of children from exploitative and too early employment. The effect of having different laws in each of the states created favored classes of children. The only recourse following *Hammer* v. *Dagenhart* was to "find a method of national limitation not repugnant to the Constitution."[35]

Even with favorable congressional sentiment toward new legislation, its passage would take time. The end of the fiscal year was near. Given the assumption that the Children's Bureau would again be given responsibility for the administration of any new federal child labor law, Abbott and Lathrop were faced with the problem of securing an appropriation so that the Child Labor Division could stay alive, retain its carefully selected and experienced staff, and be ready for prompt enforcement of new legislation when it came. The strategy they designed was a practical one that would restore some of the federal protections to children, and strengthen the position of the Children's Bureau as well. The proposal was based on an earlier solution to a problem of nonenforcement. A state labor inspector had complained to Grace Abbott that children were employed in laundries and restaurants on military reservations. Although they were working under conditions that violated his state's child labor legislation, he was powerless to enforce state standards on federally owned property. Lathrop and Abbott went to the secretaries of war and the navy and proposed that those gentlemen use their powers (which they did subsequently) to order that the federal child labor standards be enforced on all army forts and posts, naval stations, and other federal establishments under their jurisdictions.[36] Now, faced with a crisis of survival as a child labor administrative unit, Abbott and Lathrop drew upon that earlier experience and developed a proposal to put before the War Labor Policies Board.

Felix Frankfurter was chairman of this wartime board. Grace Abbott represented the Children's Bureau and served as a technical consultant. Abbott and Lathrop presented the board with convincing testimony about the increased risk of exploitation of children in a wartime economy, the importance of safeguarding children as an essential part of winning the war, and the necesity for children to do their wartime work in the schoolroom in order to be equipped for the exacting years which were sure to follow. In addition, they pointed out to the representatives of the large government purchasing agencies serving on the board that sustained efficiency in industrial production was not achieved by the employment of children. The government had a long established custom of awarding its contracts with stipulated conditions; why could not the government attach conditions related to the employment of children? As a result, the board voted that compliance with the standards of the former child labor law should be a condition of all federal contracts and that the Division of Child Labor should administer the inserted child labor clause. President Wilson subsequently allotted funds to the Children's Bureau for this purpose, which enabled Grace Abbott to continue directing inspections and enforcement procedures.[37]

Because the federal government was the largest purchasing agent, by this indirect means the wartime policy substantially reestablished the child labor protections lost through *Hammer* v. *Dagenhart*. In addition, it gave the Children's Bureau increased visibility as the sole representative of the interests of children in the federal government and enabled Lathrop and Abbott, working closely together, to assume a significant role in coordinating the activities of the reform groups seeking a second federal child labor law.[38]

Grace Abbott's administration of child labor legislation had gone on while the country was much concerned with World War I. As soon as the United States declared war, the Children's Bureau began a series of studies to learn what was happening in belligerent countries with respect to the welfare of children and the implications of those conditions for children in America. Julia Lathrop assembled a special corps of translators to read and summarize studies from Great Britain and countries of Europe—studies of child labor, infant and maternal welfare, illegitimacy, and juvenile delinquency and dependency. Findings were widely circulated through the press and bureau bulletins. Some of this work for the protection of children, carried on under war conditions, seemed extraordinary to Lathrop and Abbott. With the aid of a special grant from the president's fund, the Children's Bureau formally inaugurated the "Children's Year" in early April 1918. A series of projects was carried out in cooperation with the Woman's Committee of the U.S. Council of National Defense to alert the public to the stresses to which children are vulnerable in time of war and to attempt to minimize those influences.

As a concluding activity to the Children's Year, Julia Lathrop and Grace Abbott planned a conference on standards of child welfare. Its timing marked the passage of a decade since the auspicious first White House Conference on Care of Dependent Children.[39] On Julia Lathrop's recommendation, President Wilson appointed Grace Abbott secretary of the conference, giving her major responsibility for directing and coordinating its planning and implementation. Her child labor experience had clearly shown that if children were to be protected in work situations, a better understanding of children generally was needed by persons throughout the country so that the complexity of conditions that placed children at risk could be modified. It had shown, too, the absence of standardized norms of children's growth and development and, overall, the limits of scientific data on children. The goal of the conference set by Abbott and Lathrop was specified by President Wilson in his letter approving the Children's Year—"to set up certain irreducible minimum standards for the health, education, and work of the American child."[40]

Abbott and Lathrop intended that the standards coming out of the conference should rest on a basis of proven fact. They believed that the scientific method was the most useful tool possessed by the modern world. In arriving at child welfare standards, then, what had been proved to be true would be given highest credence; anything doctrinaire or unsupported by scientific data would be eschewed.[41]

They agreed as well that the conference should have international dimensions. Julia Lathrop and the Abbott sisters had experienced the usefulness of going abroad to "look into things you want to know about." Grace Abbott and Julia Lathrop believed that the problems of the world could be solved only by international efforts for peace and by a sharing of scientific knowledge and technical advances. They wanted to ascertain what other nations had learned about safeguarding childhood in times of war and to infuse into this country the best that was known about the nature and demands of childhood. Their plan was to bring over a small group of foreign experts to speak at conference sessions and provide new lines of thought as American conference participants set about developing a statement of child welfare standards. The conference was planned as a series, one in Washington followed immediately by eight regional conferences. The latter were to be larger and more representative of each area of the country, with the small group of foreign experts traveling to each.

To lay the groundwork for the conference and select the international representatives, Abbott and Lathrop went together to Europe via the steamship *Adriatic* during the Christmas season of 1918.[42] Each arrived in London with a roster of persons to talk with, some already known to them or to Edith Abbott or suggested by their Hull-House network and Washington officials. They made numerous visits to discuss the conference's purposes and the state of child and family welfare programs in Great Britain, France, and Belgium. Grace Abbott found time to attend a meeting of the Labour party in Albert Hall in support of Wilson's Fourteen Points.[43] In the middle of January Abbott and Lathrop went on to the Continent and repeated the search for research findings and other information about infant mortality and child care, child labor, schools, and family wage earners' protections and benefits.

At the end of January Julia Lathrop started her journey back to the United States, leaving Grace Abbott to remain until late March in order to follow through on conference arrangements and obtain a fuller view of the status of children and families at the cessation of war. She went to Rome, where she met and talked with labor officials, school personnel, judges, and directors of orphanages, maternity centers, and crèches. In all her interviews Grace Abbott was not only searching for information about children's programs and services. She was also making judgments about persons suggested to her as appropriate foreign experts for the Children's Year Conference on Child Welfare Standards.[44]

To complete her work, Grace Abbott traveled back into France and on to London and back again to the Continent before sailing home on the *Agamemnon* in early March.[45] It had been an absorbing assignment and she had considerably extended her knowledge of child welfare in other countries and had established relationships with a wide variety of influential people who would be useful to her during the rest of her career. But travel in Europe so soon after the end of the war was cumbersome and tiring and she was eager to be back to Washington, where new federal child labor legislation had been working its way through Congress.

Following *Hammer v. Dagenhart*, the Children's Bureau and the National Child Labor Committee, in consultation with their legal advisors, finally agreed that the use of the federal taxing power would be the most feasible and satisfactory means of securing federal child labor protection. If employers were required to pay an excise tax on products made with the labor of children, and if the tax was high enough, child labor would become unprofitable to the point where employers would not use it. Abbott and Lathrop felt little enthusiasm for this strategy, and they were supported in their uncertainty by the opinions of Ernst Freund, Roscoe Pound, and Florence Kelley. Yet the need was pressing to secure new legislation before the upcoming election changed the composition of Congress, so they agreed to go ahead.[46]

In November 1918, Senator Atlee Pomerene introduced a child labor measure as an amendment to the revenue bill. The employment standards were the same as in the Keating-Owen act and the coverage was somewhat more comprehensive in that it included canneries, a setting for considerable child labor abuse. However, the provisions for enforcement were different than in the 1916 act. Rules and regulations and the issuance of work certificates were all placed under the authority of a board made up of the secretary of the treasury, the commissioner of internal revenue, and the secretary of labor. The administration of the act was given to the Treasury Department where the commissioner of internal revenue was empowered to call upon the Department of Labor to issue certificates and carry out inspections.[47]

Child labor reformers objected because enforcement measures were not wholly entrusted to the Children's Bureau. However, Senator Irvine Lenroot, one of the bill's sponsors, maintained that to do so would lay the bill open to the charge of being only a subterfuge and not a true taxation measure. He offered reassurance that the bill provided for the commissioner of internal revenue to request the Department of Labor, and this would mean the Children's Bureau in that department, to issue certificates and make inspections and in other ways assist in the enforcement of the law.[48]

Julia Lathrop and Grace Abbott were not fully convinced and wanted the NCLC to withhold its endorsement until an alternative provision could be developed.[49] Their attitude may have been prompted to some extent by a desire to retain the full power and thus the prestige of enforcement in the Children's Bureau, but they were far from alone in their reluctance. Others interested in sound protection for working children believed that tax collectors would make less effective enforcement officers for child labor legislation than would bureau staff, already trained in procedures and emotionally invested in child protection. In addition, they believed, the carefully evolved federal-state relations that Grace Abbott had developed would be better maintained with enforcement clearly lodged in the Children's Bureau.

Grace Abbott pointed out that the proposed legislation was defective in other ways. An employer hiring children in January did not pay the tax until the following year and because the penalty did not increase no matter how frequently the law was violated during the year, the incentive to discharge children was seriously diminished. Also, given the stance of government on assuring secrecy about personal taxes, it would be difficult to publicize the law and offenses against it and to create a climate of support for its observance.[50]

When the bill was pending, Senator Lodge offered an amendment to the enforcement clause which would have made it the duty of the secretary of labor to cooperate in administration of the act rather than to await a request from the Treasury Department. The amendment was rejected on the basis that the bill should be a "technically perfect revenue measure and thus insure that it would be adjudged constitutional by the Supreme Court." However, the discussion had brought out clearly the intent of the Senate that issuance of work certificates and necessary inspections would be carried out by the Children's Bureau.[51] The bill passed both houses of Congress and was signed by President Wilson on February 24, to go into effect two months later. However the appropriation of $185,000 for enforcement that child labor reformers had expected to go to the Children's Bureau went instead to the Treasury Department, making it evident that the Child Labor Division of the Children's Bureau would have to await a request by the commissioner of internal revenue before becoming involved in enforcing child labor protections.

In the two months that elapsed before the bill took effect, it became evident that the Treasury Department would not be making such a request of the Children's Bureau and that the work of its Child Labor Division was ended. Grace Abbott was keenly disappointed, as were many others. Helen T. Wooley, a Cincinnati educator, wrote Carrie Chapman Catt that the Internal Revenue Service was not at all inclined to call on the Children's Bureau for its expertise in administering child labor protections, that the status of the bureau had been threatened and thereby the prestige of all women.[52]

Abbott and Lathrop were each inclined to blame the NCLC. McKelway had seriously fanned the tensions between them and the NCLC when he had gone around Julia Lathrop to the attorney general's office to get Thomas Parkinson named to assist the district attorney in *Hammer* v. *Dagenhart* instead of Roscoe Pound, to whom Julia Lathrop and

Grace Abbott had extended themselves for the assignment.[53] McKelway died before the new legislation was even planned, but Lathrop and Abbott had continued to distrust the NCLC. And with the administration of the new legislation lost to the Children's Bureau, Abbott and Lathrop, probably with some justification, believed that the committee had been seriously negligent in monitoring what was happening to the bill after it was introduced into Congress.

Julia Lathrop may not have expected the new legislation to move through Congress as quickly as it did, but it seems unfortunate that both Lathrop and Abbott were out of the country when the bill was being discussed and modified. When it came up for vote in the Senate, where it passed with little debate, they were two days at sea. It was not voted on in the House until early February, but Julia Lathrop had just begun her passage back to the United States. Given the ability each had in successful communication with members of Congress, one can speculate that at least the decision not to give the appropriation to the Children's Bureau might have been different had either Lathrop or Abbott been in Washington and in touch with Senator Pomerene and others interested in their cause. In any case, it appears that Abbott and Lathrop may have been overconfident, leading to a mistake in judgment about the wisdom of both of them being out of the country while a bill was pending in which each of them and the bureau had such a large stake.

Despite her personal disappointment at the turn of affairs, after her return from Europe Grace Abbott immersed herself in completing arrangements for the Conference on Standards of Child Welfare. A draft statement of standards had to be developed to offer to the Washington conference on May 9 and then revised and printed for consideration at the eight regional conferences. An advisory committee had to be selected to revise the standards after all the conferences were ended in order to reflect criticisms and suggestions for changes. Americans with special expertise in some aspect of child welfare had to be identified and offered a significant part in the conference programs. The foreign visitors had to be selected and their participation secured. Four came from England, one from France, three from Belgium, one from Japan, one from Serbia, and one from Italy.[54] Arrangements had to be made in each of eight cities—New York, Cleveland, Boston, Chicago, Denver, Minneapolis, San Francisco, and Seattle. When the regional conferences were held, in May and June of 1919, Grace Abbott attended each of them. The final product was a statement of minimum standards in three areas of child welfare—child labor, the health of children and mothers, and children in need of special care. The endeavor had involved a wide range of people and interests and marked a significant step of systematic development of standards as a basis for national child and family policy.[55]

With her role as administrator of federal child labor legislation ended, Grace Abbott intended to return by July to Chicago and to the Immigrants' Protective League, from which she was officially on leave. However, Julia Lathrop prevailed upon her to stay a little longer to assist with the organizational activity of the proposed International Labor Organization. The idea for the ILO had grown out of the peace conference and reflected a new awareness that economic problems were worldwide in scope and that labor and industrial relations or actions in one country affected the economy of others. Grace Abbott had served as secretary of the Children's Committee of the International Labor Conference held in Washington in the spring of 1919. Both she and Julia Lathrop were concerned that the interests of children and of women would be overlooked by the new international organization. Grace Abbott was asked to represent the Department of Labor and act as technical adviser to the official committee organizing an international labor conference, an assignment that required her to go to England in August.

Grace Abbott had acquired a breadth of knowledge about national and international labor problems, particularly in relation to children and women. This competence had grown out of her experience with industrial problems of immigrants, her child labor administrative experience in the Children's Bureau, her investigations in Europe and England earlier in the year, and her sister Edith's early research and continuing interest in the problems of women in industry. Most recently Edith had been a member of the Committee on Women in Industry of the Council of National Defense. With Josephine Goldmark and Mary Van Kleeck, she had served as an investigator of conditions at the Brooklyn Navy Yard and Frankford Arsenal in Philadelphia where, under wartime pressures for increased industrial production, labor standards were being violated.[56] Full sharing of knowledge and experience was a continuing part of the Abbott sisters' relationship and in this instance the habit had considerably extended Grace Abbott's competence to carry out the ILO assignment.

Julia Lathrop would have been glad for Grace Abbott to stay on with the Children's Bureau in some capacity, but since she was not ready to retire as chief, no available position there seemed sufficiently challenging to Grace Abbott. She had had significant national and international experience and had extended her administrative ability and areas of expertise in important ways. Her work in behalf of the Conference on

Standards of Child Welfare had expanded her contacts with women's organizations abroad and across the country and shown her capacity for a leadership role in cooperative relationships with a wide range of voluntary organizations. She had demonstrated a new creative form of collaboration in federal-state relations and secured the cooperation of states in the enforcement of a federal statute that ran counter to the traditions and special interests of large sections of the country. But it had been a demonstration limited by an abrupt ending and the long-term potential uses of the method were not yet clear. If she couldn't be in Washington, she preferred to return to Chicago, but with reservations. The Immigrants' Protective League seemed smaller and less challenging to her in 1919 than it had in 1908 and she felt apologetic to its board for having allowed it to keep her old position open to her for so long.[57] Edith Abbott, with sisterly concern, tried to arrange a place for her to live in Chicago, a flat together on the South Side or sharing her own Hull-House apartment. Unsure of her future, Grace advised that they should move slowly on committing themselves to the expense of a South Side arrangement. Yet in view of Edith's habit of living in the midst of great stacks of books and newspapers, Grace wrote that she feared "the Hull-House apartment would be very thick indeed if my things . . . were moved in on top of what is a flood situation now." In the end she decided to return to Hull-House for "this year at least and I am sure we can get along without too great a strain on our tempers for that length of time."[58]

The next eighteen months were not easy ones for the Abbott sisters. Not only Grace but Edith as well was experiencing a crisis in her professional life; it was the period in which she and Nisba Breckinridge were in conflict with Graham Taylor and negotiating the transfer of the program of the School of Civics and Philanthropy to the University of Chicago. Both of the sisters were disappointed with America's decision not to enter the League of Nations and Grace, especially, felt considerable disillusionment with the outcome of the peace settlement. Personal and family matters added stress. Their brother Ottie had lost his wife in the 1918 flu epidemic and he and his young child were now living with Othman and Lizzie Abbott in the Grand Island family home. Grace and Edith felt a keen responsibility for their parents' welfare and for the future of their little niece. Lizzie Abbott broke her hip in 1920 and although she regained her ability to walk, she suffered discomfort from the injury for the rest of her life. And in late 1920 Grace underwent a hysterectomy, an operation not simple for women today and much more serious then.[59]

Grace Abbott's renewed work with immigrants in Chicago devel-

oped differently than she had expected. The board of the Immigrants'
Protective League, and Grace Abbott when she had been its director,
had believed that the work they undertook as a voluntary agency
should be done by a public authority on a statewide scale. In the spring
of 1920 the Illinois State Legislature created an Illinois Immigration Commission and gave it broad investigative powers. Governor
Frank O. Lowden asked Grace to administer it. Again she was given a
leave of absence by the Immigrants' Protective League, which suspended its work but did not dissolve the organization. In her new position Grace had directed two pieces of social investigation—one on the
conditions of immigrants in the southern Illinois coal-mining district
and one on the educational needs of immigrants in Illinois,[60] and was on
the way to developing a sound public welfare agency when Governor
"Len" Small succeeded Governor Lowden in office. Grace Abbott had
engaged staff under civil service rules and, like Julia Lathrop, held that
public services should be nonpolitical. When one of Governor Small's
deputies supplied her with a roster of her employees and requested that
she fill in the political affiliation, ward, and precinct of each, she refused to do so. As a result Governor Small vetoed the next commission
appropriation and on July 1, 1921, the new public authority ceased to
exist. The board of the Immigrants' Protective League authorized
Grace Abbott to renew the work of that voluntary agency.[61]

By the late spring of 1921, it appeared likely that Grace Abbott, if
she wished, could succeed Julia Lathrop as chief of the Children's Bureau. Julia Lathrop had stayed longer than she might have because of
her commitment to the development of maternity and infancy legislation. With a new presidential administration—one fraught with patronage appointments—and with rumors that Lathrop wanted to retire, the
Children's Bureau position looked desirable to job seekers. One who
sought the position was Sara Walrath Lyons, a public lecturer and
writer on "Foods and Dietetic Values," who added to her lectures with
stereopticon views and exercises in deep breathing. She generated very
limited support.[62] A more serious threat to Julia Lathrop's desire to see
Grace Abbott as chief was Mrs. Harry A. Kluegel of San Francisco,
who launched a campaign in her own behalf among Republican political leaders in western states. The qualifications she claimed rested on
her service as head of the Junior Red Cross of the Pacific Coast during
the war and the work she had done in Harding's political campaign.[63]

Julia Lathrop had first been appointed chief of the bureau by a Republican president. When President Wilson assumed office, she did not
offer to resign her position, part of her strategy to guard the Children's
Bureau from political leadership, and one that became a precedent for

successive Children's Bureau chiefs during changes in national administration. When President Harding assumed office, Lathrop ignored any possible expectation that she would resign and continued to stress the scientific orientation of the work of the bureau. Mary Anderson of the Women's Bureau, as a Wilson appointee, was under pressure for her job, which intensified the concern of women's groups that neither bureau become politicized.

Julia Lathrop wrote Grace Abbott in April 1921 that she had talked tentatively with Secretary of Labor Davis about retiring and about Grace Abbott as the best choice for the position. Davis had indicated that he wanted nothing done at present and that he preferred eventually to announce the resignation and the appointment of a successor at the same time. He asked that Julia Lathrop stay on another two or three months and say nothing publicly about leaving. Julia Lathrop had also learned that Mrs. Kluegel was the only applicant of any importance; that "she makes a good appearance and a favorable impression"; that she was in Washington then, seeing people. The point Julia Lathrop wanted to make with Grace Abbott was that "if you want to come," then it would be necessary to get support organized and clearly indicated to the secretary of labor, particularly "rock-ribbed Republican" support. "I think," she wrote, "there will be a degree of political pressure here that only heroes can withstand."[64] It was expected that Secretary Davis's recommendation for the position would be honored. With some asperity Julia Lathrop characterized him as "a man who has a Men's Class in morning Sunday School . . . singularly unacquainted with any modern social theory or practice. He loves Mooseheart [a congregate children's institution in Illinois] and wishes to have 5000 children there."[65]

While it is likely that Grace Abbott from the beginning wanted the position, Lathrop's subtle challenge—"if you want to come" and the promise of a contest was enough to remove any doubts. She had had reservations, however, just as she did when she came back to Chicago from the Children's Bureau. She had met ill fortune twice now in public service from political interruptions to her career, leaving her unsure about committing herself again to public administration. She had thought, and often talked to Edith, about the possibility of running for office in Nebraska. Jeannette Rankin had done it successfully in Montana; why could not she in Nebraska? She sensed that going to the bureau as chief was likely to be a long-term career choice and she was reluctant to be so confined.

To Mollie Dewson she expressed some of her hestitation about the limitations of public jobs. "I was I quite confess altogether unhappy when Mrs. Kelley and Miss Lathrop began to close in on me and insist whether I wanted to or not it was up to me to take the job. You know as well as I do that a government job has certain difficulties." However, pressures on her to compete for the position were heavy. She was obviously the best qualified, and knew it, and she too did not want the Children's Bureau to become a third-rate bureaucracy. So she went on to acknowledge that "public service has certain opportunities greater than those of any private organization and . . . those of us who believe in the government falling to and doing things ought to be willing to help."[66]

Support for Grace Abbott's appointment was forthcoming from women's groups through word spread by Jane Addams, Florence Kelley, Sophonisba Breckinridge, Lillian Wald, Margaret Dreier Robins, and others. Florence Kelley wrote promptly, "Dear Grace Abbott, JCL has written me, and Miss Wald and I are struggling with Republicans. . . . J. A. will be here tomorrow and we shall all three have our heads together."[67] When Mrs. Kluegel's campaign seemed to be gaining strength, Harriet Taylor Upton, vice-chairman of the Republican National Committee, transmitted a telegram to the White House from Katherine Phillips Edson, a member of the Republican National Executive Committee, which said that Kluegel "has no backing from women's organizations in the west where she is known per past experience. . . . Californian women would deeply resent her appointment to Children's Bureau. . . . We prefer a specialist."[68]

Essential support came from men as well, chief among them Julius Rosenwald, Frank O. Lowden, Abel Davis, Julian Mack, Charles Nagel, Ernst Freund, and Charles L. Hutchinson.[69] Julia Lathrop let the Chicago group know that she had called on Illinois Senators Medill McCormick and William B. McKinley about Grace Abbott for the chief's post. They had evinced less that full interest by saying that they would defer to Nebraska Senator George Norris's right to make "Nebraska appointments." Abel Davis responded with "all very well about Norris but I don't like G. A.'s being driven out of Illinois." Soon after McCormick telephoned Julia Lathrop to discuss the appointment and his attitude was more conciliatory. He said he would see Norris and if Julia Lathrop would only stay on another two months or so, Grace Abbott's appointment could be made and "no water spilled." Julia Lathrop wrote Grace, "I see the fine Italian hand of such as Abel Davis and others."[70]

Not all women supported Grace Abbott. Mrs. Medill McCormick, a woman Grace Abbott later characterized as "a persistent enemy," did not. Mrs. McCormick had been opposed to the formation of an Illinois

League of Women Voters and in an organizational meeting in late 1920 had taken umbrage at Grace Abbott's response to her position. When Julius Rosenwald asked Mrs. McCormick to use her influence in behalf of Grace Abbott's appointment, she replied that she would, but only to prevent it, that Grace Abbott was not loyal to the Republican party.[71] Her evidence was Grace's absence from Social Justice Day in Marion, Ohio, a part of Harding's campaign for the presidency that occurred the day before Grace Abbott was scheduled to enter the hospital for major surgery. Mrs. McCormick's opposition, Grace Abbott believed, was due less to her absence from Marion than it was to factions within the league that reflected differences on fundamental questions about the role of women. In any case, Julius Rosenwald was sufficiently uncomfortable about his encounter with Mrs. McCormick that he asked Grace to write him a letter of explanation to the effect that she had been interested in the Marion affair and would have gone if hospitalization had not been imminent. It was not a remedy that Grace Abbott was comfortable with, but she valued Julius Rosenwald's regard, and his support for her appointment was very important, as his continued support would be for the work of the bureau. When he acknowledged receipt of Grace's letter, he added, "I may, when opportunity arises, show it to Mrs. McCormick as I would like very much to have her 'with us' should it be necessary to enlist the Senator's good offices in connection with the work of the Bureau." The matter did not entirely end there, given the strong patronage climate of Washington. Prior to her official appointment, in a final interview with Secretary of Labor Davis and a subsequent one with Albert D. Lasker, a White House staff member, Grace Abbott was reminded of "difficulties about the California woman" and asked why she had not attended Social Justice Day in Ohio.[72]

Harriet Taylor Upton carefully monitored the timing of Julia Lathrop's resignation to enhance the passage of the maternity and infancy bill. She had urged Julia Lathrop not to resign when the possibility was first mentioned because her presence was still essential to gaining support for the proposed legislation. But by August Taylor was ready to agree that the time for resignation was right. It now seemed likely that the bill would progress toward enactment if Congressman Samuel Winslow's adamant opposition could be lessened. Because he was so antagonistic toward Julia Lathrop, Taylor stated that if she were to resign he could say that he was less opposed now because he had gained what he wanted. "Of course this is just an excuse but we ought to take advantage of it." She wrote President Harding, stating this point of view and adding, "Miss Lathrop does not want to resign unless she is sure of

Miss Abbott's appointment, and, the women do not want her to resign unless Miss Abbott is sure of the appointment. . . . It is my bounden duty to watch these things and I am perfectly sure Miss Abbott is the woman for the place."[73]

Ten days later Secretary Davis sent a memo to President Harding, "Re: Miss Abbott and the Children's Bureau." He wrote, "I have known indirectly of Miss Grace Abbott's work. I know she did a fine job under Governor Lowden and I have taken some pains to look her up." Then he listed her attainments and added somewhat obscurely, "I had forgotten she had served in the Bureau."[74] He enclosed Julia Lathrop's formal resignation and his recommendation for Grace Abbott's appointment, which Harding accepted and sent to the Senate for confirmation. Davis got off a telegram to Lowden saying, "All right, old boy, the appointment will be made. Leaving for Mooseheart today."[75] And Herbert Hoover wrote Julius Rosenwald that "your heart's desire in the shape of Miss Lathrop's successor has been accomplished."[76] In other arenas the response to Grace Abbott's appointment was one of approval for Julia Lathrop's choice and grateful surprise that Harding had not replaced her with a patronage appointee. As for Julia Lathrop, some years later a former staff member who remembered the "marvelous infant and maternal mortality studies that Julia Lathrop had directed" asked her what she considered her major achievement during her years as chief of the Children's Bureau. Julia Lathrop replied simply: "I kept it from becoming politicized."[77]

Edith Abbott.

Grace Abbott.

Edith Abbott with her parents at the family home in Grand Island, Nebraska.

Grace Abbott and Charlotte Abbott, circa 1917.

Edith Abbott at the University of Chicago, 1902–3.

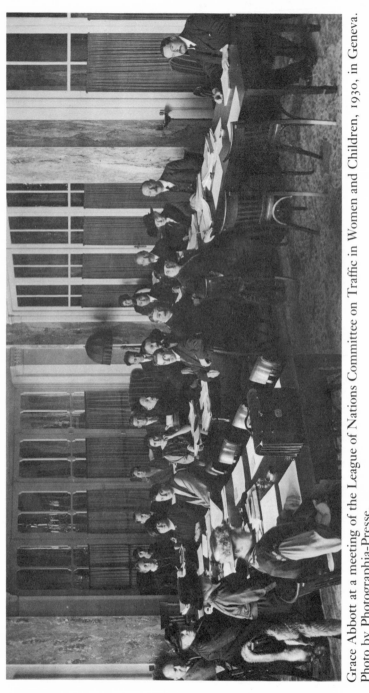

Grace Abbott at a meeting of the League of Nations Committee on Traffic in Women and Children, 1930, in Geneva. Photo by Photographia-Presse.

Grace Abbott with Frances Perkins, secretary of labor, at the opening session of the Child Welfare Conference, 1933. Photo by Underwood and Underwood.

Edith Abbott and William Hobson, executive committee member, National Conference of Social Work, Atlantic City, 1936.

Edith Abbott and Josephine Roche, Atlantic City, 1936.

Edith Abbott, mid-1930s.

Edith Abbott and Sophonisba P. Breckinridge, University of Chicago School of Social Service Administration. Photo by Bernard Hoffman.

SS *Grace Abbott*, Liberty Ship, commissioned Oct. 10, 1942. Photo courtesy of the *Baltimore Sun*.

When we are told that this country is so poor and this Congress so harassed by things of greater importance than the deaths of a quarter of a million children a year, we say to ourselves, "surely, we are not to take this seriously." . . . What answer can be given to the women who are . . . asking "why does Congress wish women and children to die?"

— FLORENCE KELLEY[1]

CHAPTER 6

Not Charity. Justice!

"NORMALCY" AND "REACTION" are characteristics commonly attributed to the Harding-Coolidge era, and certainly conditions then were not conducive to social reform. However, as Clarke A. Chambers established, the period was a "seedtime of reform," a decade that extended the groundwork for the new social programs of the 1930s. The roots of the sweeping legislation of the 1930s can be located not only in prewar progressivism but also in the period between the armistice and the beginning of the New Deal. Social reformers and social workers displayed a strong vitality which enabled them to continue to agitate, to educate, to maintain or expand established social programs, and to explore new reforms. Against the inertia of the times they kept alive the traditions of humanitarianism.[2] In this continuing search for social justice, children were of special concern.

Pioneer work by Lillian Wald, Florence Kelley, and Edward T. Devine was responsible in large part for the creation of a federal bureau for children. Continuous agitation and promotion by the National Child Labor Committee, women's organizations, the National Consumers' League, the National Conference of Charities and Correction, and the 1909 National Conference on the Care of Dependent Children was required before a bill was finally approved in April 1912, six years after one first had been introduced into Congress.[3] The act was brief but the wording of the charge to the Children's Bureau was broadly significant: to "investigate and report upon all matters pertaining to the welfare of children and child life among all classes of our people." The act gave further direction as to what urgent problems required immediate investigation—"infant mortality, the birth rate, orphanage, juvenile

125

courts, desertion, dangerous occupations, accidents and diseases of children, employment, legislation affecting children in the several States and Territories."[4]

Passage of the act represented a significant milestone. Using the general welfare clause of the Constitution as its authority, the federal government had established a function related to the social welfare of children. From its founding in 1912 until the passage of the Social Security Act in 1935, the Children's Bureau not only served the interests of children but was the central federal source to which citizens turned for authoritative information on families and their social and economic characteristics and needs.

In its early years Julia Lathrop expanded and strengthened the bureau's supporting constituency largely through her remarkable, although cautious, approach to its research function. Investigations of prenatal care, infant and maternal mortality, child hygiene, and birth registration appealed to women across the country who saw their interests being addressed. Such bureau pamphlets as *Prenatal Care* and *Infant Care*, designed for mothers and made easily available to them, became government printing office "best sellers" and won a new and loyal following. Grace Abbott's and Julia Lathrop's work during the Children's Year and in the carefully planned regional conferences of the 1919 Conference on Child Welfare Standards enlisted the active participation of millions of women representing almost all the women's organizations of the country, adding substantially to the formal constituency on which the bureau could call for backing.[5] Julia Lathrop found this expanded support when she was maneuvering to bring Grace Abbott in as her successor in preference to a political appointee. As she expressed it, "I discover that suddenly the Children's Bureau is regarded as the choice jewel of the Department of Labor; that is good trading stock."[6]

When she became the bureau's chief, Grace Abbott, as had been true for Julia Lathrop, was able to maintain a significant degree of independence in her work within the loosely coordinated Department of Labor. The successive secretaries, William B. Wilson, James J. Davis, and William N. Doak, tended to defer to them on all questions involving the status or activity of the Children's Bureau. Partly this was because the bureau had a somewhat incongruous position within the department; Congress had given it a distinctive charge, one that was broader than that given subsequently to the Women's Bureau; it was staffed almost exclusively by women; and Lathrop and Abbott were highly competent professionals, and women as well, who, the male department heads seemed to assume, surely knew best in matters related to children. Of course neither Lathrop nor Abbott could have maintained the relative independence of the Children's Bureau if they had engaged in highly controversial activities lacking a supporting constituency, or in activities in direct conflict with the general policy of the Department of Labor.[7]

If the Children's Bureau sometimes appeared to reflect elements of a favored status, it was not evident in its housing. From the time Grace Abbott went to the bureau until the early 1930s, its offices were in makeshift, temporary, lath and plaster buildings put up hastily during World War I. At one point, when the flimsy structure occupied by the Children's Bureau was destroyed by fire, its offices were simply moved to another—"Tempo No. 5," located near the stately Lincoln Memorial. These inadequate and dreary buildings were intolerably hot during the heavy Washington summers and cold and damp during other months. Yet visitors to the bureau noted an atmosphere of understanding and human sympathy, and women whose careers were launched there recalled in their later years not only the dreadful "temporaries," but more the excitement and sense of achievement they had felt.[8]

Grace Abbott's living situation was in welcome contrast to the physical environment of the Children's Bureau quarters. When she went back to Washington to assume her duties as chief of the bureau, she moved into the apartment in the Ontario which Julia Lathrop gave up to return to Illinois. It was comfortable and pleasant, with a scenic outlook over Rock Creek Park and the zoo.[9] The park offered an inducement to Sunday walks, often through the zoo, where the animals provided a balancing diversion to the behavior of some of the obdurate opponents to social programs with whom Grace Abbott had to contend.

Grace Abbott plunged into the crowded and demanding days which her work required. She was a persuasive and aggressive leader and she set a fast pace for her staff at the Children's Bureau. She expected a high level of energy and competence and complete cooperation. Her tolerance was low for any individual whose personal needs became translated into petty or self-serving impediments to getting the bureau's work done. Asked once about the qualities she considered essential in a staff member, she replied: "Intelligence, flexibility, dedication, and beyond that it doesn't matter."[10]

"It was an extraordinary thing," Elisabeth Shirley Enochs recalled. "Whenever Grace Abbott walked down a hall, you always had a feeling that a galley in full sail was passing by because everything seemed to come alive in her wake. She just infused a kind of spirit into the whole Bureau. It was an extraordinary place, an exciting place to work in those days." Dorothy Bradbury remembered Grace Abbott as "a very strong leader," not "demanding" in the usual negative sense of that word, always gracious in her expectations, but (and this with some chagrin) "you somehow always did what she wanted done." Dr. Ella Oppenheimer made a similar observation: "She didn't seem 'demanding' because we did our jobs. She had a way of letting you know what she envisioned and what she would like you to do. If you weren't able to see it and do the job, I suppose you might decide to leave."[11]

Emma O. Lundberg was one who decided to leave. She had come to the bureau during Julia Lathrop's tenure. In a period of personal difficulties Lundberg charged Lathrop with some unfairness. Lathrop responded with praise for her work and strong urging that she see a physician for exhaustion from overwork. "I feel sure that . . . the certain suggestions of unfairness which you have made will all disappear when your nerves are well stiffened and restored to the normal."[12] Although no one doubted Emma Lundberg's talents and her dedication to the children's cause, after Grace Abbott became chief, differences arose again. Lundberg, as head of the Social Service Division, liked to engage persons outside the bureau to carry out studies for which she provided general direction. She resented Abbott's policy of making such reports subject to final revision by the editorial division of the bureau. Abbott thought this was particularly essential when reports were based on work done by persons other than her own staff. She read everything herself in manuscript form before reports were published.

The differences came to a head when Lundberg demanded that her name not appear on a report and that an entire section be omitted because of the "white-washing" that she claimed had resulted from editorial revision. Abbott defended the changes on the basis that there was a great difference between setting out the facts, which no one on the bureau staff could object to, and coupling those facts with language that carried pejorative implications for the persons and programs that had been studied. When Lundberg objected to undertaking additional studies that had been planned, if they were to be subject to editing other than her own, and when her dissatisfaction continued to be expressed in memoranda with the emotional tone of one aggrieved, Grace Abbott said to her, "I don't think there is any way to reconcile our differences. What do you think you should do?" Lundberg resigned from the bureau to work for the Child Welfare League of America, although she returned to the bureau after her close friend, Katharine Lenroot, became chief.[13] Such instances in staff relations appear to have been rare, although others who could not accept the kinds of control that Grace Abbott enforced may have left the bureau more quietly.

Beatrice McConnell once described Grace Abbott as "a combination of gentleness and forcefulness."[14] Although she was an exacting administrator, she could accommodate the schedule to staff members' unexpected family responsibilities. She was sympathetic to the loneliness one staff member felt in her desire to be married and, although Grace Abbott was far from being a matchmaker or convinced that marriage was essential to all women, she asked Elisabeth Shirley to try to introduce her unhappy employee to some suitable man from among Miss Shirley's many acquaintances. When staff or friends experienced personal loss Grace Abbott was thoughtful and considerate. In recalling such a time in her own life, Elisabeth Shirley Enochs spoke of "the sweetness of Grace Abbott's character, and the tenderness that was there along with the forceful intellect."[15]

Grace Abbott watched her newest staff members for special talents that could be developed to advance the work of the Children's Bureau, shaped an assignment to the person, and then exacted maximum performance. Elisabeth Shirley Enochs was one such staff person. When a friend complained that Grace Abbott was giving the then Miss Shirley too much work and was wearing her out, Grace Abbott replied, "You don't know Elisabeth Shirley as well as I do. She is a race horse type and she can do it." Miss Shirley joined the bureau staff by chance. She had taken a civil service examination for a press relations position in the Bureau of Forestry. The examination notice had indicated that only a man would be considered, and, although her score was very high, she was given no consideration. Some time later Grace Abbott notified the Civil Service Commission of her intent to add a person to the bureau's editorial division. Its head, Isabelle Hopkins, commuted regularly on the same streetcar as did a man from the commission staff. He urged Hopkins to consider Miss Shirley for the position "to save us holding another examination for the entire United States." Miss Shirley was hired. But shortly after, Grace Abbott observed that she felt constrained by the division head's expectation that she would stay in the office and write press releases. She had innovative ideas for publicizing the bureau's work. Grace Abbott recognized her potential, gave her a free hand, and instructed her to report only to her, as chief.

One of Grace Abbott's first requests was that she produce a motion picture on breast-feeding. She wrote scripts and managed and expanded the production of radio programs that Grace Abbott had initiated earlier. She made a point of getting to know reporters and fed them human interest material that built up support and understanding of the Children's Bureau. One typical example was a response to a confirmed enemy of the bureau, Congressman A. Piatt Andrew of Massachusetts, who in an interview with the *Boston Transcript* indicated that his legislative intent for the year was to build more naval cruisers and to abolish the Children's Bureau. Elisabeth Shirley caught the irony in equating the small budget of the bureau with the cost of even one naval cruiser. She called a newspaper friend and asked him if he wanted "a hot weather story about Battleships and Babies." As a result, he wrote a humorous article that was picked up by papers across the country. Andrew's constituents began to protest his plan to abolish the Children's Bureau and the incident attracted favorable attention to the bureau in new quarters.[16]

Some months after Grace Abbott assumed her post as Children's Bureau chief, Edith suggested that her sister break her heavy schedule by joining her for a weekend holiday at Lake Mohonk, following a conference in New York. Edith wrote her mother with amusement and pretended exasperation that Grace was so much interested in her "grand new job" that she hadn't wanted to come and "may insist on going back before we get our suitcases unpacked."[17] Grace had reason to be preoccupied; the Maternity and Infancy Protection legislation, referred to generally as the Sheppard-Towner Act, had become law on November 23, 1921, and as chief of the bureau charged with its administration, she had heavy new responsibilities to prepare for.

The Sheppard-Towner legislation, which made possible the development of state programs for mothers and babies, marked a highly significant new venture into social welfare under federal auspices and provided telling evidence of the continuing chain of progressive thought and action. The very large number of babies who died during their first year of life was one of the major concerns that had influenced Congress to establish the Children's Bureau and to give it special direction to investigate infant mortality. To reformers, infant deaths represented an enormous and needless loss of human resources and a threat to the value placed upon life itself. Just how many babies died each year was impossible to ascertain because, unlike other civilized countries, the United States in the early part of the twentieth century had no uniform laws for the registration of births and deaths. The Bureau of the Census had established a death registration area in 1880 which by 1913 still included only 65 percent of the population. Registration of births was even less fully realized with only six states, New York City, and the District of Columbia included in a "provisional" birth registration area. The Children's Bureau regarded the registration of births as the first essential provision in a system of vital statistics and an indispensable practical aid in the eradication of three great evils that threatened the lives and rights of children—infant mortality, child labor, and the loss of opportunity for education.[18]

By the time the first bill for maternity and infancy legislation was introduced into Congress, the Children's Bureau and other researchers had laid a foundation of facts about why so many babies died in their first year and why so many mothers either died in childbirth or suffered long periods of invalidism following it. Preventing these infant deaths would require better care of the mother before and at the time of birth, not only to save her life but to enable her to care properly for her baby in its early months. Thus the Children's Bureau moved logically from a study of infant mortality into investigation of the problems of maternity and the circumstances under which women in all parts of the country gave birth. The findings were startling.

Childbirth in 1913 was a greater hazard to the lives of women of childbearing age than any disease except tuberculosis, with a death rate almost twice as high in the black as in the white population. Only two of the group of fifteen foreign countries which were studied showed higher rates than that of the United States.[19] The majority of maternal deaths was caused by puerperal septicemia. In the early nineteenth century "childbed fever," as it was commonly called, was one of the great scourges within hospitals where infections could spread rapidly. Death rates of women in childbirth were so high that many obstetrical hospitals were closed and commissions established to investigate the causes of such epidemics. In this country Oliver Wendell Holmes in 1843 advanced the idea that "childbed fever" was similar to a wound infection and was due chiefly to doctors who carried infection from one patient to another. His essay was then mostly ignored or discounted.[20] In Europe Ignaz Semmelweis was also studying childbed fever. He too insisted that the infection was a "cadaveric blood-poisoning" spread by doctors who did not cleanse their hands; he too was ridiculed, but went on to publish a classic work on the subject.[21] By 1875 Joseph Lister's methods of antisepsis were being applied in some hospitals to prevent infections at childbirth, and, where this was accomplished, maternal deaths dropped enormously. Yet across America, where these scientific principles were not known or not applied, women continued to lose their lives to puerperal septicemia well into the twentieth century.[22]

Other diseases or complications caused by pregnancy and childbirth caused women to die, many of whom could have been saved through proper hygiene, medical supervision during pregnancy, and better attention during labor. Not reflected in the statistics of maternal mortality were the illnesses of women that followed complications of pregnancy and left them invalided for many weeks or months or years. The continuing health or ill-health of mothers was a critical factor in the kind of care children received. Given the prevalence of unsafe milk supplies, the extent to which mothers were well enough to breast-feed their babies successfully in the early months following birth was often crucial to their survival.[23]

Why were the conditions that led to maternal and infant deaths so generally ignored? From its studies the Children's Bureau concluded that childbirth had been shrouded with an age-long mist of prejudice, ignorance, and fatalism. If a mother or baby died, it was the will of God, or in the eyes of others an unavoidable accident. Principles of proper hygiene during pregnancy and childbirth were not "public property" but almost exclusively the possession of physicians. At the same time obstetrics was not a well-developed specialization. Many physicians were indifferent to this aspect of preventive medicine because of the small fees it brought in and because it carried heavy responsibility in the face of conditions over which they had no control during pregnancy and at the onset of labor.[24]

Low standards of prenatal and early infancy care were also a result of inaccessibility to any skilled help in many areas of this country, particularly in isolated homes of the vast stretches of ranch land in the West, where a woman ready for labor had to rely upon a neighbor or husband, and often had to deliver the baby herself, alone.[25] In the South, Negro midwives provided the only care available to black women, and, in inner cities, immigrant midwives served the foreign-born woman. In contrast to the European pattern of licensed midwives educated for their function, most in this country were completely untrained, ignorant, and illiterate, dirty in their clothing and person, with only a range of superstitious practices to rely upon.[26]

The most pervasive factor in the mortality rates of women and babies was the economic one. In its first study of infant mortality the Children's Bureau found that in families where fathers' earnings were low, rates were almost twice as high as among the more prosperous group.[27] Poverty was repeatedly identified in the bureau's continuing studies as a significant factor in the deaths of mothers and babies.

The Sheppard-Towner Act was remarkable for its official attention to the injustices of women and of children, which it was intended to reduce, and for its illustration of the new power that women had won through the suffrage amendment. Jeannette Rankin introduced the first bill into Congress in 1918, marking it as a woman's issue. A powerful and persistent lobby of women fought for its passage. At the organizational meeting of the National League of Women Voters, with the suffrage amendment nearly secured, Carrie Chapman Catt, president of the soon-to-be-dissolved National American Woman's Suffrage Association, appealed to the new organization to turn its support to legislation for women and children,[28] thus opening up a large new bloc of voters. The Women's Joint Congressional Committee and its fourteen national constituent organizations made passage of the Sheppard-Towner Act a primary goal. From the time the bill was introduced until the act was passed, women deluged Congress with letters and telegrams, not only from organized feminist groups, but from women acting individually who had become aware and vocal about the oppressed status of their sex in situations of pregnancy and childbirth. Grace Abbott wrote that the Sheppard-Towner Act "constituted a demonstration not only of the political power of American women now that they have the ballot, but furnishes a concrete example of why this power is valuable to them as women."[29]

Although not all congressmen were enthusiastic about the new legislation, by the time of its passage the proposal had received the endorsement of many varied groups of citizens. Yet open opposition had emerged as well, and it continued undiminished and often strident all through the decade. This opposition came primarily from certain self-styled anti-suffrage and patriotic organizations and from the American Medical Association, and it added considerable stress to Grace Abbott's efforts to administer the act successfully.

The ultimate goal of the new legislation was to reduce the incidence of maternal and infant mortality and to promote the health of mothers and babies. To move toward this the act provided for federal matching grants to the states. The Smith-Lever Act of 1914, which promoted agricultural extension work, supplied the precedent for the method of financing. States were assured complete authority to initiate and administer their own programs in whatever state agency they designated (usually the child hygiene or child welfare division in a state department of health) subject to the approval of the Federal Board of Maternal and Infant Hygiene composed of the chief of the Children's Bureau, the surgeon general of the Public Health Service, and the United States commissioner of education. To become eligible for a federal grant, a state was required to submit to the Children's Bureau a detailed plan that would show what community services it intended to carry out to achieve the act's objectives. A clear disclaimer of any intent to limit the power or rights of parents in relation to their children was evident in the specification that no official or agent of the state administering agency and no representative of the Children's Bureau could enter any home or take charge of any child over the objections of parents.[30] At the same time, the act stood as a declaration of public policy that "the people of the United States through their federal government, share with the states and localities the responsibility for helping to provide community services that children need for a good start in life."[31] As such, it represented a notable advance in social justice for women and children.

Julia Lathrop, Grace Abbott, Florence Kelley, Lillian Wald, Grace Meigs, M.D., and others who played an important role in designing the legislation clearly believed that the programs within the states should not reflect the characteristics of "charity" available only to those unable to pay. They wanted "a community service for all classes" to solve a problem of the greatest importance to the community as a whole. On any other basis, Julia Lathrop warned, the program would degenerate into "poor relief" with its attendant stigma.[32]

If this spirit of "right to service" was to be maintained, Grace Abbott emphasized, women would have to demand the kind of services during pregnancy and childbirth that they wanted and would utilize. For this to happen they would require information about what constituted good obstetrical care. Many women were uninformed and uncertain about the kind of special attention during pregnancy and childbirth that they needed and could demand. The approach, then, would have to be fundamentally one of education with the aim of removing the whole subject of childbirth from the mysterious and unknown into its place as a subject that women had a right to know all about.[33]

As administrator of the new legislation, Grace Abbott's early task was to secure the cooperation of the states. The federal act gave permission to each of the states to use the money made available under the act, but they could not be required to do so. As in the first child labor legislation in which Grace Abbott had pioneered an original and successful form of federal-state collaboration, the success of the Sheppard-Towner Act depended in large measure upon the extent to which she could engage trust and honest cooperation with state and local officials. The act had stipulated that any reasonably appropriate state plan, adequate to meeting the act's objectives, would be approved, which accommodated Grace Abbott's preference for a liberal stance with respect to differences among the states. She observed that in contrast to legislation for birth registration, which should be the same in all states, in pioneering social legislation such as the maternity and infancy act, "uniformity is not a panacea." There could be no one model plan for all the states; each must devise its own, which would change and expand as work progressed from day to day. Federal rules should be minimal in the early stages of administration and expanded only as the experience of the several states showed an appropriate direction. To make every dollar count in saving lives of mothers and babies, she said, the program of each state must grow out of that state's particular conditions and experience.[34]

The act contained only one explicit limitation upon the states: they could not assign the money received to a private agency; these funds must be expended by public agencies to advance the development of public services for children and women. At the same time, Grace Abbott made clear, "certain fundamentals" should be addressed by each state in developing its maternity and infancy plan. It should rest on a data base about conditions in the particular state; without such facts, the plan would be at risk of relying upon experience in some other state in which conditions might be quite different. As she stated, "Unless you know where the babies are, where they are dying and why they are dying, you can't know the best plan for reducing the death rate." If a state requested approval of its plan but was outside the birth and death registration area, it should move toward inclusion. In addition, the Children's Bureau wished to know how each state expected to get results from its work. Each would be asked to show concrete outcomes year by year. She counseled state officials not to try during the first year to mount all the programs that they hoped to accomplish in the five years of the act. At the same time their plan should not be too narrowly limited: "Nothing gets public momentum if it is confined to too narrow a field."[35]

Relying upon her previous experience with state officials and child labor legislation, Grace Abbott began by sending a letter to each governor outlining the terms of the new legislation, inviting the state to present its own plan for approval, and offering consultation on technical matters such as surveying problems within the state or drafting legislation to enable the state to take advantage of the federal grants. (To accept provision of the Sheppard-Towner Act, states had to indicate their intent and commitment through legislative enactment.) Significantly, she reached out to woman's groups all over the country to urge them to work at the local and state level in proposing programs and to lobby in the state capitol so that their region could come into the benefits of the maternity and infancy legislation. By the end of the fiscal year 1923, all state legislatures had met since the passage of the act; only eight of the forty-eight states had not accepted its terms. By the time the maternity and infancy act came to an end in 1929, only Connecticut, Massachusetts, and Illinois had never accepted the aid offered by the federal government.[36] The act authorized an annual appropriation of $1,240,000 for a five-year period with $50,000 of this to be expended by the Children's Bureau for administrative purposes and for continued investigations of infant and maternal mortality. The balance was to go to the states accepting the act.[37]

The plans submitted by states, although diverse, reflected the same fundamental conception of the problem. All showed an intent to bring about better care for infants by teaching mothers, better care for women by informing them about the need for medical care during pregnancy and childbirth, and more accessible care for women and babies by bringing about more widespread health facilities.[38]

The promotion of birth registration was a prominent feature in many states. During the seven years the act was in force, birth registration was expanded from thirty states in 1922, representing 72 percent of the population, to forty-six states in 1929, representing almost 95 percent of the population.[39]

In some cities maternal and infancy work was reasonably well developed before Sheppard-Towner. However, little had been done in the rural areas of America. Although isolation was pervasive in the western states, inaccessible communities could still be found in every region. Therefore greatest emphasis was placed upon reaching the mothers and children in the country. Prenatal and child health conferences conducted by a physician and a nurse reached many women in thousands of counties. They were held wherever space was available—in churches, schoolrooms, grocery stores, or homes. These affairs were events of great interest to whole families, many of whom would pack food for the journey over plains or mountains to reach the doctor or nurse who would be there to help them. Impassable roads and swollen rivers and creeks were frequent obstacles. In one western state a nurse sent Grace Abbott a photograph of a mother and her child crossing a river in a basket swung on an overhead cable in order to attend the conference. Mothers often drove many miles with horse and buggy to bring all their children, and some rode mules over trails instead of roads.[40] At the conferences, pregnant women were examined and instructed, children were examined, weighed, and measured and their parents were given instruction in normal child growth and development. Physical defects were pointed out and follow-up work arranged to correct the conditions. Movies on health were shown and appropriate literature distributed. In some states infancy and prenatal conferences were held in every county. In addition, through the cooperation of the Children's Bureau and some of the state medical societies, rural doctors were kept informed on the most recent obstetrical practices through lectures given by an obstetrician using slides and films and a complete set of instruments.[41]

Some states requested the loan of the Children's Bureau "Child-Welfare Special," a truck compactly equipped as a child health center which had been used by the bureau for rural demonstrations since 1919. For example in 1922 thousands of preschool and school-age children in the small towns and rural counties of Tennessee and Oklahoma received attention and physical examinations in the "Child-Welfare Special," brought in at the request of the state health officer. The attention which it attracted all along the route added to the educational value. Some states adopted the model and sent their own mobile clinic to tour the countryside.[42]

The Children's Bureau also devised a widely used and unique "correspondence course"—a series of letters written by physicians and sent along with informational pamphlets to women whose names were reported by physicians or other mothers. The language of the letters was simple but scientifically correct in its instructions to women about pregnancy, childbirth, the care of the unborn child, and infant care following birth. Many thousands of letters were sent out in many states; in Texas the letters were written in Spanish as well as in English.[43]

The demand for county nurses trained in maternal and child care multiplied in excess of the supply. In response, Grace Abbott arranged during the first year of the act for a Children's Bureau staff nurse to give instruction to groups of nurses within sixteen states that requested that kind of help. County health units and public health nurses began to appear in parts of the country where they had never been before. Not all expectant mothers could get to a prenatal conference, so nurses often visited pregnant women in their homes to inform them about the care they needed. These nurses gave practical help such as how to arrange for regular urinalysis during pregnancy, they encouraged postpartum examinations, they demonstrated methods of child care and hygiene using whatever equipment the expectant mother had in her home. And they gave counsel and warm support to women who wanted to learn about their bodies and who felt alone in the travail they faced.[44]

Reaching women in very isolated areas presented the nurses with challenges which sometimes had amusing aspects, as when one was attempting to get to the home of a pregnant woman in a remote mountain area of Kentucky. When the road she was following came to an end, she asked the owner of a small general store for direction as to how to proceed further. He offered to lend her a mule to ride up the mountain trail and she gamely accepted. He would take no remuneration. When she was mounted and ready to depart, he told her she would need a spur, or else his mule would never go. He supplied that essential piece of equipment and then asked the nurse for fifty cents in payment. She was puzzled as to why he would charge her for the spur but not for the use of his valuable mule. His explanation was simple: if she was thrown off, which he thought likely, his mule would return. She might not, and she would still have his spur. The nurse later entered the fifty-cent payment into her expense account, only to have it denied unless she turned over the spur as government property.[45]

One of the most concrete accomplishments of the maternity and infancy act was in relation to the "midwife problem," a matter of concern to Grace Abbott from her days at Hull-House.[46] Although the 1920 Census listed 4,473 midwives practicing in the United States, when the Children's Bureau and the states began to survey the phenomenon, it became clear that there were at least ten times that many. The percentage of women attended by midwives varied markedly among the states, as did the conditions for the regulation of their work. The southern states with their very great number of illiterate, untrained, and aged Negro midwives were confronted with a different kind of undertaking than New Jersey, for example, where cooperation with well-trained foreign midwives was obtained, making it possible to require high qualifications before granting a midwifery license. In some states the number of practicing midwives was diminishing annually; but in Mississippi, by contrast, 48 percent of all the births were reported by midwives. The states in the Southwest with Mexican midwives and the Pacific Coast states with Japanese midwives illustrated some of the language complications.

Eighteen state health officers decided to begin training, licensing, and supervising midwives in their rural communities as the only practical means of attacking the problem. In Pennsylvania two women physicians who spoke several languages instructed midwives, using their native speech. Texas employed a Mexican nurse to train Mexican midwives. Grace Abbott added a Negro physician to the Children's Bureau staff and "lent" her to some of the Southern states to assist Negro nurses, newly employed by health departments, in developing training courses and supervising midwives. Results of these methods of work were reflected in improved care of women, more frequent calling in of a physician for difficult cases, improved registration of births, and a marked decrease in ophthalmia neonatorum, common among midwives' cases.[47]

Much of the success of a maternity and infancy program in any state depended upon community resources which could be used to promote its educational goals. The quality of collaboration with medical societies and individual physicians was critical. Cooperation was also sought from home and farm demonstration agents of granges and farm bureaus, women from a variety of state and local organizations, and school superintendents and teachers. Grace Abbott stressed that a broad base of interest was essential if the scientific care of children and pregnant women was to be promoted "since practically the entire adult population must be interested in the subject before the best results can be obtained."[48]

Administering the Sheppard-Towner Act required Grace Abbott and the three physicians and three nurses of the bureau's maternal and infant hygiene division to travel extensively into the states. They observed programs, consulted with state directors and public health nurses, and offered technical advice. They met with many groups of lay people. They also conducted special studies in states that requested them to extend the factual base of the state's work, for example in Tennessee a statistical study in six counties to show infant and maternal mortality rates as affected by the type of attendant at birth; in New Mexico a study of conditions affecting the health of mothers and infants in two counties—one with a Mexican population, the other entirely English-speaking. At the suggestion of state directors of maternal and infant hygiene, the Children's Bureau undertook to formulate standards of prenatal care and of child care which could be used by the various state agencies in their work. Grace Abbott brought together a group of prominent obstetricians to develop the prenatal standards and she secured the cooperation of the American Pediatric Society in drawing up a set of standards for conducting infant and preschool conferences.[49]

In passing the Sheppard-Towner Act Congress had authorized an appropriation for each of five years, to end in 1927. Grace Abbott believed that in large measure it had done so out of doubt as to whether the Children's Bureau would be able to enlist the cooperation of the states in any substantial way.[50] If so, the fact that productive federal-state collaboration had come about promptly and had been widely sustained suggested that there would not be excessive difficulty in getting the act extended beyond its five-year life. In addition, challenges to the act's constitutionality had been overcome.

In 1922 the Commonwealth of Massachusetts had brought an action as an original suit in the United States Supreme Court on the charge that the act was an incursion into the field of local police power reserved to the states by the Tenth Amendment and, given the fact that the money derived from federal taxation would be divided only among those states formally accepting the act (which Masschusetts had not), it also constituted an invasion of property rights of the state's citizens.[51] Edith Abbott wrote with some irony, "New England, after sacrificing her sons to defeat the principles of states' rights in 1861–65, had now come actually to regard support of that principle as a public duty."[52] Shortly after the Commonwealth suit was filed, a woman from Massachusetts filed a taxpayers suit in the Supreme Court of the District of

Columbia with virtually the same allegations as in the first case.[53] The charges ignored federal grants being accepted by Massachusetts under a score or more of other appropriation acts, for example for protection against white-pine rust and the European corn borer, suppression of gypsy and brown-tail moths, the prevention of forest fires, for vocational education and rehabilitation, for highways and the state militia. That the Sheppard-Towner Act had only extended the well-established principle of federal-state cooperation to a new field, the protection of maternity and infancy, was a point of view either unacceptable or ignored by the influential people behind the Massachusetts cases. The second case, after having been dismissed by the court, was appealed to the United States Supreme Court and both cases were argued together there.

One residue of the loss of the first federal child labor law in its test of constitutionality was a conviction held by Grace Abbott, Felix Frankfurter, Roscoe Pound, Florence Kelley, Julia Lathrop, and others that Solicitor-General James W. Beck held to a very conservative position in regard to constitutional questions and had given only cursory attention to the preparation of the government's child labor case. With a threat now to the maternity and infancy programs, Grace Abbott was much concerned that everything possible be done to defend the act. She consulted with Frankfurter, Lathrop, Kelley, and other friends of the legislation such as Gifford and Cornelia Pinchot and Senator George Pepper.[54] Just before the cases were to be heard, Grace wrote Edith Abbott a hurried note in which she indicated that "the briefs seem to me in good shape, and I think we have swung Beck into line so that he is trying to win. . . . At the rate the court is now working under the lashes of Taft we should have a decision before the summer recess."[55]

The court ruled that both cases must be disposed of for lack of jurisdiction. The statute had gone no further than to propose to share with the states the field of state power, to extend an option which the state was free to accept or reject. The question as presented was political and not judicial in character, and not a matter for the exercise of judicial power.[56] Nevertheless, enemies of the maternity and infancy act continued to claim that the question of constitutionality had not been finally settled, suggesting that optimism about an extension of the act dangerously discounted the bitterness and tenacity of the opposition. And indeed, when hearings began on a bill for the continuance of the maternity and infancy appropriation beyond 1927, the foes of the act called out the same adversaries whose arguments and attacks had been heard in the controversy over its initial passage.

The forces against the Sheppard-Towner Act carried various banners, all aimed to protect special interests—states' rights, a conservative fiscal policy, anti–woman suffrage, abhorrence of leftist ideologies, and the domain of the medical profession. As in the long debate over woman suffrage, one unremitting theme can be identified—reliance upon distinctions between the sexes with an emphasis upon biological characteristics that ascribed to women a collection of disabilities.

The "antis" reflected a view that said morality and authority hung in the balance within society.[57] The home, and an aggregate of families, more than any other factor protected against society's destruction. The critical characteristic in this line of defense was the woman in the home—the woman with her concern for stability and commitment to the future. Anything that threatened separate and distinctive sex roles threatened society. At the same time, women were perceived as inherently weak individuals. They needed care and protection from the world, which men would provide in exchange for childbearing and rearing and the special status these functions implied. Women's interests could be adequately represented through male suffrage. However, this essential willingness to care for and protect women would not last if women entered unnecessarily into the world and men became continually jostled by women in commerce and politics. Individualism for men was proper and necessary and the threat to individualism was frequently cited by the "antis" as reason to oppose the maternity and infancy legislation. To them it represented interference with individual rights by government agents who would enter into the family and "take charge" of the individual citizen; it posed an usurpation of the right of states to exercise the police power and prevent invasion of individual privacy. The maternity and infancy legislation that encouraged women to demand information about their bodies and better conditions of childbirth could only lead to rampant rejection of the proper roles of wife and mother. Thus the threat was female individualism, which must be rejected to preserve the social order. The line of reasoning facilitated a defense of individualism for men while attacking it for women.

To make their arguments, the "antis" relied upon ridicule of women as well as an image of glorified womanhood. Some of the most offensive diatribe came from Senator James Reed of Missouri. He attacked the "ambitious" character of the "scheme"; the "vast" number of people the chief of the Children's Bureau intended to employ with the "excessive" appropriations, and the immense "power and control" it would place in the hands of the Children's Bureau chief and her associates. Given that element of power and control, he said, "the question of personality becomes important." He intoned into the *Congressional Record* the names of all Children's Bureau staff who were unmarried, giving special emphasis to the title "Miss" affixed to each. "It seems to be the established doctrine of the bureau that the only people capable of caring for babies and mothers of babies are ladies who have never had babies," he said, which earned him the laughter of colleagues. He went on to deplore the employment of "female celibates . . . women too refined to have a husband." He became rhapsodical about "mother's tender love" and the "dimples in a baby's cheek [that] gather to welcome a mother's rapturous kiss." He expressed sympathy for "the yearnings . . . of the office-holding spinster . . . for the dream children she does not possess." However, he warned, "official meddling" can not take the place of mother love. "Mother love!" he went on, "The golden cord that stretches from the throne of God." He contrasted that image with the "bespectacled lady, nose sharpened by curiosity, official chin pointed and keen" who having ascertained the names of future mothers "sails majestically and authoritatively to the home of the prospective mother and demands admission in the name of the law." To laughter from the floor of the Senate, he questioned "whether one out of ten of these delightful reformers could make a bowl of buttermilk gruel that would not give a baby the colic. . . . We would better reverse the proposition," he stated, "and provide for a committee of mothers to take charge of the old maids and teach them how to acquire a husband and have babies of their own."[58]

Senator Reed was not alone in his sexist attacks. Physicians in Illinois, for example, although speaking from a different self-interest, also employed sexist language. The legislation was "a menace" sponsored by "endocrine perverts [and] derailed menopausics."[59]

In the views of the "antis" maintaining the differences between men and women not only kept society from destruction by protecting the home, it also constituted a determinant of political and economic form.[60] These opponents of social legislation held a pessimistic view of the future which narrowed the range for change which they could tolerate. Thus they were concerned with governmental power from a world view, fearful of foreign ideologies and any encroachment from pacifism or communism.

Among the various "patriotic" organizations that fought the maternity and infancy legislation was the Sentinels of the Republic, founded by Louis A. Coolidge of Boston in 1922. Although it was a small organization, its propaganda was national in scope. Its financing came from manufacturing interests, and it made no public report of income or expenditures. Its very name was a battle cry, as was its motto, "Every citizen a Sentinel! Every home a Sentry Box." The group was opposed to increased centralization of power in the federal government and its clear intent was to "stop the spread of communism," which it saw in all liberal social legislation such as the maternity and infancy act, the Equal Rights Amendment, the child labor legislation. To achieve all its goals, the Sentinels cooperated closely with the *Woman Patriot*, a publication of the Woman's Patriot Publishing Company, headed by Mary Kilbreth, former president of the National Association Opposed to Woman Suffrage, an organization that had disbanded when the Nineteenth Amendment was declared constitutional. At that time Kilbreth and four other women decided to continue publishing its organ, *The Protest*, although under a new name, the *Woman Patriot*, and to act as a self-appointed board of directors to control its editorial policy.[61]

These angry representatives of the anti-suffrage group attacked many feminists and the programs they supported. Especially they attacked the maternity and infancy legislation and Grace Abbott, who had been allied with "suspect" causes—pacifism, advocacy for immigrants, child labor regulation, unionism, and now a new conspiracy, federal programs for maternity and infancy, which to the "antis" implied control of the reproductive function and family life. The pages of the *Woman Patriot* heaped abuse upon "uplifters" and "moralists" and saw the roots of the conspiracy emanating from Jane Addams and Hull-House. "It is of the utmost significance that practically all the radicalism started among women in the United States centers about Hull-House, Chicago, and the Children's Bureau at Washington—with a dynasty of Hull-House graduates in charge of it since its creation."[62]

These "Hull-House graduates" were featured, among others, in a particularly effective, although absurd, piece of propaganda—the "spider-web chart," which drew widespread protest from women's groups for its illustration of the influence of professional patriots upon an important branch of government. The chart was prepared by Lucia R. Maxwell, a librarian of the War Department's Chemical Warfare Service, and approved by Brigadier-General Amos Fries. Inscribed to Mary Kilbreth "with appreciation for her work," the chart was apparently developed for use of the *Woman Patriot*. The document charted connecting links within a web of organizations and men and women leaders which allegedly made clear an international conspiracy, directed from Moscow, to take over this country. Various versions of the spider-web chart were given wide circulation.[63]

The anti-suffrage professional patriots saw "socialism," "communism," and "Russian influences" in the work of the Children's Bureau, which they consistently referred to as "this Socialist Bureau" or "a Socialist Propaganda agency." Grace Abbott and other backers of the legislation were charged with being more interested in the "capture of power" than in the health of mothers and babies.[64] One of the most persistent and tiresome allegations was that Grace Abbott was involved in a sinister kind of alliance with Madame Alexandra Kollontai. The origins of such an allusion went back to the Children's Year when Julia Lathrop was still chief of the Children's Bureau and had issued a useful publication entitled *Maternity Benefit Systems in Foreign Countries.*[65] In her introduction to the study Julia Lathrop wrote that "maternity benefits are not an experiment. . . . No such system, once undertaken, has ever been abandoned. Instead the tendency of changes in existing legislation has always been toward including larger and larger groups of the population . . . and toward the compulsory as contrasted with the voluntary principle of enforcement." The report had been prepared for the bureau by a competent researcher on the staff of the Library of Congress and it contained a statement that "the most comprehensive study of maternity benefits and insurance which has yet appeared in any language is the volume by Mme. A. Kollontai."[66] A distinguished advocate of social reforms, Mme. Kollantai had been in the United States in 1915–16 and again in the following year. Various Americans came to know her in Geneva in work with committees of the League of Nations. In 1917 she was appointed to the Soviet cabinet position of People's Commissar of Social Welfare. The discovery of the Children's Bureau's statement about Mme. Kollontai's study and Julia Lathrop's statement about trends generally led the professional patriots to see Julia Lathrop, and now Grace Abbott as her successor, conspiring with Mme. Kollontai and other Soviet leaders to use the Children's Bureau for "despotic power," the promotion of "revolution by legislation," and of "international control of children."[67]

This new line of attack found support from the Sentinels of the Republic, the Daughters of 1812, the Massachusetts Public Interest League, and the Daughters of the American Revolution. Grace Abbott was assailed for her supposed affiliation with leading communist and pacifist women of Europe, growing out of her 1915 participation in the International Congress of Women, her work with the League of Nations Advisory Committee on Traffic in Women and Children, and her membership in the Women's International League for Peace and Freedom.[68] She was said as well to be following Mme. Kollantai's preference for government programs over private charity, witness the change of name of the National Conference of Charities and Correction in 1917 to the National Conference of Social Work (an organization of which Grace Abbott became president in 1923) and a proposal made in 1923 (although not by Grace Abbott) for a Department of Public Welfare in the executive branch of federal government. The *Woman Patriot* made this connection: "*Miss Grace Abbott, chief of the Children's Bureau*, is president of the 'National Conference of Social Work' which has repudiated the idea of 'charities and correction' in its title, which it carried for over forty years *until the Bolshevik revolution in 1917*. It is remarkable how soon the seeds of Communism planted in Soviet Russia bear fruit in 'social work' and in proposed reorganization of the executive departments of the Government of the United States!"[69]

For the most part, Grace Abbott, more than Edith Abbott, was singularly free of resentment or anger about personal criticisms. She believed deeply in free speech, even for extremists who she felt usually damaged their position in the long run with their farfetched allegations. Although she kept herself informed about new strategies of the professional patriots (by a subscription to the *Woman Patriot*, for example), her preferred mode of response was to ignore them. When Mary Anderson, Grace Abbott's counterpart in the Women's Bureau, was caught up in the sweep of the postwar "Red Scare," she tried to persuade Grace Abbott to join her in a public rebuttal of the personal attack. But Grace Abbott would not.[70] To become defensive, she said, only "spreads it around." With her mother and friends, she took a light approach: "The hearings have been going on. Today's were amusing for a wild antisuffragist performed who embarrassed her supporters on the Committee and added to the gaiety of the morning. She is the one who describes Miss Lathrop, Mrs. Kelley and Miss Addams as Bolsheviks, Communists etc. and takes a whirl at me from time to time."[71] But to retain objectivity was not always easy. At the height of the debate on extension of the Sheppard-Towner Act, she wrote Edith Abbott: "The opposition were never meaner than yesterday. . . . At present I am going to the Capitol daily for at least several hours and last night I had to prepare replies for Sheppard late into the night."[72]

Although somewhat less publicly and personally demeaning, an even more dangerous threat to the maternity and infancy legislation, and eventually to the survival of the Children's Bureau, came from the Public Health Service and the American Medical Association. Their opposition had been slow to begin, but it gained momentum and was finally to precipitate a crisis at the 1930 White House Conference on Child Health and Protection.

Julia Lathrop had first outlined a proposal for a maternity and infancy program in her annual report of 1917;[73] it had drawn no opposing response from the Public Health Service or from physicians across the country.[74] (Haven Emerson, M.D., for example, endorsed the Sheppard-Towner Act before and after its passage, although he emerged later as a key opposing figure at the White House Conference on Child

Health and Protection.)[75] However, with the increased attention of the Children's Bureau to maternity and infancy during the Children's Year and the Conference on Standards of Child Welfare, the Public Health Service began to raise questions about proper jurisdictional boundaries of health work within the federal government. Julia Lathrop sought an interview with Surgeon-General Rupert Blue, and forthrightly explored with him his attitude toward the maternity and infancy bill, by then introduced into Congress, and the functions of the Children's Bureau in general. Privately she believed that his concern about jurisdiction of health work began after the Children's Bureau had carried out its well-received infant mortality studies and its successful publication of popular literature for individual mothers. In the interview with Dr. Blue, Julia Lathrop gave support to a new draft of the bill to allow for a joint board of the heads of the Public Health Service, the Children's Bureau, and the Bureau of Education, rather than lodging its administration solely within the Children's Bureau. Although Blue continued to appear troubled by jurisdictional health boundaries, Lathrop's assessment was that she had gained some assurance of cooperation.[76]

When Hugh S. Cumming succeeded to the office of surgeon-general, he informed Julia Lathrop that he would not oppose the maternity and infancy measure; however, it was evident that he saw its administration and control as rightfully belonging to the Public Health Service. In late 1920 when Cumming appeared before a House committee, he disclaimed opposition to the bill, but his testimony was laced with suggestions of doubt, and upon questioning he indicated his belief that as a health function, responsibility for the program should be lodged within his service. Thus he gave a signal which prompted the American Medical Association and state medical societies to bring out their forces in opposition to what was perceived as dangerous expanding governmental influence over medical practice—the specter of "state medicine," an "imported socialistic scheme." Grace Abbott was politically astute and she recognized that in the long run the resistance of the medical profession and its professional societies, and of the clearly established health interests within the federal government, was more potent in opposing an extension of maternity and infancy legislation than even the most vitriolic propaganda of the professional patriots.[77]

The controversy between the Children's Bureau and the Public Health Service was related to a deeply held philosophical view of the child which had been articulated by the founders of the Children's Bureau. These reformers had promoted a definition of child welfare theory and practice that encompassed a unified social, economic, and industrial approach to problems of childhood. Health programs for children and mothers could not be viewed as only of medical interest, but as having social, economic, and industrial components as well. Grace Abbott, like Julia Lathrop, envisioned public programs that would embrace all the interests of childhood. They intended that the Children's Bureau would bring together findings about child life from the various branches of government, and then act as a standard setter for states and communities in relation to a "whole program" of child welfare. Furthermore, Grace Abbott was opposed, as Julia Lathrop had been, to former Surgeon-General Blue's proposal to transfer the bureau functions to a Department of Health, which he desired and expected to see created. Abbott and Lathrop preferred their place in the Department of Labor, which they saw as more functionally hospitable to their broad definition of child welfare, a department "interested in securing the welfare of the masses of the wage earners of this country." Child welfare, and particularly programs for maternity and infancy, as part of a larger concern for human welfare, in their view, could not be dealt with properly as only a health concern.[78]

President Calvin Coolidge was a key figure in the contest for congressional extension of the maternity and infancy legislation. Given his preference for curtailing federal subsidies to the states, he could be expected to oppose any extension of the act that would require continuing appropriations. However, the act continued to draw strong support from women's groups, as well as from state health directors and some prominent obstetricians and pediatricians. Coolidge's solution was to approve the act in principle but oppose a renewal of the five-year appropriation, or as Grace Abbott stated in a letter to her father, "The President recommended it in one paragraph of his budget message and took it back in the next."[79] Specifically, President Coolidge stated: "I am in favor of the proposed legislation extending the period of operation of this law with . . . a view to the gradual withdrawal of the Federal Government from this field, leaving to the States, who have been paid by Federal funds and schooled under Federal supervision, the privilege and duty of maintaining this important work without aid or interference from the Federal Government. . . . The States should now be in a position to walk alone along this highway of helpful endeavor."[80] His choice of metaphor led Edith Abbott to a biting comment: "President Coolidge, like many other brave New England men, was quite willing to accept a ninety million federal subsidy for good roads . . . but his searing New England conscience made him afraid of a subsidy of $1,249,000 for mothers and babies."[81]

In January 1927, an extension of the Sheppard-Towner Act and an appropriation was finally secured, but not without serious loss. An eight-day filibuster by four vehemently opposed senators[82] was finally broken by a compromise amendment, accepted by Grace Abbott and the proponents of the legislation when cloture seemed unattainable. The amendment provided for a two-year extension of the act and then its repeal at the end of that period.

The fight for extension of the maternity and infancy legislation had been demanding and, to many friends of the act, to look forward to the repeal of the initial legislation in two years felt like defeat. Florence Kelley, that staunchest of women in the network of women reformers, confided to Julia Lathrop her sense of failure over the limited renewal of the Sheppard-Towner Act. "As I understand it, the great sin of omission of the women's organizations really occurred in March 1926, when we failed to concentrate all our efforts on the Senate immediately after the House had, in February, authorized the prolongation of the Act and adequate appropriations for two years. If we had made a sufficient demonstration of power and zeal before the end of the long session, I do not believe the Senate would have dared to act as brutally as it did from July 1926 on. It is always hard to make up afterwards for a neglected demonstration of strength. . . . My only excuse for falling down last year is that I really was ill, . . . unfit and unable to fight when the fighting was good." Now Florence Kelley, with renewed energy, proposed to Julia Lathrop that "it is of very great importance that we should keep up a continuous series of demonstrations of public approval of her [Grace Abbott] and her work, all kinds of organizations of men and women being gradually put on record before the time comes for the new Sheppard-Towner." Grace Abbott also preferred to concentrate on a drive for new legislation in 1929, and took an optimistic view: "It requires absolutely the same legislative procedure for the extension as it does for a new bill, and so under the circumstances we yielded very little."[83]

Grace Abbott also took some prompt and carefully developed action. Dr. Martha Eliot, who had become a close friend of hers, remembered a conversation between the two of them which took place when the Sheppard-Towner Act appeared likely to end. Grace Abbott recognized that new legislation would be almost impossible in 1929 without the cooperation of organized medicine, and to her this meant that something had to be done that would "show the doctors what they are doing" by opposing maternity and infancy legislation.[84] The result was the launching of an unprecedented and imaginative investigation of maternal mortality. Infant mortality rates had begun to show some improvement, but maternal deaths assigned to causes associated with pregnancy and child birth continued high. Although not fully documented, earlier studies strongly suggested that these deaths were in most instances preventable.[85] The intent of the new study was to identify the conditions contributing to the tragic loss of life in the United States attributed to causes associated with pregnancy and childbirth.

Working closely with Dr. Robert L. De Normandie of the Harvard Medical School and other physician members of the bureau's Obstetric Advisory Committee, Grace Abbott designed a comprehensive study of maternal mortality which was then carried out by her staff with the cooperation and consultation of the committee and of physicians from selected state departments of health. The research included states in the birth-registration area in which both the state board of health and the state medical society formally requested to be included in the study. In thirteen states, each maternal death that occurred in 1927 and in 1928 was investigated. In 1928 two more states came into the study and each maternal death for that year in those states was studied. In all, the deaths of 7,537 women were investigated. Data were obtained from certificates of deaths attributed to puerperal causes, birth certificates when they were available, and hospital and clinic records where the woman had received care. (Relatively few of the women who died in hospitals had planned hospitalization; it usually had been an emergency measure.) In addition, as soon as possible after a death certificate had been filed, the physician or midwife or other attendant at birth was interviewed individually by a physician from the staff of the Children's Bureau or a state department of health using a standard interview schedule. Although few of the doctors had kept case histories, most appeared to remember vividly the circumstances of the woman's death.[86]

When the study was complete a very serious situation had been found with regard to the quality of care that women received during their pregnancies. An almost total lack of adequate prenatal care prevailed. In fewer than 1 percent of the cases was the care given up to the standards of prenatal care previously developed by the Children's Bureau in collaboration with its Obstetric Advisory Committee.[87] The incidence of death from puerperal septicemia was enormous, "nothing short of appalling," the Obstetric Advisory Committee noted. One-fourth of the maternal deaths followed abortion. Unwed women were especially vulnerable to death following abortion. More than half of the women studied had had some operative procedure before death, often unwisely undertaken or performed by physicians untrained in surgical techniques. Use of pituitrin was common and associated with serious accidents of pregnancy such as sepsis, hemorrhage, and ruptured uterus. The cruel waste in human life was also evident in the number of stillbirths, infant deaths following live births, and damaged infant survivors.[88]

Detailed findings of the study with evaluative comments and recommendations by the Obstetric Advisory Committee were widely circulated. Did the study make any difference? Almost twenty years later the value of the study was recalled by a distinguished obstetrician from Chicago's Lying-In Hospital who testified before a Senate committee in relation to pending maternal and child welfare legislation. He recalled how he had first heard about the unusual study of maternal mortality that the Children's Bureau had conducted in the late 1920s, one that had brought about an interest in conditions of childbirth well beyond what that interest had been. "We had to have some organization, some group of individuals," he said, "who would call our attention to the fact that many women that had no business dying in childbirth were losing their lives every year in the United States."[89]

During the same years that Grace Abbott's time and energy were being poured into the administration of the maternity and infancy legislation and the struggle for its continuance, another matter of social justice was demanding equal time. The child labor legislation passed in 1919 and administered by the Treasury Department was declared unconstitutional when a challenge to it reached the Supreme Court in 1922.[90] In view of this second rejection of federal child labor regulation, advocates for the protection of children concluded that it was now evident that Congress could not successfully deal with child labor under the Constitution as it stood and that a new strategy was imperative—a constitutional amendment which would give Congress clear power to regulate conditions of children's work. The Abbott sisters agreed that an amendment was necessary. Federal child labor regulation had shown itself to be effective and it was still needed. In January 1923, Grace Abbott told a Senate committee that only thirteen states measured up to the standards that were in the first child labor law. Once the second decision of unconstitutionality was rendered, not only did the employment of children increase, but states with lower standards returned to enforcing, often ineffectively, only those lower standards. In addition, there were disturbing disclosures about the ways in which some manufacturers were dodging their own state child labor laws and reviving sweatship employment of young children. For example, New York manufacturers were found to be sending their work to New Jersey to escape New York's more stringent regulations about tenement home work.[91]

Samuel Gompers had been long opposed to child labor. He arranged a conference at the American Federation of Labor headquarters to which representatives of varied national labor, civic, social, and religious groups were invited to consider what should be done. Grace Abbott represented the Children's Bureau. Out of the meeting the Permanent Conference for the Abolition of Child Labor was formed.[92] Support for an amendment came from diverse groups, including persons other than recognized reformers. President Harding recommended passage and submission to the states, as did Calvin Coolidge when he assumed the office. Herbert Hoover advised seeking an amendment to erase a condition that was "poisoning the springs of the nation at their source."[93]

Julia Lathrop, however, issued an astute warning. She wrote Grace Abbott that Owen Lovejoy had wired her for advice on what the National Child Labor Committee should do in view of the court decision, and that she had replied that it should make the strongest possible effort to raise standards in the states then providing the least protection, that the times seemed inhospitable for the launching of a new constitutional amendment and that perhaps a waiting policy was best for awhile. She reflected further in her letter to Grace Abbott that "it is extraordinary how much sentiment exists against central control. The resentment . . . has been played upon or fostered by the amiable thinkers who are fighting the Sheppard-Towner. I have been bewildered by the indignant ignorant talk of 'business men'—'too much money being spent for education' is a common criticism. . . . A mob opinion by most respectable financial pillars is not easy to alter by increasing their provocation."[94] Felix Frankfurter, certainly a friend of child welfare, also questioned whether an amendment to the Constitution was necessarily a desirable strategy to end exploitation in child labor, and urged the League of Women Voters to a "deeper statesmanship" which would be "to awaken the community to the need of its removal."[95]

Support for a child labor amendment came from important national feminist groups and organizations, chief among them the Women's Joint Congressional Committee, the National League of Women Voters, the General Federation of Women's Clubs, the National Consumers' League, and the Women's Trade Union League. All during the months when an amendment was being drafted and moved through congressional committees, Grace Abbott's role in its behalf was one in which her expertise was unsurpassed. Day after day she worked with leaders of the various interest groups, presenting facts, developing and clarifying diverse points of view, proposing resolutions of conflicts about strategies, enlarging the base of support by reaching out to additional potential constituencies, and holding the tenuous coalition together when tensions were high. She assertively sought advice and other forms of assistance from noted lawyers who respected her and her cause—Ernst Freund, Felix Frankfurter, Edward P. Costigan, then on the Tariff Board and later a U.S. senator, Roscoe Pound, and Reuben Oppenheimer, a protégé of Felix Frankfurter.[96] With Frankfurter, Grace Abbott maintained an ongoing two-way exchange of ideas on matters of social justice. Their correspondence reflects a friendship and shared respect often enlightened by humor and brief exchanges of challenging banter.[97] Mutual interest in a child labor amendment also led Grace Abbott to a lasting friendship with Costigan and to accruements to each in the coming years of controversy over public relief.

Grace Abbott was a most able and effective witness before congressional committees. Her experience with the first federal child labor legislation enabled her to clarify elusive administrative and legal nuances of regulatory administration. She was careful to appear with the facts organized and in good humor she gave candid replies to sometimes prickly or obscure questions. Senators whose knowledge about administering child labor legislation was unequal to Grace Abbott's sometimes espoused proposals that she recognized as clearly unworkable. So she would say, "Well now may I just give you two or three points as to how it seems to me." And then her straightforward and convincing response moved the discussion further toward acceptance of the kind of amendment she wanted. At one point Senator Colt was led to observe, "Miss Abbott, you are a master on this whole subject."[98] Because she was just that, and because senators sometimes were condescending or pompous in manner, impatience sometimes lay close to the surface of her replies. After Felix Frankfurter had read the minutes of the Senate hearings on the amendment, he wrote to congratulate Grace Abbott on her testimony. "I don't dare put on paper the thoughts that were aroused in me. They are not seemly. I thought I knew before how much guff my profession was addicted to. . . . The only fellow who seemed to know what he (or she) was talking about, was Grace Abbott. But how do you get away with such brazen contempt for United States senators as you managed to smuggle in several times?"[99] "Contempt" was too strong a word for the quality that underlay some of her responses. If she was not in awe of senators, she respected the legislative process, slow-moving and roundabout as it often was. She was too politically astute to show open discourtesy to lawmakers. However, she didn't hesitate to expose their ignorance of the critical issues, to disagree energetically with their views, or to interrupt them when her thoughts raced ahead of their verboseness. Whether they liked her or not, and generally most appeared to, they recognized her competence, her command of the facts and realities of public administration.

Out of her administrative experience, her long-standing interest in law, and her consultation with Roscoe Pound, Felix Frankfurter, and Ernst Freund, Grace Abbott developed strongly held preferences about the form a child labor amendment should take. She wanted an amendment that would be a straightforward and unambiguous grant of power to Congress to regulate child labor, leaving the minimum and mandatory standards of child labor protection to be specified by Congress in separate legislation that could be modified as changing times required. The power to regulate should not be held exclusively by the federal government; the individual states should be free to continue to exercise the police power to enact and enforce child labor legislation with higher (although not lower) standards than those provided by a federal statute. Uniformity among the states, in her view, was essential only in the observance of a federal minimum standard. At the same time she believed that the only way to give all children protection from premature employment, even with the distinct progress being made in many states, was to enact a federal standard. To wait until all the states voluntarily set an appropriate level of protection, she said, would deny perhaps a whole generation of children the protection "which science indicates is needed at the present time."[100]

An inordinate expenditure of Grace Abbott's time and energy went into trying to bring diverse proponents of an amendment into some agreement about phraseology that would leave no room for litigation as to its meaning. No friendly difference over terms was involved; discussions were sometimes unyielding and bitter. Achieving agreement on the simple phrasing "the labor of persons under eighteen years of age" as the condition to be regulated, and on the negative aspects of "power concurrent with the several states" had to be persuasively and repeatedly interpreted to congressmen who were jostling each other for the right to claim authorship of the final draft and to members of the National Child Labor Committee who were adamantly committed to their own draft and reluctant to see it revised.

Throughout efforts to secure an amendment, Grace Abbott worked closely with Florence Kelley. Each distrusted the judgment of Owen Lovejoy of the NCLC. Their distrust grew when, without warning to the organizations with whom it was allegedly cooperating, the NCLC sent its legal adviser, William Draper Lewis, before the Senate committee, where he presented an entirely new form for the amendment, thus throwing other proponents of the amendment into disarray.[101] Kelley and Abbott were convinced that the NCLC draft contained contentious language that could only lead to legal disputes. Florence Kelley was a fearless and open fighter and she never disguised her dismay over the actions of the NCLC. Grace Abbott's distrust of the NCLC was of long standing, but she wanted to avoid an appearence of the struggle as one of Abbott and Kelley versus the NCLC, which would tend to force others to take sides and intensify the difficulties in holding the varied proponents into some kind of coalition.

Congress adjourned in 1923 without final action on an amendment. Grace Abbott was convinced that the disagreement and confusion created by the NCLC's legal representative had brought about the loss of the bill in that session. Looking ahead, Grace Abbott asked Julia Lathrop to find an opportunity to "talk over with Mr. La Follette the question of legislative tactics. His crowd, of course, is going to have enormous influence in the next Congress. . . . The question of the language is going to be difficult . . . and between Mr. Gompers and Mr. Lovejoy, the sledding is not always easy." [102]

By November, Edward Costigan was warning Grace Abbott that it was vital that "the Amendment's most important supporters know clearly what they want and stand resolutely united." An impression that friends of the amendment are "wavering and uncertain" about its form would risk hastily made changes by members of Congress who, he said, "would like nothing better than an opportunity to secure . . . the public credit which will follow if the accepted Amendment is stamped with their names." He entreated Grace Abbott to continue her leadership in trying to keep the friends of the amendment together. [103]

Conferences and informal exchanges went on at a heavy pace. In December the Women's Joint Congressional Committee and the Permanent Conference for the Abolition of Child Labor came together on a form which each was willing to accept. The NCLC was not, however. Grace Abbott asked Senator George Pepper to help find some last-minute way that concessions could be made that would not weaken the amendment and yet make it possible to move it along. [104]

In February 1924, en route to New York, Grace Abbott wrote her mother a hurried note. Lillian Wald had telephoned at midnight and urged her to attend a conference with NCLC members in one more effort to secure agreement. "Incredible," she termed the continuing ups and downs with the NCLC. She arrived in the early evening and left at midnight after the conference ended because she had to get back to Washington to prepare for her testimony before the House committee, scheduled within a few days. [105]

Finally, in June 1924, an amendment was passed by both houses of Congress and offered to the states for ratification. [106] By the time the amendment was passed, it was not a partisan measure, giving hope for early ratification. However, as Grace Abbott later recorded, "The amendment encountered unexpected opposition which misrepresented its history, its authors and its supporters, its terms and its objectives, with the result that . . . it seemed doomed to defeat." Edith Abbott recorded that initially her sister "was not prepared for the propaganda of animosity, of deliberate falsehoods, and of personal attacks that poured forth."[107]

The professional patriots who so bitterly fought the Sheppard-Towner Act redoubled their efforts to defeat the child labor amendment. The Sentinels of the Republic led the attack in Massachusetts, where the question was submitted to voters in November 1924 for an expression of opinion. The Sentinels used the worn themes of threat to the family and of communist conspiracy, and, joined by the National Association of Manufacturers and the Catholic Church, brought about a rejection of the amendment by a wide margin. The process in Massachusetts had been watched across the country and the outcome was a serious setback for proponents of ratification in other states.

The spider-web chart and charges of communism hit hard and were listened to. The *Woman Patriot* attacked "the Kelley-Abbott gang" and claimed that "Communists, under direct order of the Communist International, are backing the improperly termed 'Child Labor' Amendment, for the purpose of 'nationalizing' the care and education of youth up to 18 years as a preliminary to revolution." "Is it conceivable," they asked, "that American mothers and fathers will tamely submit to turning over their sons and daughters to Miss Grace Abbott as an overparent?"[108]

Although opposition to ratification was not universal among Catholics, many saw it as an entering wedge to "nationalization of education" and direct power over every child by the federal government. One authority on Catholic attitudes toward child labor believed the most telling opposition began in the Catholic weekly, *America*, where the link between child labor and education was made explicit. "The most obvious way in which children can be kept from gainful employment is by requiring them to attend school, and under the proposed amendment school attendance could be required by Federal Law. But if the Federal Government can send children to school, it can also define what constitutes a satisfactory school. It can prescribe the studies for the children and the training of the teachers, and erect or subsidize schools to give the required training."[109]

Manufacturers' associations turned their large resources to defeat the amendment. As Grace Abbott observed, "No other important national labor program was under discussion in 1924 and [they] were free to devote themselves to an extensive and aggressive campaign against the amendment."[110] Businessmen feared that its adoption would lead to more federal labor legislation. They claimed that the amendment was a "union labor scheme" to reduce the number of employees available to factories, farms, and commercial houses so as to drive up wages. They also directed propaganda to farmers and others with agricultural interests where opposition became keen. Farmers were told that boys would no longer be permitted to do farm work of any kind, not even "driving up the cows, or hoeing the vegetables . . . even for their own parents." Nor would a mother have the right to "teach her daughter to do any housework whatever, whether it be the sweeping of floors or the washing of dishes."[111]

The amendment had specified age eighteen, instead of sixteen, to make it possible to keep youth from premature employment in mines and other dangerous work settings. The reformers never intended that the federal government would undertake to regulate all labor of young persons under eighteen years. However, this provision was widely misrepresented and became a means to fan the fear of many that Congress would misuse its grant of power.

Some newspapers, resisting any move toward stricter control of newsboys, used their pages to tout the virtues accruing to the experiences of "the little merchant," free to sell newspapers on the streets of the cities at night. But to the Abbott sisters, one of the most devious approaches came from the National Association of Manufacturers in its challenge to the usefulness of education as offered in the public schools to children of working-class parents. Invited to speak before the annual convention of the National Education Association, Grace Abbott struck hard. She questioned the motives of businessmen who opposed the amendment and she charged selfishness. "When manufacturing associations and other big business organizations could not find another reason for opposing child labor laws," she asserted, "they spread the idea that poor boys and girls should not be sent to school past the lower grades." Back of this opposition, she said, was "the desire of manufacturers and big businessmen to get poor boys and girls into their kitchens and factories." She charged industry with fighting unfairly and disguising its own true interests. Grace Abbott was a formidable opponent. She knew that her speech would be given publicity and she showed in her appearance a clear illustration of what Julia Lathrop termed her "courage and amicable fighting blood."[112]

By early 1925, six states had rejected the amendment and only three had ratified it. Florence Kelley complained that "ratification seems always to move somewhat like a slow infection." Most people seemed to regard the amendment as dead, leading Grace Abbott to tell the Illinois League of Women Voters that "the two great obstacles to securing a minimum standard of protection and of opportunity for all children have always been the selfish interest in the exploitation of children by

the few and the patient toleration of injustice to children by the many."
By 1931 only six states had accepted the proposed amendment.[113]

Two years later, in the depth of the Depression, the public generally
looked to Washington for more guidance. President Roosevelt urged
ratification and old supporters of the amendment rallied their efforts
again. However, as Grace Abbott recorded, "the old story that this was
not a child labor amendment but a communistic youth-control measure
was repeated and listened to."[114] Employers took advantage of the
cheapness of children's labor and sweatshops became common again. In
Pennsylvania, led by Cornelia Pinchot, girls and boys working for star-
vation wages called attention to this trend and became front page news
by going on strike against their employers.[115] Regression toward the
worst of the old abuses of child workers was checked temporarily by
the administration of the National Industrial Recovery Act of 1933.

Grace Abbott was keenly disappointed in the failure of the states to
ratify "the children's amendment." She had seen it as having the potential to pave the way for other federal labor legislation and to stand in the
Constitution as a clear declaration of child rights, a landmark achievement that could hasten other reforms and benefits for children. The
amendment to her was a symbol for all aspects of social justice for children. She never thought of exploitive child labor as an isolated social ill,
but one that was inextricably linked with loss of education, depleted
health, undeveloped human potential, and, most of all, tied to poverty.
Repeatedly she pointed out that "child labor and poverty are inevitably
bound together and if you continue to use the labor of children as the
treatment for the social disease of poverty, you will have both poverty
and child labor to the end of time."[116]

Grace Abbott continued to say that she believed the amendment
would eventually be accepted by the states. Given her quality of facing
up to the realities of losses, perhaps she was only reflecting a commitment she could not relinquish. When the Fair Labor Standards Act was
being developed in 1937, she wrote Frances Perkins that "child labor
seems still to be in some sense a special responsibility of mine."[117] According to Frances Perkins it was primarily Grace Abbott's persuasive
plea that brought last-minute insertion of child labor provisions in the
new federal labor legislation. Grace Abbott had said, "You are hoping
that you have found a way around the Supreme Court. If you have,
why not give the children the benefit by attaching a child labor clause
to this bill?" President Roosevelt agreed.[118]

Reformers' hopes for eventual ratification of the child labor amendment were renewed once more when on June 5, 1939, the U.S. Supreme Court answered two important questions at issue—whether

or not the child labor amendment was still alive for ratification, and whether a state that had rejected the amendment could reverse itself by later voting for ratification. Both question were answered in the affirmative. Grace Abbott was by then too seriously ill to rally to the children's cause.[119]

Perhaps you may ask, "Does the road lead uphill all the way?" And I must answer, "Yes to the very end." But if I offer you a long, hard struggle, I can also promise you great rewards. — GRACE ABBOTT[1]

CHAPTER 7

Well Babies — Well Mothers

Persons who knew and worked with the Abbott sisters agreed that they were much alike and very different. Edith Abbott by all accounts was a scholar, "an intellectual down to her finger tips." Grace Abbott also possessed keen intellect, but she was more disposed to action and was the moving force in implementing the ideas the sisters generated. Their relationship was congenial, based on loyalty and trust.

It has not been possible to clearly define which sister originated the many ideas and undertakings central to their partnership. Both were far ahead of their times in conceptualizing and endorsing social programs to reduce the hazards of life. Sometimes they worked in tandem but mostly they seemed to be moving along abreast of each other. Both were daring in the way they seized opportunities and accepted risks. Each was assertive and provided forceful leadership in whatever program or movement they became involved in. Each was sometimes termed "dominating," a correct observation if taken to mean that she was confident of her facts and judgments and intent upon making her point of view prevail.

Edith Abbott was a more intense personality than Grace Abbott. She felt injustice in a personal way, a quality discernable in her writing, which earned for her a title first applied to Florence Nightingale— "passionate statistician."[2] Both sisters worked long hours at office and at home but Edith Abbott worked under more stress. In what her father termed "your workshop of a home,"[3] she often sat propped up in bed poring over piles of books and papers about her. Grace Abbott was more flexible, more able to remain objective and find a way around difficulties, more able to relax from work by attending a play or a concert or going to a good restaurant with good company, all diversions which

159

Edith enjoyed with her when she came to Washington or they met in New York, but not ones she often sought out for herself. Outside her work environment, Edith Abbott was not particularly comfortable. She avoided social situations unless they were tied to work in some way. Grace Abbott, on the other hand, gave small dinner parties for congenial friends like the Costigans, where their common legislative goals might be discussed for hours but without the intensity that Edith would have brought to the exchange.

Edith Abbott usually hid the softness in her personality. She was often abrupt, almost bristling in manner. One of her students recalled an incident that was not atypical. In the midst of a two-hour class in public welfare administration, she broke off her lecture, called his name, followed by "I want to see you after class." As he described it, he "sweat out" the second hour and then slowly walked down the law school ampitheatre steps for some admonishment. She looked at him pointedly with her bright dark eyes and said, "Do you wear those loud sport coats when you are in the field interviewing clients?" His reply was a quiet, "No, Miss Abbott." During the next session of the class she again directed him to see her after class. Again his guilt and apprehension came to the fore. This time she looked him over and asked, "Why the somber oxford grey, Mr. Coop? I don't want you to overdo it." Despite her manner, like many other students he felt the positive force of her personality and her immense conviction and breadth of knowledge. He said that she had touched his life in a very personal way.[4]

Grace Abbott could also be abrupt if she was faced with requests she considered a waste of time, for example for information about her early life and work to use in an account of "women who are doing interesting things today,"[5] or when she was asked for advice by someone who she felt was overlooking the obvious appropriate action, in which case she would lay out a prescription in a very forceful rapid-fire way. Overall, however, Grace Abbott demonstrated what Frances Perkins once termed "her fine equalitarian manner."[6]

Frank Bane described an incident that illustrates Edith Abbott's discomfort with social amenities that brought attention to her. Together they were preparing some draft legislation for Governor Henry Horner. Bane was in favor of employee contributions for unemployment compensation; Abbott was not. As Bane recollected it, "Edith was in my [American Public Welfare Association] office every day fighting as only she could fight for everything she wanted." After a particularly strenuous argument, Edith Abbott prepared to leave and said as she reached the door "Frank, I just want to make one last comment. Viciousness is bad, but stupidity is worse." Bane enjoyed these encounters. On his way home he remembered that it was the night of the faculty dinner so he stopped at a florist's shop and had an orchid sent to her. She came to the event wearing her usual black lace evening dress, but no corsage. Bane approached her and in his rather gallant manner said, "Edith, where is that orchid I sent you?" She flashed a straight look at him and said emphatically, "The orchid is in a vase on my bureau, and there it shall stay. I never had an orchid in my life, and you are not going to make a fool of me in my old age."[7] In contrast, Grace Abbott knew how to avoid social situations she wasn't interested in, but with more aplomb. She once replied to an invitation to a dance given by the Nevada State Democratic Labor Club with "The only reason I am not accepting at once is that I quit dancing when the two-step was still the fashion, and I am afraid I should only be a wallflower!"[8]

Grace Abbott sometimes seemed amused by her sister's singular or eccentric ways. In other instances, however, she would try to temper Edith's approach or gently reprove her. When she sent Edith an article critical of the American Red Cross to publish in the *Social Service Review*, she wrote, "I don't care how you cut it up. I think though it will be more convincing if you don't bring in all the heavy artillery you can locate for the attack." Sometime after Nisba Breckinridge had been narrowly defeated by Porter R. Lee of Columbia University for the presidency of the National Conference of Social Work (a contest that had ramifications for competing points of view about social work education), Grace admonished Edith with "I am sorry you said what you did to Dunham about Conference Presidents. It really isn't true you know. . . . I don't think it pays to show one's sores to a man like Dunham."[9]

By no means was Edith Abbott always austere. When the pressures she felt were somewhat lessened, her manner with students and friends was often considerate, even charming. Florence Kelley once observed to Grace Abbott that "a dear letter has come from Edith. She is always too heartening about my humble endeavors. I wish I could make anyone feel like standing up straight, and taking a fresh, long breath and then starting all over new, as her letters make me feel."[10] Often after an argumentative encounter, Edith Abbott realized she might have offended and she would try to make amends, but not at the expense of softening her convictions. Phyllis Osborn once had a heated discussion with Edith Abbott at a meeting in Philadelphia. Osborn was then a regional representative for the Public Assistance Bureau of the Social Security Administration and Abbott became upset and angry with her because she had defended some administrative aspect of the Aid to Dependent Children program. By the time Phyllis Osborn had returned to her office in Kansas City, a letter had come from Edith Abbott, four handwritten pages stating again her reasons for the position she had taken and ending by saying that she had meant no personal attack; she had only wanted Miss Osborn "to see the light."[11]

An interesting aspect of the Abbott sisters' partnership is the way they used the resources of government and higher education to get the most out of each. Edith Abbott supplied carefully selected personnel for the Children's Bureau from among her more promising students. Grace Abbott in turn frequently made student financial aid available to Edith by contracting with her for research to be carried out under Children's Bureau sponsorship and Edith's research direction. If either Edith or Nisba Breckinridge had concluded an investigation which merited wide circulation, Grace might arrange to purchase it from the University of Chicago and publish it in Washington. A promising exploratory study by one of Edith Abbott's students sometimes provided the basis for Children's Bureau staff to embark upon a larger piece of research.

In her speeches and in the pages of the *Social Service Review*, Edith Abbott articulated points of view that Grace as chief of the Children's Bureau felt she could not say publicly. Edith or Nisba Breckinridge might sign such commentary or publish without signature. "You may think this is too hot to use," Grace once wrote Edith with an enclosed draft of a manuscript, [but] "these things need to be said!"[12] Edith and Grace Abbott each read the other's manuscripts and discussed them at length to the end that the final publication sometimes seemed to be as much the work of one as the other. The annual reports of the chief of the Children's Bureau were the work of Grace Abbott and her staff, but Edith's finer editorial hand can sometimes be discerned. Occasional sentences appear that could only be Edith's, as in a discussion of the labor of farm children in North and South Dakota: "The wild geese racing southward at the close of the Indian summer cheer the cold and lonely children as they go round and round the field, counting the days until the ground freezes too deep for plowing."[13] Eight years before it was completed and published, Edith Abbott had proposed the idea for Grace's classic work, *The Child and the State*, and had suggested a division of labor.[14] Although the introductions to each of the sections of documents in the two volumes clearly reflect Grace Abbott's wide experience and points of view, the completed work represented many hours of research, discussion, and writing by each.

Studying the record of the Abbott sisters' activity during the 1920s and 1930s leaves an impression of year after year of crowded schedules, hastily arranged meetings in train stations as their paths crossed in travel, one book after another that had impressed one sister being mailed for the other to read, and letters, telegrams, and manuscripts speeding back and forth between them. Whenever either was in New York, she usually stayed at the Cosmopolitan Club, where one could be easily in touch with other women in the network of reformers. The club had been established originally by a group of women from the Murray Hill district as a place where their homesick French, German, and British governesses could get together and establish friendships. At some point the wealthy founders became interested in having the club for themselves, a club for women of means who shared an interest in theater, art, and music. Gradually women with philanthropic or civic interests began to be admitted, which then led to bringing in leaders from the network of women reformers. Women like the Abbotts, Alice and Edith Hamilton, Josephine Roche, and Frances Perkins preferred it to staying in a hotel where they found no companionship or opportunity to "do business" with other women with common interests and commitments. Women who wanted to get Eleanor Roosevelt's ear in the 1930s could sometimes find her there for lunch.[15]

Changes came in Grace Abbott's way of life when in 1925 her twelve-year-old niece, Charlotte, came to live with her in Washington. Ever since the death of Charlotte's mother in 1918, the Abbott sisters had been concerned for their niece's welfare. They were keenly conscious of her as a child growing up without her own mother and, although she lived with two loving grandparents and her father, the Abbott aunts carried a feeling that she was somehow their special responsibility. As their parents grew older and more infirm, the Abbott sisters planned for Charlotte to live with one of them. Not surprisingly, given the weight they attached to the development of intelligence, one large factor in their concern was their wish for Charlotte to have better educational opportunities.

Edith Abbott's letters provide evidence of her love for her young niece, her desire to do what was best for her and insure that Charlotte always felt part of the family group and saw Grand Island as "home." However, as Charlotte Abbott once expressed it, "Aunt Edith could find a way to communicate with any reasoning adult but she was at an utter loss with a child." Grace Abbott was more relaxed with Charlotte, more able to enjoy and appreciate her individual personality. She also maintained a more open relationship with Charlotte's father. Her letters to her brother usually included some news of Charlotte that would add to his appreciation of his daughter or that contained an element of camaraderie, as when he was elected mayor of Grand Island and Grace and Charlotte together composed a telegram to send him:

"We celebrated your victory last night. Don't lose the keys of the city. We are coming back soon and want to get in." Edith Abbott, in contrast, wrote to him more in this style: "Herewith find account for white dress and jacket the child got on the way home in June."[16] A gift of money from Edith to Charlotte might be accompanied with expressions of love but also be laced with directions for its use. A similar gift from Grace was usually "for something you want."

Similar traits are seen in letters to their parents. Grace Abbott's were more devoted to her activities on the national scene that she knew they would be interested in and warm inquiries about home and family. Edith's letters reflected vestiges of her childhood homesickness, her anxiety about her parents, and gave numerous directions as to activities they should engage in and ones they should avoid. Yet no undertaking was too much for her if she thought it would add to her parents' happiness and self-fulfillment. Edith Abbott was responsible for her father's writing his *Recollections of a Pioneer Lawyer*. She provided encouragement, suggested what to include, and gave editorial and publishing help. It was she who planned and carried out a Golden Wedding Anniversary celebration in Grand Island that brought her parents heartfelt recognition and reflected the esteem in which Othman and Lizzie Abbott were regarded in Nebraska.[17]

An unexpected development in Grace Abbott's state of health sent her into "exile," as Edith Abbott always referred to Grace's two periods of absence from Washington because of tuberculosis. In December 1927, Grace Abbott had a heavy cold and cough but she continued with her rigorous schedule. In early January she telegraphed Edith Abbott that she had had some rather alarming opinions from doctors and asked her sister to come to Washington to help her with necessary decisions. A diagnosis of tuberculosis had been made with the prescription of the day, a "good rest in a favorable climate." By the middle of January Katharine Lenroot had become acting chief of the Children's Bureau, Charlotte Abbott had changed from day status to residential status at the National Cathedral School, and Grace Abbott was on her way to Colorado Springs, where she came under the care of Dr. Gerald Webb. Edith accompanied her as far as Chicago where, as she recorded, "I said goodbye to her . . . with a very heavy heart. It was the beginning of the long struggle with tuberculosis."[18]

Grace lived at the Broadmoor Hotel (where other of Dr. Webb's patients also lived) and began a period of bed rest, most of it on a screened porch adjoining her room and overlooking the mountains. Although she had had other experiences with convalescence following serious illnesses, the sudden and enforced inactivity placed new kinds of demands upon her. Her hopes about an early improvement in her condition were soon dashed. By the sixth week she had begun to reconcile herself to a long period of treatment.[19] She cancelled plans to attend summer meetings in Europe and thought of resigning her position with the bureau. Julia Lathrop promptly advised her against it. She knew the demands and restrictions attached to the position of bureau chief, and she understood that Grace Abbott might eventually choose to leave it, but she didn't want her to resign from a defensive position—"only when you are strong and confident, fully refreshed and quite yourself." She also gave Grace facts about the legal status of a presidential appointee and her right to continue to draw her salary.[20]

Grace Abbott gradually addressed herself to a new kind of self-discipline in an effort to get full value from the enforced rest. Yet the days were long and quiet. She listened to the radio and studied the birds and surrounding terrain outside her porch with a small set of binoculars that Nisba Breckinridge sent her. Dr. Webb brought her a small clipboard for writing, and after an initial somewhat scornful rejection of it as a poor substitute for a desk, she found she could write on it without sitting up. Her communication with the world outside the Broadmoor Hotel picked up immediately. Katharine Lenroot wrote often, enclosing memos and correspondence and requests for advice. Grace Abbott began to work, at first about two hours a day, giving a measure of direction to bureau affairs. Edith Abbott began to send books to review. Katharine Lenroot sent material for a paper which Grace blocked out to be filled in at the bureau and then returned to her for "a final whack."

The extent to which Grace Abbott was often lonely and bored, however, is reflected in the pleasure and appreciation she expressed when Nisba Breckinridge spent her spring vacation at the Broadmoor. She had a room next to Grace's and her presence gave Grace a distinct lift in spirits. Edith Abbott made plans to spend the summer in Colorado Springs. Dr. Webb gave approval to Grace's moving into a rented bungalow with Edith, which the Costigans located; Josephine Roche found a reliable maid; and Edith undertook to plan activities for Charlotte Abbott, who spent the summer with her aunts. Gradually Grace was allowed to be out of bed and by the end of summer get out each day for a drive.[21]

It was a difficult two months for Edith Abbott. She responded poorly to the high altitude. Housekeeping tasks always exasperated her, and she brought work to finish and received more in the mail each week. But nothing was too much for her to do for her sister. The knowledge that Grace had tuberculosis had been more overwhelming for

165

Edith Abbott than for Grace. Edith loved and admired her sister immensely and was deeply hurt by the interruption of her career and the threat to her vitality.

Dr. Webb held out encouragement that Grace Abbott could return to her position at the bureau in the fall, which she finally was able to do in October 1928.[22]

The Abbott sisters were among those who supported the election of Herbert Hoover to the presidency in 1928. At Grace Abbott's suggestion, Edith and Julia Lathrop undertook to organize support for Hoover among social workers. Hoover's appeal to the Abbotts and to Lathrop stemmed from his stated concern for the welfare of children, his opposition to premature child labor, his pioneering record in administering the Commission for Relief in Belgium, and an assumption that he would be a strong friend of the children's cause. After eight years of Harding and Coolidge, Hoover seemed to promise renewal of an energetic government and new opportunities in the search for social justice. In her enthusiasm Edith Abbott said, "I can hardly believe that anything so good as Herbert Hoover in the White House can come to pass in these days. It is like rubbing the lamp."[23] Her exhilaration was short-lived.

After taking office, Hoover wrote the director of the budget that "I would be obliged if you would treat with as liberal a hand as possible the application of . . . the Children's and Women's Bureaus. I have great sympathy with the tasks they are undertaking." At the same time, Hoover was known to prefer voluntary charitable efforts rather than new public social programs, and he was on record as cautioning against building a child health program "on the shifting sands of overcentralization."[24]

With the maternity and infancy legislation due to expire at the end of June 1929, the Women's Joint Congressional Committee, early after Hoover's inauguration, brought to his attention the necessity of prompt congressional action. Senator Wesley L. Jones and Congressman John G. Cooper introduced the needed legislation but no word came from the White House and the Sheppard-Towner Act was allowed to lapse. Agitation for its renewal continued but Congress adjourned in late November without action on the Jones-Cooper bill.

Reports had reached Grace Abbott that President Hoover could not be counted on to press for a renewal of the maternity and infancy work within the Children's Bureau and that he had "other plans." In late August she requested an appointment with the president. Her purpose in coming, she told Hoover, was to talk about the maternity and infancy work, the pressure from all sections of the country for its continuance, and the many inquiries about what was being planned. Much of what she was able to draw from the conversation was ambiguous, but three points seemed clear. President Hoover wanted to find a way to substitute voluntary funding as far as possible, to decentralize the work by developing a county unit plan, and to wait for a recommendation that he expected from the upcoming White House conference for "something more comprehensive." Abbott believed that relying on voluntary funding would allow the work to go forward only in a small way, and that county health units in many parts of the country were still so undeveloped as to insure that little would be done if major responsibility for planning and extending services shifted to the local level.[25]

In his State of the Union message to Congress in December President Hoover gave a signal of the intent of his administration when he said that the purpose of the Sheppard-Towner Act should be continued through the Children's Bureau "for a limited period of years" and he made reference to a greater role for the Public Health Service.[26]

Grace Abbott believed there had been support enough to pass the Jones-Cooper bill had it been brought to a vote. The reason it had not came to light in the next session of Congress when Hiram W. Johnson became the new Commerce Committee chairman. To explain the committee's continuing inaction on the Jones-Cooper bill, he revealed to Belle Sherwin of the League of Women Voters that he was honoring requests found in the committee files from the Department of the Treasury, where the Public Health Service was lodged, and from the Department of the Interior, headed by President Hoover's personal friend, Dr. Ray Lyman Wilbur, to the effect that the president would be gratified if action was deferred until after the While House Conference on Child Health and Protection, which he had called for a year hence.[27]

Resentment over the expiration of the Sheppard-Towner Act was strong among members of the Women's Joint Congressional Committee and further intensified when Senator Cooper abandoned the Jones-Cooper bill and introduced a new one which would give the maternity and infancy functions to the Public Health Service. By way of explanation Cooper said that he had acted in response to a direct request from the White House.[28] In the face of a flood of letters from women leaders in all sections of the country, Cooper made a third and then a fourth revision, each time leaving his proposed legislation less acceptable to supporters of the old Sheppard-Towner Act. Grace Abbott wrote her father: "I am meeting Miss Lathrop in a few minutes to go over the history of the Washington battle and plan the next engagement. It is in the main guerilla warfare!"[29]

By the time the White House Conference on Child Health and Protection was convened in November 1930, the objectionable Cooper bill had not been brought to a vote. The Senate apparently was waiting to know the outcome of the conference.

In July 1929, President Hoover had announced his decision to call a White House Conference on Child Health and Protection. It was to be a large conference made up of representatives from the important voluntary bodies and public officials throughout the country. The subjects to be covered included "problems of dependent children; regular medical examination; school or public clinics for children; hospitalization; adequate milk supplies; community nurses; maternity instruction and nurses; teaching of health in the schools; facilities for playgrounds and recreation; voluntary organization of children; child labor and scores of allied subjects." The conference would not take place for at least a year to give time for "exhaustive examination" of the problems and the preparation of conference materials.[30]

Amid rumors that Grace Abbott was being deliberately ignored in the conference planning and that the Children's Bureau was in danger of being seriously affected, Julius Rosenwald asked Abbott to give him a confidential account about how things stood. Because the Children's Bureau had played a major role in the initiation of the 1919 Conference on Standards of Child Welfare, Abbott replied, she had been approached in 1928 by citizen groups about initiating a plan for a conference on children to be held in 1929 to coincide with efforts to renew maternity and infancy legislation. She had thought it best to wait until a new administration was installed. Soon after the inauguration, she sent Secretary of Labor Davis a memorandum on the matter but Davis reported back that the president was too busy at that time to consider it. Then Grace Abbott began to hear reports that such a conference actually was being arranged, that Dr. Wilbur was to be in charge, and that various persons were being drawn into the planning. Nothing official was said to her, however, until she was asked to serve on the planning committee. At its first meeting, she was given a minor role. Mrs. F. Louis Slade, a member of the committee, protested to the president and to Wilbur that the public expected the Children's Bureau to play an important part in the conference. Wilbur then announced that Abbott would serve as secretary of the executive committee, an assignment Abbott perceived as nominal since the executive committee was not functioning as such.

Abbott told Rosenwald that she believed Wilbur had come to the cabinet hoping to build up the Public Health Service and eventually transfer it to the Department of the Interior, and in addition to bring into the Public Health Service all the work of the Children's Bureau, except for the Industrial Division. She believed that Wilbur intended to organize the conference so as to ensure those ends, which would mean that the maternity and infancy work with the states would no longer be administered by the Children's Bureau, and that the bureau would be severely weakened and its overall broad purpose destroyed. "I have come to this conclusion slowly," she wrote, "but now I feel quite sure of it."[31]

The constituency that had supported a renewal of Sheppard-Towner reached the same conclusion and the protest grew. Lillian Wald opened up the subject in the pages of *The Survey* with an article with the provocative title, "Shall We Dismember the Child?" She reviewed the original purpose of the Children's Bureau and cited its outstanding contribution: having successfully tested a "unified approach to the problems of childhood," and having fully documented the "effectiveness of a single agency dealing with childhood as a whole."[32] When Paul U. Kellogg, editor of *The Survey*, received the manuscript, he asked Dr. Haven Emerson to read it in his capacity as associate editor for the field of public health and preventive medicine. In a series of letters of more emotion than substance, Emerson termed Wald guilty of loose and specious arguments, journalistic opportunism, assigning an offensive title to her article, and offering evidence that Grace Abbott had found herself overwhelmed and had run to her friends for support of the Children's Bureau.[33] Kellogg exercised his editorial prerogative, went ahead with publication, and offered Emerson space in *The Survey* to reply, which Emerson declined to do. As diplomatically as possible Kellogg gave Emerson a forthright statement of his own position:

> If there is such a considerable move to change the province of the Bureau as you suggest, surely it is high time for friends of its working conception and its work to be heard. You must count me as one. . . . The things that the Children's Bureau has done could have been done years ago by either the U.S. Public Health Service or the Bureau of Education. That it was the group which was interested in the conservation of childhood that fought the fight for creating the Bureau, and got the backing for such work . . . is, I think, significant . . . a dynamic we want to conserve. The fact that it is in the Labor Department has been a useful accident. The need for continuing its synthetic service is to me the primary issue. . . . Fundamentally, . . . children are bundles of varied possibilities; refuse to be cramped into all the neat categories of our adult and scientific scheming. . . . That's life as distinguishable from ab-

straction. And as long as children remain so, we will be losing something . . . as an energizing force for concern and action if we scatter this organic approach to the child as an entity.[34]

Kellogg captured the essence of why the controversy involved much more than a contest for dominance and control among professions and governmental departments, and why it was not simply a controversy between physicians and social workers, or between women and men. Although complicated by personality conflicts and other current social and political developments, the controversy rested on a clear philosophical difference about the nature of childhood and how the needs and problems of children should be conceptualized and addressed.

The Children's Bureau view of the child as needing protection in certain situations rested on a conviction that the rights of children should be established in order to attain goals of social justice. National leadership was essential to reinforce and extend the efforts of states and localities for the protection of children and families against the hazards of life. Social reform legislation would be required to combat ignorance, poverty, disease, and the other social ills that underlay problems of child welfare, including child health. The quality of child health (or child care or child education) was in large measure a reflection and function of the well-being of society and had to be addressed within the larger societal context, utilizing the concept of "the whole child." Actions taken to improve any part of a comprehensive child welfare program should grow out of scientific findings that should be widely disseminated to parents and others in the community. Persons trained under a variety of disciplines were needed for a comprehensive approach to the welfare of children.

In contrast, a transcript of the White House conference sessions shows that conference leaders and section chairpersons (predominantly comprised of male physicians) expressed a somewhat sentimental view of the child with the child's welfare closely coupled with religious and moral values. Ideas of charity were favored over ideas of child rights and social justice. In order to address a multiplicity of interests and initiatives, local responsibility and local autonomy should be relied upon for leadership except as local leadership might be required to yield to the "beneficent tyranny" of scientific findings or the burdens of irrational general public opinion. The federal government should follow, rarely lead or initiate actions except at the request of states and localities or when necessary to bring wide-scale threats to the nation's people under control. The remedy for the problems of child welfare usually required individual initiative, personal reform on the part of parents, the elimination of faults of character, and teaching children to grapple with life. The individual organism was the unit of concern. Great weight was placed on the findings of science but these should be transmitted to the public through "competent philanthropy." Child health lay within the purview of public health and medically trained personnel. The clock of progress would be set back if "incompetents" began to "clatter around in the field of epidemiology."[35]

As part of the planning process for the White House conference Grace Abbott was named to the Conference Section Committee on Public Health Service and Administration, made up mainly of physicians and chaired by Surgeon-General Hugh S. Cumming. Abbott was subsequently assigned to a small subcommittee, chaired by Dr. Haven Emerson and charged to study and make recommendations on federal health organization. It was this subcommittee that became the center for what Emerson termed the "Children's Bureau fracas." In any case it was the work of this committee that provided the fuel to disrupt the White House conference when it finally met in late November 1930.[36]

The conference opened with an address by President Hoover in which he said: "We approach all problems of childhood with affection. Theirs is the province of joy and good humor. They are the most wholesome part of the race, the sweetest, for they are fresher from the hands of God."[37] Trouble had already begun, however. When delegates arrived in Washington they were given a 600-page bound preliminary report marked confidential. The volume included a report from Surgeon-General Cumming's Committee on Public Health Service and Administration and one from Dr. Emerson's subcommittee with a recommendation for the transfer of the maternity and infancy programs of the Children's Bureau to the Public Health Service. No reference was made in the bound volume to Grace Abbott's dissent from the recommendation and her minority report.[38]

Delegates responded angrily, leading Rodney Dutcher to report: "Not since the days of the suffrage fight have so many trained, able women been so full of wrath about anything as specialists in child welfare, health, education, medicine and social work became at the recommendation to transfer the bureau's child health work to the U.S. Public Health Service. For a time the protest these delegates staged overshadowed all other doings of the conference. Only after the unfortunate males who had tried to jam the proposal through had been badly rattled and had decided to eliminate it from the conference findings did the meeting conclude in peace and harmony."[39]

On the first day of the conference Dr. Emerson's small subcommittee was scheduled to meet to formally adopt its report. An array of over two hundred people surged into a room designed to hold about fifty persons. Emerson stood at the door trying to stem the tide. When the area outside the meeting room began to fill, he brought a chair into the lobby, stood upon it and with asperity told those assembled outside to leave, that the committee meeting did not concern them. There were angry murmurs from the crowd. When Emerson got down from the chair to leave, Josephine Goldmark fanned his resentment when she reached for the chair, stood upon it, and addressed those waiting. She told them what the recommendation was going to be, that they should stay but be orderly and let the meeting go on.

Emerson sat at a table at the front of the room as did a state public health official, an official of the American Medical Association, and Grace Abbott. The audience, largely women, contained nationally distinguished persons and many others eminent in their own states and communities. Among them were Lillian Wald, Florence Kelley, Edith Abbott, Sophonisba Breckinridge, Dr. Martha Eliot, Dr. Alice Hamilton, Dorothy Kirchway Brown, and others of like stature and interest in the Children's Bureau.

Emerson read the majority report and then faced a challenge from the audience about not reporting Grace Abbott's minority position. He agreed to read her report and did so, stopping now and then to deny her statements. There were indignant protests. Delegates demanded that the majority report be rejected and withdrawn from circulation. Emerson allowed a vote and then announced, to challenges, that the motion had not passed. Another motion was made to the effect that Grace Abbott's report be adopted in every instance in which it differed from the majority report. That motion passed by an unmistakably large majority. No one among the delegates spoke for the majority report.

The atmosphere throughout the meeting was tense, sometimes openly hostile. At one point Dr. Emerson characterized remarks by Grace Abbott as "malicious, mischievous misstatements of fact."[40] Those who knew Grace Abbott well realized that she was making a tremendous effort not to lose control of herself under the sustained hostility of Emerson and the other committee members.

In other subsection meetings elsewhere, protest was growing about the proposed transfer of the Children's Bureau health functions. That evening Grace Abbott was a speaker at a session on the prevention of child dependency. Ignoring President Hoover's benign stance at the opening of the conference, she gave the conference listeners hard facts about unemployment, the inequitable distribution of wealth for children and families, about what low wages cost a community and who paid that cost, about current worldwide unemployment that was causing large-scale suffering among children, and the long-term costs to those children, not only in health, but also in psychological well-being. "There are many children tonight," she said, "who have not known security in their homes for over a year. . . . many families that will not be taken care of by charity this winter where the family standards have gone steadily down . . . such as to produce almost nothing at all to share. You can never make up to those children for that." She went on to cite the confusion prevailing about relief for that distress and advocated that "as long as this kind of dependence is the result not of personal difficulties or character complications, but is simply due to the absence of the wage earner's wages . . . then we should make payments for children during the unemployment."[41] Her speech was interrupted repeatedly by applause and brought such prolonged applause at the end that Homer Folks, who was chairing the session, finally had to terminate it so that the next speaker, Surgeon-General Cumming, could be heard.

The following day, Dr. Emerson presented his report to the full body of the conference. He announced that the Section Committee on Public Health Service and Administration had met the night before and had reaffirmed his subcommittee's majority report. He then proceeded to read a paper. The large audience sat through four more speeches (not always patiently) before Chairman Cumming asked for discussion of the Report of the Commission on Public Health Service and Administration. Delegates had come expecting to act on controversial issues, but Cumming announced that there would be no votes taken and that any controversial subject would be referred to the president's continuing conference committee.

One by one, delegates rose to speak in behalf of the Children's Bureau and the importance of not transferring its health functions. Among them was J. Prentice Murphy, administrator of a large Philadelphia voluntary children's agency; Marguerite Wells, with instructions to speak for twelve national women's organizations; Dr. Dorothy Mendenhall, speaking for women physicians; Dr. Robert L. De Normandie, distinguished obstetrician of Harvard University; Edwin C. Hollenbeck, for the American Legion's welfare committee; Josephine Goldmark, with a message from the head of Yale University's School of Medicine; Rose Schneiderman, president of the National Women's Trade Union League, who tried valiantly to persuade Chairman Cumming to allow a vote expressing the sense of the meeting; John P. Frey, for the American Federation of Labor; and others. Dr. William F.

Snow of the American Social Hygiene Association voiced what others felt when he objected to confusion in procedural rulings that undemocratically appeared to be bent as needed to a special interest.

Cumming tried to end the meeting but Florence Kelley persisted. She recalled the great achievements that had flowed from the 1909 Conference on Dependent Children and said, "I am sadly wondering whether instead of any glorious recollections associating themselves with this conference, this will be remembered as the conference which recommended the dismemberment of the Children's Bureau against the protest of the organized womanhood of this country."[42]

That night Secretary Wilbur met with selected conference leaders and told them that President Hoover did not want any conflict with his "Child's Bill of Rights." Wilbur read them a yet very rough draft of the nineteen points which eventually became the "Children's Charter," printed attractively in blue and gold and hung on walls in many school buildings and churches.

By the next day, the last of the sessions, some degree of goodwill had been brought to the badly damaged conference. With Secretary Wilbur presiding, Surgeon-General Cumming proposed that the recommendation of his committee for the transfer of the bureau's functions be stricken from the record in the interest of harmony and sent to the president's continuing committee for disposition, along with an opposite one from another section. Before adjourning Grace Abbott asked that Secretary Wilbur take to President Hoover the pledge of all there that "from this day forward we will work harder and more intelligently for the health and protection of children."[43] The audience rose, applauded heartily, and with relief dashed for their trains. In the weeks and months ahead nothing was heard from the president's continuing committee about transfer of the bureau's health functions.

Extraordinary support for Grace Abbott and the Children's Bureau was shown at the conference in the face of powerful and hostile opposition. Women were justifiably amused when Mary Anderson reported that Secretary Davis had warned Secretary Wilbur that Grace Abbott had a "tremendous political following" and that if he wasn't careful he would find himself "sitting on a park bench singing 'I wish I had left her alone.'"[44] Nevertheless, the experience had been taxing and not a little disheartening. When the publicity attending the conference died down, some questioned what tangible achievements had resulted from a year of intensive study by experts beyond an uninspiring and noncontroversial "string of platitudes" contained in a "Children's Charter."[45] Renewed efforts to obtain acceptable maternity and infancy legislation were unsuccessful; more urgent claims were heard as the shadows of the long depression pressed more heavily and unemployment soared. Sheppard-Towner proponents acknowledged the matter to be closed for the time being.

The process that ran the White House conference aground reflected a number of contests and forces. One was the unyielding resistence of the AMA to health programs linked to nonvoluntary social welfare auspices. Although the AMA favored bringing together in one agency all the health work at the federal level, so entrenched was its opposition to any kind of "state medicine" that its representatives at the conference vigorously opposed any extension at all of federal aid for state infancy and maternity programs, even under the aegis of the Public Health Service.[46]

As part of, but going beyond, that traditional wall of resistance was a power struggle between male physicians and organized women for a primary role in the shaping and delivery of preventive health services for women and children. By the time the White House conference convened, it was clear that physicians initially had seriously underestimated the strength of women proponents of Sheppard-Towner and their determination and commitment to its principles and programs. Sheppard-Towner represented a first round in what was to become a recurring confrontation between women and physicians. Within this drive was a demand by women for the right to know about their bodies and to exercise control over their reproductive functions. The initial step was to insist upon the elimination of unnecessary deaths and continuing poor health connected with childbirth. For the needed information and knowledge to remain only in the possession and control of physicians was no longer tolerable. Most male physicians saw these tasks as purely medical ones, belonging only to them and not to be yielded by sharing the channels of medical care, certainly not with women.

Failure to renew Sheppard-Towner brought gains and losses for women. To their credit they succeeded in influencing medicine to assume responsiblity for preventive services. The maternity and infancy programs that appeared in the states acted as a catalyst to modifying private medical practice. When the push for legislation was first made, preventive programs of the Public Health Service were largely directed toward improving water supplies, community conditions of sanitation, eliminating the threat of yellow fever, and similar efforts at broad-scale environmental control of disease. Family doctors were concerned with individual pathology; they treated the sick. Seldom was there an expectation of regular and systematic health examinations for family members. Prenatal care, if any, was usually one visit. However by 1930 general practitioners had begun to encourage regular health care, to keep better records of their patient's state of health, to respond to minor ailments, and to encourage attention to correctable handicaps. "The shift does not reflect scientific advances. General practitioners did not suddenly discover new techniques that dramatically increased their diagnostic abilities. . . . Rather, . . . [it] was a social, not a medical, phenomenon. It reflected, as its timing makes clear, a medical response to a political innovation."[47]

The loss of Sheppard-Towner, however, interrupted the drive by women to be recognized as having a particular expertise and a broader outlook about preventive health care for women and other family members. In addition the shift from public maternity and infancy programs to care by private physicians meant that new preventive services would be available mostly for women able to consult private physicians. Poor women and women in remote geographical areas would still be disadvantaged. Also, Sheppard-Towner did not last long enough to make birth control methods easily available to women, an essential step in gaining control over their own bodies. By charging that it was a measure intended to promote birth control, the implacable opposition had endangered the enactment of Sheppard-Towner and its extension five years later.[48] The extent to which societal attitudes constricted the Children's Bureau maternity and infancy work in matters of contraception is evident in Grace Abbott's report that "there were States where it was not 'good form' to speak of the prenatal period of childhood and the causes of the deaths of mothers in childbirth. . . . There were States in which the Children's Bureau film 'Well Born' could not be shown because its general theme was held to be included in those prohibited by the censorship law."[49] During the seven years of Sheppard-Towner, Julia Lathrop and Grace Abbott knew that they could not politically sustain the principle of public money for birth control. It was too early.[50]

Another development influenced the course of the White House conference. Grace Abbott's following had emerged as clearly political, highly visible, and vocal. In May, James J. Davis became the Republican candidate for senator from Pennsylvania. His election seemed assured and speculation began as to whom President Hoover would name to succeed Davis as secretary of labor. A spontaneous movement in behalf of Grace Abbott began. Newspapers all over the country picked up the suggestion. Many were clearly aware of her public record and her qualifications; others responded to the fact that she was a popular public official, and a woman at that, and saw her candidacy as a good story in the heat of summer and the uncertainty as to when Davis would formally resign and what Hoover would do about a replacement.[51]

Grace Abbott, always frank and open with her sister, wrote, "I do not know who or what is responsible for this publicity about my appointment. The Scripps-Howard papers carried a story which went to all their papers. I do not know what other papers did besides the Tribune and News which you telegraphed about. I am sure there is nothing to it. Mr. Hoover knows me well enough to know he does not want me close to him." [52] In any case, newspaper articles and editorials all over the country responded with accounts of Grace Abbott's achievements and suitability for the office. Only two women then held government executive positions in labor, Margaret Bondfield, minister of labor in England, and Frances Perkins, commissioner of labor in New York State under Governor Franklin Roosevelt.

Grace Abbott's impressive support system went into action. Clara Beyer, after consulting and planning with others in the women's network, launched a full-scale campaign to mobilize support through letters and petitions to President Hoover. Thousands of signatures and letters were collected and forwarded to him. Support came not only from women's organizations but from university and college faculties, the Urban League, and from the influential men who had supported Grace Abbott since her days with the Immigrants' Protective League in Chicago.

Persistent reports indicated that William Doak of the Brotherhood of Railway Trainmen would be appointed. Labor's dislike of Doak and its failure to unite on any other candidate fed the hopes of Grace Abbott's advocates. The Abbott sisters, however much they may have liked the idea, agreed that Hoover knew Grace and her record of independence too well ever to appoint her to his cabinet; besides each doubted that Hoover, conservative and cautious as he was, would under any circumstances be the first president to appoint a woman to a cabinet position. [53]

When James J. Davis was elected senator in November, and still the president had not appointed a new secretary of labor, support for Grace Abbott intensified. The timing coincided with the convening of the White House conference and did nothing to calm President Hoover's and Secretary Wilbur's irritation at the rebellious atmosphere in their long-touted White House Conference on Child Health and Protection. Whatever chances Grace Abbott might have had with Hoover, and they were slim from the outset, evaporated with the White House conference. Doak was appointed in early December. But as Clara Beyer summed it up: "It was splendid stuff for the future of women and paved the way for Frances Perkins a few years later." [54]

With his commitment to efficient management, President Hoover must have seen the Children's Bureau with its broad charge and age-population base, in contrast to immigration or labor statistics, as something of an anomaly. Given Abbott's backing from organized women, perhaps he was also a little rankled to find upon assuming office that he had little choice about continuing her as chief of the bureau. At least he once complained to Jane Addams that he had had to appoint a Democrat as chief of the Children's Bureau.[55] By the end of the White House conference, if not before, Hoover and Wilbur were convinced that Grace Abbott was unduly suspicious, self-righteous, and inflexible.[56] No doubt their opinions were not altered by her response to a request from the White House as the 1932 election drew near.

The Women's Division of the Democratic National Campaign Committee had circulated campaign material that challenged Hoover's support of the Children's Bureau. Secretary Doak sent Grace Abbott a copy of the statement and asked her to comment upon "its inaccuracies." In Abbott's absence from Washington, Katharine Lenroot prepared a reply that concluded that what was needed was not denial but a strong public statement from the president of his appreciation of the bureau's work and his desire to see it remain intact and its work go forward. A week later Grace Abbott received a second request to prepare a memorandum on the "Highlights of Labor and Welfare Records of the Candidates," issued by the Democratic National Campaign Committee, and to get it over to Secretary Doak so that he could have it with him when he went to a cabinet meeting the following morning. Abbott prepared a response, laying out the events that had led to the Democratic women's allegations and endorsing Lenroot's suggestion for a strong public statement of support for the bureau by President Hoover.

That reply, as had Lenroot's, did not supply what was wanted, and subsequently Secretary Doak's office sent on to the Children's Bureau a letter that President Hoover had dictated with a request that Grace Abbott sign it for immediate release. Franklin Roosevelt was scheduled to speak by radio to discuss a series of questions including his position with regard to the Children's Bureau. If signed, the letter would have had Grace Abbott vigorously denying and labeling as "absolutely untrue" allegations of the Democratic women that Hoover had not given full support to the bureau, that he had called the White House Conference on Child Health and Protection without adequate representation of the Children's Bureau, and that he had attempted to have the health functions of the bureau transferred to the Public Health Service. Grace Abbott refused to sign the letter and it went into her files with her handwritten comments on the margins to show the source and nature of the request.[57]

For a bureau chief to oppose the president so directly was decidedly uncommon. Had Hoover's chances for reelection been better, the consequences could have been extremely serious for the future of the bureau as well as for Abbott's future in it.

For Grace Abbott the decade of the twenties had indeed been "uphill all the way" and the promised rewards were not yet all in sight. She had drawn too heavily from her great wells of strength and was required once more to go to the mountains of Colorado to seek recovery from tuberculosis.

Although Grace Abbott's second absence from the Children's Bureau because of health problems was longer than the first (eleven months stretching from the middle of June 1931) she made the adaptation to her enforced bed rest without the dashed hopes and time lost through depression that had been an early part of her first bout with tuberculosis. From the onset she knew what to expect from Dr. Webb's regimen, and, as she wrote her brother, it would be a "damned slow job."[58] Occasionally her letters reflected frustration with her enforced absence from Washington, but on the whole her self-discipline was impressive. Although this period of exile was compulsory, and it required a certain kind of surrender to outside forces, it was hardly retirement for Grace Abbott. Throughout it she remained actively involved in the administration of the bureau. The clipboard technique again served her and even in periods when she was required to lie inactive, she used the hours as she told Nisba Breckinridge "to think and plan."[59]

From the standpoint of an administrator who was required to be away but did not want to relinquish her hold, Grace Abbott found in Katharine Lenroot the nearly perfect acting chief. Lenroot had come to the Children's Bureau only two years after it was established. She was committed to the philosophy of the bureau's founders and knew its work from a variety of assignments. She was loyal, careful and conscientious about administrative tasks, and ready to carry as much responsibility as was required day by day. She respected Abbott's wider experience and ability and recognized that Abbott would not turn over her responsibilities completely. Happily for Abbott's peace of mind, Lenroot was willing to solicit her advice, and did so in long detailed letters usually several times a week or more, in which she reported on bureau activities and problems, sought direction for important decisions, and frequently asked that Abbott reply by airmail or telegraph.

If Lenroot sometimes felt that her assignment was one of heavy responsibility with only partial authority, her letters gave no hint of it. She was conciliatory and moved quickly to follow Abbott's advice, even when it meant changing the direction she had felt inclined to fol-

low initially. The relationship between Abbott and Lenroot did not reflect the element of personal friendship that Grace Abbott experienced
with Julia Lathrop or Martha Eliot or Josephine Roche, but it appeared
to be one of cordial ease and mutual trust. Yet Katharine Lenroot was
ambitious in her own right, and she must have found the long-distance
administrative directives sometimes unsettling, for example when Abbott wrote directly to the head of the bureau's statistical division with a
sharp letter of reprimand for falling behind the previously agreed upon
schedule of work.[60] Abbott followed this with instructions for changes
in monthly division reporting forms in order to "get a better picture of
how work is really progressing." It was important, Abbott admonished
Lenroot from her sanitorium bed, "to keep track of what is *not* being
done as well as what is being done."[61] In another instance Abbott made
her judgment about allocation of resources prevail over that of both
Lenroot and Martha Eliot when Eliot wanted to undertake a new study
that Abbott felt was unwise. "We cannot take on a project [at this time]
that requires long time field work or expanded organization in another
city." To soften her veto, Abbott added, "Dr. Eliot is so fine that I can't
bear to refuse anything but I am sure I am right on this."[62] At one point
in the press of Abbott's absence and bureau work, an article carrying
Abbott's name as author was sent for publication without her having
seen it. She wrote Lenroot briefly but explicitly to instruct the head of
the editorial division that nothing was to carry her name as author without her express permission. "I don't like signing things I have not written or rewritten even though they are better written than my own
work."[63] If it was not always an easy role that Lenroot fulfilled, her loyalty to Grace Abbott and their mutual commitment to the Children's
Bureau made it possible.

The correspondence between Abbott and Lenroot during this period
is remarkable for its illustration of strong leadership within an atmosphere of collegiality and respect. It reflects too a pattern of work
within the Children's Bureau, established by Julia Lathrop and extended by Grace Abbott, a pattern that helps to understand how the
Children's Bureau was able to accomplish so much and bring influence
to bear so widely, all with very limited resources.[64] The intent was to
push for maximum efficiency in the assignment and performance of the
too few staff members, and at the same time to retain enough flexibility
to permit an innovative response to new opportunities in behalf of children and families. To accomplish these aims Grace Abbott tried to
maintain a balance in the range of bureau activities, select new projects
with an alertness to how each would reinforce ongoing work, and continually evaluate and reevaluate staff and applicants for positions in or-

der to match tasks to special competencies. Regular staff was supplemented from time to time with temporary appointments. Edith Abbott was called upon repeatedly to identify from among former students someone in Texas, Oregon, Pennsylvania, or some other state who could supply a particular talent at some phase of a bureau project. This often turned out to be a woman who could not accept long-time employment because of family responsibilities. Edith Abbott was regarded by her students as being very opposed to marriage; those who wed before their training was completed feared her disapproval and delayed telling her of their plans as long as possible; some kept it secret from her. Edith Abbott's opposition was not so much to the institution of marriage as such as to the loss to the profession which so often followed a woman's marriage and childbearing. Such a loss, after she had invested her school's hard-won resources in that person's professional education, seemed to Edith Abbott a personal defeat, particularly if the student had been a promising one. Being able to "bring her back in," even temporarily, gave her satisfaction.

Keeping in touch with the women leaders among the bureau's supporting constituencies, as well as with important men who demonstrated consistent and telling support for the bureau, was central to Grace Abbott's pattern of administration. Her intent was twofold: to nurture and reinforce that base of support and to protect the public image of the bureau so that it could continue its influence. Bureau accomplishments were placed ahead of any one individual's desire for personal recognition. Grace Abbott was continually watchful for undercurrents of dissatisfaction that might diminish the bureau's independence and ability to lead. When she had been in Colorado for six months in her second battle against tuberculosis, Prentice Murphy, head of a large Philadelphia voluntary child care agency, wrote Edith Abbott that "so many people have [your sister] on their minds. The lack of information about her health has led certainly to overstatements as to a long long absence from Washington. In discussing the Costigan bill for federal relief last week [a bill that if enacted would have given the Children's Bureau a major new administrative responsibility], I was told that 'since Miss Abbott was not coming back for some time that the bill would have to be modified.'"[65] Edith Abbott promptly sent Murphy's letter to Grace who in turn mailed it at once to Katharine Lenroot so that Lenroot could "make sure that the impression that I am really down and out should not get abroad. . . . The head of an organization always gets more credit for what is done than she should and as I said before, everyone who knows you is not worried about anything."[66]

By May 1932 Dr. Webb was willing to say that Grace Abbott could leave Colorado even though she had had a flare up of an old gall bladder problem and her medical records were being evaluated at Mayo Clinic, posing the possibility of surgery sometime in the future.[67] She went back to Washington by way of Grand Island to reassure her family about her condition and to satisfy her own concerns about her now aged parents.

The National Conference of Social Work met in Philadelphia in the middle of May. The year marked the twentieth anniversary of the founding of the Children's Bureau and, as part of the conference program, Grace Abbott and Julia Lathrop were honored. It was a poignant occasion, particularly for Grace Abbott, for Julia Lathrop had died only a month earlier. Abbott and Lathrop had had a special understanding between them and, as Grace Abbott expressed it a few days after her death, "the loss seems greater as the days go by and I recall so many things she said and we did together."[68]

Lillian Wald and Prentice Murphy presided at the conference dinner where Grace Abbott was honored. She responded to their remarks with the kind of encompassing touch that always engaged her listeners: "I am sure those social workers who are in public office, in either federal, state, or local units, my comrades in arms in the struggle for better public services, will understand me when I say that I have had to learn how to sit through a meeting and arrange my countenance so as to display no emotion when I am assailed, but I have not learned how to behave when praise is meted out as it has been tonight. It is for a public official an unusual experience." Then in a moving way she recalled for the audience when Jane Addams had returned to Hull-House from the 1909 White House Conference and the satisfaction Miss Addams had expressed about the recommendation to establish a federal Children's Bureau. It seemed "to give promise of reality for the ideas and ideals expressed at the Conference." She also recalled the affectionate and noisy farewell party that the Hull-House residents had given Julia Lathrop when she left to become the first chief of the Children's Bureau—the first governmental bureau dedicated to "the welfare of children and child life among all classes of our people" and the first woman to hold a major executive office in national government. She paid high tribute to Julia Lathrop for setting up a program aimed at prevention of conditions adversely affecting children, rather than one that only pointed the way for treatment of the symptoms of child neglect, dependency, and delinquency. She described clearly the philosophy and concepts of childhood that underlay the bureau's program. She gave tribute to others to whom the Children's Bureau was indebted, including some with whom she had often disagreed, A. J. McKelway and Owen

Lovejoy. And she paid special homage to two other long-term and trusted friends of the Children's Bureau who had died within the year—"two who traveled very different roads but often reached the same objective." One was Florence Kelley, who "during the last years walked with increasing difficulty; but until the autumn of 1931 she was able to travel faster, farther, and more courageously than most of us." Grace Abbott also recalled with affection Julius Rosenwald, "a friend and supporter of the Children's Bureau throughout its history." She spoke of her last meeting with him in the summer of 1930, when she had visited him in his home to seek counsel and support in the face of the threat from the Public Health Service. "Remember," he had said several times, "any time I can be of service to the Children's Bureau, you say the word and I will come to Washington."[69]

When the conference ended, friends of Grace Abbott who expected her back in Washington were both disappointed and alarmed to learn that she was now on her way to Mayo Clinic where she faced surgery for removal of her gall bladder. Given her history of lung problems, her case was regarded as carrying more than usual risk. Dr. Martha Eliot accompanied her to Rochester, stayed with her throughout the surgery, and helped to assuage Edith Abbott's great anxiety. In a lighter vein, Edward and Mabel Costigan, masking their concern, telegraphed Grace, "Will you never stop adventuring?" Some weeks after her ordeal Grace Abbott was able to write her niece that "the black days are over for me altho I still get pathetically tired by evening. Every day is better tho so that another week you will find it hard to believe I have parted with another part of my anatomy."[70]

When Grace Abbott returned to Washington she was still kept on a restricted schedule. Gradually she moved into her old pace of work, although for the rest of her life she was medically compelled to spend most of the heavy hot days of summer away from Washington and in the benign climate of Colorado Springs or Santa Fe.

There are great reaches of territory . . . the great fields of public charitable organization, of law and government in relation to social work, of social economics, of social insurance, and modern social politics—all of which are required if the social worker is to be an efficient servant of the state.

— EDITH ABBOTT[1]

CHAPTER 8

Defining a Profession

THE LATE 1920s and the decade of the 1930s provided the arena for the mature unfolding of Edith Abbott's career. The times demanded a great expansion of the program of social work education which she and Sophonisba Breckinridge had begun. These years also opened the door for Edith Abbott to exert major influence upon the building of a public welfare system throughout the United States.

Moving the Chicago School of Civics and Philanthropy to the University of Chicago in 1920 had been a remarkable achievement on the part of Edith Abbott and Nisba Breckinridge. Once accomplished, this pioneer undertaking carried heavy risks. Announcement of the new affiliation of the "old School" as Edith Abbott later reported to her alumni "was received very coldly and critically by a discouraging number of friends among social workers."[2] The new School of Social Service Administration was the first instance in which social work education came fully into the structure and educational policy of a major coeducational university. Such an affiliation was widely disapproved, not only by Graham Taylor and his followers, but in the eastern part of the United States as well. Reasons for the opposition were embedded within the origins of social work training.

In the late nineteenth and early twentieth century, preparation for social work, as had been true earlier for the professional schools of law, medicine, engineering, and teaching, was supplied largely by the apprenticeship system. A new employee in a charitable organization was given instruction from a regular staff member who assigned reading, offered conferences, and supervised the learner in carrying out specific tasks within the single organization. Obviously no well-rounded view

184

of the whole field was gained. The apprenticeship system operated only in the large charitable organizations of a few cities. These philanthropic organizations trained only the number of persons needed for their own staff turnover and looked after their own interests further by requiring new employees to agree to stay with the agency for a specified length of time. Even though charity organization societies were multiplying and the need for trained workers was acute, no readiness was shown to train workers from other cities if they expected to return to those cities after training. In addition, public support for charitable agencies was limited and there was little general recognition that philanthropy was work requiring technical skills.[3]

In 1897 Mary Richmond spoke at the National Conference of Charities and Correction on the need for systematic training in applied philanthropy. She proposed that a training school be established in a large city with direct access to philanthropic agencies and, significantly, that any affiliation with a college or university not be allowed to interfere with an emphasis upon "practical work" over theory and academic requirements.[4] Other leading charity workers also resisted looking to universities and colleges to develop social work training because they feared that universities as research institutions would not place appropriate value upon "practical" fieldwork for students.

In turn, higher education was reluctant to become involved in social work education because social work appeared to be a profession mainly for women. Eastern universities, patterned after the early colleges for men, carried on the academic tradition of preparing only for the professions in which men engaged. Colleges for women largely followed the curriculum model set in colleges for men.[5]

The scant interest in social work that did exist in academe came mainly from the developing field of social science, and even there issues in philanthropy made up a very small part of the curriculum. Indeed, as sociology developed as an academic discipline, it became more concerned with the study of normal human relationships and societal processes and reflected less interest in the social problems that were of immediate concern to social workers. The sociologists' growing disenchantment with charities and correction was matched by that of leaders in charitable organizations who found the social science emphasis upon developing theory insufficient to meet the insistent challenges in their day-to-day problems. As Frank Bruno stated it: "The numbers of insane were increasing at an alarming rate; children were being brought up in almshouses; the mentally deficient were an increasing menace to the well-being of society; dependency was placing an ever increasing burden on taxpayers, and efforts to treat it were apparently waging a losing battle. . . . These were pressing exigencies which could not wait long for an answer."[6]

As a response to these frustrations, the Conference of State Boards of Charities, which had functioned as a section of the American Social Science Association, broke away from that parent body in 1879 to form the National Conference of Charities and Correction. With an expanded clientele it rapidly became a more vigorous organization. Significantly, however, upon separating from the Social Science Association, the conference gave up its strong interest in scientific inquiry into social problems. Attention shifted to methods of administering charitable organizations and techniques for giving help to individuals.

Edith Abbott saw social work as a discipline separate from sociology. Yet the historical perspective that she brought to all her undertakings led her to denounce the early break from social science with its resultant premature concentration upon the development of treatment techniques. She was concerned that social theory was then very tentative and much in need of consistent criticism and testing, some of which social workers were in a position to supply. She believed that social workers could and should develop their own competence to determine whether or not certain subjects in the field of social treatment were suitable for a particular application of social statistics. In her view the diversion from research, which was a consequence of social work's move away from social science, unnecessarily handicapped the profession for many years in developing better scientific methods in social welfare program development and administration.[7]

In 1898 the New York COS took a step toward establishing the kind of professional school that Mary Richmond had called for a year earlier. A school similar to the New York effort was established in Boston in 1904, with some degree of affiliation with Simmons College and Harvard University. The demand for social work training in other cities led Graham Taylor of the Chicago Commons and Julia Lathrop of Hull-House to establish the Chicago Institute of Social Science in 1903 as part of the Extension Division of the University of Chicago. The Chicago effort reflected a significant difference from the eastern schools: leadership for the training program had come out of the settlements instead of the COS. The Chicago Institute became the completely independent School of Civics and Philanthropy in 1908. Subsequently schools were opened in St. Louis, Philadelphia, Richmond, and Houston. All of these independent schools of philanthropy, except for the Philadelphia school, at some time had an affiliation of sorts with a university or college. However, the relationship was nebulous and no institution of higher learning was given a clear responsibility for standards of instruction or other educational policy of the professional schools.

Edith Abbott's preference for locating social work education firmly within the universities was reinforced by papers given at the 1915 National Conference of Charities and Correction. Abraham Flexner, a noted authority on medical education, questioned the status of social work as a profession. He was dubious about how well social work had translated a clear definition of a profession out of its potential scientific base. Social work appeared to him to be "not so much a defined field as an aspect of work in many fields." His evaluation implied a lack of specificity in aim that seriously affected the development of education for social work.[8]

Flexner was followed on the program by Felix Frankfurter, who fueled Edith Abbott's interest in seeking university affiliation for social work education. Frankfurter called for the same adequacy in training for "the very definite, if undefined profession we call social work" as was required for the established professions of law and medicine. He maintained that schools for social work should seek "a complete association with a univerity" where there could be intimate contact with the other branches of a university's work and the school could be part of "a single intellectual community."[9]

So strong was the opposition to schools of philanthropy being moved into universities that the Russell Sage Foundation, which had agreed to award the School of Civics and Philanthropy a new grant, withdrew its offer when the plan to move the school to the University of Chicago was announced, thus seriously endangering the financial stability of the new School of Social Service Administration. Years later Edith Abbott recalled that "it hurts me still to remember how cruelly we needed that money, and how hard it was to do without it."[10]

Julius Rosenwald urged Edith Abbott to seek money from the Rockefeller family and lent his influence to a formal request. In 1926, after two years of negotiation, the Laura Spelman Rockefeller Memorial provided a gift of money to use for operating expenses of the school for a period of five years. In 1927 additional support was made available by the Rockefeller Foundation, including an additional $500,000 for a thirty-year endowment with the provision that the university find a way to match it with one million dollars by 1931. All through the 1920s and early 1930s, Edith Abbott worked under considerable pressure to help generate outside funds, first for operating expenses and then to ensure the endowment.[11]

The two-year period of negotiation for the Laura Spelman Rockefeller grant served as a test of Edith Abbott's conviction about the proper form for social work education. The Wieboldt Foundation in Chicago was willing to spend up to $500,000 for a downtown social work "training school" where all the private social agencies would be housed in a center for the practical training of social work. Desperate as she was for funds, Edith Abbott showed a kind of Puritan courage by rejecting the proposal outright. She saw it as offering only a somewhat more systematic form of the old apprenticeship system and as posing a clear denial of her concept of professional education. Harold Swift, chairman of the board of trustees, and President E. D. Burton matched Abbott's faith in the proper direction for social work education by giving her assurance that the university would find a way to continue the school's program even after the expiration of the five-year guarantee given by the former trustees of the old School of Civics and Philanthropy.[12] A significant endowment had been at stake but Edith Abbott and her close associate Sophonisba Breckinridge, supported by Swift and Burton, did not yield in their determination to develop a model of social work education based on social science theory and research within a major university.

The funding from the Laura Spelman Rockefeller Memorial made it possible to begin a period of great growth and development at the School of Social Service Administration. For Edith Abbott it meant a reasonable assurance of permanence for the school, and a base from which to attract a strong faculty and to address more substantially than had yet been possible that task of inquiry and publication and the development of a scientifically based curriculum. Edith Abbott influenced social work education in a major and lasting way not only by bringing it under the aegis of a university. As her published papers show clearly, she followed this achievement by serving in large measure as an architect of today's social work curriculum. Her differences with the opponents of university affiliation went beyond that single issue and reflected distinctions in underlying beliefs, objectives, and strategies of social work education from those held at the time by leaders in the schools of philanthropy.

When Abbott and Breckinridge took the School of Civics and Philanthropy into the University of Chicago, social work in a very real sense was family casework in voluntary agencies. Prior to the 1920s, casework was still broadly defined to include any activity that was meant to influence behavior and improve the client's welfare. By the 1920s, however, the early training schools began to invest their curricula with narrow specialization and a concrete practical instruction which subordinated theory and research to an intensive quest for skill and technique.[13]

Caseworkers discovered Freudian doctrine and began to incorporate psychiatric thought and techniques into their work. The revelation of the unconscious and the idea that social workers could now learn about their client's inner life with its dynamic effects upon motivation and behavior influenced social workers to move away from a form of social treatment based on rational assumptions, information, and environmental manipulation. Skilled casework now required insights into the client's psyche; older ways of working suddenly appeared superficial. Psychoanalysis had become the scientific method for understanding the individual.[14]

Outside of Chicago a new philosophy began to appear in social work education. Brackett forecast it by saying that "what is needed most in social work is human beings rich in the subtle, compelling power of personality."[15] Casework leaders began to view education for social work as a process of affecting and molding the student's personality. The intent was to eliminate attitudes and behaviors that could interfere with casework effectiveness and to add to technical skill in ways that made possible a stronger and more psychodynamically helpful professional relationship. Porter R. Lee, director of the New York School of Social Work, considered casework to be "fundamentally the influence of one personality on another . . . a deliberate human relationship at its best." Social work education was incomplete unless the training process facilitated within the individual student "certain definite personality developments which are quite as important in the practice of social casework as are experience and education in the more limited sense."[16]

Edith Abbott disparaged this new emphasis upon personality, which she saw as accompanied by a downgrading of "knowledge courses." To her, the new interest was a seriously misguided use of the profession's energy. She had limited understanding of the psychologist's current conception of personality or the nuances of the client's psychic life that consumed the interests of psychiatric social workers. She was, in fact, little interested. She had been much influenced early in her education by the writings of John Stuart Mill and his interest in the formation of an exact science of human nature and the true causal laws of human character.[17] To Edith Abbott reason and character, so fashioned as to be steady and constant, rather than psychic life, should govern behavior. For her, reality was in the objective environment of the client, in the crowded homes and workplaces of adults and children, in the jails, the inadequate schoolrooms, and the hospital wards they inhabited. Reality for the poor and disadvantaged and handicapped was reflected in rates of unemployment, in the punitive environment of relief offices, and in the incidence of infant mortality. For her, little more needed to be said.

In discussing basic principles of professional education for social work before a large audience at the National Conference of Social Work in 1928, Edith Abbott stated her conviction that becoming truly professional meant following in the footsteps of the so-called learned professions. "A good medical school is concerned with medical science and takes little interest in the bedside manner; . . . the law schools . . . properly concern themselves not with the idiosyncrasies or personalities that make for the success of practicing lawyers but rather with the science of the law." No doubt she startled, offended, or amused some among her large audience by saying with assurance, "Some of you may not agree with me about this matter of personality but I am convinced that this is only because you are using the word 'personality' when you really mean character."[18]

To Edith Abbott, "character" was superior to "personality." Character was a reliable set of behaviors that enabled the individual, despite obstacles, to react in a consistent way in matters of moral and social justice issues. One did not need to question or study character, only form it, acquire it. Its components included, as Edith Abbott enumerated them, "honesty, courage, fair and square dealing, respect for human rights and for all human beings even if they are very poor and very troublesome, willingness to make personal sacrifices for a good cause, and above all the ability to assume grave responsibility." These qualities, she said, often latent in the student, were the ones the professional school should discover and strengthen.[19] If she had not chosen to ignore Freudian doctrine, Edith Abbott might have said that character (and personality if she had to be concerned with it) resided in the superego.

Edith Abbott wanted "a solid and scientific curriculum in social welfare." With a remarkable show of honesty before faculty of established disciplines, she told a convocation audience at the University of Chicago in the early 1930s that the distance yet to go in social work education was great indeed. "We are still in the early stages of organization, our scientific literature is just beginning to be written, our clinical facilities are still to be developed. . . . The academic curriculum of most of the professional schools is now poor and slight and covers in many schools only the various aspects of a single field—casework. . . . But casework," she emphasized, "is very far from being the whole story."[20]

The whole story to Edith Abbott included interrelated fields of study of which every social worker should have a competent understanding. First was social treatment, covering the principles of dealing with diverse families and individuals in need of assistance and advice. Social treatment, if not defined narrowly, was the "unique and the most fruitful of the recent contributions of social workers to the social order." Abbott wanted wide boundaries to the conception of "treatment" so that "the application of casework principles to our public services should not be forever neglected." A broad understanding was required—of social psychiatry, social aspects of medicine, immigration, and the principles of penology and criminal justice. In fact, she said, social treatment encompasses "the whole science of human relations."[21]

Edith Abbott believed that there were no more fundamental subjects of study for the social work profession than social legislation bearing upon the major problems of social work, the structure of government and its processes, public welfare administration and its history, basic economic principles, and social research. "Must these always be referred to, slightingly, as 'background courses'? They are professional courses to be enjoyed not by a well-educated few but by the rank and file who are to carry on our social service traditions in the future." Enriched by Sophonisba Breckinridge's background of scholarship in law and political science and Abbott's in history and economics, students were expected to devote themselves to gaining an understanding of statutes and statute-drafting, administrative law, the court system, and economic principles as they applied to questions of social insurance, workmen's compensation, the minimum wage, and family allowances. How else, Abbott asked, can social workers intelligently initiate, support, or reject programs of social reform? Acquiring knowledge about the history of social experimentation involving the lives of human beings was also of first-rate importance. "So little do people know," Abbott said, "of the social reformers of the past and of their work that old experiments are wastefully repeated and outworn theories adopted."[22]

Unlike most of the training schools for philanthropy, the Chicago curriculum emphasized social research and social statistics. Edith Abbott wanted every social worker to be able to give a competent reading to the statistical literature of the profession, and to be able to deal critically with statistical arguments which she said are "so often and, too frequently, so fallaciously, marshaled in support of some proposed measure of reform." She deplored instances when persons from other disciplines who did not properly understand the purpose and methods of social work were called in to do "special surveys" because social workers were untrained in research and not expected to analyze and interpret their own data.[23] Abbott and Breckinridge were active researchers, of course, and they firmly led other faculty in this direction, not only to push the boundaries of social work knowledge wider, but also to raise the standard of instruction. Developing a doctoral program of study was a first order of business for Abbott and Breckinridge when they moved the old School of Civics and Philanthropy into the university. The first Ph.D. degree in social work from among their students was awarded in 1924.

Edith Abbott thought that the provision of adequate fieldwork was the most difficult side of social work education. The great problem that she saw was the necessity to make fieldwork truly educational. She deplored the confusion between fieldwork and inspection visits, the latter which she saw as "purely observational and informational," from which the student gained nothing of the "actual experience in doing under expert supervision, which is the invaluable asset of properly organized fieldwork." She believed the question of credit for fieldwork in its somewhat unstandardized condition would pose the greatest difficulty to university affiliation for most training schools. She was equally concerned about "farming out" of students to social agencies without adequate linkage to the academic side of the curriculum.[24] In an attempt to provide a rigorous and integrated learning experience for students, she chose to employ field instructors as full-time faculty members who supervised students in their agency placements and taught in the school's social treatment courses as well.

Much of the Chicago curriculum focused on what was closest to Edith Abbott's heart, "the great field of public welfare administration." Neither of the Abbott sisters ever fell prey to the legacy of suspicion of government welfare which Lubove found associated with the evolution of social work as a profession.[25] From the beginnning of their careers, each was oriented toward public services. Each was convinced that the great advances in social welfare must come from public rather than private agencies. Each was part of the social class of the Progressive era that was continually occupied with social problems.[26] The Abbott sisters, as part of that class, were problem-solvers who sought an understanding of the entire social system and a specialized expertise to deal with it. From their positions of leadership in the federal government's Children's Bureau and in a great university, each was intent upon expanding and transmitting that expertise and integrating it into government action. Edith Abbott chided social work educators who continued to envelop themselves in the affairs of long-established voluntary social work agencies and resisted the development of public services. "Are we building on the foundation [our first social workers] so wisely laid or have social workers become so concerned about case work methods and such phenomena as the *ego libido* and various psychiatric diagnoses and such exigencies as community chest financial campaigns that they have lost their sense of responsibility for this great division of public welfare that should be their professional concern?"[27]

Finding themselves lamentably handicapped in their early teaching by the absence of adequate social welfare learning sources readily available to students, Abbott and Breckinridge undertook to provide scientifically based materials that would illustrate the historical, legal, and social aspects of social problems. With financial help from Julius Rosenwald, who continued to serve as a great friend, they established a Social Services Series of ten books that are still of interest today, nine of which were authored by one of the Abbotts or by Breckinridge. Their intent was to provide easy access to source materials—not "readings," as Edith Abbott emphasized, but public documents, treaties, and unpublished case records to which they added cogent commentary. The series represented an original contribution to teaching and research in the social services and met an urgent need. Interest in the new series extended well beyond social work education to others in the social sciences. A reviewer in the *Harvard Law Review* termed the first of the series, Abbott's *Immigration*, "a novel and striking . . . collection" useful to students of administrative law. An economist reviewing the same volume in the *Journal of Political Economy* commented: "To those who may have felt that Miss Abbott has been at times too much moved by the human tragedies involved in our immigration policy and administration, the case records in this volume must come as an arresting if not decisive answer. . . . No more striking illustration of the function of sympathetic rational first-hand knowledge and insight in the scientific treatment of a social problem could be found."[28]

Abbott and Breckinridge also launched a professional journal, the *Social Service Review*, which attracted immediate interest in this country and abroad. The time was hardly propitious for assuming a responsibility as exacting as initiating a scholarly journal. The faculty was small; the school's financing was uncertain; promising students had to be recruited and, upon graduation, assisted with an appropriate job placement; and relations had to be maintained with social agencies providing student field placements. All of the editorial work and, until articles began to come in that met their exacting standards, much of the writing for the new journal fell to Abbott and Breckinridge. Less determined individuals would have hesitated. To them, however, beginning the journal was "a plan long cherished as a way of strengthening the educational program of a graduate professional School."[29]

The new journal covered a remarkable range of topics—historical, legal, economic, social, political, and international. It contained a special section of illuminating summaries of significant official reports from public social agencies, legislatures, official investigative commissions, and research organizations. A series of monographs, largely based upon student theses under Abbott's and Breckinridge's supervision, added to the impressive flow of professional literature for social work.

For Edith Abbott, developing the literature through the publication of research was one of the ways to extend the proper definition of her profession. She cited a parallel stage in the history of the Harvard Law School when the generosity of Nathan Dane established a professorship bearing his name. "Dane's original and primary purpose 'was not so much the development of lawyers as of law. . . . He expressly stipulated that . . . [the first holder of the Dane professorship] should be allowed time to publish as well as to teach'; and this is believed to explain the long-established Harvard tradition that scholarly publication is one of the main objects of her School of law."[30] Edith Abbott believed that American universities had a comparable opportunity to strengthen and lead the schools of social work to a new science and art of social welfare administration. For her, the purpose of research carried within it the concept *pro bono publico*. She rejected the assumption that "social research could only be 'scientific' if it had no regard for the finding of socially useful results and no interest in the human beings whose lives were being studied."[31]

When Robert Hutchins first became president of the University of Chicago in 1929, the Abbott sisters and Nisba Breckinridge were not a little patronizing in their attitude toward his appointment. Grace Abbott referred to him privately with her sister as "your boy president." Breckinridge was said to have described him as "much too young to know anything of importance."[32] However, the three women soon became intrigued with his leadership and modified their private reference to a more accepting one—"our young president." Among the many stories that are told by former students of Abbott and Breckinridge is one that has to do with a meeting sponsored by the School of Social Service Administration. Hutchins attended but found it necessary to leave before the meeting was over. As he made his way to the exit, Nisba Breckinridge, presiding at the microphone, using her best southern manner called out, "Mr. President! Mr. President! You need not leave. Nothing will be said here that you are too young to hear."

The initial skepticism expressed by the Abbotts and Breckinridge was short-lived. Whatever doubts Hutchins may have held about social work education were also softened as Edith Abbott began at once to inform him about the School of Social Service Administration, its philosophy, aims, and faculty. Hutchins in later years stated that Abbott and Breckinridge "were very kind to me. They knew that I was quite young and inexperienced and that I didn't know anything about social work. I had had nothing to do with it at New Haven and they took special pains to see to it that I understood what they were talking about. They were extremely generous in every way."[33]

Edith Abbott liked Hutchins's definition of a university as a community of scholars. Her outreach to him was given solid reinforcement as she discovered in their exchanges that they shared a common set of beliefs about the purposes of a university and the direction that should be taken in education for the professions. Hutchins, like Edith Abbott, deplored the current thrust toward careerism that stressed the training of technicians in the professions. Both Abbott and Hutchins saw this as an abandonment of the possibilities in university education. Both believed that the goal of a university was to produce educated individuals and that the professions needed, not "apprentices already trained," but educated persons who knew something about the world, about their society and how it was organized, about their duties and responsibilities to society and how social work (or law or medicine) related to it. Hutchins also took the point of view that the university had too many constituencies and that some should become technological institutes, or even be disbanded. "Very early, however," he said, "Miss Abbott convinced me that the social work profession had an intellectual content that had to be mastered in itself and that her intent was to turn out individuals who understood both the social science base and the special content of social work." He came to believe that the School of Social Service Administration was the best professional social work school anywhere, and he added with amusement, "Miss Abbott did not try to disabuse me of that impression."

Hutchins recalled the regular meetings that he held with deans and Edith Abbott's influence upon that august assembly of males. He said that "of course the school of social service administration was not regarded by medicine, law, and theology as quite in their class." So he found it very interesting to see the way in which Edith Abbott came to dominate discussion after discussion, not because of the prestige of her institution—which the other deans did not acknowledge—but "because of the clarity and force of her mind." The discussions in the deans' meetings, Hutchins said, were long and often wandering. Edith Abbott could scarcely tolerate a wandering discussion. So at intervals she would say, "Now gentlemen, I would like to remind you of a few facts!" As a result, Hutchins said, "Edith Abbott had an influence in the administration of the university through the other Deans which she gained entirely through her personal qualities." He remembered her as "extremely direct, never bothering to try to indulge in circumlocution for the purpose of making what she said more agreeable. She simply said it, in the simplest possible language and she was always enormously effective."

In Hutchins's judgment, were the Abbott sisters "domineering," as some had suggested? "It could easily be true," he said. "In groups of powerful individuals Edith Abbott could not only assert herself but she could get her way. And I suppose the same habits and traits were carried over into the administration of the School." But the point to be emphasized, he said, was that "she commanded the respect of all these people." Hutchins remembered Grace Abbott as "a woman of tremendous experience that entitled her to think that she knew what she was talking about. She knew what was effective to say and not to say. She was less likely to act in a way that seemed domineering even though her intentions were the same as her sister's." Reflectively he added, "They were remarkable people. Remarkable people are not common, and not common in universities." He talked of characteristics he had observed among many university faculty and administrators who sought to "get ahead" by developing habits of being obliging, logrolling, and assenting to a series of compromises, finally to sink into apathy. "But these women," Hutchins said, "had none of these characteristics at all. They were never obliging at any stage of their lives, certainly not for the purpose of advancing their careers."

The relationship between Edith Abbott and Robert Hutchins became one of personal and professional regard, made comfortable perhaps for each by a certain indulgence in his manner toward her. Wilma Walker once accompanied Edith Abbott to a reception for Hutchins and his new wife. As Abbott reached Hutchins in the receiving line, he held on to her hand and, in what Wilma Walker characterized as a "very sweet kind of way," introduced Edith Abbott to his wife and said, "I want you to know her especially because she's been the one who's told me many, many times when to get on and when to get off."[34] Even though Hutchins initiated a policy of mandatory faculty retirement, he never applied it to either Edith Abbott or Nisba Breckinridge. Nor were rules of nepotism enforced when Grace Abbott joined the faculty. Hutchins remembered each of these circumstances with a good-humored tolerance: as to retirement, "I'm sure each one stayed on

196

as long as she wanted to." As to nepotism, "The question just never came up."

Edith Abbott sometimes came to late afternoon classes looking tired and distracted. Nevertheless she usually began her lecture in her strong voice with a preemptive "Now Class!" as she entered the room and began walking to the lectern. In the 1920s and 1930s and into the 1940s few students failed to feel the impact of her personality, the breadth of her knowledge, and her passionate concern for the poor and unfortunate people of the world. Among the courses that Edith Abbott taught was the history of philanthropy. Her research in this area was far-reaching and she felt a special investment in the subject. One former student recalled that "the material unrolled before me like a great drama, and my mind was opened to ideas that have influenced my entire life."[35] Elizabeth Wisner, one of Abbott's substantial group of graduates who became deans of schools of social work, wrote, "I do not recall that she ever talked about methods of social action, but one felt involved in the causes in which she was engaged and ready to do battle by her side."[36]

Subject-centered rather than student-centered, Edith Abbott defied many of the rules for effective teaching. She was confident that the intellectual pleasure of analyzing a case or reporting a new research finding was sufficient to merit student attention. Her research assistant once asked Edith Abbott about the "art of teaching" and recalled that "she looked at me as though I had uttered an obscenity." Lectures were sometimes dramatic with an artful use of Abbott's rich voice, and sometimes "a monotonous mixture of lecture and recitation." She did not invite class participation; when she chose to pause in her lecture, she began calling on individual students, using a set formula. "Mr. Dodge of Virginia, please comment on the case on page 200." Students were exasperated by their inability to know when their names would be called. Nevertheless, to many students "recognition as a representative of the state from which they came, the dignity of being addressed in a commanding contralto from the judicial bench of Law Commons, was a rewarding experience."[37]

The intensity with which Edith Abbott worked and lived increased her impatience with less than a student's best effort. The enormous energy that Abbott and Breckinridge each poured into their endeavors quickly became evident to new students and faculty alike. When Wilma Walker first joined the faculty of the School of Social Service Administration, no office was immediately available for her. On a Sunday morning Breckinridge telephoned Miss Walker that she had found an office and would meet her at Harper Hall to look it over. As they climbed the stairs to the fourth floor, Breckinridge said, "The only trouble with working here is that the elevator doesn't run on Sundays or after 10:30 at night. But of course one does not mind walking down so much as walking up." Like other newcomers to the world of Abbott and Breckinridge, Wilma Walker wondered what lay ahead.[38]

Edith Abbott was demanding of all about her; faculty and students in turn tended to work very hard "because she expected it of us." She was sometimes objectionably compulsive in her driving effort to avoid interruptions in the flow of work. Wayne McMillen recorded what became an often told campus story about "the young woman student who was being married and was leaving the following day on a wedding trip. Miss Abbott handed her a lofty stack of statistical schedules. 'Here,' she said, 'you can tabulate these while you are on vacation.'" McMillen did not remember the end to that episode, but he thought it quite likely that the young bridegroom had spent part of his honeymoon as an assistant statistical clerk.[39]

Student assistants to Edith Abbott were apt to feel somewhat like "eraser carriers" as they sat in her class with the books she might call for, or went hurrying back and forth between her home and office in Cobb Hall, or dashing to the library stacks for a reference to a case she needed immediately, or in search of Nisba Breckinridge whom, as one assistant perceived, Abbott regarded as a "good substitute for an original source." Often Edith Abbott worked in her bedroom with her student assistant at hand. At such times "Miss Abbott sat stiff against the high wooden headboard. There must have been a pillow against her back but I was not aware of it. Her focus was the lapboard on which she wrote and the books and papers scattered across the white counterpane. I had no sense of Miss Abbott being in bed, she might have been lecturing from the judicial bench in the Common Room of the Law Building, except that she wore no hat."[40]

Edith Abbott considered a hat essential to her proper appearance. Keeping it at hand in her office, she would pull it stoutly down on her head before a student came in for a conference. As she grew older she became insistent that new clothing be tailored to a comfortable familiarity in style and fit. She often bought dresses too large so that she could then require a seamstress to refit and shape them to a satisfactory resemblance of her former garments. She was apt to become attached particularly to hats. Once a friend persuaded her to let her take a well-worn one to a milliner for cleaning and reshaping. When Abbott called for it, the milliner could see she was not fully pleased with her work.

Abbott studied the hat, then said, "It needs a little—like this—," and she tugged at the brim and the crown until the milliner protested that she was making it look like it did when she had sent it in. "*That's* the idea," Edith Abbott replied with satisfaction. "Yes, *that's* the idea." Changing styles in clothing held little interest for Edith Abbott. Feeling like herself in whatever she wore was the important thing; then she was free to pursue her work without distraction.[41]

The sight of Edith Abbott and Sophonisba Breckinridge in their long dresses talking and walking together from the Law Building to Cobb Hall was a familiar sight to many of the university's inhabitants. One observer described it thus: "Their preoccupation and leisurely pace gave them a pathway to themselves. Students walked around them on the grass. These diminutive Victorian [appearing] ladies seemed larger because of their dress . . . Miss Abbott . . . in her black hat and dark dress . . . Miss Breckinridge's floppy Panama hat and voile dress [setting] off a soft vivacious face and slender feminine figure. Their faces were almost obscured by their hats, but one could see Miss Abbott's firm chin and lovely aquiline nose; her exquisitely molded face, however, seemed remote, almost frozen."[42]

To many students Edith Abbott was formidable indeed. Those who found her awesome and unapproachable used expressions to describe her such as "possessing a mind like a steel trap," or "a mind that came down on things whole—no working around through the problem." One said Abbott was "so competent that she scared the hell out of me."[43] Many students never had an opportunity to appreciate her incisive sense of humor or to glimpse the gentle sensitivity and personal compassion behind her austerity, or to realize the regard in which she held her students. Some who were less threatened and more perceptive understood more. A county welfare director in a southern state reminisced about his days as her student.

> I had four classes with her. I took anything she taught. She was also my faculty advisor. She had more than one personality. Quite human too. . . . One day when Edith Abbott had appointments with students, Jane Hoey came in unannounced from Washington. Miss Abbott went on seeing students; only when she had finished would she see her important visitor from that chaotic Washington public assistance scene. . . . She always followed a crowded schedule. Sometimes when she wanted more time with a student, she might say, "You come along and ride down to Hull-House with me." Those rides in her old Ford—it happened to others too. She would drive through those Chicago streets talking and waving her hand, still conferring with the student, going and coming from

Hull-House. . . . I ask myself, do you consider these the type of things that help students? They helped me. The kindly personal things. And the tremendous dedication to right what was wrong. What made her so devoted? So far advanced? I worked harder there at longer hours than anywhere else. Others did the same.[44]

Sternly devoted as she was to her vision of social welfare education, Edith Abbott was still capable of responding to exigencies that came with the times. As interest in psychiatric aspects of social work grew stronger, she became somewhat reconciled to including a psychiatric component in the curriculum. Some of her faculty urged it, Ruth Emerson for one, who wanted psychiatric content for her medical social work students at Billings Hospital. In addition, Commonwealth Fund grants for social work education were attractively liberal and to obtain them a school was expected to include psychiatric theory and practicum in its instruction. Edith Abbott undoubtedly held a belief that if government did what it should for people in the provision of services and income, then therapy for personal problems would seldom be needed. Yet she could bend when the times required it and the opportunity arose to do so effectively. Bringing Charlotte Towle to the faculty of the University of Chicago in 1932 provided a convincing demonstration of Abbott's practical streak and willingness to yield ground to someone who had something she needed, promised brilliance, and had a supply of energy that rivaled her own.[45]

Before coming to Chicago Charlotte Towle had been affiliated with the Smith College and the New York schools of social work. She was well known in social work and psychiatric circles, where her competence was unquestioned. Certain other aspects of her background appealed to Edith Abbott. Towle was born and grew up in Montana, which enabled Abbott to perceive her not as an easterner but as someone who could appreciate the "western heritage" which the Abbott sisters treasured. In addition, Towle had worked as a social worker at the U.S. Neuropsychiatric Hospital in Tacoma, Washington, and to some extent in state hospitals, which Abbott viewed as evidence of a broader background than experience in eastern voluntary agencies offered. Towle's work style suited Abbott as well. She expected to carry a heavy load of work; she accepted large classes; she provided consultation to community agencies, and was willing to fill in with fieldwork supervision of individual students when it was necessary. Her interest in publishing especially pleased Edith Abbott. In the face of her own heavy work schedule and her need for Towle's competence and special knowledge, Abbott probably was glad to give Towle a nearly free hand to develop the casework curriculum and set a new pattern of generic casework.

During the course of their association Abbott and Towle influenced each other. Edith Abbott learned from Charlotte Towle how serious deprivation and problems could cause an individual to internalize those hardships and then be unable to function adequately even when income was provided or the deprivation was otherwise removed. In turn, Abbott influenced Towle to see the reality of the harsh environment in which so many people lived. In Charlotte Towle's words, "she made the means test, legal settlement, relative support laws, and similar restrictive statutory and administrative practices come alive for me in terms of what they were doing to people psychologically." Towle acknowledged that Edith Abbott had enabled her to add an entirely new dimension to her thinking, one that sprang from Abbott's influence rather than from her own training as a psychiatric social worker.[46] The influence was clearly discernible in Towle's little classic book, *Common Human Needs*. In it she emphasized the principle of public assistance as a right and demonstrated the nature of psychological needs in interaction with social forces.[47]

Although Edith Abbott was willing to alter her perception of casework as a result of her relationship to Charlotte Towle, she had little understanding of the emerging field of group work, as Elizabeth Wisner once observed.[48] Abbott's lack of interest in group work can be traced to her early association with Neva Boyd, who directed the Chicago Training School for Playground Workers, established in 1911. Largely through the interest of Jane Addams and the program's informal association with Hull-House, the playground training program was transferred in 1914 to the Chicago School of Civics and Philanthropy.

Boyd was an early explorer in formal education for persons interested in the potential of work with small social groups. To Abbott and Breckinridge, however, Boyd's interests were peripheral to their convictions about the direction social work education should take. They saw the playground movement as too directly rooted in recreation and education. Boyd's instructional style was one that Abbott and Breckinridge did not understand nor value. She rarely used a didactic approach: instead she used the class as an experience in group life, the essence of which was psychological intimacy. Her interest in research was slight and she showed little inclination to write. When the Chicago School of Civics and Philanthropy moved to the University of Chicago, the recreation program was left behind. Probably the separation was mutually acceptable. Boyd later recorded that she had feared that a university would not give sufficient freedom to develop her ideas and so she had chosen to remain at Hull-House.[49]

It was many years before group work was fully developed enough to be accepted generally into social work education. The demand in the 1920s and 1930s for group work instruction was not as insistent as for psychiatric casework, and a group worker counterpart of caseworker Charlotte Towle did not appear, leaving Edith Abbott free to ignore the emerging field of social group work in which she had little interest.

Always Edith Abbott had "outside assignments" to work into her crowded schedule. A chief one was to serve as an expert researcher into the matter of crime and the foreign-born for the Wickersham Commission on Law Observance and Enforcement appointed by President Hoover in 1929. Abbott assembled a staff and directed a broad investigation. Public opinion on the matter at different periods of American history was carefully studied. Statistics were gathered from cities with high and low proportions of foreign-born populations, including data on the incidence of crime, police arrests, convictions, and commitments. Factors that were bringing individuals into conflict with the law were studied, particularly those peculiar to the foreign-born as distinct from the native-born. Intensive investigation was made of the Mexican immigrant in relation to criminal justice. Special studies in selected cities were carried out. The findings documented that the foreign-born in the United States, in proportion to their numbers, were committing considerably fewer crimes than were the native-born, leading Edith Abbott to comment:

> For more than a century there has been continuously in this country a clamorous group who have tended to emphasize only the difficulties connected with immigration and to lose sight of all its beneficial effects. Unfortunately these attacks on the alien have frequently laid stress on the popularly supposed relation between immigration and crime. Statistics have never justified their assumptions. . . . It is easier . . . to charge our crime record against immigrants than . . . an inefficient and corrupt system of police and an outworn system of criminal justice. Charging our high crime rates against the foreign born . . . is the "easy way"—the line of least resistance. . . . But an attempt to face squarely the more difficult problems of life is more in line with our American traditions.[50]

In 1919 concern about standards of social work education led Abbott and Breckinridge to help establish the first national association of schools of social work, which later became the American Association of Schools of Social Work. Edith Abbott pressed for adoption of standards by which social work education could be measured and accredited. She described the some twenty-five schools in 1927: "Their differences 'leap to the eyes,' and when you study their announcements and catalogues they seem to have nothing in common except a name—and of course, a purpose." She proposed standards of curriculum, admission of students, required resources, and accreditation procedures and urged their adoption.[51] Other deans of schools felt her dominating presence in meetings of the association. "Once she rose to speak there was a stir in the audience, and her clear and forthright opinions created excitement and controversy." Others worked for high standards but, in the view of many, Edith Abbott was "the most articulate and effective spokesman on every issue that related to the development of professional education."[52]

The curricula of schools of social work today strongly reflect the broad outlook that Edith Abbott pioneered. Many of the principles about which she spoke and wrote are so generally accepted that it would be easy to overlook the enormous contribution that she made to education for social work and to the social welfare system. When she and her close associate, Nisba Breckinridge, launched social work education within a university, the great developments in public welfare were yet to come. Most social work training schools, keenly preoccupied with casework narrowly defined and with field work in voluntary agencies, continued to hold a very limited conception of professional education. Edith Abbott's own advanced study in economics, in the history of legal and medical education, and her affiliation with the American Economic Association and the American Statistical Association gave her a distinctly different perspective than that of other social work leaders of her day. Abbott and Breckinridge believed that they were engaged in a "great experiment" when they undertook to develop a wholly new pattern of professional education for social work. They were regarded by many of their social work contemporaries as "too academic" in their approach to social work training. Their endeavor was risky and, given the undeveloped state of professional social work in the 1920s, it was highly fortunate for them as individuals, for the university, and for the social work profession that each was a scholar of impeccable standing.

Local government, local taxes, local poor relief had some significance in pioneer days—and so did slavery, squatter sovereignty, free soil, and the controversy over the 'subjection of women'—but they have no relation to the facts of modern life.
— EDITH ABBOTT [1]

CHAPTER 9

Permanence and Change

THE LATE YEARS of the Hoover administration and the emergence of the New Deal provided an arena in which the Abbott sisters acted as nationally recognized advocates for the old and new poor who endured distress and destitution in the Great Depression. They astutely collaborated to gain fullest use of the resources each brought to their partnership. Edith Abbott's long years of scholarship had given her vast knowledge of the antiquated public relief system and the limits of private philanthropy. Her editorial control over an influential social service journal made it possible for the Abbotts to get prompt public attention to their views, fully laid out. Access to the *Social Service Review* allowed Grace Abbott to channel information to her sister from the Washington scene, and, writing under her sister's name, to take positions that she could not state publicly as a member of the presidential administration. In addition Grace Abbott brought to the partnership the influence of her political following, her access to government and other national leaders, and the facts she uncovered from Children's Bureau studies of the effects of the Depression on children, families, transient boys, and other special groups. Each worked with the other to document the extent and nature of the suffering, and used every opportunity to speak and write about the need for federal aid and public policy which would make possible a modern system of social security.

As unemployment and poverty spread and became a way of life for thousands of families who had never before known it, nationwide social statistics were lacking on the extent of relief being provided to families, children, and homeless and transient persons. Even before the Depression Edith Abbott had seen that cities needed access to uniform methods of securing accurate data for use in community social planning. She had been influential in instituting a project at the University of Chicago in 1927 under the joint direction of the Association of Community Chests and Councils and the university's Local Community Research Committee. The intent was to establish uniform recording and reporting procedures for the collection of financial and service data useful to public and private social agencies. The project outgrew its parent base, and under Edith Abbott's influence it was transferred in 1930 to her sister in the U.S. Children's Bureau, where monthly reports continued to be issued on public and voluntary relief expenditures, as well as aspects of health, dependency, and delinquency. By absorbing a similar project that had been carried on by the Russell Sage Foundation, the collection of statistics was expanded and, at the request of Fred C. Croxton, acting chairman of the President's Emergency Committee for Employment, the Children's Bureau began assembling reports for the use of the committee.[2] Data from ninety-seven cities, geographically well distributed, showed that public and private relief expenditures had increased over 90 percent between 1929 and 1930—as Edith Abbott expressed it, "a tale told numerically of the accumulated misery that social workers have been trying to provide for during these tragic months." The families receiving the relief were "the normally hard-working, small-spending families who through no fault of their own slip farther and farther down until they become applicants for charity." Furthermore, despite Hoover's repeated insistence that voluntary agencies were meeting all charity needs, the proportion of the relief load met by public relief agencies had grown to 72 percent.[3]

Grace Abbott warned the President's Emergency Committee for Employment that it was imperative to "get the children out of the breadlines." In the last period of depression it was the children who suffered most, she said. Thousands had been undernourished and their health permanently injured. "The same thing is happening today and the national economy makes it imperative to come to the relief of the children before it is too late." She stressed the effects of the Depression on the morale of homemakers if relief was not available promptly—"the father idle about the house, unsettled, disheartened; the mother going out to work, if she can secure it, and using up every bit of her strength in the double task of providing for the family's maintenance and caring for the household and the children; and the children suffering from . . . uncertainty of what the future may mean."[4]

Children's Bureau studies of "transient boys" warned of the dangers in continuing neglect of the health, education, and general welfare of young people and pointed to the need for federal-state cooperation. Alarming numbers of boys (and some girls) were leaving their families that for the first time had been reduced to dependency on community aid. Some were too proud to stay under those circumstances; some left home to relieve the family of at least one hungry mouth; some thought that employment, nonexistent in their own community, would be found elsewhere. Social workers, police, and railroad men in constant touch with this new army of transient boys saw them overwhelmingly as youth who under normal economic conditions would be in school in their own communities; they were not the pre-Depression hobos. They came from every state. As winter came on, they drifted into warm climates or areas where rumor promised employment.

Approved community methods of handling transients had almost completely broken down and the old practice of "passing on" had taken over. Communities lacked money to help the boys return home; they were unable to take care of their own unemployed. In city after city boys found that if they paused to rest or seek food, they could stay only twenty-four hours. Shelter facilities were occasionally in well-regulated lodging houses with beds and bath and laundry facilities. More often they were basement jails without sanitary arrangements or the sand houses on railroad property. The boys suffered demoralization, untreated illness, hunger, and the damaging influences of an irresponsible life on the road. Steady increases were found in injuries or deaths in policed freight yards where trains had to be boarded while in motion. Grace Abbott urged federal and state cooperation to secure shelter and food of acceptable standards, registration and interviewing, an end to "passing on," and training programs for those who could not be sent home. Most important, Grace Abbott maintained, was the need to address the causes which made these boys transients.[5]

A newspaper report that Secretary of the Interior Ray Lyman Wilbur had returned from a trip around the country and "saw no abject poverty in any of the great centers of population" came to Edith Abbott's desk at the same time as a report of conditions in the Angelus Building, once a popular hotel and now housing some of the most destitute of all Chicago's hungry people. Edith Abbott responded with the passionate outrage which she felt at the Hoover administration's continuing disclaimer of a national crisis. In a letter to the *New Republic*, she observed that "Secretary Wilbur apparently did not visit Chicago in his search for abject poverty." She traced vividly the suffering of the unemployed in Chicago and conditions in the Angelus—dark halls requiring search lights to inspect the conditions, unheated rooms except for those who could get a little warmth out of bits of "relief fuel" burned in old gas grates or charcoal buckets, poorly clad and hungry people who clung to the old building because there was no other shelter. Electricity had been disconnected and tenants were using kerosene lamps—"in Chicago, in the twentieth century!" Edith Abbott exclaimed. She referred those who might want further information about the Angelus to the Chicago Urban League, "which has made a valiant effort to help the unfortunate people clinging to the haven there offered . . . [and to] the various relief agencies, which are doing the best they can with the very inadequate funds they have been able to get from public or private sources for a disaster that is too vast for any local government to deal with in the fourth bread-line winter."[6]

As the Depression lengthened, concern grew about children in coal-mining families. The President's Emergency Committee for Employment asked Grace Abbott to carry out a series of surveys in typical coal-mining counties to assess the available resources for local relief. Children's Bureau investigators visited counties in eleven states where unemployment had been reported to be especially severe. Strikes in the coalfields during the 1920s and a decade of underemployment had left the miners even more than most of the American workers at the mercy of the Depression. The needs of miners and their families were found to be in stark contrast to the resources and experience in their rural counties. The Children's Bureau studies provided a dramatic demonstration of the inability of an outmoded system of poor relief to meet modern social and industrial conditions.[7]

Grace Abbott was deeply distressed by the extent of malnutrition of children and serious deprivation among the mining families, and she seldom let opportunities to advance her interests slip by. In the spring she was a speaker at Bryn Mawr College, where Jane Addams was being honored. During the tea which followed the ceremonies, Grace Abbott sought out Rufus Jones of the American Friends Service Committee. She told him about the children in the coal-mining regions of the Allegheny and Blue Ridge Mountains—the very serious shortage of food, the cold and barren houses, the widespread illness. She asked whether the American Friends Service Committee might undertake to feed these children. Jones was excited by the possibility. Grace Abbott returned to Washington, discussed the matter with Fred C. Croxton, and the two of them then returned to Philadelphia to lay the full situation before the Friends' Board of Directors. Abbott and Croxton arranged an appointment with President Hoover for Rufus Jones and Clarence E. Pickett. Seeing an opportunity to support voluntary charity, Hoover responded by transferring $225,000 to the AFSC from an unexpended balance in the World War I American Relief Administration Children's Fund. True to his values, Hoover then imposed a requirement that Jones should not only raise additional private funds, but make sure that local governments were giving as much help as possible. Grace Abbott supplied technical assistance and lent Children's Bureau staff to assist in launching the program.[8]

Grace Abbott continued to call attention to opportunities to help groups of dependent children. She emphasized that machinery for administering mothers' pensions, authorized in statutes during the Progressive era, still existed in forty-four states. She cited these statutes as evidence that government had already affirmed a responsibility to make financial aid available as a right without individuals having to be dependent upon the paternalistic altruism of certain segments of society. In many families, she said, poverty due to the loss of employment and wages was the sole problem. She pressed for the use of the mothers' pension statutes in the current emergency. Thirty years before the federal government gave states the option to grant Aid to Families of Dependent Children where a parent was unemployed, Grace Abbott urged states to add unemployment of a father to the list of conditions for which aid could be given for dependent children living in their own homes.[9]

As the fourth winter of the Depression drew near, Hoover faced heavy challenges to his adamant stand against federal aid for local relief. Finally he was compelled to agree to broadening the lending power of the Reconstruction Finance Corporation, his weapon against the Depression, by authorizing loans to the states from which aid could be given to individuals in extreme need. In the pages of the *New Republic* Edith Abbott attacked Hoover's solution. She contended that the Emergency Relief Act of 1932 contained a tragic joker that allowed the RFC to nullify the intent of Congress. It stipulated that the governor of any state must certify that the resources of that state, "including moneys then available and which can be made available" by the state, the political subdivisions, or by private contributions, were inadequate to meet the relief needs. Consequently, Edith Abbott said, no matter what degree of destitution existed in a given state, "the political pundits of the Reconstruction Finance Corporation . . . can sit comfortably back, refusing the applications for relief loans and tell the Governors to go home and raise local public or private funds, while the families of the unemployed are forgotten." Then she challenged, "Should the families of the destitute be allowed to go hungry while the various governmental units play battledore and shuttlecock with someone's neglected obligations? Millions of people are supported on very inadequate relief rations, and the icy winds of winter are on the way." Abbott repudiated the theory of local responsibility for relief which President Hoover held tenaciously. The major difficulty, she said, was in the antiquated "pauper laws" still on the statute books and little changed from the English poor laws of 1601. She found no principle involved—"only an old tradition embodied in some very musty statutory regulations. . . . Local relief is not like parental love. There is nothing immutable and sacred about it." Furthermore, the principle of local responsibility had been applied by the RFC only to "the human victims of the depression and not to the corporations. The administration did not tell General Dawes and other private bankers . . . that they must wait until the city council or the county board or the state legislature did its part."[10]

President Hoover continued to say that the Depression was only temporary and that voluntary charity, chiefly the American Red Cross, was able to meet the emergency and human need in any national disaster. A prolonged drought in the summer of 1930 brought new suffering and near-starvation to countless rural families. Hoover responded by asking Congress to authorize loans secured on the next crop so that farmers could buy seed, fertilizer, and feed for cattle. Challenged to provide for hungry people as well as livestock, Hoover reiterated his deeply felt conviction that America stood for individual and local responsibility and mutual self-help and that it was dangerous to sacrifice those principles by providing federal relief funds to individuals.[11]

The situation among the drought-stricken farmers was acute. While Congress was debating the question of federal relief in January 1931, several hundred tenant farmers, black and white, some with rifles, came to the Red Cross office in England, Arkansas, and asked for food. When the Red Cross staff person said that his stock of relief forms had been exhausted, the farmers moved against the food supplies and seized flour and lard.[12] The Senate responded by appropriating $25,000,000 for relief needs to be administered by the American Red Cross. Before the House could act on the matter, the Red Cross refused the appropriation as a threat to its voluntary spirit. President Hoover praised the organization for refusing to yield during the drought crisis to insistent pleas that it abandon its voluntary character and independence. To have done so, he said, would have "meant the destruction of the spirit of the Red Cross" and "a step on the pathway of Government doles."[13]

The incident of the ARC and the drought-relief crisis highlighted a controversy in public opinion. Even in the face of stark portrayal of desperate need among persons who had been independent and had expected to remain so, many federal, state, and local officials and prominent citizens continued to be extraordinarily concerned that private almsgiving be maintained as the proper way of meeting the pervasive national crisis. An editorial in the *New York Times* was illustrative. To give public appropriations for relief in the drought-stricken states "would be a confession of the loss of that spirit which has given America her leadership in philanthropy." Edith Abbott found this reaction unparalleled in American history. She said that to find such stress laid on the virtue of private charity, as President Hoover was endorsing, it was necessary to go back to sixteenth-century England. In that epoch-making period various statutes had led to tax-supported poor relief; that action, however, had been laced with national admonitions about the necessity of private charity. Edith Abbott maintained that the current faith in private almsgiving was not "rugged individualism" but "Malthusian sophistry," nourished by the poorly administered poor laws of the eighteenth century. Arguments against public relief in the 1930s belonged to the discredited social theory that destitution is the fault of the person in need.[14]

The monthly statistical reports issued by the Children's Bureau continued to show that voluntary agencies were completely unable to shoulder the burden of relief to hungry families. Such regular repetition of evidence by Grace Abbott's bureau that President Hoover was wrong about the capacity of private philanthropy did nothing to soften his distaste for her, which had begun in the disputes over Sheppard-Towner and the White House conference. Even though she was still a member of Hoover's administration, Grace Abbott increasingly disagreed publicly (but discreetly) with positions he took in relation to the present crisis. The nature of remarks each made in separate speeches at an annual convention of the Red Cross affords an example.

President Hoover praised the Red Cross for again demonstrating "that it can meet and relieve human suffering in any national disaster." Many of his statements were sentimental, acclaiming the "great spiritual value [that] comes to those who give from the thankful heart" and commending the Red Cross for its "sense of personal responsibility of neighbor for neighbor, . . . its spirit of charity and benevolence in the individual [and for] holding alight the lamp of voluntary action in American life." One statement angered social workers across the country, who were struggling to administer inadequate public relief funds honestly and fairly: "The very spirit which makes the Red Cross possible assures it a probity and devotion in service which no government can ever attain."[15]

Grace Abbott addressed the same assembly the following morning. She gave facts about the extent of suffering and destitution, the dangers to childhood, the significant expansion in general public relief for families compared to private relief grants. And she challenged the Red Cross as the largest national relief-giving agency to acknowledge the very serious conditions in the country and to meet its special responsibility in the education of public opinion as to what was needed and how it could be accomplished.[16]

Grace Abbott analyzed an official report of the American Red Cross on its relief work in the drought of 1930–31.[17] Her sister's editorial hand worked it over before their hard-hitting attack was published in the *Social Service Review*. They stated that the bitterness of the controversy over the Red Cross and drought relief was due to the unfortunate quasi-public character of the ARC with the president of the United States as its ex officio president. "His political policies . . . must therefore become the policies of the organization." In their view, the attitude of the Red Cross on one of the most important political questions before Congress—the question of federal grants for public relief—appeared to have been determined by political considerations. They labeled as meaningless the words of the president in describing assistance given by the Red Cross as "neighborly aid." The organization had more staff and higher annual expenditures than most government bureaus; those who administered local chapters' work were often imported from outside the locality and the national office determined how much would be locally expended and for what general purposes. "A reading of this report shows more central—more 'bureaucratic'—control, if that offensive term has any meaning, over the local expenditures of the Red Cross nationally raised fund than the La Follette-Costigan bill contemplated in the expenditure of federal funds for unemployment relief."

When the Red Cross limited its field to calamities that could be classed as "acts of God," it was done more as a matter of expediency than principle, the Abbott sisters wrote. Only because disasters are temporary and less expensive to relieve could the Red Cross assume full responsibility for assistance. Limiting its field to what it could do adequately was a proper judgment in the Abbotts' view. At the same time, however, unemployed industrial workers were left at the mercy of a worldwide depression. They regretted that the ARC, in refusing the drought-relief appropriation, had not given a proper reason—that public funds should be administered by public agencies. And they reproved the organization for including in their report Hoover's unfortunate remark about "probity and devotion in service" that was only possible in voluntary services. "Social workers employed by the Red Cross know that the best of them exemplify no greater devotion in service than do the best of our public relief workers. Moreover, they know that belittling our essential public services serves no useful purpose. . . . Our largest national private agency may well speak with candor and honesty about the limitations of its services as well as their extent and excellence."[18]

In the depths of the Depression, burdened social workers who were witnesses daily to almost unbelievable suffering and stress among the nation's people were outraged when Ray Lyman Wilbur addressed the National Conference of Social Work in May of 1932 and said, "Unless we descend to a level far beyond anything that at present we have known, our children are apt to profit, rather than suffer from what is going on." Listeners responded with cries of "Shame!" Wilbur went on to talk about the value of adversity in family life and made other shallow statements about what social workers regarded as an unparalleled national emergency. One newspaper reporter satirized Wilbur's speech as "a rare contribution to the humane literature of the Administration." To agitation for an organized protest, Grace Abbott responded characteristically: "I think there is such widespread knowledge of the fact that he made an ass of himself that it is unnecessary."[19]

Each of the Abbott sisters was encouraged and excited by the nomination and election of Franklin Roosevelt to the presidency. Grace Abbott was constrained from any public announcement of her support, but promptly after the Democratic convention Edith declared herself for Roosevelt. She wrote Mollie Dewson in the Women's Division of the Democratic Campaign Committee that although she was a "lifelong Republican by heritage, education, and years of allegiance," she saw no hope for the various social welfare measures she cared so much about except through Roosevelt's election. She gave three reasons. The Hoover administration had failed completely to understand that the American doctrine of relief had always been the doctrine of public responsibility, in contrast to Roosevelt who, in New York, had promptly recognized the urgency of the need and the remedy—large state appropriations for relief and work for the unemployed. She cited Roosevelt's "generous attitude toward women in public life" reflected in his recognition of Frances Perkins's competence by appointing her to the position of industrial commissioner. And last, Edith Abbott said that although she believed "the gains resulting from prohibition have greatly outweighed any possible losses," she agreed with Senator Borah that Hoover was no longer a dry candidate; there was really nothing to choose in that respect, so she would vote on the more pressing issues of the campaign.[20]

Edith Abbott rejected Hoover for another reason, one she did not state except to close friends and family. She harbored bitter feelings toward him and his administration as a result of the loss of Sheppard-Towner and the stress that Grace Abbott had endured during the White House conference controversy. In a deeply felt, personal way, Edith Abbott held Hoover and his appointee, Ray Lyman Wilbur, accountable for her sister's recurrence of tuberculosis and a second enforced "period of exile."

When Franklin Roosevelt was elected to the presidency, Grace Abbott relied again on the precedent set by Julia Lathrop and did not offer to resign her position when the new administration came in. Democrats after patronage brought pressure on James Farley to force her out. He turned to Eleanor Roosevelt for advice. Although she was interested in building up the women's division of the party, Eleanor Roosevelt wanted appointments to be on the basis of merit and she would not sanction removing competent women because they were of Republican background. She suggested that Farley say simply that "no change is being made in the Children's Bureau and that Miss Abbott has the backing of most of the organized women interested in child welfare."[21]

The Abbott sisters were among the many in women's organizations, in the professions, and among state labor officials who acclaimed the appointment of Frances Perkins as secretary of labor. Grace Abbott wrote Nisba Breckinridge that Roosevelt had "really come through." She hoped stress would be placed on Perkins's competence rather than on "the first woman" aspect of the appointment.[22] Perkins's biographer recorded that when Roosevelt was considering whom to appoint as labor secretary, he gave a signal to those close to him that whether he appointed Frances Perkins would depend upon a call for her around the country. Committees sprang up to solicit telegrams and letters from businessmen, bankers, and labor groups. Social workers and organized women did not have to be urged. Although Grace Abbott could not give public statements in support of Perkins, she understood the use of influence in Washington and had other means at hand. In December she arranged a conference on the problems of children in the Depression and invited Perkins to be the principle speaker. When Perkins arrived in Washington, she was astonished to find that Abbott had also arranged for her to be photographed, interviewed, and introduced to senators and congressmen on Capitol Hill.[23]

From the outset Grace Abbott generously extended herself to Perkins. She arranged for Perkins to stay at "the club" in Washington after the inauguration until she could decide what housing she wanted. When Perkins arrived in Washington she had heard from no one in the Department of Labor except for personal notes from Grace Abbott and Mary Anderson. Perkins answered Abbott's letter with appreciation, and said she counted on Abbott for "a great deal of help and knowledge." She added meaningfully, "we shall have to make an arrangement for a conference that will not scandalize the Department." And she asked Abbott to obtain a copy of the department payroll or budget that would give her an idea of the titles, duties, and positions under Civil Service "or otherwise," and to get it to her promptly.[24] It was the first of many requests that Perkins made of Abbott during their association together.

From the perspective of her long years of experience in Washington, Abbott felt free to offer advice to Perkins or disagree with her. She did it in an objective, easy way that Perkins responded to and that helped to keep Children's Bureau interests clear, even in the fast pace of the New Deal. For example, when Perkins was searching for ways to reorganize the Labor Department to save money and improve coordination, remarks she made to Abbott and to Mary Anderson suggested that she was considering a consolidation of the Children's Bureau and the Women's Bureau. Abbott responded in a concise way that allowed Perkins to dismiss the matter as a misguided idea among many good ones. "I think this would be a serious mistake," Abbott wrote. "The assumption that from an industrial standpoint women and children should be classed together is unjust to both women and children. Women are adults, are in industry to stay, and such handicaps as they have and should be taken into account are not those of children. There is a real scientific basis for an integrated and correlated service for children which would be lost if the Bureau were to be consolidated with an adult service." Perkins acknowledged the memo with: "The matter of the consolidation of the two Bureaus . . . is only vaguely in my mind and I am very glad indeed to have you clarify the situation." Anderson responded to the suggestion of consolidation with excessive attention and emotion. She recorded later in her autobiography that the incident had complicated her relationship to Perkins thereafter.[25]

After Grace Abbott's death, Frances Perkins stated that when she had first come into the Department of Labor, she had found Grace Abbott "an invariable authority on the whole Department of Labor. She had given long and practical thought to its problems, and her advice was so sound that I recognized her more often than any one else."[26] And indeed, reports and memoranda between them show that Perkins consulted Abbott frequently, not only on matters affecting the Children's Bureau, but on the larger problems of departmental organization and policy.

Even after Grace Abbott left her government post, she continued to send Perkins information and suggestions. The degree of trust between them is illustrated by an incident when Grace Abbott served as chairperson of the American delegation to the seventh Pan-American Child Congress in Mexico City in 1935. Upon her return Abbott wrote Perkins that "while I was in Mexico I took the liberty of calling on the Chief of the Department of Labor and extending your greetings and offering the assistance of the Department, etc." Perkins replied: "It was a beautiful thing to think of doing, and just right. 'Ever loyal' ought to be your motto."[27]

Within a small circle of friends whose discretion was assured, Grace Abbott confided that Perkins was "not really a first class administrator." However, her selection of personnel had been good on the whole, an important test. Abbott regretted Perkins's relations with the press; she could have done better was the implication. However, Abbott emphasized, "people have applied perfectionist standards to Miss Perkins as they generally do to a reform candidate and to a woman."[28] Within the immediate family circle of her sister, her two brothers, and her niece, Grace Abbott shared these same observations. But she made it clear, her niece remembered, that "it was not to be talked of outside the family."

By the end of 1933 Grace Abbott was fairly certain that she wanted to resign as chief of the Children's Bureau and join her sister's faculty at the University of Chicago's School of Social Service Administration. Her formal resignation on June 15 brought an outpouring of commendation for her long service, and regret for her departure.[29] Many people shared Eleanor Roosevelt's sentiments: "For so long I have thought of you as a tower of strength in the Children's Bureau that I can hardly bear to think of anybody else trying to take your place." Carrie Chapman Catt thanked Grace Abbott for all she had done for the women's cause, and then added a perceptive touch: "I have put myself in your place in the imagination and for that reason I am rather glad you have resigned. I am sure you must be desperately tired after these long years . . . the new post will be a little easier, a little less controversial, a little more peaceful."[30]

Grace Abbott was indeed very tired. She told friends that there had been occasions when she had been ill and had wanted to resign but the times were wrong to do so. Now with Frances Perkins in a position to defend the Children's Bureau against those who wanted to weaken or destroy it, she could safely resign and feel confident that a qualified successor would be appointed. She said too that "I want to be freer than I can be in official life and the university gives me this opportunity." In addition, she claimed to be "thoroughly midwestern," which made her want to return to Chicago.[31]

Grace Abbott's resignation was unquestionably on her own initiative, and she was sincere when she said that she felt she could now resign because the bureau was safe in Frances Perkins's hands. Abbott had been highly impressed with Perkins's success in improving the department's organization, quality of personnel, and its prestige.[32] Abbott could feel a measure of gratification that her supporters' attempts to have her named secretary of labor in 1930, although unsuccessful, had helped to pave the way for Perkins. The new secretary's active leadership, however, meant that the bureau no longer functioned so independently as it had under Secretaries Davis and Doak. And, too, some of the challenge was gone with the loss of Sheppard-Towner and the child labor amendment which left the bureau's function almost entirely one "to investigate and report." These factors may have somewhat diluted Abbott's satisfaction with her job and reinforced her readiness for change.

Upon Grace Abbott's departure from the Children's Bureau in June, Katharine Lenroot once more became acting chief. No successor to Grace Abbott was named until late November. In that interim, supporters of Lenroot waged an active campaign in her behalf. Although a number of women were suggested to Frances Perkins at one time or another, the significant contest was always between proponents of only two, Katharine Lenroot and Dr. Martha Eliot. Lenroot had the strong support of the American Association of Social Workers, championed most strongly by Prentice Murphy of the Children's Bureau of Philadelphia, Allen T. Burns, executive director of the Association of Community Chests and Councils, and Homer Folks of the State Charities Aid of New York.[33] Eliot was strongly urged by the American Pediatric Society, as well as by Josephine and Pauline Goldmark and others associated with the Consumers League.[34]

Frances Perkins turned to Grace Abbott for a frank appraisal of each contender for the position. Abbott replied, "I feel sure that the Bureau's constituency expects Miss Lenroot to be appointed and that it will be very hard to pass over her." She stressed Lenroot's nineteen years' experience in the bureau, her popularity with Congress and with the general public. "From the standpoint of the Department, she would swing the job with less friction, fewer mistakes and misunderstandings in Washington and outside than anyone I know of." Abbott also spoke of Martha Eliot's strengths. Appointing her "would simplify all our medical relationships (they are very important) and she is extraordinarily successful in her relationships with people. Her attitude on industrial and social questions is absolutely right."[35]

Grace Abbott could see the strengths and weaknesses of both Lenroot and Eliot. In 1921 Abbott had been slow to decide on Lenroot for assistant chief and had done so only after urging Mollie Dewson to accept the position.[36] In the 1920s Abbott and Lenroot's professional relationship became a strong and trusting one. Yet despite the respect she held for Lenroot, Abbott shared the view of some others that Martha Eliot showed more creativity and reforming spirit. She stressed too that Eliot would be able to resolve some of the animosity between the Public Health Service and the Children's Bureau without sacrificing its integrity.[37] However, Eliot was a very independent person and Abbott had some concern as to whether she would always be willing to postpone action until she had an adequate balance of support for what she wanted to do. Abbott feared too that Eliot would be continually frustrated with the day-by-day administrative minutia and detailed decision-making unless she had an assistant chief like Lenroot, and Lenroot gave no assurance that she would stay on if she were passed over for chief.[38] All these thoughts Grace Abbott undoubtedly shared with Frances Perkins in their conversations together.

In July, Allen T. Burns became upset about a conversation with Harry Hopkins in which Hopkins asked him, "Who should be appointed to succeed Grace Abbott?" When Burns replied with Lenroot's name, Hopkins had said emphatically that Secretary Perkins would never risk her appointment because of political difficulties.[39] The exchange led Burns to introduce an acrimonious tone to the public controversy. He wanted Abbott to use her relationship with Perkins to lobby for Lenroot and stated that she had hurt Lenroot's chances by discussing doubts about her with Perkins. Burns apparently did not understand the objective and candid way that Grace Abbott and others in the network of women reformers appraised for each other the strengths and weaknesses of a particular person for a particular job. Abbott replied evenhandedly to Burns. She had, she reminded him, recommended both Lenroot and Eliot very highly. In doing so she had "talked with Miss Perkins as frankly and honestly as I know how to—as I would to you if you asked me the strong and weak points of some Bureau staff member you were considering for a particular position." She pointed out that the decision was Frances Perkins's to make and that whenever an appointee had to be confirmed by the Senate, as the chief of the Children's Bureau did, the secretary necessarily had to consider possible political complications in her selection. Roosevelt had safely ignored patronage demands when he retained a Republican as chief; asking a Democratic Senate to confirm a new Republican bureau chief presented a higher level of difficulty. "I have been convinced from the beginning," Abbott wrote Burns, "that there are real political difficulties in connection with Lenroot's appointment—not originating with the Secretary or the President but with the Southern Democrats who are looking for opportunities for attack on the President's patron-

age policies and K. L. would offer one. . . . If the President were prepared to make an issue of it as he did in the case of Tugwell he would
probably win. But such victories usually mean concessions on other issues and the President certainly does not want to knowingly take on
such skirmishes unless they are necessary." And then from her years of
experience in Washington she wrote with commendable restraint,
given the tone of Burns's letter to her: "I have not been told all this. I
know it, without being told."[40] To others, Abbott advised that Perkins needed information and honest evaluation of the candidates,
not pressure.[41]

Grace Abbott, Katharine Lenroot, and Martha Eliot were loyal
friends and the months of uncertainty about Abbott's successor were
uncomfortable for each of them. The situation was not made easier for
Lenroot by the realization that Abbott and Eliot were personal friends
outside their shared professional activities while her own cordial relationship with Abbott rested almost entirely on their shared professional
responsibilities and interests.[42] At different times each of the three tried
to ease the potential for misunderstanding. At one point Abbott wrote
Lenroot with affection and concern, "Of course, you cannot but have
been hurt by questions of your competency which some few people
may have raised. . . . There are always differences of opinion about
people and the capacities to do certain kinds of jobs. . . . To me, the
wonderful thing has been the unanimity of support [that] I have heard
everywhere from people who have worked with you and were really
competent to judge your capacities. I was happy about it for you
and for the Bureau, too. . . . These differences in judgment, often
influenced by very small things, are inevitable. They come with
prominence."[43]

By late July it appeared to most observers, including Abbott, that
Eliot would become the new chief of the bureau.[44] But social workers
redoubled their efforts and in November Lenroot was named to the
post. Given the opportunities for suspicion and resentment during the
debate about Abbott's successor, it is not a little remarkable that Abbott, Lenroot, and Eliot moved through it without rancor or lasting
misunderstandings. Whatever their private feelings, each appeared to
ignore rumors that would have aroused animosity among persons less
professional and less dedicated to preserving the integrity of the Children's Bureau programs. They remained congenial colleagues and
friends for the rest of their lives.[45]

The Federal Emergency Relief Administration, launched by President Roosevelt in May 1933 to provide grants-in-aid to the states for

relief needs, meant drastic changes in federal relief policy, an acknowledgment that unemployment was national in scope and that only the federal government had sufficient power and resources to deal with the extent of human needs across the country. The action was fiercely opposed by those who clung to the belief that voluntary agencies and local resources could meet the emergency. Social workers who knew the inadequacy of local taxes and private charitable gifts to care for the increasing poor of the nation generally welcomed the FERA, none more than the Abbott sisters.

The appointment of Harry Hopkins as FERA administrator came just as the *Social Service Review* was going to press, but Edith Abbott found time to express in it the satisfaction she felt at the announcement of his appointment.[46] He was, after all, a qualified and experienced social worker who had climbed steadily up the social welfare ladder, attested to by his early work with Christadora House in New York, his supervisory and administrative work for the Association for Improving the Condition of the Poor, the Board for Child Welfare, and the New York Tuberculosis and Health Association. His service as Roosevelt's relief administrator in New York had given the Abbotts recent opportunity to study his goals and methods. Nevertheless, the Abbott sisters, particularly Edith Abbott, were ambivalent toward Hopkins. They applauded the principles and standards he built into the requirements that the states must meet to receive federal aid, for example his intent to give adequate relief and to get it as quickly as possible into the homes where breadwinners were out of work; the prohibition against turning over public funds to private agencies and his mandate that relief should be furnished directly to an applicant by a public agent; his encouragement of cash relief in place of demeaning grocery and coal orders; and his insistence that social workers administering the new relief funds should have lighted, cheerful offices in which to carry out their work with the nation's needy citizens. Hopkins's intense energy, his nononsense approach, and his ability to make decisions rapidly were all to the good in Edith Abbott's view. However, he gave social workers an early signal of his independence when he addressed them at their annual conference in Detroit. He acknowledged that social workers supported many "perfectly fine and worthy objectives" but the intent of FERA was specific and limited—"to see that the unemployed get relief, not to develop a great social-work organization throughout the United States."[47] Edith Abbott noted that all the powers were to be in his hands as administrator of FERA and that he was given large discretionary authority in the distribution of vast sums of money. She understood the magnitude of the undertaking and saw its hazards. Three months after Hopkins took office, Edith Abbott wrote that "everyone is watching and waiting to see that national standards are really put into effect along with federal funds" and that "the vigor of some of the new 'Rules and Regulations' [not] be diminished as local pressure is applied."[48]

From the outset Edith Abbott regretted that the FERA was made only a temporary organization, exempt from civil service regulations. Each state was required to set up its own emergency relief administration, which meant that "one state after another carefully avoided laying the groundwork for a new public assistance administration [to] permanently supplant the inadequate and inefficient local poor relief system." She recognized the danger in allowing Hopkins to use half of the federal funds as unmatched grants to states that he thought could not reasonably be expected to supply matching monies. As a result, each governor felt impelled to drive the best possible bargain with Hopkins. Inevitably, decisions often appeared personal and partisan. The federal government, trying to alleviate unprecedented suffering, began to emphasize anew the old principle of local responsibility. Thus "the game of 'pull and haul' between the federal and local relief authorities [came into] full swing again," Abbott said. When Hopkins launched his work relief program to provide for "the employables," and said that "unemployables" were to "go back to the states," Edith Abbott entreated him to take a position of leadership and demand that the states abolish their old pauper laws. Using the best from the old poor-law foundation, she wanted the federal government to set up a modern system of public assistance. She deplored what she regarded as an inevitable loss of standards if the federal government withdrew from "general relief" in states that could not possibly take back the relief burden. "It is hard to believe that the President can wish to perpetuate the old theory of local government which makes the small property-tax payer responsible for the relief that his poor neighbors need. This outgrown theory of local taxation has been condemned root and branch by political scientists and economists as well as by social workers." Already in the states, she observed, school systems dependent upon local property taxes were being destroyed, child guidance clinics given up, hospitals planned and approved but not built, and relief was still cruelly inadequate.[49]

Other prominent social workers and reformers also were disappointed with the premature ending of the FERA and discontented with the New Deal's record of partial responses to the drastic social challenges of the times. Edith Abbott was impatient. Having waited long for a national administration that seemed committed to using its power to meet the critical exigencies ushered in by the Great Depression, she was intolerant of decisions that seemed to say that the time was not expedient for more far-reaching social legislation. She offered her advice freely to Harry Hopkins, sometimes much as she might admonish one of her students. Once when he was in Chicago, he consented to meet with some of her faculty and students. Hopkins talked about the bright future when the long-term social goals so important to Edith Abbott would be accomplished. From the back of the room came Edith Abbott's resonant voice, "When, Harry? When!"[50]

Edith Abbott thought it had been a serious mistake to dismantle the FERA to make way for another work relief program. It had been wrong, she believed, to place upon a single federal administrator the responsibility for expenditures of billions of dollars, which inevitably meant hasty decisions and counter-decisions and some ill-considered developments. Federal grants were made on an uncertain emergency basis, leaving no opportunity for long-term planning. Like many other social workers she could not accept the justice of the federal government's ending "this business of relief" before the assistance programs of the Social Security Act were ready to function and before any permanent, modern public welfare substitute could be put in place. Grace Abbott also believed that federal aid could have been a lever for building upon state programs; however that objective had been sacrificed to other ends.

Yet the Abbott sisters acknowledged that the FERA had achieved great success in meeting the country's needs for a time. They respected Hopkins for conceding that the most truthful allegation against his program had been made by the families who depended upon it: "We have never given adequate relief." The Abbotts recognized, too, that to Hopkins's credit he had chosen to try to get relief through to desperately needy people within the framework of generally accepted social work principles, even though the political fallout was far and wide. Despite its shortcomings, the Abbotts believed that the FERA "on the whole, represented great gains in the relief program, and, more than this, in the social welfare program on a national scale."[51]

In June 1934, President Roosevelt appointed the Committee on Economic Security to assemble findings and make recommendations which he could use in proposing a social security program to Congress. Edwin E. Witte, executive director of the committee, met with Katharine Lenroot and Dr. Martha Eliot to learn what the Children's Bureau wanted for children. He expressed his intent to consult Grace Abbott as well and Lenroot promptly wrote Abbott, urging her to try to be available to him. Witte said to Abbott that he wanted to draw on her "thought and experience" with respect to care of dependent children but also "to bring into the picture the entire problem of mothers' pensions, maternity and infancy care, and education and health work among children." He urged her to respond by September 15 when he had to make a preliminary report to a cabinet commitee. "I rely upon you," he wrote, "more than anyone else, to guide our committee in its thinking on what ought to be done for children."[52]

Grace Abbott was in Colorado without access to background documents and she responded with what she termed a "hastily prepared and preliminary memorandum," promising a more detailed one with budget estimates and references at a later time.[53] She proposed four services as a basis for a broad and comprehensive children's program. Two reflected her experience with the Sheppard-Towner Act. The first was a cooperative program with state departments of health for parent education, health supervision of children by means of school inspections and child health centers, and physical examinations of children leaving school. The second proposal was for a rural maternal nursing and educational program and for maternity care of all women not able to pay for it. (Abbott had been corresponding all summer with the president of the National League of Women Voters as to how the league might help to recover the lost Sheppard-Towner legislation. By late summer Abbott favored placing such provisions in the social security program if it looked possible to get strong support from the Committee on Economic Security.)[54] Abbott's third suggestion was in a new direction; she urged the provision of medical care for crippled children and for those with problems that frequently led to physical handicaps.[55] Witte later recorded that the Children's Bureau had suggested the crippled children's service "because it was thought that President Roosevelt would be peculiarly interested in it." Roosevelt approved it without question but without any evident special interest.[56] Whether Roosevelt's potential support motivated Abbott's proposal is unclear. Eliot believed she wanted a health program for crippled children because she saw a chance to legislate a form of health care that the American Medical Association would find hard to oppose and that such a program might help to break the way for federal health insurance.[57] Lastly, Abbott proposed a program of mothers' pensions to meet the essential financial needs of young children living in their own homes where fathers were dead, had deserted, or were mentally or physically incapacitated. Grace Abbott, like Julia Lathrop, had consistently emphasized that the welfare of children was dependent upon the welfare of parents and their ability to meet basic economic family needs.

Abbott, as former bureau chief, Lenroot, and Eliot, both still under consideration for the post, worked closely together to refine their ideas about effective and feasible programs for children within the developing social security legislation. In October Abbott (acting not only as a friend but as a dollar-a-year consultant to the Children's Bureau) went to Washington for several days of deliberation with Lenroot and Eliot to work out last details. Many years later Eliot remembered with keen satisfaction how the three had sat around a table together deciding the proposals for children on which they would stand together.[58] These included maternal and child health (a revised and extended version of the Sheppard-Towner Act), child welfare services (for homeless, dependent, and neglected children and children in danger of becoming delinquent), crippled children's services, and aid to dependent children (based on the experience of the states with mothers' pensions). Given the Children's Bureau experience and longtime interest in the aspects of childhood addressed by each of these proposals, the Abbott-Lenroot-Eliot triumvirate believed that all four should be administered by the Children's Bureau.

Aid to states for crippled children's services encountered no significant difficulties at any stage of the legislative process. The maternal and child health proposals held the potential for opposition from the same groups that had fought the Sheppard-Towner Act. Witte credited Abbott and Lenroot's "consummate skill" in designing strategic changes that helped to overcome the opposition of Catholics as well as the Public Health Service. In addition, as Witte noted, "the American Medical Association was far too alarmed about the possibility of health insurance to present any serious objections to the administration of the child and maternal health services through the Children's Bureau." Abbott and Lenroot and Eliot were also substantially aided by representatives of women's organizations over the country who had never accepted the loss of Sheppard-Towner, and who loyally appeared at congressional hearings to express their continuing interest in this program, as well as in the other proposals related to security for children. The request for aid to the states for child welfare services was threatened for a time by opposition from Catholic groups who feared intrusion by federal and state authorities into private charitable institutions for children. Compromises were reached however which enabled leading Catholics to support the legislation. All three of these children's programs, at all stages of consideration for inclusion in the social security bill, were regarded as most appropriately administered by the Children's Bureau.[59]

The Committee on Economic Security agreed that the aid to dependent children proposal also belonged to the Children's Bureau. However, in the late stages of the committee's work, that consensus began to shift under pressure from representatives of the FERA, particularly Aubrey J. Williams and Josephine C. Brown, who took the position that aid to dependent children was not a child-centered service but was public assistance with a focus on adult responsibilities and income maintenance. Congress was preoccupied with old age and unemployment insurance issues and gave little time or interest to children's affairs in economic security. As a result, the administration of aid to dependent children, in a late revision, was vested in the Social Security Board, along with the other categorical assistance programs. Lenroot wrote Abbott, "It was only at the last minute that I knew the administration of mothers' pensions had been changed." Eliot wrote, "No one seems to know why."[60]

Grace Abbott was keenly disappointed by this development. She saw the aid to dependent children program as an extension of mothers' pensions. In 1911 she had worked for the passage of mothers' pension legislation in Illinois, the first state to take such a forward step. The founding of the Children's Bureau had been linked closely to the mothers' pension movement. Like many others, she wanted aid to dependent children given to the Children's Bureau where it could be integrated into a program of social services. Despite the limitations of the mothers' pension programs, she believed that many children had been enabled to remain in their own homes who otherwise would have grown up in institutions. She feared that placing the aid to dependent children program in a large new administrative structure, completely outside the states' mothers' pension laws, would result in loss of standards and a program that would take on vestiges of poor relief.

In contrast, FERA spokesmen charged that the Children's Bureau constituency was unwilling to acknowledge the widespread positive influences of FERA on local poor relief attitudes and practices. They said that mothers' pension programs in the states had not kept pace with changes in society and that the Social Security Act provided an opportunity to build a sound general public assistance program out of the FERA's experiences with all its assets and liabilities.[61]

Public hearings during the legislative process had given evidence that social work leaders were opposed to splitting off a promising children's program from the Children's Bureau. Why their judgment was not accepted in the final draft of the bill is unclear. Josephine Brown suggested that the political repercussions from FERA had left Congress disenchanted with "standards" and the authoritative efforts of FERA to raise and maintain standards of relief-giving and administration by qualified personnel. As Gertrude Springer expressed it, "The Children's Bureau was known to have 'standards' and many congressmen, governors, and local political leaders were pretty fed up just then with standards."[62]

From the summer of 1934 until the passage of the Social Security

Act, Grace Abbott worked for its development and enactment. She testified in behalf of proposals before House and Senate committees[63] and served as one of the twenty-three members of the Advisory Council on Economic Security appointed by President Roosevelt to advise the Committee on Economic Security and assist in interpreting various proposals to the public.[64] The ambiguous charge given the council, and its large size, lessened its effectiveness. Meetings were long and frustrating as differences over the scope of the council's charge arose between Abbott and Paul Kellogg, a professional friend, journal editor, and longtime advocate of social legislation. Frances Perkins's biographer noted that Kellogg "poured into the council greater intensity than its advisory role could contain. . . . On one such occasion, Abbott, with far greater experience of government, lost her temper and moved that the meeting be ended." Witte felt in retrospect that the advisory council for a number of reasons "did not work out very well."[65] Abbott's attendance at meetings in Washington all through the fall of 1934 was at considerable inconvenience and cost to her physical well-being. Yet if she was disappointed in the council's effectiveness, the frequent visits to Washington gave her opportunities to talk with congressmen and other persons whose support for the social security bill was crucial.

When the bill's passage was endangered during six weeks of hearings by the House Ways and Means Committee, Frances Perkins sought a conference in her office with a small group of persons whom she knew to be staunchly in support of the proposal. Grace Abbott was there along with Frank Bane, John G. Andrews, Katharine Lenroot, Father John O'Grady, and Arthur Altmeyer. Following the conference, as a longtime member of the advisory committee of the American Association for Labor Legislation, Grace Abbott took the lead in organizing a small committee to get signatures of prominent people to a public statement, presented to Congress and to the president, urging action on the pending bill. Leaders of organizations friendly to the social security bill also were urged to contact members of Congress.[66] The activity was given widespread publicity and came at a time when the measure appeared to be lost. "The story has never been told," Edwin Witte wrote Edith Abbott, "how very near the [House] committee was to ditching the entire bill." Townsendites deluged committee members with demands for old-age pensions at levels that the House committee regarded as impossible. Businessmen opposed the bill because of the taxes it called for. Criticisms were pouring in from "self-styled experts and liberals" who favored social security but viewed the pending bill as unacceptable because it departed from some of their prized recommendations.[67] The public statement that Abbott spearheaded emphasized that even though the economic security bill did not guarantee all that many of its backers wanted, it was "imperative that the government recognize its responsibility for enacting a program which would insure the workers against the hazards which have wrecked their lives during these last years. . . . It is of the greatest practical importance that a decision be promptly made. The State legislatures which must act with reference to several titles of the bill are adjourning. The public is growing confused and discouraged. The high hopes of millions of distressed people, raised by the Administration in its 'solemn covenant with the people,' should be promptly fulfilled."[68]

President Roosevelt had thought major obstacles to passage would not come until Senate hearings. The statement transmitted to him and to Congress, in Witte's assessment, helped to influence the president to tell congressional leaders that he wanted the bill passed substantially in its present form. Witte believed this composite of activity "marked a distinct turning point in the history of the measure," and he said, "I give Miss Abbott much of the credit."[69]

Not everything the Abbott sisters wanted was included in the social security bill that finally passed. Yet they were realists who believed that it was better to accomplish as much as possible in "the here and now" and then attempt to build on that new base. Grace Abbott wrote Elisabeth Shirley Enochs about the thrill she felt at reading the text of the act in the *New York Times* and her belief that it had been an enormous accomplishment "even though there are those who will weep that the millennium is not yet." Edith Abbott assigned as much significance to securing a base of social security for America's citizens as she had to winning suffrage for women. Each had marked a major departure from the inhibitions of the past.[70]

When the bill became law and the Social Security Board was established to administer the act, Frances Perkins asked Grace Abbott to serve as one of its three members. Abbott, newly established as a professor of public welfare, was tempted to accept. She wrote Perkins that she was attracted to "the administrative pioneering that will have to be done and the importance of developing from the outset the right kind of federal-state relationships. . . . Then too, I like to do what you ask me to." But she declined and cited the need for more time away from the demands of administration to rebuild her health.[71]

> *When [sisters] . . . agree, no fortress is so strong as their*
> *common life.*   — ANTISTHENES[1]

CHAPTER 10

Sisters and Comrades

THE PROGRAMS of the Federal Emergency Relief Administration and of the Social Security Act brought a marked expansion in public relief and social services across the country and placed new demands upon social work education. All at once professional social workers were urgently needed and in short supply. The days when Edith Abbott searched for ways to attract enough able applicants to her school were gone; the problem had reversed to one of how to handle the heavily increased requests for admission. From the outset, Edith Abbott refused to offer "short training courses for emergency relief work," believing that these new students would set the tone of social work practice in public welfare. Like students who came before the Depression, they should meet the regular standards of admission and be given sound and basic social work education.

In the spring of 1934, Harry Hopkins announced that through the FERA the government would underwrite a special training program on a national scale to assure that persons employed by the various state relief administrations were qualified for the responsibilities that went with the expenditure of billions of dollars. Representatives of universities and colleges that had not previously developed a social work curriculum began to demand federal grants to establish programs of instruction to train personnel for relief administration.

When Hopkins launched his proposal, there were twenty-six schools in the American Association of Schools of Social Work. Most had struggled to reach and maintain acceptable standards of professional instruction. Most were capable of serving more students if students could be enabled to pay their tuition and board and room. Edith Abbott and Sophonisba Breckinridge viewed with alarm Hopkins's hastily organized plan of granting federal funds in aid of newly announced and poorly thought-out training plans. Breckinridge was currently the president of the American Association of Schools of Social Work, a circumstance that facilitated a prompt and effective application of Chicago influence on social work education. Breckinridge appointed a committee from the membership of the AASSW and charged it to develop a plan for meeting the emerging need for staff in the public welfare services and to present this plan to Hopkins as a sound means of obtaining personnel. As a result, requests for federal funds to establish poorly conceived social work schools were discouraged in Washington and the FERA plan became one of training necessary personnel in the already organized and accredited professional schools with the aid of federally funded scholarships.[2]

Edith Abbott and her faculty, even before the federal program was in operation, had begun to serve state relief administrations. In May 1933, the Georgia state relief administrator asked Edith Abbott to accept twenty-five members of his staff, all of whom were college graduates. President Hutchins provided new funds to Abbott for the costs of additional fieldwork supervision. By the summer quarter the School of Social Service Administration had enrolled nearly fifty persons from the Georgia relief services, some coming at state expense, others on their own funds.[3]

In evaluating the effect of the FERA scholarship program on social work education, Edith Abbott noted that it had enabled her school to raise its requirements for admission. Responding to the emergent needs of the difficult times had not meant a loss of standards. She attributed this to the expansion of relief work at a time when other employment opportunities were scarce and the publicity given to opportunities in public welfare, a career about which college graduates previously had been poorly informed. Abbott gave FERA its due by citing its firm support of effort to maintain standards. Selection of students to receive scholarships was left to the various states, but at no time, she noted, did state relief administrators bring pressure on the schools to admit poorly qualified applicants. Edith Abbott's graduate student enrollment increased markedly after 1934. The school became a nationally recognized educational institution with students enrolled from every state.[4]

Edith Abbott assumed a broker role in the placement of her students in the developing public welfare system. Even before the 1930s she had felt free to make her judgment prevail as to the kind of work a particular student should do with little attention to the individual's preference. Ethel Verry described herself as an early example. She entered the school in 1926 with a master's degree, intending to pursue a doctorate.

She had begun a research project at the Illinois Children's Home and Aid Society when Abbott and Breckinridge saw the opportunity they had long awaited to help modernize the Chicago Orphan Asylum, a well-endowed agency founded in 1849 in response to the devastating consequences for children of a cholera epidemic in Chicago. The asylum for years had resisted efforts to bring it into community social planning for children. An occasion to intervene successfully arose following a lecture by C. C. Carstens, the first executive of the Child Welfare League of America. Abbott had brought him to the University of Chicago for consultation with students, faculty, and community people. A few of the more progressive board members of the asylum attended one of Carstens's lectures and afterwards tentatively proposed to him that the league conduct a survey of their institution as a basis for recommending changes in its program. Breckinridge overheard the request. Abbott and Breckinridge lost no time in assuring the asylum board members that it was unnecessary to "go east" for such a study. Under their direction Miss Verry could do it. Ethel Verry protested that she felt ill prepared for such an important project, but they brushed aside her objections and "just put me there," as Verry described it. She set aside her dissertation, hoping to undertake another at the Orphan Asylum, a goal that seemed to Abbott and Breckinridge less important than putting to work the potential they saw in her for creative innovation in social service programs for children. (Verry did indeed fulfill their expectations by building the asylum into a leading professional community program, eventually renamed the Chicago Child Care Society.) In recollection, Verry acknowledged that Abbott and Breckinridge had seemed able to recognize where a particular student could be most effective and "having put you there, they would do all they could to see to it that it worked."[5]

Lilian Ripple gave a telling illustration of Edith Abbott's readiness to commit her students to employment. Ripple was attending the 1934 National Conference of Social Work. She sat down in a hotel lobby only to find that she was a few feet from Edith Abbott, although Abbott's chair was turned aside from where Ripple sat. Abbott almost appeared to be "presiding over court." One public welfare director after another from all over the country came to talk with her about critical staff needs. Abbott would listen and then with assurance name a student who would be "just the right person." A student herself then, Ripple grasped that her friends' employment was almost certainly arranged, whether they knew it or not. Thus did Abbott advance her concept of social work in the public sector by educating and sending out staff all over the country.[6]

Edith Abbott seemed to feel justified in tapping former students as well to fill particular posts. Phyllis Osborn gave an account of having been "summoned by Edith Abbott" to go elsewhere. She was working comfortably in the Kalamazoo, Michigan, public schools as one of the first visiting teachers in the system when Abbott informed her that she should leave and go to Nebraska where she was badly needed. Each of the Abbott sisters had been upset by the inept and insensitive leadership in the Relief Division in Nebraska and complained to Harry Hopkins that it was doing "great harm both to the development of the public welfare movement in Nebraska as well as to you and the Relief Administration." From the relatively benign climate of the public schools in 1934 Kalamazoo, Osborn resettled herself in Lincoln, Nebraska. Her first impressions were of "multiple forms, federal instructions, and wondering in something of a daze 'does Miss Abbott know what she sent me into.'" The Great Plains were burning hot and the dust storms were almost unbearable, the hours long and exhausting. Osborn survived by staying at the Cornhusker Hotel, one of the first buildings in Nebraska to be air-conditioned, although unreliably. She was told to develop a WPA project to study all the Nebraska social services, including jails, detention and youth correctional facilities, probation, and state hospitals. She put out two volumes of work which were used extensively by the state legislature and the other public bodies.[7]

Why did competent social workers accept Abbott's high-handed management of their affairs? Verry said it was because "you knew she was always building for the future, building the profession. And too, accepting her training and her scholarship aid made you feel that you owed her allegiance." Without hesitation Osborn said that "when Miss Abbott said to someone 'you must go' to a certain place, you were convinced it was for your own good and even the good of the country!" In another view, Ripple pointed out that of course students were reluctant to endanger their relationship with someone who could open the job market to them. But, she added, "it was more than that. One felt a sense of mission. Edith Abbott gave status to social work; students saw her almost as the master of their profession. If she saw you as a person to assume a certain responsibility, then you must be that person, and you rose to it."[8]

After Grace Abbott returned to Chicago, the two sisters lived comfortably together in a large house on Woodlawn Avenue which met the specifications of Grace's physician, close proximity to workplace and a screened porch on which to sleep. Students who had referred to Edith

Abbott and Nisba Breckinridge as A and B soon modified the appellation to A²B. In addition to teaching public welfare administration, Grace Abbott assumed the formal responsibility for the *Social Service Review* editorship, an assignment that was easily shared with her sister.

Grace Abbott continued to receive more requests than she could meet for public service on a national and international scale. She accepted Secretary of State Cordell Hull's appointment as chairperson of the United States Delegation to the seventh Pan-American Child Congress in Mexico City in 1935. In that same year she served as government delegate to the meeting of the International Labor Organization in Geneva, and in 1937 went again to the ILO conference, this time as head delegate for the United States. The following year she served the Wage and Hours Division of the Department of Labor as a member of the Textile Industry Committee to recommend wage scales for the cotton, rayon, and silk industry under the Fair Labor Standards Act.[9]

Given her desire to continue activities involving pressing public issues, and the many requests for her to do so, not surprisingly she found the first year of the teaching and editing schedule unexpectedly confining. Afternoon classes four days a week, and her sister's implicit expectation that one failed to meet a class only for pressing exigencies, restricted her sense of freedom to take on outside commitments. She found daily class preparation to be ever with her, observing to Wilma Walker with some exasperation that she had used up in one hour of lecture what it had taken her many times that number of hours to assemble. She wrote often to Children's Bureau staff for hurry-up mailings of current data, once saying, "I am living from hand to mouth as far as preparation for class is concerned."[10] Her teaching style was not too different from her method of instruction in Grand Island high school, calling upon students for recitation at intervals in her lectures and showing surprise and disapproval if they could not answer well. Yet she could relax with students and be informal, as in a discussion of juvenile delinquency when she observed that it was just as well that there had been no juvenile officers in Grand Island when she was growing up there. She and her brother, Ottie, had watched with longing the track crew of the railroad spinning along in its open-air hand-pumped car. One evening after the workmen had finished for the day and put the car away, temptation overcame them, and Grace and her brother got it out on the tracks and sped off. They were into the next county before an aghast railroader, aware of the schedule of an express from California, flagged them down.[11]

Grace Abbott's classes were usually intellectually stimulating. To students with highly conservative backgrounds, she appeared as a vigorous liberal and their exposure to her in the classroom had a tonic effect on their social outlook. She introduced, some said, the reality of what was "out there" in public welfare administration. "She had a warmth about her that was different, a warmth of one who was of the world."[12]

The Abbott sisters by now were receiving varied kinds of recognitions, including honorary degrees.[13] They were highly visible in social welfare circles and attracted notice wherever they were. Edith Abbott was president-elect of the 1936 National Conference of Social Work, which met for a sunny spring week in Atlantic City. Conferees moved pleasurably along the boardwalk as they went back and forth between meetings. On one side was the fascination of the sea and on the other a long chain of fine hotels and enticing shops. Yet over sixty-five hundred social workers addressed themselves in their meeting rooms to the pressing problems of human insecurity. Gertrude Springer gave the flavor of the Abbott sisters' presence at the conference: "If it had any heroines they were Grace and Edith Abbott—'The Abbotts of Nebraska'—whose direct and forthright expressions of conviction coupled with keen comments on the current scene drew quick response from people confused by indirection and uncertainty. 'My big mistake,' said a chairman whose meeting drew but a scanty crowd, 'was in not getting an Abbott on the program.' Either one of them 'packed the house' whenever she spoke and invariably received what everyone but the Abbott concerned recognized as an ovation."[14]

People who didn't know the Abbotts well often thought of them as formidable. Some feared to disagree with them or felt threatened by their influence. When Grace Abbott's book, *The Child and the State*, was published, Edith waited monthly for a review of it in *The Survey*. Finally she added a handwritten postscript to a more formal letter to Gertrude Springer: "Confidential from me to thee is this: I am terribly disappointed to have another Survey come in and still *no review* of that fine 2 vol. work of G.A. on 'State and Child'. I attach herewith a review from Harvard Law Review,—but it burns me up that our social work mag's completely ignore it. . . . If you'd stick a pin in your book review editor you'd oblige this disgruntled E.A." Springer replied that no doubt Abbott had by now seen Clara Beyer's review that made quite clear Grace's "notable contribution to social history." And then she added, "And now a confidential word from me to thee. We had a good deal of difficulty in getting a competent reviewer to accept this assignment. To put it bluntly, a lot of people seem to be 'afraid of the Abbotts.' Of course I was myself a good while . . . [but now,] I like you best when you are 'this disgruntled E.A.'"[15]

The companionable years of the Abbott sisters' maturity were from the outset clouded by intervals of concern over Grace's health. Given her serious bouts with tuberculosis, she watched carefully any signs of excessive fatigue or lingering colds. In turn her physicians tended to study any new symptoms for their relationship to her history of lung disease. Family correspondence from the summer of 1935 on contains increasingly frequent references to Grace's health. She was delayed in leaving Colorado in August because "Dr. Webb thinks I had better wait until the special kind of blood count he takes is reported." By the fall of 1937 Grace said to Elisabeth Shirley Enochs that she was improving from an illness that she acknowledged was "not lungs this time."[16]

In April of the following year, Grace Abbott entered a hospital in Chicago for a series of tests of bone marrow. Dr. Martha Eliot came to be with her. When the tests were completed, Abbott asked her friend to "go to the laboratory and see what they found and then come tell me." The diagnosis was multiple myeloma. Grace Abbott accepted the diagnosis and its implications stoically. Although she and Dr. Eliot were together a number of times in the months to come, Eliot stated that they never discussed the ultimate consequences of her illness again. It was different for Edith Abbott. She was heartbroken. Grace asked Eliot to try to explain her illness to Edith, to help her understand and accept it. Eliot felt she was unsuccessful in her attempt. At the first indication of a terminal illness for her sister, Edith Abbott could feel only despair. Cancer then was such a dread disease that it was spoken of only in very guarded circles. Edith insisted that no one be told the nature of her sister's illness. So successful was she in concealing the diagnosis that the literature of the time of Grace Abbott's death and after refers only vaguely to "anemia." More than two decades later, inquiries of Abbott's former colleagues and students yielded no reliable information about the nature or duration of her illness.[17]

Physicians began giving Grace Abbott a series of x-ray and calcium treatments. She wrote her niece: "It seems my bones were softening. Dr. Palmer has been having me take enough calcium by mouth and by a vein in my arm to turn me into a statue. . . . The pains are disappearing entirely. I am really without them for the first time in months." She spent the summer in Santa Fe and reported to her niece that she was "enormously better, not limping anymore." She returned to teaching in the fall and outwardly appeared to be cheerful and composed about herself. Depression came through occasionally in expression of concern about the war outlook: "One thinks of the European situation constantly—it forms an ominous background to everything."[18]

All during the fall and early winter of 1938 Grace Abbott was well enough to teach, to travel, and to carry out editing duties. She put special effort into completing the editorial work on a manuscript written by Walter Friedlander that described a remarkable child welfare program in the Weimar Republic of Germany following World War I, a unique system of public care for children and youth that was completely destroyed by the Nazis. Grace Abbott had first become interested in this social experiment in the early 1920s and when she was in Europe in 1930 she called upon Dr. Friedlander in Berlin. He was then executive director of the Bureau of Public Assistance and Child Welfare. Given the unsettled status of youth in America in 1930, Abbott wanted to learn about the innovative centers Friedlander had developed for unemployed youth. Six years later, after Friedlander had fled the Nazi terror, Grace Abbott influenced her sister to invite him to serve on her faculty, an offer he accepted. Completing her work on Friedlander's manuscript helped to place into the literature an account of a highly significant and lost experiment in child welfare.[19]

Grace Abbott hoped as well to finish an account of Julia Lathrop's Children's Bureau years, a project she had begun much earlier in collaboration with Jane Addams. Her writing was intended to complement Addams's account of Lathrop's early career. Jane Addams's section was published after her death as *My Friend, Julia Lathrop*. Abbott's account, which held so much promise, remained among her unfinished work.[20]

In October Grace Abbott was well enough to go to Washington for a meeting of the Textile Industry Committee and a month later was looking forward to a trip to New York with a schedule that gave her a free evening for dinner and theater with her niece. In late December the two Abbott sisters went together to California for a combination of vacation and lectures. Grace reported to her niece the great pleasure she had in the sunshine and flowers, but even more in the snow-covered mountains. "It was lovely but my three days of lectures at the end took away the vacation atmosphere."[21]

The shadows darkened rapidly for Grace Abbott in 1939. She entered the hospital soon after returning from California and was there except for brief intervals until her death. In a somewhat random effort to control a little-understood form of cancer, she was given x-ray therapy, radium, and "fever treatment," which she found extremely uncomfortable. She broke her arm in March, an accident common to her disease, and thereafter could not use her right arm or hand. Pain was always present and sometimes intense. She resented the pain because it caused her to limp "and makes my difficulties so conspicuous." From the beginning of the hospitalization, Edith Abbott responded to inquiries with a series of postponements: "Expected to be away for another week," "Not expected back until the end of March," "Will not be able to resume her duties for at least two more months," "Not expected to return until the fall."

By early June Grace Abbott's condition had worsened. The Abbott sisters' brother Arthur came from Grand Island, but he wrote Othman Abbott, Jr. that "I seem to be an extra bother to Edith." Martha Eliot was there as well, but no one could help Edith. She was worn out, distraught, and unreconciled to her beloved sister's impending death. On June 19 Grace "was relieved of her awful struggle to breathe," as her brother termed it. A simple Quaker service was held in the Abbott sisters' home on Woodlawn Avenue, and afterwards Grace was cremated and her ashes returned to Grand Island to the family cemetery plot.[22] Notices of her death at sixty years and accounts of her achievements appeared in newspapers across the country. Telegrams and letters of condolence and admiration for Grace Abbott's years of work in the public good poured in, mostly directed to Edith Abbott. They came from the president of the United States, senators, and other public officials, jurists, and many other citizens of all walks of life who had known her work and had felt touched by it. Perhaps no accolade came closer to defining her particular genius than that given by Felix Frankfurter: "I do not believe that American experience would disclose a finer illustration of the rare art of public administration. I do not mean to minimize the triumphs of . . . mechanical inventions, but social inventions apparently entail much subtler gifts. . . . The manner in which Grace Abbott translated the blueprints of social policies into effective operating institutions for the benefit of society at large made her work, in every true sense of the phrase, that of social invention."[23]

The days and nights following Grace Abbott's death were harsh ones for her sister. For some months she sought surcease through extensive recollections of her sister's work and achievements and then of their childhood together. She wrote carefully designed answers to every expression of sympathy. She became possessive of her sister's personal effects and for a long time would allow nothing to be changed in her sister's room. Dorothy Bradbury spent some months in 1943 in Chicago developing a history of the Children's Bureau and worked closely with Edith Abbott. Although she had conquered the outward evidences of her loss, Edith Abbott still found it hard to speak of Grace and to review the results of her work without tears coming to her eyes. Always she strived to keep her sister's presence alive in the minds and hearts of others. For some years she sent flowers or a telegram to Martha Eliot on Grace's birthday. Any recognition of Grace Abbott was intensely meaningful to her sister, particularly those that fixed Grace's name to a cause—to scholarships, a children's home in South Dakota, a housing division near Hull-House, and a children's hospital wing. Edith Abbott derived special pleasure from the naming of a Liberty Ship in October of 1942—the S.S. *Grace Abbott*. With friends and family she attended the christening ceremony in the Bethlehem Fairfield Shipyards in Baltimore.[24]

The primary effort to bring her grief under control was made through the use of her tremendous capacity for work. Edith Abbott's lifelong pattern of concentration and steady movement toward goals held her fast. Nevertheless, some believed that her work was significantly affected by her sister's death. It was said that she had no one to pull her back to reality, no political action outlet for her ideas. It was as though a dam had been put over the river.

Edith Abbott retired as dean of the school in 1942, after eighteen years in that demanding post. She retained teaching responsibilities and the editorship of the *Social Service Review*. Nisba Breckinridge, now retired, left her quarters at Green Hall, which had been her home since she came to the University of Chicago, so that she could live with Edith Abbott, who was lonely in the house she had shared with her sister. Letters to Charlotte Abbott from her aunt between 1942 and 1945 give evidence of Edith's growing older. She was unwilling to give up all responsibility at the school but finding it arduous in a new way—the meetings to go to, the papers to grade, the travel, and the weight of a schedule that had always been too heavy. Nisba Breckinridge was growing more dependent upon her as well. Their relationship in their late years was a reflection of love and commitment to each other based on long years of shared responsibility and caring, mixed with tiring demands by Breckinridge as she grew increasingly isolated from professional affairs and young people, and impatience on the part of Edith Abbott when fatigue and work were too heavy. Yet when Nisba went into her last illness, Edith Abbott put her own needs aside, and attended her lovingly, coaxing her to eat, and to sleep, and reassuring her.

The loss of her sister and then of her close compatriot Breckinridge in 1948 left Edith Abbott more alone than she could bear. She became more brusque, sometimes suspicious and quarrelsome. In the view of some she had stayed too long and, although her intellectual capacities were unimpaired, she had lost the ability to communicate meaningfully with many students and faculty. Yet her old vitality still came to the fore under challenge. She was opposed to America's involvement in the war and, when the lend-lease bill was under discussion, she vigorously and publicly protested the support given it by the League of Women Voters, of which she was a member. She saw Frances Perkins in Washington, and, as Edith Abbott described the encounter, Perkins asked "what was the trouble with all of us out here about the Lease-lend bill. She asked me if this was my Nebraska isolationism and my reply was, 'It was Nebraska isolationism in part, but it was also Quaker pacifism.' We had quite an argument."[25]

In the fall of 1949 Russell Ballard of Hull-House delighted Edith Abbott by inviting her to move into the same apartment at Hull-House that she had given up years before when she moved into the university area.[26] She hastened to accept his offer, even against the wishes of Wilma Walker, who loved her and knew that the distance between Hull-House and the university would make it difficult to continue to visit her each day. Abbott taught only one small seminar but held onto the editorship of the *Social Service Review*. Gradually those close to her persuaded her that she should relinquish this assignment to Helen Wright, who had succeeded her as dean and deserved a chance to put her own stamp on the *Review*, an issue of fairness that was convincing to Abbott.[27]

The final professional triumph of Edith Abbott's career was her acceptance speech when she was given the Survey Award at the 1951 National Conference of Social Work. The bronze plaque noted her "imaginative and constructive contributions to social work." The conference had been largely devoid of calls for social action and the slight, frail seventy-five-year-old woman who came to the podium "startled and delighted the large general session audience by turning her acceptance speech into a strong-voiced demand that something be done to abolish the means test and to establish children's allowances."[28]

To those who had known Edith Abbott well, her presence continued to hold them. Between trains in Chicago, Dorothy Bradbury once telephoned Edith Abbott, who prevailed upon her to change her ticket so that she could take a few hours and spend them with her at Hull-House. Later that night, Edith insisted upon walking to the corner with Bradbury because, she said, the neighborhood was getting dangerous. Looking back at Abbott under the street lamp, a slight, old-fashioned but strangely beautiful figure, it occurred to Bradbury that she was unlikely to see Edith Abbott again, and as the taxi drove away she wept at the realization.

The days at Hull-House grew harder for Edith Abbott. Glaucoma clouded her vision and made reading and mobility difficult. The weight of the past and unresolved sorrows led her to turn to her father's old remedy for ills, a glass of wine. When it became evident she could no longer live alone, Wilma Walker wrote Arthur Abbott that it was time to come for his sister. Thus did Edith Abbott return to Nebraska, as she had always expected to.

A beautiful passage in Edith Abbott's writing is a description of her heritage and childhood home: "Grace and I often talked over the vivid memories which we shared of the pioneer days in our part of the Great Plains. . . . And we used to say that if we lived in Chicago a hundred years, we could never forget the call of the meadow larks along the roadside; the rustling of the wind in the corn; the slow flight of the sand-hill cranes over the prairie creek near our home; and the old Overland Trail, a mile from the main street of our town—where the wild plums were hidden and the bittersweet berries hung from the cottonwoods in the early fall."[29]

But these were her memories and the Nebraska she returned to was a new environment. The old family home had been converted to three apartments. Her brothers, Arthur and Othman Jr., each occupied one of them and Edith Abbott now the third. They lived independently of each other, but with old loves and old rivalries renewed. Edith Abbott was lonely despite her younger brother's close attention. She complained that no one came to see her, that neighbors were afraid of her. Her glaucoma worsened, her body weakened, and her spirit diminished.

On July 22, 1957, Arthur Abbott telegraphed his niece that "Edith is down in bed now and I do not believe she will get out of it." A week later he sent a message that "Edith Abbott died without pain tonight."[30] It had been hard to think of Edith Abbott in a weakened condition, as Wayne McMillen wrote Arthur, "but perhaps it was a relief to her indomitable spirit to lay aside the burden of a body that no longer served her."[31] The last years of Edith Abbott's life had not been happy ones. Her cherished values, her goals, and her fighting spirit were not particularly conducive to happiness in the times in which she lived. Nor did Edith Abbott consider happiness the object of life. Her life partnership with her sister, the legacy she left her profession, and the work that earned her the tribute "the noblest Roman of them all in public welfare"[32]—all that had been enough.

BIBLIOGRAPHICAL ESSAY

Cʜᴀᴘᴛᴇʀ ɴᴏᴛᴇꜱ show sources of direct quotations within the narrative and of primary and secondary sources drawn upon more generally. The following manuscript collections were consulted at various stages of my investigation.

Papers of Grace and Edith Abbott, Regenstein Library, University of Chicago.
Jane Addams Memorial Collection, University of Illinois at Chicago.
Archives, London School of Economics and Political Science.
Clara Beyer Papers, Schlesinger Library, Radcliffe College.
Sophonisba P. Breckinridge Papers, Library of Congress. (Separate from Breckinridge family collection, and hereafter referred to as Breckinridge Papers.)
Sophonisba P. Breckinridge Manuscripts, Regenstein Library, University of Chicago.
Children's Bureau Papers, National Archives.
Edward P. Costigan Papers, University of Colorado.
Mary Dewson Papers, Schlesinger Library, Radcliffe College.
Martha E. Eliot Papers, Schlesinger Library, Radcliffe College.
Felix Frankfurter Papers, Library of Congress.
Alice Hamilton Papers, Schlesinger Library, Radcliffe College.
Warren G. Harding Papers, (Microfilm) Ohio Historical Society.
Immigrants' Protective League Papers, University of Illinois at Chicago.
Esther Loeb Kohn Papers, University of Illinois at Chicago.
Katharine Lenroot Papers, Columbia University.
Passfield Papers, Beatrice Webb Diaries, Library of London School of Economics and Political Science.
Presidential Papers, Herbert Hoover Library, West Branch, Iowa.
Josephine Roche Papers, University of Colorado.
St. Hilda's Settlement, London.
Survey Associates Papers, and the Paul U. Kellogg Papers, Social Welfare History Archives, University of Minnesota.

The papers of Grace and Edith Abbott constitute the principal collection focused primarily upon one or both of the Abbott sisters. The majority of the collection consists of Grace Abbott's papers, largely devoted to her work as chief of the Children's Bureau between 1921 and 1934, and her tenure as professor of public welfare at the School of Social Service Administration between 1934 and 1939. Especially useful were her manuscripts, speeches, correspondence, and the notebooks of publicity in various newspapers and journals of the day that gave insight into her activities, the controversies which arose during her years as chief, and the constituencies upon which she drew for support.

Academic papers comprise the largest part of the papers of Edith Abbott. These include documents, lectures, and bibliographies that she used in her classes in English and American philanthropy, public welfare administration, and immigration, and material relevant to her service as dean of the School of Social Service Administration from 1924 to 1942.

The papers of each sister contain useful correspondence between one or both of them and other prominent people with whom they were associated, for example, Jane Addams, Florence Kelley, Julia Lathrop, Lillian Wald, Sophonisba P. Breckinridge, Julian Mack, Julius Rosenwald, Felix Frankfurter, Katharine Lenroot, Martha Eliot, M.D., Raymond Fosdick, Herbert Hoover, Harry Hopkins, Frances Perkins, and others.

The Abbott Papers were enriched in 1981 by the addition of family correspondence and other personal documents made available by Charlotte Abbott. She generously gave me access to these materials prior to making her gift to the Regenstein Library. Citations to this material appear as Abbott Papers, C. A. Addenda. This addition fills many missing links in the original collection. Notably it documents the Abbott sisters' adolescence and early adult years in Nebraska and the influences, both familial and societal, that led them to Chicago. Particularly interesting are letters written by Edith Abbott to her family during her adolescent years at Brownell Hall, by Grace Abbott to her family during her employment as a teacher in the Broken Bow high school, and other records kept by the Abbott sisters such as notebooks and college themes. The C. A. Addenda also contains useful copies of correspondence between Grace Abbott and Katharine Lenroot, Martha Eliot, M.D., and Frances Perkins.

Edith Abbott left copies of a manuscript in different stages of revision from her effort to write a biography of her sister. She hoped the manuscript would be accepted for publication by the University of Chicago Press, but it was not. She had written most of the manuscript under great pressure in her later years when she felt alone and burdened with the loss of her sister and of her great friend, Sophonisba P. Breckinridge. The manuscript is useful chiefly for its guidance to primary sources and as an indication of what Edith Abbott regarded as landmark developments in her sister's career. The section on family heritage and childhood years was written somewhat earlier. Even before Grace Abbott's death, Edith Abbott had begun to make notes for this portion of the biography. Hurried phrases to trigger her memory later were found jotted down between appointments or during meetings in the pages of a small pocket calendar. This early part of the manuscript conveys the impression that her memories of childhood had flowed easily and were recorded authentically as she recalled them. Therefore, I have drawn heavily on this material to portray the Abbott sisters' childhood in their little frontier town. At the same time, I examined reports in Nebraska newspapers and histories of Nebraska to test the validity of Edith Abbott's account of these early times and the place her family occupied in Grand Island and in Nebraska.

The papers of Martha E. Eliot, M.D., Alice Hamilton, M.D., Clara Beyer, and Mary Dewson were especially useful as a resource for filling out an understanding of the network among women reformers of which the Abbott sisters were a part.

The Survey Associates Papers and the Paul U. Kellogg Papers provide a significant source for documenting the social, political, and economic developments during the most active years of the Abbott sisters' careers and for grasping more fully the perspectives of other leaders in the developing social welfare system and the profession of social work.

I consulted the Children's Bureau Papers in the National Archives, but found them in the middle 1970s so poorly catalogued and housed as to make access to desired data unduly time-consuming. Fortunately much of the material pertinent to my interests was available in duplicate copies in the papers of Grace and Edith Abbott.

Katharine Lenroot generously gave me access to a copy of the interviews which she had given for Columbia University's Oral History Project, and also to her personal file of correspondence with Grace Abbott from 1921 to 1939. The latter was especially useful for documenting the collegial relationship between Grace Abbott and Katharine Lenroot and the administrative style that Grace Abbott demonstrated. Lenroot later gave that file of correspondence to Columbia University. Much of it is also found in the papers of Grace and Edith Abbott.

Correspondence between Grace Abbott and Sophonisba P. Breckinridge, found in the Sophonisba P. Breckinridge Papers, was enlightening about Breckinridge's personality and relationship to the Abbotts.

The Sophonisba P. Breckinridge Manuscripts (Regenstein Library) are very brief, but provide poignant insights into her character and relationship to Edith Abbott.

I consulted a microfilm of the Warren G. Harding Papers for evidence of his position on Grace Abbott's appointment as chief of the Children's Bureau and the Sheppard-Towner legislation.

I found the Herbert Hoover Presidential Papers helpful to my study chiefly for documenting the wide support of Grace Abbott for secretary of labor that was conveyed to President Hoover.

The diaries of Beatrice Webb in the Passfield Papers for the years in which she was heavily involved in the Royal Commission on the Poor Law supplied a sense of the excitement generated by the issues she raised, to which Edith Abbott was exposed during her year at the London School of Economics.

Correspondence between Grace Abbott and Felix Frankfurter, in the Felix Frankfurter Papers, was illuminating for understanding Abbott's friendship with Frankfurter and her reliance upon him for consultation at numerous times.

I also examined correspondence between Grace Abbott and Edward P. Costigan and between Abbott and Josephine Roche, both collections in the University of Colorado library. Although this did not provide new insights, it did add a general corroboration of other data.

The Immigrant's Protective League Papers provided a limited supplement to the Annual Reports of the league and the correspondence of Grace Abbott during this period of her career, found in the Abbott Papers.

The Annual Reports of St. Hilda's Settlement can hardly be said to reside in a manuscript collection, but they did supply essential information to understanding Edith Abbott's residence in that settlement and her work in its neighborhood. St. Hilda's today is very different than in 1906. My visit to the settlement in behalf of my study aroused the curiosity of the young director and he allowed me to search in a cupboard at the settlement where, amidst an array of diverse materials, copies of the old annual reports were unearthed.

CHAPTER NOTES

PREFACE

1. Jill Conway, "Women Reformers and American Culture, 1870–1930," *Journal of Social History*, 5 (Winter 1971–72), 164–77.

2. Julia Lathrop, Reporting for the State Board of Charities of Illinois, in the Sixth Session of the Conference, *Proceedings of the National Conference of Charities and Correction at the Twenty-First Annual Session, May 23–29, 1894* (Boston: Press of Geo. H. Ellis, 1894), pp. 305–6.

3. Because Grace Abbott effectively championed the children's cause, she was sometimes assumed to be motivated by maternal interests. References to her as "the mother of America's children" and other such emotional allusions were common. Those who made such assumptions often quoted from one of her speeches: "Sometimes when I get home at night in Washington, I feel as though I had been in a great traffic jam . . . moving toward the Hill where Congress sits in judgement on all the administrative agencies of the Government. In that traffic jam there are all kinds of vehicles . . . the kinds of conveyances, for example that the Army can put into the street—tanks, gun carriages, trucks, the dancing horses of officers. . . . There are other kinds of vehicles in this traffic jam—great numbers of them . . . hayricks and the binders and the ploughs . . . [of] the Department of Agriculture. . . . There are . . . the handsome limousines [of] the Department of Commerce. . . . and the barouches in which the Department of Justice officials sometimes appear. . . . I stand on the sidewalk watching it become more congested and more difficult, and then because the responsibility is mine and I must, I take a very firm hold on the handles of the baby carriage and I wheel it into the traffic." G. Abbott, "New Measures of Values," address in accepting the Gold Medal of the National Institute of Social Sciences, *Journal of the National Institute of Social Sciences*, 16–19 (May 1931–Dec. 1934).

To assume from this quotation that Grace Abbott chose her responsibilities for children because of her feminine temperament or maternal needs is to overlook the fact that she also championed just as vigorously the cause of the immigrant man and woman, the rights of women in industry, fair labor standards for the labor force of America, and the interests of women who wanted education and a career. Circumstances created an opportunity for her to become chief of the Children's Bureau. Under different circumstances, she might have been head of another governmental bureau. She had wanted to be a lawyer and to run for public office. Quite clearly had circumstances been different in 1930 she might have been the first woman to be named to a president's cabinet. Metaphors are sprinkled throughout Grace Abbott's speeches and writing, even in early family correspondence. She liked colorful symbols, and she used them freely. Commonly they embodied distinctly nonmaternal emphases, as in, "I am meeting with Miss Lathrop to go over the history of the Washington battle and plan the next engagement. It is in the main guerilla warfare."

4. Arnold C. Koenig to E. Abbott, July 3, 1940, Abbott Papers, C. A. Addenda.

5. G. Abbott, "The Changing Position of Women," in Charles A. Beard, ed., *A Century of Progress* (Chicago: Harper & Bros., Publishers, 1933), p. 289.

CHAPTER 1: *Western Heritage*

For family background and childhood and adolescent experiences, I relied principally upon: O. A. Abbott's *Recollections of a Pioneer Lawyer;* a partial manuscript and notes by E. Abbott, intended to become a biography of her sister; early family correspondence; conversations with C. Abbott; newspapers and histories of early Nebraska. When not otherwise noted, material came from O. A. Abbott's memoirs or E. Abbott's notes and manuscript. Direct quotations from O. A. Abbott's publication are referenced, but not those from E. Abbott's incomplete notes and manuscript.

1. Edith Abbott, "A Sister's Memories," *Social Service Review*, 13 (Sept. 1939), 351–52.

2. Othman A. Abbott, *Recollections of a Pioneer Lawyer* (Lincoln: Nebraska Historical Society, 1928), xi, 123–25.

3. Population figures supplied by Nebraska State Historical Society.

4. Abbott family scrapbook and photograph album: "The officers of the Rockford Female Seminary hereby certify that Miss Elizabeth M. Griffin . . . has attained the highest standard in deportment and scholarship and is a valuable member of the institution. To her diligent application to study, to her exemplary deportment and respectful treatment of the teachers they render a cheerful and unqualified testimony and most willingly award to her this expression of their high and favorable regard. Rockford, Illinois, July 12, 1866." (Signed) Anna P. Sill;

notation from Miss Sill's notebook, p. 31, Rockford College, Howard Colman Library; reference letter from R. A. Childs to "All Whom It May Concern," re: Miss Lizzie Griffin, Feb. 12, 1872, Abbott Papers, C. A. Addenda.

5. O. A. Abbott, *Recollections*, p. 141.

6. Hiram Mattison, *Atlas Designed to Illustrate Burritt's Geography of the Heavens* (New York: Sheldon and Co., 1856).

7. Edith Abbott, "A Sister's Memories," p. 353.

8. A. F. Buechler, R. J. Barr, and Dale P. Stough, eds., *History of Hall County* (Lincoln: Nebraska Historical Society, 1920), p. 189. For documentation of the status of Othman A. Abbott at this time, see "Model Government of the 'Third City,'" Grand Island *Daily Independent*, Apr. 27, 1910, sec. 2, p. 1. The petition to incorporate Grand Island as a city was written by Othman A. Abbott in 1872. As a leading member of the 105 petitioners, he was designated in 1910 as "honored and highly esteemed" by his fellowmen. A photograph of Othman A. Abbott was part of the newspaper story.

9. Six letters from E. Abbott to Lizzie Abbott; one to O. A. Abbott, to G. Abbott, to Arthur Abbott, and to O. A. Abbott, Jr., n.d., Abbott Papers, C. A. Addenda.

10. "Announcement of Twenty-Fifth Annual Commencement," Brownell Hall, June 13, 1893, Abbott Papers, C. A. Addenda.

11. W. Jett Lauck, *The Causes of the Panic of 1893* (Boston: Houghton Mifflin and Company, Riverside Press, 1907); James C. Olson, *History of Nebraska* (Lincoln: University of Nebraska Press, 1955), pp. 232–36; Buechler et al., *History of Hall County*, pp. 297–316.

12. "Last of Roll of Men Gone," Grand Island *Daily Independent*, n.d., for account of death of William A. Hagge, close friend of O. A. Abbott, and for reference to their joint losses in bank failure and their "sturdy character" as seen in their determination to meet their financial obligations to their investors.

13. Reminiscence of Charlotte Abbott, June 14, 1973.

14. Olson, *History of Nebraska*, pp. 232–36.

15. As a framework for evaluating the Abbott sisters' response to Populism, I have relied upon the treatment given it by Richard Hofstadter in *The Age of Reform* (New York: Vintage Books, 1955).

16. Letter from G. Abbott to E. Abbott, June 19, 1897; from Lizzie Abbott to E. Abbott, June 20 and 30, 1897, Abbott Papers, C. A. Addenda.

17. Notebook of poetry, stories, and other notes kept by G. Abbott, Abbott Papers, Addenda II, Box IV, Folder 11; E. Abbott's college themes, Abbott Papers, C. A. Addenda.

18. W. C. Gaston and A. R. Humphrey, *History of Custer County, Nebraska* (Lincoln: Nebraska State Historical Society, 1919), pp. 192–97.

19. Letters from G. Abbott to Lizzie Abbott, Sept. 28, Oct. 3, 17, 23, and 31, 1898, Feb. 13, 1899; to E. Abbott, Sept. 7 and 24, Oct. 9, 19, and 30, 1898, Jan. 25, Feb. 19 and 21, 1899; to Arthur Abbott, Sept. 23, Nov. 2, 1898; to "all the Family," Jan. 22, Feb. 17, 1899, Abbott Papers, C. A. Addenda.

20. G. Abbott to Lizzie Abbott, Mar. 3, 1899; Mrs. Jewett to Lizzie Abbott, Mar. 4, 1899; telegram from T. H. Jewett to E. Abbott, Mar. 4, 1899; Lizzie Abbott to family at home, Mar. 6, 1899, Abbott Papers, C. A. Addenda.

21. G. Abbott to Claudia Carlos Snyder, Mar. 24, 1933, Abbott Papers, Box 75, Folder 9.

22. Louise Pound to E. Abbott, Nov. 15, 1897, Abbott Papers, C. A. Addenda.

23. E. Abbott to Lizzie Abbott, n.d.; four letters to G. Abbott, n.d., Abbott Papers, C. A. Addenda.

24. Abba Bowen, *Anchora of Delta Gamma*, 75 (Winter 1958), p. 10; R. McLaran Sawyer, *Centennial History of the University of Nebraska* (Lincoln: Centennial Press, 1969), II, 34–35; Ida Shaw Martin, *The Sorority Handbook*, 8th ed. (Boston: privately published, 1923), pp. 43–51, for insights into the role played by sororities for early generations of college women.

25. Thirty years later when Edith's niece, then a University of Chicago undergraduate, learned that her aunt had been a favored student of Thorstein Veblen, she displayed the eager interest of the young in the talked-about affairs of the former Chicago professor. Edith's only response was a prim, "He was always a gentleman with me."

26. Joseph G. Svoboda, University of Nebraska Archives, Nov. 25, 1975; Elisabeth Shirley Enochs, "Childhood Scenes," *The Child*, 4 (Aug. 1939), 34; E. Abbott to Mrs. Hopkins, Aug. 11, 1939, letter supplied by E. S. Enochs.

27. Arthur G. Abbott to G. Abbott, Oct. 4, 1905, Abbott Papers, C. A. Addenda.

28. Interview, C. Abbott; photograph supplied by C. Abbott.

29. Abbott Papers, Addenda II, Box IV, Folder 11.

30. Interview, James Brown IV, July 14, 1976.

31. In 1936, at age 91, Elizabeth Griffin Abbott was given an honorary M.A. degree from Rockford College, her alma mater, in recognition of her public service in Nebraska for suffrage and other civic endeavors, for example, her appointment by the governor to serve as delegate to the thirteenth National Conference of Charities and Correction; her in-

fluence in obtaining Carnegie Funds in 1905 for a new library building in Grand Island; her service as a member of the visiting and examining board of the Nebraska Soldiers and Sailors Home. *1937 Rockford College Bulletin of Information*, p. 4; letter of appointment by Governor Dawes to Mrs. O. A. Abbott, July 6, 1886; letter of appointment by Governor Lorenzo Crounse to expire Apr. 1, 1896; Grace Bentley Paine to E. Abbott, Dec. 2, 1941, Abbott Papers, C. A. Addenda.

32. *Omaha World-Herald*, July 6, 1930.

33. Willa Cather, *My Antonia* (Boston: Houghton Mifflin Co., Riverside Press, 1918 and 1926), p. ix.

CHAPTER 2: *The Scientific Spirit and Human Purposes*

1. Franklin D. Roosevelt, from a speech prepared the day before his death for delivery by radio to the Jefferson Day Dinner, Apr. 14, 1945.

2. James Rowland Angell, "Some Reflections upon the Reaction from Coeducation," *Popular Science Monthly*, Nov. 1902, pp. 21–22.

3. Helen R. Wright, "Three against Time: Edith and Grace Abbott and Sophonisba P. Breckinridge," *Social Service Review*, 28 (Mar. 1954), 42.

4. Sophonisba P. Breckinridge mss; Edith Abbott, *Women in Industry. A Study in American Economic History* (New York: D. Appleton and Co., 1910).

5. Abbott Papers, Box 2, Folder 14.

6. E. Abbott to Lizzie Abbott, Sept. 1905, Abbott Papers, C. A. Addenda.

7. Allen F. Davis, "The Women's Trade Union League: Origins and Organization," *Labor History*, 5 (Winter 1964), 3.

8. Gladys Boone, *The Women's Trade Union Leagues in Great Britain and the United States of America* (New York: Columbia University Press, 1942).

9. E. Abbott to G. Abbott, n.d., Abbott Papers, C. A. Addenda.

10. E. Abbott and S. P. Breckinridge, "Employment of Women in Industries: Twelfth Census Statistics," *Journal of Political Economy*, 14 (Jan. 1906), 14–40.

11. The Abbott sisters had access to fine books of art purchased in limited editions by Othman and Lizzie Abbott prior to the hard times of the 1890s and now in the possession of Charlotte Abbott. Examples: *Mr. Vanderbilt's House of Collection, Described by Edward Strahan*, vol. 1, copy no. 632 (Philadelphia: George Barrie, 1883–84); *Une Centaine De Peintres. The Works of One Hundred Great Masters*, Engraved, with Descriptive Text under the Direction of Alphonse Bacheret, copy no. 858

(Philadelphia: George Barrie, n.d.); *From the Works of Distinguished British Painters* (engravings on steel) (New York: D. Appleton & Co. Publishers); *One Hundred Crowned and Laurelled Masterpieces of Modern Painting*, Grand Imperial Japan edition, copy no. 143.

12. Edith Abbott to Grace Abbott, Feb. 16, 1906, Abbott Papers, C. A. Addenda.

13. See list of Edith Abbott's publications, p. 287.

14. E. Abbott to Lizzie Abbott, Oct. 4, 1906, Abbott Papers, C. A. Addenda.

15. Record of E. Abbott's registration at the London School of Economics and Political Science for the Michaelmas, Lent, and Summer terms of 1906–7, Archives, London School of Economics.

16. Beatrice Webb Diaries, July 7, 1891, Passfield Papers.

17. Syllabus of "Methods of Social Investigation," Calendar, 1906–7, London School of Economics and Political Science, Archives.

18. Richard Henry Tawney, "Beatrice Webb," *Proceedings of the British Academy*, 29 (London: Geoffrey Cumberlege Amen House, E. C. 4, 1945); Norman and Jeanne MacKenzie, *The Fabians* (New York: Simon and Schuster, 1977), p. 120.

19. Othman A. Abbott to E. Abbott, Mar. 5, 1907, Abbott Papers, C. A. Addenda.

20. E. Abbott to Othman A. Abbott, June 6, 1907, Abbott Papers, C. A. Addenda.

21. Karl de Schweinitz, *England's Road to Social Security* (New York: A. S. Barnes and Company, Perpetua ed., 1961), pp. 184–85.

22. Beatrice Webb Diaries, Feb. 17, 1908.

23. Extract from the "Cheltenham Examiner," 1898, St. Hilda's Settlement Archives.

24. Annual Report no. 18, St. Hilda's Settlement, Apr. 1, 1906 to Apr. 1, 1907, St. Hilda's Settlement Archives.

25. Werner Picht, *Toynbee Hall and the English Social Settlement Movement* (London: G. Bell and Sons, 1914), pp. 113, 232.

26. Charles Booth, *Life and Labour of the People in London*, third series (London: Macmillan and Co., 1902), p. 76.

27. Annual Report no. 18, St. Hilda's Settlement.

28. E. Abbott to Lizzie Abbott, Apr. 27 and May 7, Abbott Papers, C. A. Addenda.

29. Edith Abbott recounted this incident in "Grace Abbott and Hull-House, 1908–21, Part II," *Social Service Review*, 24 (Dec. 1950), 508. In that account she indicated that the suggestion of "made work" came from Grace Abbott. This attribution contradicted her own early notes of the incident in which she recorded that she had made the suggestion

initially with Grace issuing the warning. The idea was characteristic of Edith Abbott at that period of her thinking; it was a suggestion that Grace Abbott was unlikely to have made.

30. Edith Abbott, "English Poor-Law Reform," *Journal of Political Economy*, 19 (Jan. 1911), 47–59.

31. E. Abbott to Lizzie Abbott, Dec. 11, 1906, Abbott Papers, C. A. Addenda; E. Abbott "Woman Suffrage Militant: The New Movement in England," *The Independent*, 61 (Nov. 29, 1906), pp. 1276–78.

32. E. Abbott to Lizzie Abbott, May 7, 1907, Abbott Papers, C. A. Addenda; Picht, *Toynbee Hall and the English Settlement Movement*, p. 123.

33. E. Abbott to Lizzie Abbott, Nov. 10 and Dec. 11, 1906; Mar. 25, May 22, and July 10, 1907, Abbott Papers, C. A. Addenda.

34. Interview with Charlotte Abbott, Mar. 8, 1973.

35. Arthur Abbott to E. Abbott, Oct. 3, 1907, Abbott Papers, Box 1, Folder 10.

36. E. Abbott to Grace Abbott, n.d.; to Lizzie Abbott, n.d., Abbott Papers, C. A. Addenda.

37. G. Abbott to E. Abbott, June 9, 1907, Abbott Papers, C. A. Addenda.

38. S. P. Breckinridge to E. Abbott, Oct. 23, 1907, Abbott Papers, Box 1, Folder 10.

39. Louise de Koven Bowen, *Growing Up with a City* (New York: Macmillan Company, 1926), pp. 115, 120; G. Abbott to O. A. Abbott, Jr., n.d., Abbott Papers, C. A. Addenda.

40. S. P. Breckinridge to E. Abbott, Apr. 13, 1908, Breckinridge Papers, Box 1, Folder 1.

41. Julia C. Lathrop to E. Abbott, Mar. 25, 1908, Abbott Papers, Box 57, Folder 5; S. P. Breckinridge to Edith Abbott, Apr. 13, 1908, Breckinridge Papers, Box 1, Folder 1.

CHAPTER 3: *Chicago — New Frontiers*

1. Carl Sandburg, "Chicago," *Chicago Poems* (New York: Henry Holt and Company, 1916), pp. 3–4.

2. E. Abbott, Notes and ms.

3. Louise C. Wade, *Graham Taylor, Pioneer for Social Justice 1851–1938* (Chicago: University of Chicago Press, 1964), pp. 58–62.

4. Grace Abbott, "A Study of the Greeks in Chicago," *American Journal of Sociology*, 15 (Oct. 1909), 380–81.

5. "The Early Hull-House" (Chicago: University of Illinois, n.d.), pp. 1–4.

6. *Hull-House Yearbook 1910,* Jane Addams Memorial Collection, University of Illinois at Chicago.

7. Allen F. Davis, *Spearheads for Reform. The Social Settlements and the Progressive Movement. 1890–1914* (New York: Oxford University Press, 1967), pp. 33–38.

8. Nicholas Kelley, "Early Days at Hull-House," *Social Service Review,* 28 (Dec. 1954), 424–29.

9. Davis, *Spearheads for Reform,* pp. 26–29.

10. Allen F. Davis, *American Heroine. The Life and Legend of Jane Addams* (New York: Oxford University Press, 1973), pp. 74, 118.

11. G. Abbott to Lizzie Abbott, July 12, 1908, Abbott Papers, C. A. Addenda.

12. Jane Addams, *The Second Twenty Years at Hull-House* (New York: Macmillan Company, 1930), p. 405.

13. Davis, *Spearheads for Reform,* pp. 171–72.

14. E. Abbott, Notes and ms.

15. Ibid.

16. G. Abbott to O. A. and Lizzie Abbott, n.d., Abbott Papers, C. A. Addenda.

17. Francis Hackett, "Hull-House—A Souvenir," *Survey Graphic,* 54, no. 5 (1925), 276.

18. Alice Hamilton, *Exploring the Dangerous Trades* (Boston: Little, Brown and Co., 1943), p. 69.

19. Eleanor Flexner, *Century of Struggle. The Woman's Rights Movement in the United States* (New York: Atheneum, 1973), p. 248.

20. Letter to Lyman Abbott from Theodore Roosevelt, Nov. 10, 1908, cited in William L. O'Neill, *Everyone Was Brave* (Chicago: Quadrangle Books, 1969), pp. 61–62, n. 4.

21. Edith Abbott, "Grace Abbott and Hull-House, 1908–21, Part II," *Social Service Review,* 24 (Dec. 1950), 502.

22. *Proceedings of the National Conference of Charities and Correction at the Thirty-ninth Annual Session, June 12–19, 1912,* ed. Alexander Johnson (Fort Wayne, Ind.: Fort Wayne Printing Co., 1912).

23. Paul U. Kellogg, "The Industrial Platform of the New Party," *The Survey,* 28, no. 21 (1912), 668.

24. *Proc. of NCCC, Thirty-sixth Annual Session, June 9–16, 1909,* ed. Alexander Johnson (Fort Wayne, Ind.: Fort Wayne Printing Co., 1909).

25. *Proc. of NCCC, 1912,* pp. 376–80.

26. Ibid., pp. 388–95.

27. Davis, *Spearheads for Reform*, pp. 196–97; Addams, *Second Twenty Years at Hull-House*, pp. 24–27.

28. Davis, *American Heroine*, pp. 184–85.

29. E. Abbott, "Grace Abbott and Hull-House, Part II," pp. 501–2.

30. G. Abbott, "Women in Government," Abbott Papers, Box 25, Folder 3.

31. William Allen White, *Autobiography* (New York: Macmillan Co., 1946), p. 484.

32. G. Abbott to Lizzie Abbott, Sept. 4, 1912, Abbott Papers, C. A. Addenda.

33. G. Abbott to Lizzie Abbott, Mar. 11, 1911, Abbott Papers, C. A. Addenda.

34. Flexner, *Century of Struggle*, p. 261.

35. E. Abbott, "Grace Abbott and Hull-House, Part II," pp. 502–4.

36. Ibid., pp. 505–6; *Chicago American*, June 8, 1916, editorial page.

37. E. Abbott, "Grace Abbott and Hull-House, Part II," p. 501; J. Addams to G. Abbott, Oct. 16, 1914, Abbott Papers, Box 3, Folder 3.

38. E. Abbott and S. P. Breckinridge, *Wage-earning Women and the State: A Reply to Miss Minnie Bronson* (Boston: Equal Suffrage Association for Good Government, 1912).

39. E. Abbott, "The Copycat Vote," *New Republic*, 2 (Apr. 24, 1915).

40. E. Abbott, "Are Women a Force for Good Government?" *National Municipal Review*, 4 (July 1915), 435–47; and "The Woman Voter and the Spoils System in Chicago," ibid., 5 (July 1916), 460–65.

41. G. Abbott, "What Have They Done?" *The Independent*, 115 (Oct. 24, 1925), 475.

42. G. Abbott, "Women in Government."

43. Ibid.

44. G. Abbott, "After Suffrage—Citizenship," *The Survey*, 44 (Sept. 1, 1920), 655–57.

45. G. Abbott to Lizzie Abbott, Mar. 30, 1909, Abbott Papers, C. A. Addenda.

46. G. Abbott, "The Immigrant as a Problem in Community Planning," in *Twelfth Annual Meeting of the American Sociological Society, . . . December 27–29, 1917* (Chicago: University of Chicago Press, 1918), pp. 166–73.

47. Marie Louise Degen, *The History of the Woman's Peace Party*, Johns Hopkins University Studies in Historical and Political Science, 1939, series LVII, no. 3.

48. "Is the Women's Peace Movement 'Silly and Base'?" *Literary Digest*, 50 (1915), 1022–23.

49. G. Abbott to Lizzie Abbott, Apr. 11 and 16, 1915, Abbott Papers, C. A. Addenda.

50. *Chicago Record-Herald*, Apr. 13, 1915.

51. *Report of the International Congress of Women. The Hague—The Netherlands*, Apr. 28th to May 1st, 1915 (Printed by the Woman's Peace Party, 1915), pp. 5–6.

52. Mercedes M. Randall, *Improper Bostonian: Emily Greene Balch* (New York: Twayne Publishers, Inc., 1964), pp. 157–58.

53. Jane Addams, Emily G. Balch, and Alice Hamilton, *Women at The Hague: The International Congress of Women and Its Results* (New York: Macmillan Company, 1915), pp. 150–59.

54. Lela B. Costin, "Feminism, Pacifism, Internationalism, and the 1915 International Congress of Women," *Women's Studies International Forum*, 5, no. 3/4 (1982), 300–315.

55. G. Abbott to Lizzie Abbott, postcard, 1915, Abbott Papers, C. A. Addenda.

56. G. Abbott to her family, May 17, 1915, Abbott Papers, C. A. Addenda.

57. Alice Hamilton to her family, May 15, 1915, Alice Hamilton Papers, A22, Folder 5.

58. G. Abbott, *The Immigrant and the Community* (New York: Century Co., 1917), p. 276.

59. *Program of the Conference of Oppressed or Dependent Nationalities*, Washington, Dec. 10th and 11th, 1916, under the auspices of the American Delegation to the Congress-after-the-War of the International Committee of Women for Permanent Peace, Abbott Papers, C. A. Addenda; G. Abbott to Paul U. Kellogg, Nov. 2, 1916, Survey Papers.

60. E. Abbott, Notes and ms.; Bruno Lasker, "Spokesman of Submerged Peoples. The Conference of Oppressed or Dependent Nationalities," *The Survey*, 37 (Dec. 16, 1916), 293–95.

61. E. Abbott to Josephine Roche, n.d., Edward P. Costigan Papers.

62. G. Abbott to S. P. Breckinridge, 2 letters in 1916, undated, Breckinridge Papers, Box 1, Folder 2.

63. Helen R. Wright, "Three against Time: Edith and Grace Abbott and Sophonisba P. Breckinridge," *Social Service Review*, 28 (Mar. 1954), 41–53; "The Common Welfare. Miss Lathrop and the Chicago Institute," *Charities and the Commons*, 18 (Apr.–Oct. 1907) 701–2.

64. Julia C. Lathrop to E. Abbott, Mar. 25, 1908, Abbott Papers, Box 57, Folder 5.

65. S. P. Breckinridge to E. Abbott, Apr. 13, 1908, Breckinridge

Papers, Box 1, Folder 2; Wright, "Three against Time," p. 44; Jane Addams, *My Friend, Julia Lathrop* (New York: Macmillan Co., 1935), p. 159.

66. "The Common Welfare. Miss Lathrop and the Chicago Institute," pp. 701–2; "The Common Welfare. The New Academic Year in the Training Schools for Social Work," *Charities and the Commons*, 19 (Oct. 1907–Mar. 1908), 893–95.

67. S. P. Breckinridge and E. Abbott, "Chicago's Housing Problem: Families in Furnished Rooms," *American Journal of Sociology*, 16 (Nov. 1910), 289–308; "Housing Conditions in Chicago, III: Back of the Yards," ibid., 16 (Jan. 1911), 433–68; "Chicago Housing Conditions, IV: The West Side Revisited," ibid., 17 (July 1911), 1–34; "Chicago Housing Conditions, IV," ibid.; "South Chicago at the Gates of the Steel Mills," ibid., 17, no. 2 (Sept. 1911), 145–76.

68. S. P. Breckinridge and E. Abbott, *The Delinquent Child and the Home* (New York: Russell Sage Foundation, 1912).

69. Maude Marshall to E. Abbott, Aug. 12, 1912, Breckinridge Papers, Box 1, Folder 2.

70. E. Abbott and S. P. Breckinridge, *Truancy and Non-Attendance in the Chicago Schools: A Study of the Social Aspects of the Compulsory Education and Child Labor Legislation of Illinois* (Chicago: University of Chicago Press, 1917).

71. E. Abbott, *The Real Jail Problem* (Chicago: Juvenile Protective Association of Chicago, 1915); *The One Hundred and One County Jails of Illinois and Why They Ought to Be Abolished* (Chicago: Juvenile Protective Association of Chicago, 1916), p. 1.

72. E. Abbott, "Cheap Clothes and Nasty," *New Republic*, 3 (Jan. 1, 1916), 217–19.

73. Edith Abbott, "Field-Work and the Training of the Social Workers," in *Proceedings of the National Conference of Charities and Correction at the Forty-second Annual Session, . . . May 12–19, 1915* (Chicago: Hildmann Printing Co., 1915), pp. 615–21.

74. E. Abbott, "Are Women Business Failures?" *Harper's Weekly*, (Apr. 8, 1905), 496.

75. Wade, *Graham Taylor*, pp. 161–85; E. Abbott to Julia Lathrop, Aug. 17, 1920, Abbott Papers, C. A. Addenda.

76. E. Abbott to Julia Lathrop, Aug. 17, 1920, Abbott Papers, C. A. Addenda; Felix Frankfurter, "Social Work and Professional Training," in *Proc. of NCCC, 1915*, pp. 591–96.

77. Wade, *Graham Taylor*, p. 174.

78. E. Abbott, "Field-Work and the Training of the Social Workers," pp. 615–21.

79. E. Abbott, "Twenty-one Years of University Education for the Social Services, 1920–41," *Social Service Review*, 15 (Dec. 1941), 670–705.

80. Wade, *Graham Taylor*, p. 177.

81. Ibid., p. 176.

82. E. Abbott to Julia Lathrop, Aug. 17, 1920, Abbott Papers, C. A. Addenda.

83. Ibid.

84. Wade, *Graham Taylor*, pp. 176–77.

85. "Bulletin of Information," University of Chicago, Graduate School of Social Service Administration, 20 (June 1920), 3.

86. For example, E. Abbott to Gertrude Vaile, May 20, 1920, letter made available by the School of Social Service Administration.

87. Julia Lathrop to E. Abbott, Aug. 10, 1920, Abbott Papers, Box 3, Folder 11.

88. E. Abbott, "Twenty-one Years," p. 671.

89. Wade, *Graham Taylor*, pp. 176, 177.

90. Ibid., p. 183.

91. E. Abbott to Julia Lathrop, Aug. 17, 1920, Abbott Papers, C. A. Addenda.

92. E. Abbott to Gertrude Vaile, May 20, 1920.

93. E. Abbott, "Twenty-one Years," p. 705.

94. Wade, *Graham Taylor*, p. 175, n. 33.

CHAPTER 4: *Advocacy and Immigrants*

1. Message of President Grover Cleveland, vetoing the Immigration Bill of 1897, which provided a literacy test for the admission of aliens, U.S., 54th Cong., 2nd Sess., Senate Doc. no. 185.

2. "Eleven Years of Community Service. A Summary of the Work of the Immigrants' Protective League," Jane Addams Memorial Collection, pp. 2, 10; E. Abbott, Notes and ms.

3. E. Abbott, Notes and ms.

4. Harry Barnard, *The Forging of an American Jew. The Life and Times of Judge Julian W. Mack* (New York: Herzl Press, 1974).

5. E. Abbott, "Grace Abbott and Hull-House, 1908–21, Part II," *Social Service Review*, 24 (Dec. 1950), 498–99.

6. "Ernst Freund, 1864–1932," *University Record*, 19 (Jan. 1933), 39–47.

7. IPL, *Annual Report* (Chicago: Immigrants' Protective League, 1908–9).

8. James R. W. Leiby, "How Social Workers Viewed 'The Immigra-

tion Problem'—1880–1930," in *Current Issues in Social Work Seen in Historical Perspective*, no. 62-18-26 (New York: Council on Social Work Education, 1962), pp. 30–42.

9. S. P. Breckinridge, *New Homes for Old* (New York: Harper and Brothers, Publishers, 1921), p. 223.

10. IPL, *Annual Reports*, see staff rosters for 1908 to 1920.

11. G. Abbott, *The Immigrant and the Community* (New York: Century Company, 1917), p. 16.

12. Edith Abbott, "A Sister's Memories," *Social Service Review*, 13 (Sept. 1939), 357–58; E. Abbott, Notes and ms.

13. Allen F. Davis, *American Heroine. The Life and Legend of Jane Addams* (New York: Oxford University Press, 1973), pp. 117–18.

14. IPL, *Annual Reports*, particularly 1914, pp. 7–11, and 1916, p. 20.

15. Ibid., 1913, pp. 17–20; E. Abbott, *Immigration: Select Documents and Case Records* (Chicago: University of Chicago Press, 1924), pp. 695–718.

16. IPL, *Annual Reports*, 1911, pp. 20–21; 1913, pp. 17–20; 1915, pp. 10–12; 1917, pp. 19–20; G. Abbott, *Immigrant and the Community*, pp. 81–104.

17. E. Abbott, "A Sister's Memories," pp. 371–74.

18. E. Abbott, "Statistics Relating to Crime in Chicago," in *Report of the City Council Committee of Chicago on Crime in the City of Chicago* (Chicago: City Council Committee, 1915), pp. 19–88.

19. G. Abbott, "The Chicago Employment Agency and the Immigrant Worker," *American Journal of Sociology*, 14 (Nov. 1908), 289–305.

20. Ibid., pp. 297–98; G. Abbott, "The Bulgarians of Chicago," *Charities and the Commons*, 21 (1909), 658–60.

21. IPL, *Annual Report*, 1909–1910, pp. 27–29; E. Abbott, "A Sister's Memories," p. 360.

22. Personal generosity to professionals active in causes of interest to them was characteristic of the Dauchys. See Mary Anderson, *Woman at Work. The Autobiography of Mary Anderson* (Minneapolis: University of Minnesota Press, 1951), pp. 79–80.

23. O. A. Abbott to G. Abbott, Jan. 26, 1909; G. Abbott to Lizzie Abbott, n.d.; E. Abbott to O. A. Abbott, Jr., Mar. 8, 1909, Abbott Papers, C. A. Addenda.

24. Matthew Josephson, *Sidney Hillman. Statesman of American Labor* (New York: Doubleday and Co., 1952), pp. 38–57.

25. "The Common Welfare—Garment Workers' Strike in Chicago," *The Survey*, 25 (Nov. 19, 1910), 273.

26. "End of the Chicago Garment Strike," *The Survey*, 25 (Feb. 11, 1911), 796.

27. E. Abbott, "Grace Abbott and Hull-House, 1908–21, Part I," *Social Service Review*, 24 (Sept. 1950), 393–94, for Hillman's letter, n.d. (but probably 1939).

28. G. Abbott, "A Study of the Greeks in Chicago," *American Journal of Sociology*, 15 (Oct. 1909), 379–93; "Bulgarians of Chicago," pp. 653–60.

29. IPL, *Annual Report*, 1911–12, p. 21.

30. E. Abbott to Lizzie Abbott, Sept. 22, 1911, Abbott Papers, C. A. Addenda.

31. E. Abbott to Lizzie Abbott, Sept. 22, 1911, and n.d.; G. Abbott to Lizzie Abbott, Nov. 10, 1911, Abbott Papers, C. A. Addenda.

32. IPL, *Annual Report*, 1910–11; G. Abbott's Notebook of 1911 trip to Central Europe, Abbott Papers, Box 81, Folder 2; G. Abbott to E. Abbott, ibid., Box 2, Folder 13; G. Abbott to Lizzie Abbott, Sept. 23 and Oct. 12, 1911, ibid., C. A. Addenda; Leiby, "How Social Workers Viewed 'Immigration Problem,'" pp. 40–41.

33. IPL, *Annual Report*, 1910–11, p. 30.

34. E. Abbott, *Immigration*, pp. 198–99; "The Common Welfare. The U.S. Immigration Commission Report," *The Survey*, 25 (Oct. 1910–Mar. 1911), 517–19; "Recommendations of the United States Immigration Commission," ibid., pp. 603–4; Edward T. Devine, "Immigration as a Relief Problem," *Charities*, 12 (Feb. 6, 1904), 129–33; and Devine, "Social Forces," *The Survey*, 25 (Feb. 4, 1911), 715–16.

35. Henry Cabot Lodge, *Congressional Record*, Mar. 16, 1896, 54th Cong., 1st sess., pp. 2817–20.

36. IPL, *Annual Report*, 1910–11, pp. 6–7.

37. G. Abbott, "Adjustment—Not Restriction," *The Survey*, 25 (Jan. 7, 1911), 527–29.

38. E. Abbott, "Grace Abbott and Hull-House, Part II," p. 493, n. 20.

39. E. Abbott to Lizzie Abbott, n.d., Abbott Papers, C. A. Addenda.

40. "Testing a Race by Its Literacy," *New Republic*, 2 (Feb. 6, 1915), 8. The four veto messages in *Congressional Record*, Feb. 1, 1917, pp. 2691–94.

41. G. Abbott, *Immigrant and the Community*, pp. 55–56.

42. Ibid., p. 61.

43. IPL, *Annual Report*, 1909–10, pp. 21, 25.

44. Ibid., 1911–12, p. 11; G. Abbott, *Immigrant and the Community*, pp. 71–75.

45. G. Abbott, *Immigrant and the Community*, pp. 77–78.

46. IPL, *Annual Report*, 1909–10, pp. 6–8, 15–19.

47. Roy Lubove, "The Progressive and the Prostitute," *The Historian*, 24 (May 1962), 308–30; John C. Burnham, "The Progressive Era Revolution in American Attitudes toward Sex," *Journal of American History*, 59 (Mar. 1973), 885–908; Egal Feldman, "Prostitution, the Alien Woman and the Progressive Imagination, 1910–1915," *American Quarterly*, 19, no. 2 (1967), 192–206; George Kibbe Turner, "The City of Chicago. A Study of the Great Immoralities," *McClure's Magazine*, 28 (Apr. 1907), 575–92.

48. G. Abbott, *Immigrant and the Community*; IPL, *Annual Report*, 1909–10.

49. Children's Bureau, *Annual Report*, 1923, pp. 31–32.

50. G. Abbott to S. P. Breckinridge, Nov. 22, 1922, Breckinridge Papers, Box 1, Folder 3. Florence Kelley to E. Abbott, n.d., Abbott Papers, Box 57, Folder 1.

51. Arthur Sweetser to G. Abbott, Nov. 14, 1922, Abbott Papers, Box 61, Folder 1; Manley O. Hudson to G. Abbott, Oct. 29, 1922, ibid., C. A. Addenda; Harriett B. Laidlaw to G. Abbott, Oct. 19, 1922, ibid., Box 61, Folder 1.

52. Advisory Committee on the Traffic of Women and Children, *League of Nations Reports*, 2d sess., Mar. 22 to 27, 1923, and 4th sess., May 20 to 27, 1925, C 225 M. 129, 1923, IV, pp. 27, 30–31, and Annex 10, p. 61; C 382 M. 126, 1925, IV, p. 15; E. Abbott, "Three American Pioneers in International Social Welfare," *The Compass*, 28 (May 1947), 6.

53. G. Abbott to Raymond B. Fosdick, May 21, 1923; Fosdick to G. Abbott, Oct. 4, 1923, Abbott Papers, Box 61, Folder 1.

54. "Trade Routes of White Slavers," *The Survey*, 59 (Jan. 15, 1928), 486–88.

55. *League of Nations Report*, 4th sess., pp. 16–22, 29, 104–9, 112; Children's Bureau, *Annual Report*, 1925, pp. 35–38; "Memorandum re proposed child welfare program, submitted by Miss Grace Abbott of the United States of America," Abbott Papers, Box 61, Folder 1.

56. "Memorandum re proposed child welfare program," ibid., pp. 401–13.

57. John Palmer Gavit, "The World Notices the Child," *The Survey*, 54 (July 1, 1925), 401, 413.

58. Raymond B. Fosdick, Letter to the editor, *New York Times*, May 24, 1925, Sect. 2, p. 6.

59. G. Abbott to Kenneth Eslinger, Dec. 17, 1937, Abbott Papers,

Box 61, Folder 1; Manley O. Hudson to G. Abbott, Feb. 10, 1923, ibid., C. A. Addenda.

60. Julius Rosenwald to S. P. Breckinridge, Jan. 24, 1918, IPL Correspondence and Reports, Immigrants' Protective League Papers, Box 11.

61. Davis, *American Heroine*, pp. 74–75; E. Abbott, Notes and ms.

62. J. Addams to F. Kelley, June 27, 1922, Abbott Papers, Box 3, Folder 3.

63. J. Addams to G. Abbott, Mar. 30, 1934; Alice Hamilton to G. Abbott, May 20, 1935; Louise de Koven Bowen to G. Abbott, Aug. 5, 1935; Alice Hamilton to G. Abbott, Aug. 12, 1935, Abbott Papers, Box 55, Folder 1.

64. Grace Abbott was given a leave of absence from the IPL in 1913 to direct the work of a special Immigration Commission appointed by the Massachusetts legislature for the purpose of making a full investigation of the status of the immigrant in that state. Only six months and a budget not to exceed $15,000 were allowed for the undertaking. Grace Abbott completed her report on time and returned an unexpended balance of $2500 to the state. A member of the commission gave this commendation: "she planned and carried through a comprehensive investigation of conditions and wrote a report of which it was said 'on State Street' that it was the ablest State paper ever issued in the Commonwealth." Commonwealth of Massachusetts, *Report of the Commission on Immigration. The Problem of Immigration in Massachusetts*, House Report no. 2300 (Boston: Wright and Potter Printing Co., 1914); E. Abbott, "Grace Abbott and Hull-House, Part II," pp. 496–97 and n. 21.

CHAPTER 5: *The Iniquity of the Fathers*

1. Grace Abbott, *The Child and the State*, vol. 1 (Chicago: University of Chicago Press, 1938), p. 79.

2. Jane Addams, *My Friend, Julia Lathrop* (New York: Macmillan Co., 1935), p. 49.

3. Quoted in Dorothy Bradbury, "A History of the Children's Bureau," p. 147 (manuscript in possession of Dorothy Bradbury).

4. S. P. Breckinridge to Julia C. Lathrop, Apr. 30, 1917, Abbott Papers, Box 59, Folder 4.

5. E. Abbott, "A Study of the Early History of Child Labor in America," *American Journal of Sociology*, 14 (Nov. 1908), 16.

6. Robert H. Bremner, ed., *Children and Youth in America. A Documentary History*. II, 1866–1932, Parts 1–6 (Cambridge: Harvard University Press, 1971), p. 601.

7. E. Abbott and S. P. Breckinridge, "Employment of Women in

Industries: Twelfth Census Statistics," *Journal of Political Economy*, 14 (Jan. 1906), 14–40; Mary E. McDowell, "The Need for a National Investigation into Women's Work," *Charities and the Commons*, 17 (Oct. 1907), 634–36; Allen F. Davis, *Spearheads for Reform. The Social Settlements and the Progressive Movement. 1890–1914* (New York: Oxford University Press, 1967), pp. 133–35; Eleanor Flexner, *Century of Struggle. The Woman's Rights Movement in the United States* (New York: Atheneum, 1973), p. 213.

8. U.S., Cong., Senate, *Report on the Condition of Women and Child Wage-Earners in the United States*, Senate Doc. no. 645, 19 vols. (Washington, D.C., 1910–13).

9. G. Abbott, *Child and the State*, p. 265.

10. Ibid., p. 462.

11. Arthur S. Link and William B. Catton, *American Epoch*, vol. I (New York: Alfred A. Knopf, 1973), p. 123.

12. "An Act to Prevent Interstate Commerce in the Products of Child Labor," 39 Stat. 675–76 (1916).

13. Children's Bureau, *Annual Report*, 1917, p. 6.

14. G. Abbott to E. Abbott, May 9, 1917, Abbott Papers, C. A. Addenda.

15. Grace Abbott, *Administration of the First Child-Labor Law*, Legal Series no. 6, Industrial Series no. 6, C. B. Pub. no. 78, 1921, p. 7.

16. G. Abbott, untitled speech, Abbott Papers, Box 25, Folder 11.

17. Ibid.

18. Robert W. McAhren, "Making the Nation Safe for Children: A History of the Movement for Federal Regulation of Child Labor. 1900–1938" (Ph.D. dissertation, University of Texas, 1967); Louis J. Covotsos, "Child Welfare and Social Progress: A History of the United States Children's Bureau, 1912–1935," (Ph.D. dissertation, University of Chicago, 1976).

19. Covotsos, "Child Welfare"; Walter I. Trattner, *Crusade for Children* (Chicago: Quadrangle Books, 1970), pp. 85–87, 100–101, 133–35.

20. Florence Kelley to G. Abbott, Nov. 27, 1917, Abbott Papers, C. A. Addenda.

21. G. Abbott, *Administration of the First Child-Labor Law*, pp. 21–25, 53.

22. Ibid., p. 54.

23. G. Abbott to Frances Perkins, Mar. 21, 1933, Abbott Papers, C. A. Addenda; untitled speech, ibid., Box 25, Folder 11.

24. Julia Lathrop to Anna Rochester, Sept. 15, 1916, and Owen Lovejoy to Julia Lathrop, Nov. 13, 1916, Children's Bureau Papers, Drawer 25-1-1, cited in Covotsos, "Child Welfare," pp. 175–76.

25. G. Abbott, *Administration of the First Child-Labor Law*, p. 54.

26. Ibid., pp. 29–30.

27. Ibid., pp. 32–52.

28. For example, see Mrs. L. P. Dillon to G. Abbott, Apr. 22, 1918, and G. Abbott to Mrs. L. P. Dillon, Apr. 27, 1918, Children's Bureau Papers, RG 102, Folder 25-2-1-1.

29. "Strategy for Testing the Act," letter to the editor, *Southern Textile Bulletin*, Aug. 24, 1916, p. 10, in Bremner, *Children and Youth*, pp. 710–11.

30. Trattner, *Crusade for Children*, p. 135.

31. Children's Bureau, *Annual Report*, 1918, pp. 6–7; G. Abbott to E. Abbott, n.d., Abbott Papers, C. A. Addenda.

32. *Hammer* v. *Dagenhart*, 247 U.S. 251, 268 (1918).

33. G. Abbott to Lizzie Abbott, June 4, 1918, Abbott Papers, C. A. Addenda.

34. Children's Bureau, *Annual Report*, 1918, p. 7.

35. Ibid.

36. Ibid., pp. 7–8.

37. G. Abbott, *Administration of the First Child-Labor Law*, p. 134.

38. Covotsos, "Child Welfare"; Children's Bureau, *Annual Reports*, 1917, pp. 32–49, and 1918, pp. 23–25.

39. Neither the 1909 or 1919 conferences were termed White House conferences. Only after Herbert Hoover used that term for the 1930 Conference on Child Health and Protection were the earlier ones also referred to generally as White House conferences.

40. Children's Bureau, *Annual Report*, 1918, p. 25.

41. *Standards of Child Welfare. A Report of the Children's Bureau Conferences, May and June 1919*, C. B. Pub. no. 60, 1919, p. 12.

42. *New York Times*, Dec. 15, 1919, p. 9, col. 3.

43. G. Abbott's notebook of her European activities, 1919, Abbott Papers, C. A. Addenda.

44. Ibid.; G. Abbott to E. Abbott, Dec. 27, 1918, Abbott Papers, Box 2, Folder 13.

45. G. Abbott's appointment book, Abbott Papers, C. A. Addenda.

46. McAhren, "Making the Nation Safe for Children," p. 113.

47. "Taxes to Drive Out Child Labor," *The Survey*, 41 (Nov. 23, 1918), 221.

48. Lilian Brandt, "A Program for Child Protection. Fourteenth National Conference on Child Labor," *The Survey*, 41 (Dec. 14, 1918), 338–42.

49. Transcript of a telephone conversation between Owen Lovejoy

and Julia Lathrop, Nov. 22, 1918; Julia Lathrop to Owen Lovejoy, Dec. 5, 1918, Children's Bureau Papers, File 26-1-o, cited in McAhren, "Making the Nation Safe for Children," p. 112.

50. G. Abbott to Carrie Chapman Catt, Sept. 1, 1921, Children's Bureau Papers, File 10-9-1 (1), cited in McAhren, "Making the Nation Safe for Children," p. 116.

51. "Working Papers," *The Survey*, 41 (Mar. 22, 1919), 895.

52. Helen T. Wooley to Carrie Chapman Catt, May 10, 1919, Abbott Papers, Box 62, Folder 5.

53. Trattner, *Crusade for Children*, p. 135.

54. From England: Sir Arthur Newsholme, Chief Medical Officer of the Local Government Board, who had made strong contributions to measures designed to lessen the infant mortality rate in England; Mrs. Eleanor Barton, of the Women's Cooperative Guild, an organization of the wives of British wage earners that had advocated the national protection of maternity and infancy; Sir Cyril Jackson, Board of Education, London; and Mr. R. C. Davison, director of the Juvenile Labor Exchanges; from France: Dr. Clothilde Mulon, of the War Department, supervisor of crèches maintained in connection with munitions plants; from Belgium, Dr. René Sand, professor of social and industrial medicine at the University of Brussels and advisor to the Ministry of Labor; Miss L. E. Carter, principal of High School C, Brussels; Mr. Isador Maus, director of the Division of Child Protection, Ministry of Justice; from Japan: Mr. Takayuki Namaye, Interior Department, in charge of reformatory and relief work and the protection of children; from Serbia: Dr. Radmila Lazarevitch Milochevitch, a physician and leader in social activities; from Italy: Professor Fabio Frassetto, professor of anthropology, University of Bologna.

55. *Standards of Child Welfare*, pp. 431–44.

56. S. P. Breckinridge to Edith Campbell, Dec. 18, 1917; "Employment of Women at Frankford Arsenal, Philadelphia, PA., inspected Nov. 26, 1917," Breckinridge Papers, Box 3, Folder W, cited in J. Stanley Lemons, *The Woman Citizen: Social Feminism in the 1920s* (Urbana: University of Illinois Press, 1973), p. 28.

57. G. Abbott to S. P. Breckinridge, July 26, 1919, Breckinridge Papers, Box 1, Folder 3.

58. G. Abbott to E. Abbott, June 19, 1919, Abbott Papers, Box 2, Folder 13.

59. Lizzie Abbott to G. Abbott, June 18, 1920; Lizzie Abbott to G. Abbott, Nov. 1, 1920; O. A. Abbott to G. Abbott, Oct. 31, 1920, Abbott Papers, C. A. Addenda.

60. G. Abbott, *Educational Needs of Immigrants in Illinois*, and *The Immigrant and the Coal-mining Communities in Illinois* (Springfield: Illinois State Immigrants' Commission, 1920).

61. E. Abbott, "Grace Abbott and Hull-House, 1908–1921, Part II," *Social Service Review*, 24 (Dec. 1950) 493–518; Grace Abbott to Esther Loeb Kohn, July 9, 1921, University of Illinois at Chicago Special Collections, Correspondence with Hull-House Associates VII, Box 13.

62. Letters of support and application of Sara W. Lyons, Record Group 174, Chief Clerk's File 150-7, National Archives.

63. Letters of support and application of Mrs. H. A. Kluegel, Record Group 174, Chief Clerk's File 150-7, National Archives.

64. Julia Lathrop to G. Abbott, Apr. 1, 1921, Abbott Papers, Box 57, Folder 7.

65. Julia Lathrop to G. Abbott, June 4, 1921, Abbott Papers, Box 57, Folder 7.

66. G. Abbott to Mary Dewson, n.d., Mary Dewson Papers.

67. Florence Kelley to G. Abbott, Apr. 8, 1921, Abbott Papers, C. A. Addenda.

68. Warren G. Harding Papers (microfilm), Roll 140, Box 436, Presidential Case Files, File 14, Children's Bureau, Ohio Historical Society.

69. Letters re. G. Abbott's Appointment as Chief of Children's Bureau, Record Group 174, Chief Clerk's Files 141–12, National Archives.

70. Julia Lathrop to G. Abbott, Apr. 6 and Apr. 15, Abbott Papers, Box 57, Folder 7.

71. Each of the Abbott sisters was a registered Republican throughout her voting years, but Grace, as her father termed it, tended to stray from the fold. She referred to herself as a "Progressive Republican." She voted for Theodore Roosevelt when he was the Progressive candidate in 1912, for Woodrow Wilson in 1916, for Robert La Follette in 1924, for Herbert Hoover in 1928, and for Franklin Roosevelt in 1932 and 1936. No clear evidence indicates whether she voted for Harding in 1920, although remarks she made to her niece suggest that she did not.

72. S. P. Breckinridge to Grace Abbott, Oct. 11, 1921, Breckinridge Papers, Box 1, Folder 3; G. Abbott to Julius Rosenwald, Oct. 17, 1921, Abbott Papers, Box 60, Folder 4; Julius Rosenwald to G. Abbott, Oct. 19, 1921, ibid., C. A. Addenda; E. Abbott, Notes and ms.; G. Abbott's notes on interview with Secretary Davis and Lasker, Aug. 19, 1921, Abbott Papers, Box 21, Folder 9.

73. Harriet Taylor Upton to President Warren G. Harding, Aug. 8, 1921, Warren G. Harding Papers (microfilm), Roll 140, Box 436, Presidential Case Files, File 14, Children's Bureau.

74. James J. Davis to President Warren G. Harding, Aug. 19, 1921, Warren G. Harding Papers (microfilm), Roll 140, Box 436, Presidential Case Files, File 14, Children's Bureau.

75. James J. Davis to Honorable Frank O. Lowden, Apr. 19, 1921, Record Group 174, Chief Clerk's Files 141-12, National Archives.

76. Herbert Hoover to Julius Rosenwald, Aug. 22, 1921, Presidential Papers, Herbert Hoover Library, Commerce Official.

77. Interview with Ella Oppenheimer, M.D., Apr. 25, 1974.

CHAPTER 6: *Not Charity. Justice!*

1. U.S., 66th Cong., 3rd Sess., House, Committee on Interstate and Foreign Commerce, *Public Protection of Maternity and Infancy, Hearings on HR 10925*, Testimony of Florence Kelley, Dec. 20, 1920, pp. 27–29.

2. Clarke A. Chambers, *Seedtime of Reform. American Social Service and Social Action 1918–1933* (Minneapolis: University of Minnesota Press, 1963).

3. Florence Kelley, *Some Ethical Gains through Legislation* (New York: Macmillan, 1905), pp. 99–104; Josephine Goldmark, *Impatient Crusader. Florence Kelley's Life Story* (Urbana: University of Illinois Press, 1953), pp. 94–100; Dorothy E. Bradbury, *Four Decades of Action for Children. A Short History of the Children's Bureau*, C. B. Pub. no. 358, 1956, pp. 1–4; Lillian Wald, "The Idea of the Federal Children's Bureau," in *Proceedings of the National Conference of Social Work*, 1932, pp. 33–37.

4. "An Act establishing the Children's Bureau," 37 Stat. 79 (Apr. 9, 1912).

5. Children's Bureau, *Annual Report*, 1921, p. 7.

6. Julia Lathrop to G. Abbott, Apr. 8, 1921, Abbott Papers, Box 57, Folder 7.

7. Louis J. Covotsos, "Child Welfare and Social Progress: A History of the United States Children's Bureau, 1912–1935" (Ph.D. dissertation, University of Chicago, 1976), p. 54.

8. I found this recollection repeatedly in interviews I conducted with persons who had worked with Grace Abbott during her years as chief of the Children's Bureau.

9. G. Abbott to Lizzie Abbott, n.d., Abbott Papers, C. A. Addenda.

10. Conversation with Beatrice McConnell, Apr. 1974.

11. Interviews with Elisabeth Shirley Enochs, June 4, 1973; with Dorothy Bradbury, June 4, 1973; with Ella Oppenheimer, M.D., Apr. 25, 1974.

12. Julia Lathrop to Emma O. Lundberg, Jan. 14, 1916, Abbott Papers, Box 59, Folder 3; Lundberg to Lathrop, Jan. 17, 1916, ibid.

13. Emma O. Lundberg to G. Abbott, 1924, Children's Bureau Papers, RG 102, 1921–24, 1-3-01; G. Abbott to Isabelle Hopkins, Dec. 6, 1924, ibid., Box 281; G. Abbott to Lundberg, Apr. 15, 1925, and Lundberg to G. Abbott, Apr. 16, 1925, Abbott Papers, Box 36, Folder 3.

14. Beatrice McConnell interview.

15. Interview with Elisabeth Shirley Enochs, June 4, 1973, and Oct. 7, 1973.

16. Ibid.; "Battleships and Babies," Children's Bureau publicity scrapbook 12 (July 1931–Nov. 1933), Abbott Papers, Box 53; "A. Piatt Andrew Would Abolish Children's Bureau," *Boston Evening Transcript*, Nov. 5, 1927, sec. 5, p. 8.

17. E. Abbott to Lizzie Abbott, n.d., Abbott Papers, Box 53.

18. Grace L. Meigs, M.D., *Maternal Mortality from All Conditions Connected with Childbirth in the United States and Certain Other Countries*, C. B. Pub. no. 19, 1917; *Birth Registration: An Aid in Protecting the Lives and Rights of Children*, C. B. Pub. no. 2, 1914.

19. Meigs, *Maternal Mortality*, pp. 7–8.

20. Oliver Wendell Holmes, "The Contagiousness of Puerperal Fever," in *Medical Essays, 1842–1882* (Boston: Houghton Mifflin and Co., 1889), pp. 104–72.

21. Ignaz Semmelweis, "The Etiology, Concept and Prophylaxis of Childbirth Fever," in Sir William J. Sinclair, *Semmelweiss, His Life and His Doctrine. A Chapter in the History of Medicine* (Manchester: University Press, 1909), pp. 48–61.

22. Meigs, *Maternal Mortality*, p. 18.

23. Ibid., pp. 10–13.

24. Ibid., pp. 24–25.

25. Viola I. Paradise, *Maternity Care and the Welfare of Young Children in a Homesteading County in Montana*, C. B. Pub. no. 34, 1919, pp. 27–34; extracts from letters of Mrs. ———, of Southwestern Wyoming, to the Children's Bureau, 1916–17, Abbott Papers, Box 62, Folder 10–11; Children's Bureau, *Annual Report*, 1917, pp. 18–19.

26. Grace Abbott, "The Midwife in Chicago," *American Journal of Sociology*, 20 (Mar. 1915), 684–99; Maurice J. Lewi, "What Shall Be Done with the Professional Midwife?" *Transactions of the Medical Society of the State of New York*, 1902, pp. 282–84, cited in Robert H. Bremner, ed., *Children and Youth in America. A Documentary History*, II, 1866–1932 (Cambridge: Harvard University Press, 1971), pp. 983–84; Josephine Baker, *Fighting for Life* (New York: Macmillan Co., 1939), pp. 111–17;

Ellen A. Stone, "The Midwives of Rhode Island," *Providence Medical Journal*, 13 (1912), 58–59, in Bremner, *Children and Youth*, pp. 988–89.

27. Emma Duke, *Infant Mortality; Results of a Field Study in Johnstown, Pa.*, C. B. Pub. no. 9, 1915, pp. 1–99.

28. Mildred Adams, *The Right to Be People* (Philadelphia: J. B. Lippincott Co., 1967), pp. 171–72.

29. G. Abbott to Mrs. W. E. Barkeley, Dec. 1921, Children's Bureau Papers, Drawer 430, cited in Covotsos, "Child Welfare," p. 140.

30. "An Act for the Promotion of the Welfare and Hygiene of Maternity and Infancy" (Sheppard-Towner Act), 43 Stat. 135 (Nov. 23, 1921).

31. Martha M. Eliot, "The Children's Bureau: Fifty Years of Public Responsibility for Action in Behalf of Children," *American Journal of Public Health*, 52 (Apr. 1962), 576.

32. Meigs, *Maternal Mortality*, p. 26; Julia Lathrop to Bleeker Marquette, Dec. 1, 1920, Children's Bureau Papers, Drawer 408, cited in Covotsos, "Child Welfare," p. 123.

33. Grace Abbott, "Administration of the Sheppard-Towner Act: Plans for Maternal Care," *Transactions of the American Child Hygiene Association*, 13 (1922), 194–201, found in Bremner, *Children and Youth*, pp. 1006–7.

34. Excerpts sent to Illinois newspapers from the address of G. Abbott, on "Building Child Welfare Programs," Annual Convention of Illinois League of Women Voters, Peoria, Ill., Nov. 15, 1927, Abbott Papers, C. A. Addenda; address by G. Abbott before the conference of state and provincial health authorities, May 15, 1922, Children's Bureau Papers, RG 102, 1921–24, 8225 and 8231.

35. Address by G. Abbott before conference of state and provincial health authorities.

36. *The Promotion of the Welfare and Hygiene of Maternity and Infancy. The Administration of the Act of Congress of November 21, 1921, for the Period of March 20, 1922 to June 30, 1923*, C. B. Pub. no. 137, 1924, p. 5; Children's Bureau, *Annual Report*, 1929, p. 1.

37. Children's Bureau, *Annual Report*, 1922, p. 5.

38. U.S., 69th Cong., 1st Sess., House, Committee on Appropriations, *Appropriations, Department of Labor, 1927: Hearing before Subcommittee*, Statement by Grace Abbott, Feb. 3, 1926, p. 92.

39. Statement by G. Abbott, *Congressional Digest*, 10 (Feb. 1931), 38.

40. U.S., 69th Cong., 1st Sess., House, Statement by G. Abbott, p. 93.

41. Ibid.; Children's Bureau, *Annual Reports*, 1922–29.

42. Children's Bureau, *Annual Reports*, 1922–29.

43. Ibid.
44. Ibid.
45. Interview with Elisabeth Shirley Enochs, June 4, 1973.
46. Grace Abbott, "Midwife in Chicago," pp. 684–99.
47. U.S., 69th Cong., 1st Sess., House, Statement by G. Abbott, pp. 94–95; Children's Bureau, *Annual Reports*, 1922–29.
48. U.S., 69th Cong., 1st Sess., House, Statement by G. Abbott, p. 95.
49. Ibid., pp. 95–96; *Standards of Prenatal Care. An Outline for the Use of Physicians*, C. B. Pub. no. 153, 1925; U.S. Children's Bureau, Committee on Standards for Physicians Conducting Conferences in Child-Health Centers, *Standards for Physicians Conducting Conferences in Child Health Centers* (Washington, D.C.: Government Printing Office, 1926).
50. E. Abbott, Notes and ms.
51. *Commonwealth of Massachusetts* v. *Andrew W. Mellon, Secretary of the Treasury, Grace Abbott, Chief of the Children's Bureau of the Department of Labor, Hugh S. Cumming, Surgeon General of the Public Health Service, John J. Tigert, Commissioner of Education*, 262 U.S. 447.
52. E. Abbott, "A Sister's Memories," *Social Service Review*, 13, (Sept. 1939), 390–91.
53. *Harriett Frothingham* v. *Andrew W. Mellon et al.*, 262 U.S. 447.
54. G. Abbott to Sec. of Labor James J. Davis, May 18, 1922, Children's Bureau Papers, Box 430, 1921–24, Folder 11052—U.S. Supreme Court 1923; Julia Lathrop to G. Abbott, May 24, 1922, Abbott Papers, Box 57, Folder 8; G. Abbott to Julia Lathrop, May 27, 1922, ibid., Box 62, Folder 6; Felix Frankfurter to G. Abbott, Oct. 17, 1922, ibid., C. A. Addenda; Felix Frankfurter to G. Abbott, Oct. 23, 1922, ibid.; Cornelia B. Pinchot to Florence Kelley, Sept. 23, 1922, ibid.; G. Abbott to Julia Lathrop, May 2, 1923, Abbott Papers, Box 57, Folder 9.
55. G. Abbott to E. Abbott, Spring 1923, Abbott Papers, C. A. Addenda.
56. *Commonwealth of Massachusetts* v. *Mellon et al.*; *Frothingham* v. *Mellon et al.*; also in 43 Sup. Ct. Rep. 597, found in Bremner, *Children and Youth*, pp. 1021–24.
57. For insights into the character of the opposition to Sheppard-Towner, I am indebted to Judith Papachristou and her paper "Suffrage and ERA: A Richness of Similarities. The Hostage to Civilization," presented at the annual meeting of the Organization of American Historians, April 1980, San Francisco.
58. U.S., 67th Cong., 1st Sess., *Congressional Record*, 1921, 61, Pt. 9,

pp. 8759–60, 8764–65, 8767, in Bremner, *Children and Youth*, pp. 1012–19.

59. *Illinois Medical Journal*, 39 (1921), 143, in Bremner, *Children and Youth*, pp. 1019–20.

60. Papachristou, "Suffrage and ERA."

61. Norman Hapgood, ed., *Professional Patriots* (New York: Albert and Charles Boni, 1927), pp. 80–94, 170–72.

62. *Woman Patriot*, 7 (Dec. 15, 1923), 8; ibid., 10 (Aug. 1, 1926), 117.

63. Hapgood, *Professional Patriots*, pp. 10–31.

64. *Woman Patriot*, 10 (June 1, 1926), 86.

65. Henry J. Harris, *Maternity Benefit Systems in Foreign Countries*, C. B. Pub. no. 57, Legal Series no. 3, 1919, p. 9.

66. Ibid., p. 175; A. Kollontai, *State Insurance of Motherhood* (Petrograd, 1916).

67. *Woman Patriot*, 12 (May 15, 1928), 75–76.

68. Ibid., 11 (May 1, 1927), 66.

69. Ibid., 7 (Dec. 1, 1923), 20.

70. Mary Anderson, *Woman at Work. The Autobiography of Mary Anderson* (Minneapolis: University of Minnesota Press, 1951), p. 190. Abbott did, however, yield to a request from Senator Sheppard that she write a response to the professional patriots' charges of communism, which he inserted into the *Congressional Record*. See 69th Cong., 2nd Sess., Dec. 11, 1926, vol. 68, p. 1.

71. G. Abbott to Lizzie Abbott, Mar. 1, 1924, Abbott Papers, C. A. Addenda.

72. G. Abbott to E. Abbott, Jan. 5, 1926, Abbott Papers, C. A. Addenda.

73. Children's Bureau, *Annual Report*, 1917, pp. 44–49.

74. James G. Burrow, *A.M.A. Voices of American Medicine* (Baltimore: Johns Hopkins Press, 1963), p. 158, n. 16.

75. Abbott Papers, Box 62, Folder 6.

76. Notes by Julia Lathrop on interview with Dr. Rupert Blue, May 25, 1919, Abbott Papers, Box 62, Folder 5; Julia Lathrop to the Secretary of Labor, July 19, 1921, ibid., Box 62, Folder 6; interview with Katharine Lenroot, July 7, 1973.

77. Hugh S. Cumming to Julia C. Lathrop, Dec. 9, 1920, Abbott Papers, Box 62, Folder 6; Burrow, *A.M.A. Voices*, pp. 152–58; *Journal of the American Medical Association*, 78 (1922), 1709, in Bremner, *Children and Youth*, pp. 1020–21.

78. Julia Lathrop to the Secretary of Labor, July 19, 1921.

79. G. Abbott to O. A. Abbott, Dec. 12, 1926, Abbott Papers, C. A. Addenda; E. Abbott, Notes and ms.

80. U.S., 69th Cong., 2nd Sess., *Congressional Record*, Dec. 6, 1926–Jan. 6, 1927, 68, Pt. 1; quote from Dec. 16, p. 97.

81. E. Abbott, Notes and ms.

82. Senators Hiram Bingham of Connecticut, William M. King of Utah, Edwin S. Broussard of Louisiana, and James A. Reed of Missouri.

83. Florence Kelley to Julia Lathrop, Mar. 22, 1927, Abbott Papers, Box 57, Folder 1; G. Abbott to Florence McKay, Jan. 18, 1927, ibid., Box 62, Folder 7.

84. Martha M. Eliot, M.D., Rockefeller Colloquia, May 9, 1975 (transcript of tape-recorded series of colloquia), Schlesinger Library.

85. Meigs, *Maternal Mortality*; Robert Morse Woodbury, *Maternal Mortality: The Risk of Death in Childbirth and from All Diseases Caused by Pregnancy and Confinement*, C. B. Pub. no. 158, 1926.

86. *Maternal Deaths. A Brief Report of a Study Made in 15 States*, C. B. Pub. no. 221, 1933. For the full report see *Maternal Mortality in Fifteen States*, C. B. Pub. no. 223, 1933.

87. *Standards of Prenatal Care.*

88. *Maternal Deaths. A Brief Report*, pp. 16–20, 21–27, 35–36, 40–55.

89. U.S., 79th Cong., 2nd Sess., Senate, Committee on Education and Labor, Testimony of M. Edwards Davis, M.D., June 21 and 22, 1946, Senate Doc. no. 1318, pp. 101–5.

90. *Bailey* v. *Drexel Furniture Co.*, 259 U.S. 20 (1922).

91. Testimony of Grace Abbott: U.S., 67th Cong., 4th Sess., Senate, Committee of the Judiciary, *Child Labor Amendment to the Constitution*, Jan. 10, 1923, p. 24, and Feb. 15, 1924; U.S., 68th Cong., 1st Sess., House, Committee of the Judiciary, *Proposed Child Labor Amendments . . . Hearings*, 1924, pp. 37–38; Grace Abbott, *The Child and the State*, vol. 1 (Chicago: University of Chicago Press, 1938).

92. *New York Times*, June 2, 1922.

93. President Harding: *New York Times*, Dec. 9, 1922, p. 6; President Coolidge: Dec. 7, 1923, in E. Abbott, Notes and ms.; Hoover's remark in an address to the American Child Hygiene Association, *American Child*, 2 (Nov. 1920), 204.

94. Julia Lathrop to G. Abbott, n.d., Abbott Papers, Box 57, Folder 8.

95. Felix Frankfurter, "Child Labor and the Court," *New Republic*, 31 (July 26, 1922), 248–50.

96. G. Abbott to Felix Frankfurter, 1922, Frankfurter Papers; Frankfurter to Abbott, Jan. 25, 1923, Abbott Papers, C. A. Addenda; Frankfurter to Abbott, Jan. 27, 1923, ibid.; Abbott to Frankfurter, Feb. 20

and July 27, 1923, Frankfurter Papers; Frankfurter to Abbott, Sept. 21, 1923; and Abbott to Frankfurter, Sept. 25, 1923, E. Abbott, Notes and ms.; telegram from Abbott to Frankfurter, Feb. 9, 1924; and Frankfurter to Abbott, Feb. 10, 1924, Abbott Papers, Addenda II, I-Folder 4; Abbott to Frankfurter, Feb. 5, 1925, Frankfurter Papers; Ernst Freund to G. Abbott, July 12, 1923, Costigan Papers; Edward P. Costigan to G. Abbott, June 3, 1922; Abbott to Costigan, July 14, 1923; Costigan to Abbott, July 15, 1922; telegram from Abbott to Costigan, Jan. 14, 1923; Costigan to Abbott, Feb. 19, 1923, ibid.; Roscoe Pound to G. Abbott, June 28, 1923, Frankfurter Papers; Pound to Abbott, July 5, 1923, Costigan Papers; Abbott to Pound, July 10, 1923; Pound to Abbott, July 14, 1923; Abbott to Pound, July 27, 1923; Pound to Abbott, Aug. 1, 1923; Abbott to Pound, Aug. 6, 1923; Pound to Abbott, Mar. 13, 1924; Pound to Abbott, Mar. 17, 1927; Pound to Hon. Israel M. Foster, Apr. 3, 1924, E. Abbott, Notes and ms.

97. For example see Frankfurter to Abbott, Feb. 27, 1925; Abbott to Frankfurter, n.d.; Frankfurter to Abbott, Sept. 15, 1925, Abbott Papers, C. A. Addenda, for an exchange between them regarding Roscoe Pound's having been offered the presidency of the University of Wisconsin. Given her midwestern loyalties and preference for coeducational institutions of higher learning, Abbott hoped Pound would accept. Frankfurter in turn did not want Pound's leadership in law diverted, doubted his administrative abilities, and challenged Abbott with "You know how keen R. P. is to educate women, don't you?"

98. U.S., 67th Cong., 4th Sess., Senate, Committee of the Judiciary, *Child Labor Amendment*, p. 47.

99. Frankfurter to G. Abbott, Sept. 21, 1923, in E. Abbott, Notes and ms.

100. U.S., 67th Cong., 4th Sess., Senate, Committee of the Judiciary, *Child Labor Amendment*, p. 48.

101. Ibid., p. 81.

102. Statement by E. Abbott, Abbott Papers, Addenda II, Box II, Folder 6; G. Abbott to Julia Lathrop, July 5, 1923, ibid., Box 57, Folder 9.

103. Costigan to G. Abbott, Nov. 23, 1923, Abbott Papers, Addenda II, Box III, Folder 6.

104. G. Abbott to George Pepper, Dec. 7, 1923, Feb. 7 and Feb. 11, 1924, Abbott Papers, Addenda II, Box III, Folder 6.

105. G. Abbott to Lizzie Abbott, Feb. 6, 1924, Abbott Papers, C. A. Addenda.

106. The proposed amendment read: "Section 1. The Congress shall have power to limit, regulate, and prohibit the labor of persons under

eighteen years of age. Section 2. The power of the several States is unimpaired by this article except that the operation of State laws shall be suspended to the extent necessary to give effect to legislation enacted by the Congress."

107. G. Abbott, *Child and the State*, vol. 1, p. 467; Abbott Papers, Addenda II, Box III, Folder 6.

108. *Woman Patriot*, 8, no. 12 (June 15, 1924), 7; and 8, no. 10 (May 15, 1924), 8.

109. Vincent A. McQuade, "The American Catholic Attitude on Child Labor since 1891" (Ph.D. dissertation, Catholic University of America, 1938), pp. 73–74.

110. G. Abbott, *Child and the State*, vol. 1, p. 467. Also see J. E. Hulett, Jr., "Propaganda and the Proposed Child Labor Amendment," *Public Opinion Quarterly*, 2 (Jan. 1938), 105–15; and Anne Kruesi Brown, "Opposition to the Child-labor Amendment in Trade Journals, Industrial Bulletins, and Other Publications for and by Business Men" (M.A. thesis, University of Chicago, 1937).

. 111. *Manufacturers' News*, 25 (Aug. 20, 1923), 3–4; 26 (Aug. 9, 1924), 4–5; 26 (Sept. 6, 1924), 14; 26 (Oct. 25, 1924), 14.

112. *New York Times*, June 29, 1926, p. 6; Julia Lathrop to G. Abbott, Mar. 17, 1925, Abbott Papers, Box 57, Folder 10.

113. Florence Kelley, "Present Status of the Federal Child Labor Amendment," Feb. 24, 1927, Abbott Papers, Addenda II, Box IV, Folder 4. For a comprehensive account of the course of ratification and the eventual rejection of the proposed child labor amendment see Chambers, *Seedtime of Reform*, pp. 29–58; also Richard B. Sherman, "The Rejection of the Child Labor Amendment," *Mid-America*, 45 (Jan. 1963), 3–17.

114. G. Abbott, *Child and the State*, vol. 1, p. 468.

115. Paul Comly French, "Children on Strike," *The Nation*, 136 (May 31, 1933), 611–12; "Industry. Children on Strike," *The Survey*, 69 (June 1933), 229.

116. Quoted in Dorothy Bradbury, *Four Decades of Action*, p. 39.

117. G. Abbott to Frances Perkins, Nov. 4, 1937, Frances Perkins Papers.

118. Frances Perkins, *The Roosevelt I Knew* (New York: Viking, 1946), p. 257. Martha Eliot, M.D., also attributed the inclusion of the child labor provisions of the Fair Labor Standards Act to Grace Abbott's foresight and the basic administrative procedures that she had developed and successfully demonstrated. Found in Jeannette Cheek, series of interviews on "The History of Women in America," p. 303, Schlesinger Library.

119. *Coleman et al.* v. *Miller*, 59 S. Ct. 972 (1939); *Chandler* v. *Wise*, 59. S. Ct. 992 (1939).

CHAPTER 7: *Well Babies — Well Mothers*

1. Commencement Address at the New Jersey College of Women, New Brunswick, N.J., June 2, 1934, Abbott Papers, Box 24, Folder 13. Grace Abbott apparently relied upon her memory to paraphrase Christina G. Rossetti's poem, "Up-Hill."

2. *The Nation*, Jan. 23, 1924, p. 77.

3. O. A. Abbott to E. Abbott, Mar. 5, 1924, Abbott Papers, C. A. Addenda.

4. Nathan Cooper to the Memorial Committee for Edith Abbott, Oct. 22, 1957, letter supplied by School of Social Service Administration, University of Chicago.

5. Abbott Papers, Box 21, Folder 2.

6. Interview with Elisabeth Shirley Enochs, Oct. 7, 1973.

7. Interview with Frank Bane, June 5, 1973.

8. Abbott Papers, Box 75, Folder 11.

9. G. Abbott to E. Abbott, Mar. 2, no year, Abbott Papers, C. A. Addenda.

10. Florence Kelley to G. Abbott, July 23, 1923, Abbott Papers, C. A. Addenda.

11. Interview with Phyllis Osborn, May 16, 1977.

12. G. Abbott to E. Abbott, n.d., Abbott Papers, C. A. Addenda.

13. Children's Bureau, *Annual Report*, 1922, p. 22.

14. E. Abbott to G. Abbott, Nov. 24, 1930, Abbott Papers, Box 2, Folder 13.

15. Background to the Cosmopolitan Club supplied by Ollie Randall in an interview on Nov. 20, 1974.

16. G. Abbott to O. A. Abbott, Jr., Apr. 7, 1927, Abbott Papers, Box 2, Folder 13; E. Abbott to O. A. Abbott, Jr., 1927, ibid., C. A. Addenda.

17. A. E. Sheldon to E. Abbott, Nov. 26, 1928, Abbott Papers, C. A. Addenda; E. Abbott to G. Abbott, Feb. 10, 1923, ibid. Also see letters and telegrams of congratulation to O. A. and Lizzie Abbott, ibid.

18. E. Abbott, Notes and ms.

19. G. Abbott to E. Abbott, Feb. 1928, Abbott Papers, Box 2, Folder 13; G. Abbott to E. Abbott, Mar. 1 and Mar. 7, ibid., C. A. Addenda.

20. Julia Lathrop to G. Abbott, Feb. 8, 1928, Abbott Papers, Box 58, Folder 2; Julia Lathrop to G. Abbott, Feb. 17, 1928, ibid.

21. G. Abbott to S. P. Breckinridge, Feb. 28, Abbott Papers, C. A. Addenda; G. Abbott to E. Abbott, Mar. 1, ibid.; G. Abbott to S. P. Breckinridge, Mar. 11, ibid.; G. Abbott to S. P. Breckinridge, Apr. 15, 1928, Breckinridge Papers, Box 1, Folder 3; Katharine Lenroot to G. Abbott, May 22, 1928, Abbott Papers, Box 36, Folder 8; Edith Abbott to Julia Lathrop, June 11, 1928, ibid., Box 56, Folder 6.

22. E. Abbott to Lizzie Abbott, Aug. 5, 1928, Abbott Papers, C. A. Addenda; G. Abbott to E. Abbott, Oct. 2, 1928, ibid.

23. E. Abbott to Julia Lathrop, June 11, 1928, Abbott Papers, Box 56, Folder 6.

24. Herbert Hoover to the director of the budget, Oct. 16, 1929, in Ray Lyman Wilbur and Arthur Mastick Hyde, *The Hoover Policies* (New York: Charles Scribner's Sons, 1937), p. 58; "Presidential Address," American Child Hygiene Association, *Transactions*, 13 (1922), 13–15, in Robert H. Bremner, ed., *Children and Youth in America. A Documentary History*, II, 1866–1932 (Cambridge: Harvard University Press, 1971), pp. 1063–64.

25. Memorandum re: interview with the president, Aug. 29, 1929, Abbott Papers, Addenda II, Box III, Folder 6.

26. *New York Times*, Dec. 4, 1929.

27. William John Cooper to the secretary of the interior, Sept. 11, 1929, Presidential Papers, Herbert Hoover Library, Presidential Subject—Maternity Legislation; Ray Lyman Wilbur to Wesley L. Jones, Sept. 28, 1929, ibid.; Wilbur to Walter H. Newton, Feb. 7, 1930, ibid.; Hiram W. Johnson to Mrs. J. C. Whitman, Mar. 11, 1930, ibid.; "Relationship of the Controversy to the Sheppard-Towner Act," Abbott Papers, Box 62, Folder 8; "The Children's Bureau," *New Republic*, 62 (Apr. 2, 1930), 179–80; David Burner, *Herbert Hoover: A Public Life* (New York: Alfred A. Knopf, 1979), p. 340.

28. E. Abbott Notes and ms.; Abbott Papers, Addenda II, Box II, Folder 12.

29. G. Abbott to O. A. Abbott, Jan. 10, 1930, Abbott Papers, Addenda II, Box II, Folder 12.

30. "Notes and Comments," *Social Service Review*, 3 (1929), 481–82.

31. Julius Rosenwald to G. Abbott, Apr. 24, 1930, Abbott Papers, Box 36, Folder 10; G. Abbott to Julius Rosenwald, Apr. 28, 1930, ibid.

32. Lillian D. Wald, "Shall We Dismember the Child?" *The Survey*, 63 (Jan. 15, 1930), 458.

33. Haven Emerson to Paul U. Kellogg, Nov. 26, 1930, Survey Papers, Box 68, Folder 511; Emerson to Kellogg, Dec. 20, 1929, ibid.;

Emerson to Kellogg, Dec. 23, 1929, ibid.; Emerson to Kellogg, Jan. 7, 1930, ibid.

34. Kellogg to Emerson, Dec. 23, 1929, Survey Papers, Box 68, Folder 511.

35. Supplement to *U.S. Daily News*, sec. 11, vol. 5 (Nov. 28, 1930).

36. Haven Emerson to Paul U. Kellogg, Nov. 26, 1930.

37. Herbert Hoover, *The Memoirs of Herbert Hoover. The Cabinet and the Presidency, 1920–1933* (New York: Macmillan Co., 1952), p. 260.

38. For material on the conference sessions I have relied upon a transcript of the conference sessions in the supplement to the *U.S. Daily News*, sec. 11, vol. 5, (Nov. 25, 1930); *Washington Post*, Nov. 21, 22, 23, 1930; *New York Times*, Nov. 21, 22, 23, 1930; *Time*, 16 (Dec. 1, 1930); J. Prentice Murphy, "When Doctors Disagreed," *The Survey*, 65 (Dec. 15, 1930); Bess Furman, *Washington By-Line. The Personal History of a Newspaperwoman* (New York: Alfred A. Knopf, 1949); Josephine Goldmark, *Impatient Crusader. Florence Kelley's Life Story* (Urbana: University of Illinois Press, 1953), and interviews with persons present at the conference sessions. Direct quotations are noted separately.

39. Rodney Dutcher, "Delegates Angered at Treatment They Received at Child Health Conference," *Washington Star*, Nov. 23, 1930.

40. "Child Experts Fail to Close Rift in Ranks," *Washington Post*, Nov. 21, 1930, p. 1.

41. Supplement to *U.S. Daily News*, sec. 11, vol. 5, pp. 19–20.

42. Ibid., p. 35.

43. Ibid., p. 55.

44. Mary Anderson to G. Abbott, Dec. 22, 1931, Abbott Papers, C. A. Addenda.

45. *The Nation*, 131 (Dec. 3, 1930), 595.

46. James G. Burrow, *A.M.A. Voices of American Medicine* (Baltimore: Johns Hopkins Press, 1963), p. 163.

47. Sheila M. Rothman, *Woman's Proper Place. A History of Changing Ideals and Practice. 1870 to the Present* (New York: Basic Books, 1978), p. 143.

48. *Woman Patriot*, 5 (Oct. 15, 1921); Mary Ware Dennett to Julia Lathrop, Jan. 7, 1922, Abbott Papers, Box 62, Folder 6; Martha M. Eliot, M.D., Rockefeller Colloquia, May 9, 1975, Schlesinger Library.

49. G. Abbott to the Conference of State and Provincial Health Authorities of North America, Apr. 29, 1931, Abbott Papers, C. A. Addenda.

50. A decade later Grace Abbott believed that public attitudes had changed and that the continuation of the Children's Bureau "hands-off policy" on birth control could no longer be justified. Grace Abbott to

Katharine Lenroot, Nov. 14, 1938, Abbott Papers, Box 62, Folder 1.

51. See E. Abbott, "Grace Abbott for the Cabinet," Abbott Papers, C. A. Addenda, a collection of newspaper articles and commentary.

52. G. Abbott to E. Abbott, May 24, 1930, Abbott Papers, C. A. Addenda.

53. E. Abbott, "Grace Abbott for the Cabinet."

54. Interview with Clara Beyer, May 11, 1977.

55. E. Abbott, "Washington and the Children's Bureau Years," Abbott Papers, C. A. Addenda.

56. Ray Lyman Wilbur to Dr. Richard C. Cabot, Nov. 20, 1930, Esther Loeb Kohn Papers, Box 1, Folder 1; Burner, *Herbert Hoover*, p. 222.

57. Katharine Lenroot to the secretary of labor, Oct. 7, 1932; W. N. Smelser to G. Abbott, Oct. 13, 1932; G. Abbott to the secretary of labor, Oct. 14, 1932; unsigned letter to Honorable W. E. Doak, Oct. 13, 1932, Abbott Papers, C. A. Addenda.

58. G. Abbott to O. A. Abbott, Jr., Sept. 4, 1931, Abbott Papers, C. A. Addenda.

59. G. Abbott to S. P. Breckinridge, Abbott Papers, C. A. Addenda.

60. Elizabeth Tandy to G. Abbott, Oct. 2 and Oct. 5, 1931, Katharine Lenroot Papers; G. Abbott to E. Tandy, Oct. 12, 1931, ibid.; Tandy to Katharine Lenroot, Oct. 20, 1931, ibid.; K. Lenroot to G. Abbott, Oct. 20, 21, and 23, 1931, ibid.

61. G. Abbott to Katharine Lenroot, Oct. 23, 1931, Katharine Lenroot Papers.

62. Katharine Lenroot to G. Abbott, Oct. 19, 1931, with handwritten comments by G. Abbott in margin, Katharine Lenroot Papers; Martha M. Eliot to G. Abbott, Oct. 19, 1931, with handwritten comments by G. Abbott in margin, ibid.; G. Abbott to Katharine Lenroot, Oct. 23, 1931, ibid.

63. Katharine Lenroot to G. Abbott, Apr. 4, 1932, with handwritten comments by G. Abbott in margin, Katharine Lenroot Papers.

64. Robert Allen Karlsrud, "The Hoover Labor Department: A Study in Bureaucratic Decisiveness" (Ph.D. dissertation, University of California at Los Angeles, 1972), p. 353. Karlsrud concluded that "from its beginnings, the Children's Bureau with the support of its very avid proponents, had followed the policy of bureaucratic aggrandisement, accruing more and more functions . . . greater and greater numbers of projects." This conclusion seemed to be based largely on a comparison of the budget of the Children's Bureau and the Women's Bureau. A study of the correspondence over the years between Julia

Lathrop and Grace Abbott and between Grace Abbott and Katharine Lenroot does not lend credence to a finding of "bureaucratic aggrandisement."

65. Prentice Murphy to E. Abbott, Jan. 4, 1932, Abbott Papers, Box 75, Folder 8.

66. G. Abbott to Katharine Lenroot, n.d., Katharine Lenroot Papers.

67. G. Abbott to E. Abbott, Apr. 5, 1932, Abbott Papers, C. A. Addenda.

68. G. Abbott to Josephine Roche, Apr. 19, 1932, Josephine Roche Papers.

69. Grace Abbott, "Address," in *Proceedings of the National Conference of Social Work*, 1932, pp. 45–51; quotes on pp. 45–46, 47, 51.

70. E. Abbott to Charlotte Abbott, June 24, 1932, Abbott Papers, C. A. Addenda; Edward and Mabel Costigan to G. Abbott, June 29, 1932, ibid.; G. Abbott to Charlotte Abbott, n.d., ibid.

CHAPTER 8: *Defining a Profession*

1. Edith Abbott, *Social Welfare and Professional Education*, 2nd ed. (Chicago: University of Chicago Press, 1942), p. 13.

2. E. Abbott, *Twenty-one Years of University Education for the Social Services, 1920–1941* (Chicago: University of Chicago Press, 1943), p. 3.

3. E. Abbott, "Education for Social Work," in Department of Interior, Bureau of Education, *Report of the Commissioner of Education for the Year Ended June 30, 1915*, vol. 1 (Washington: Government Printing Office, 1915); Jesse Frederick Steiner, *Education for Social Work* (Chicago: University of Chicago Press, 1921), pp. 6–8.

4. Mary E. Richmond, "The Need of a Training School in Applied Philanthropy," in *Proc. of NCCC, 1897* (Boston: Geo. H. Ellis, 1898), pp. 181–88.

5. James H. Tufts, *Education and Training for Social Work* (New York: Russell Sage Foundation, 1923), pp. 111–20; Jeffrey Richardson Brackett, *Supervision and Education in Charity* (New York: Macmillan Co., 1903), pp. 156–58, 162; Amos G. Warner, *American Charities, a Study in Philanthropy and Economics* (New York: Crowell, 1894).

6. Frank J. Bruno, *Trends in Social Work 1874–1956. A History Based on the Proceedings of the National Conference of Social Work* (New York: Columbia University Press, 1957), pp. 133–34.

7. E. Abbott, *Social Welfare and Professional Education*, pp. 131–73.

8. Abraham Flexner, "Is Social Work a Profession?" in *Proc. of NCCC, 1915* (Chicago: Hildmann Printing Co., 1915), pp. 576–90.

9. Felix Frankfurter, "Social Work and Professional Training," in *Proc. of NCCC, 1915*, pp. 591–96.

10. E. Abbott, *Twenty-one Years of University Education*, p. 3; E. Abbott to Sydnor Walker, Jan. 25, 1937, letter supplied by School of Social Service Administration.

11. E. Abbott, *Twenty-one Years of University Education*, p. 7; E. Abbott to Sydnor Walker, April 19, 1931, and Jan. 25, 1937, letters supplied by School of Service Administration.

12. Rayman Solomon, "The Founding and Development of the Graduate School of Social Service Aministration at the University of Chicago: A Study of Foundations and Public Policy Research," unpublished paper, May 1976, citing the following sources: Laura Spelman Rockefeller Memorial, *Memorial Policy in Social Science*, Oct. 1922, Beardsley Ruml Papers; Barry D. Karl, *Charles E. Merriam and the Study of Politics* (Chicago, 1974), pp. 132–36, 150–52; Trevor Arnett to E. D. Burton, May 23, 1924, Presidential Papers; Memorandum, Harold Swift to E. D. Burton, June 10, 1924, Swift Papers; Ferris F. Laune to Burton, Nov. 3, 1923, Presidential Papers; L. C. Marshall to Burton, Nov. 9, 1923, Presidential Papers; Burton's memorandum of conversation with Swift, June 10, 1924, Presidential Papers; Swift to Burton, June 13, 1924, Swift Papers; Swift to Trevor Arnett, June 20, 1924, Swift Papers (all this correspondence in the Regenstein Library, University of Chicago).

13. Roy Lubove, *The Professional Altruist. The Emergence of Social Work as a Career. 1880–1930* (Cambridge: Harvard University Press, 1965), p. 80, 85–89, 143.

14. Ibid.

15. Jeffrey R. Brackett, "The Curriculum of the Professional School of Social Work," in *Proc. of NCCC, 1915*, p. 612.

16. Porter R. Lee, "Committee Report: The Professional Basis of Social Work," in *Proc. of NCCC, 1915*, p. 603; Lee, *Social Work as Cause and Function and Other Papers* (New York: Columbia University Press, 1937), pp. 79, 82; Lee and Marion E. Kenworthy, *Mental Hygiene and Social Work* (New York: Commonwealth Fund, 1929), p. 215.

17. John Stuart Mill, *System of Logic. Ratiocinative and Inductive: Being a Connected View of the Principles of Evidence and the Methods of Scientific Investigation*, 8th ed. (New York: Harper and Bros., Publishers, 1893), Book VI, pp. 578–659.

18. E. Abbott, "Some Basic Principles in Professional Education for Social Work," in *Social Welfare and Professional Education*, pp. 44–80, quote on p. 47.

19. Ibid., pp. 47–48.

20. E. Abbott, "The University and Social Welfare," in *Social Welfare and Professional Education*, pp. 12–13.

21. E. Abbott, "Some Basic Principles," pp. 49–50.

22. Ibid., quotes on pp. 80, 56.

23. Ibid., p. 52.

24. E. Abbott, "Education for Social Work," pp. 351–59, quote on p. 356; "Some Basic Principles," pp. 57–60.

25. Lubove, *Professional Altruist*, pp. 52–54.

26. Robert H. Wiebe, *The Search for Order. 1877–1920* (New York: Hill and Wang, 1967); Robert L. Buroker, "From Voluntary Association to Welfare State: The Immigrants' Protective League, 1908–1926," *Journal of American History*, 58 (Dec. 1971), 643–60.

27. E. Abbott, "Some Basic Principles," p. 51.

28. Ernst Freund, Review of E. Abbott's *Immigration: Select Documents and Case Records*, *Harvard Law Review*, 38 (Dec. 1924), 274–76; A. B. Wolfe, Review of same book, *Journal of Political Economy*, 33 (Feb. 1925), 115–17. Also see "Chicago Brings Gifts," *The Survey* 54 (May 15, 1925), 250.

29. Wayne McMillen, "The First Twenty-Six Years of the Social Service Review," *Social Service Review*, 27 (Mar. 1953), 1–14.

30. E. Abbott, "University and Social Welfare," pp. 17–18.

31. E. Abbott, "Notes and Comments," *Social Service Review*, 6 (June 1932), 305.

32. G. Abbott to E. Abbott, n.d., Abbott Papers, Box III, Folder 2; Eleanor K. Taylor, "The Edith Abbott I Knew," *Journal of the Illinois State Historical Society*, 70 (Aug. 1977), 183.

33. Interview with Robert Hutchins, Nov. 5, 1974. Additional references to Hutchins are from this same interview.

34. Interview with Wilma Walker, July 12, 1973.

35. Wayne McMillen, "Edith Abbott: Her Contribution to Professional Education for Social Work," *S.S.A. Newsletter for Alumni*, 5 (Dec. 1957), 8.

36. Elizabeth Wisner, "Edith Abbott's Contributions to Social Work Education," *Social Service Review*, 32 (Mar. 1958), 7.

37. Taylor, "Edith Abbott I Knew," p. 180.

38. Interview with Wilma Walker, July 12, 1973.

39. McMillen, "Edith Abbott: Her Contribution," p. 8.

40. Taylor, "Edith Abbott I Knew," p. 179.

41. Interview with Wilma Walker, July 12, 1973.

42. Taylor, "Edith Abbott I Knew," pp. 178–79.

43. From comments of former students of Edith Abbott who knew of my interest in her and volunteered recollections.

44. Interview with Virgil Hampton, Nov. 16, 1972.

45. For insights into Edith Abbott's relationship to Charlotte Towle I am indebted to Helen Harris Perlman and Bernece Simon, with whom I consulted on July 21, 1976.

46. Quoted in McMillen, "Edith Abbott: Her Contribution," pp. 6–7; also see Wisner, "Edith Abbott's Contributions," p. 6, and Towle to E. Abbott, Aug. 17, 1954, Abbott Papers, C. A. Addenda.

47. Charlotte Towle, *Common Human Needs, An Interpretation for Staff in Public Assistance Agencies*, Federal Security Agency, Social Security Board, Bureau of Public Assistance, Public Assistance Report no. 8 (Washington: Government Printing Office, 1945). During the McCarthy period of the early 1950s, this very useful and perceptive publication was withdrawn by the Federal Security Agency. The action was strongly protested by social workers. The volume has since been reissued by the National Association of Social Workers, Inc.

48. Wisner, "Edith Abbott's Contributions," p. 6.

49. Paul Simon, ed., *Plan and Game Theory in Group Work. A Collection of Papers by Neva Leona Boyd* (Chicago: Jane Addams Graduate School of Social Work, University of Illinois at Chicago Circle, 1971); E. Abbott to Sydnor Walker, Dec. 12, 1925, letter supplied by the University of Chicago School of Social Service Administration.

50. E. Abbott, *Report on Crime and Criminal Justice in Relation to the Foreign Born*, National Commission on Law Observance and Enforcement (Washington: Government Printing Office, 1931). Also see "Find Foreign Born Commit Fewer Crimes," *New York Times*, Aug. 24, 1931, p. 1.

51. E. Abbott, "Backgrounds and Foregrounds in Education for Social Work," in *Social Welfare and Professional Education*, pp. 24–25.

52. Wisner, "Edith Abbott's Contributions," p. 8.

CHAPTER 9: *Permanence and Change*

1. E. Abbott, "Federal Relief Sold Down the River," *The Nation*, 142 (Mar. 18, 1936), 346.

2. "Notes and Comments," *Social Service Review*, 4 (1930), 486–87; Children's Bureau, *Annual Report*, 1931, pp. 36–39.

3. "Relief Statistics in 1930," *Social Service Review*, 5 (Mar. 1931), 109–10.

4. *New York Times*, Nov. 4, 1930, p. 14.

5. U.S., 72nd Cong., 2nd Sess., Senate, Committee on Manufacturers, *Relief for Unemployed Transients: Hearings before the Subcommittee on S. 5121*, Jan. 23, 1933, pp. 23–35; Children's Bureau, *Annual Report*,

1932, pp. 5–9; "Perils to Children in Crisis Stressed," *New York Times*, Dec. 14, 1932, p. 2.

6. E. Abbott, "Poor People in Chicago," *New Republic*, 72 (Oct. 5, 1932), 209.

7. Grace Abbott, "Improvement in Rural Public Relief: The Lessons of the Coal-Mining Communities," *Social Service Review*, 6 (June 1932), 183–222.

8. Clarence E. Pickett, *For More than Bread* (Boston: Little, Brown and Co., 1953), pp. 19–21; Mary Hoxie Jones, *Swords into Ploughshares. An Account of American Friends Service Committee 1917–1937* (New York: Macmillan Co., 1937), p. 313; Pickett to E. Abbott, June 22, 1939, Abbott Papers, Box 21, Folder 5; Katharine Lenroot to G. Abbott, Aug. 6, 1931, letter supplied by Lenroot; Lenroot to G. Abbott, Aug. 19, 1931, Abbott Papers, C. A. Addenda; Lenroot to G. Abbott, Nov. 20, 1931, letter supplied by Lenroot.

9. "Guardian of the Children of America," *New York Times Magazine*, Nov. 9, 1932, pp. 11, 17.

10. E. Abbott, "The Fallacy of Local Relief," *New Republic*, 72 (Nov. 9, 1932), 348–50.

11. Arthur M. Schlesinger, Jr., *The Age of Roosevelt. The Crisis of the Old Order. 1919–1933* (Cambridge, Mass.: Houghton Mifflin Co., 1957), p. 170.

12. Ibid., p. 175.

13. "Red Cross Stand on Federal Aid Is Commended," *United States Daily*, Apr. 14, 1931.

14. "The Voluntary Spirit," *New York Times*, Jan. 24, 1931; E. Abbott, *Public Assistance* (Chicago: University of Chicago Press, 1940), pp. 656–58; "Notes and Comments, Public Relief and the American Spirit," *Social Service Review*, 5 (Mar. 1931), 112–15.

15. "Red Cross Stand on Federal Aid Is Commended."

16. "The Challenge in Child Welfare," address by G. Abbott, before Annual Convention of the American National Red Cross, U.S. Chamber of Commerce Bldg., Washington, D.C., Apr. 14, 1931, Abbott Papers, C. A. Addenda.

17. *Relief Work in the Drought of 1930–31*, Official Report of the Operations of the American Red Cross, Covering Activities from August, 1930, to End of Fiscal Year June 30, 1931 (Washington, D.C., 1931), p. 109 (ARC 901, Oct. 1931).

18. "Notes and Comments. The Red Cross and the Great Drought," *Social Service Review*, 6 (June 1932), 297–300. The article was published unsigned after controversy among the Abbott sisters and Nisba Breckinridge. The latter offered to sign the article to protect the Abbott sis-

ters from criticism for so openly challenging interests of Hoover in whose administration Grace Abbott was a significant appointee. Grace wired Edith that SPB should not do so; she had not written the article, and she should not have to shoulder the responsibility. Finally unsigned, the article still was clear to most readers as authored by the Abbott sisters.

19. Ray Lyman Wilbur, "Children in National Emergencies," in *Proceedings of the National Conference of Social Work*, 1932, pp. 25–31; Claude G. Bowers, "Secretary Wilbur and Marie Antoinette," newspaper clipping (name of newspaper missing from clipping), May 20, 1932, Breckinridge Papers, Box 5; G. Abbott to E. Abbott, May 21, 1932, Abbott Papers, C. A. Addenda.

20. E. Abbott to Mary Dewson, July 5, 1932, Abbott Papers, Box 69, Folder 2.

21. Eleanor Roosevelt to James Farley, n.d., cited in Joseph P. Lash, *Eleanor and Franklin* (New York: W. W. Norton and Co., 1971), p. 389.

22. G. Abbott to S. P. Breckinridge, Mar. 1, 1933, Breckinridge Papers, Box 5.

23. George Martin, *Madam Secretary. Frances Perkins* (Boston: Houghton Mifflin and Co., 1976), p. 234, citing *New York Times*, Dec. 11, 1932, p. 12, and interview by Martin with Clara Beyer.

24. Mary Dewson to G. Abbott, Mar. 1933, Abbott Papers, Box 69, Folder 2; Martin, *Madam Secretary*, p. 5; Frances Perkins to G. Abbott, Feb. 27, 1933, Abbott Papers, C. A. Addenda.

25. G. Abbott to the secretary, Apr. 13, 1934, Abbott Papers, C. A. Addenda; Frances Perkins to Miss Abbott, Apr. 27, 1934, ibid.; Mary Anderson, *Woman at Work. The Autobiography of Mary Anderson* (Minneapolis: University of Minnesota Press, 1951), pp. 184–85.

26. *New York Times*, June 21, 1939.

27. G. Abbott to Frances Perkins, Oct. 24, 1935, Abbott Papers, Box 68, Folder 4; Perkins to G. Abbott, Oct. 30, 1935, ibid.

28. G. Abbott to Ernestine Evans, Nov. 29, 1935, Abbott Papers, Box 68, Folder 7.

29. See letters in Abbott Papers, Box 36, Folder 16, and extensive newspaper reports of the day.

30. Eleanor Roosevelt to G. Abbott, June 13, 1934, Abbott Papers, C. A. Addenda; Carrie Chapman Catt to Grace Abbott, n.d., ibid.

31. G. Abbott to S. P. Breckinridge, Breckinridge Papers, Dec. 1933, Box 5; G. Abbott to Julian Mack, July 6, 1934, Abbott Papers, Box 76, Folder 3; G. Abbott to Paul U. Kellogg, July 6, 1934, ibid., C. A. Addenda.

32. Grace Abbott to Allen T. Burns, July 23, 1934, Abbott Papers, Box 37, Folder 1; Grace Abbott to Prentice Murphy, July 6, 1934, ibid.

33. Copy of Minutes of the Steering Committee Meeting, Division on Government and Social Work, American Association of Social Workers, June 20, 1934, Abbott Papers, C. A. Addenda.

34. Grover F. Powers, M.D., to G. Abbott, June 21, 1934, Abbott Papers, C. A. Addenda; Samuel McC. Hamill to Frances Perkins, June 9, 1934, ibid.; Edwards A. Park, M.D., to Josephine Goldmark, July 15, 1934, ibid.; J. Prentice Murphy to Martha Eliot, July 15, 1934, ibid.

35. G. Abbott to Frances Perkins, June 19, 1934, Abbott Papers, C. A. Addenda.

36. G. Abbott to Mary Dewson, n.d., Mary Dewson Papers.

37. G. Abbott to J. Prentice Murphy, July 6, 1934; interview with Katharine Lenroot, July 7, 1973, in which Lenroot reminisced about the controversy: "I was not as much a fighter as Martha. My tendency was to be rather conservative. Martha and Grace were of the personality of the real reformers. . . . I was never what you would call a crusader as Miss Addams and the Abbotts were. Martha and Grace were more similar in their temperament and makeup."

38. See interviews by Jeannette Cheek with Martha M. Eliot, M.D., Schlesinger Library, p. 443, for Eliot's acknowledgment of an independence and administrative style summed up in her statement, "But, you know, there were losses and gains by the way I did things. Sometimes it was a gain; sometimes it was a loss." Interview with Charlotte Abbott for evidences of Grace Abbott's comments to her about Eliot's characteristics as they affected her administrative style; K. Lenroot to G. Abbott, Aug. 6, 1934, Abbott Papers, C. A. Addenda, for Lenroot's attitude toward staying on.

39. J. Prentice Murphy to G. Abbott, June 28, Abbott Papers, C. A. Addenda; Murphy to E. Abbott, July 5, 1934, ibid.; Murphy to G. Abbott, July 20, 1934, ibid.

40. J. Prentice Murphy to G. Abbott, July 20, 1934; Allen T. Burns to G. Abbott, July 21, 1934, Abbott Papers, Box 37, Folder 1; G. Abbott to Burns, July 23, 1934, ibid.; Burns to G. Abbott, July 27, 1934, ibid.

41. G. Abbott to J. Prentice Murphy, July 6, 1934.

42. Abbott's friendship with Eliot developed quickly after Eliot came to the Children's Bureau in 1923 at Abbott's request to discuss Eliot's interest in the prevention of rickets in children through the use of cod liver oil and the possibility of a community program that would

demonstrate that rickets could be prevented in all children. Abbott was excited by the prospect of using a program of preventive social action to translate scientific findings into gains for children and was willing to use Sheppard-Towner funds. Eliot was immediately impressed with Abbott's vision, her quick mind, and readiness to make decisions without delay once the supporting facts were laid out. Abbott in turn liked Eliot's creative bent, her interest in the prevention of children's health problems, and her readiness to introduce a scientific rigor into the demonstration. For description of the rickets studies and demonstrations, see Children's Bureau, *Annual Reports*, 1923–30. The personal friendship between Abbott and Eliot was illustrated even at the height of the controversy over the new bureau chief when they (with Ethel Dunham, M.D.) explored Colorado and the Southwest by automobile for a vacation of several weeks. See Cheek interviews with Eliot, p. 355, and Eliot to Abbott, July 1934, Abbott Papers, C. A. Addenda.

43. G. Abbott to Katharine Lenroot, n.d., Abbott Papers, C. A. Addenda; Lenroot to G. Abbott, Aug. 6, 1934, ibid.; Martha M. Eliot to J. Prentice Murphy, July 25, 1934, ibid.; Eliot to G. Abbott, July 1934, ibid.

44. G. Abbott to Elisabeth Shirley Enochs, 1934, copy of letter supplied by E. S. Enochs; J. Prentice Murphy to G. Abbott, Aug. 3, 1934, Abbott Papers, C. A. Addenda; Martha M. Eliot to G. Abbott, July 1934.

45. Katharine Lenroot to Louis J. Covotsos, with copy to Lela B. Costin; interview with Katharine Lenroot, July 7, 1973; interview with Martha Eliot, M.D., July 6, 1973.

46. "Notes and Comments," *Social Service Review*, 7 (June 1933), 327.

47. Harry L. Hopkins, *Spending to Save. The Complete Story of Relief* (Seattle: University of Washington Press, 1936); Hopkins, "The Developing National Program of Relief," in *Proceedings of the National Conference of Social Work*, 1933, pp. 65–71.

48. "Notes and Comments," *Social Service Review*, 7 (Sept. 1933), 516–17.

49. E. Abbott, *Public Assistance*, pp. 669–90; E. Abbott, "The Crisis in Relief," *The Nation*, 137 (Oct. 11, 1933), 400–402; E. Abbott, "Don't Do It, Mr. Hopkins!" *The Nation*, 140 (Jan. 9, 1935), 41–42; E. Abbott, "Federal Relief," pp. 346–71.

50. Interview with Wilma Walker, July 12, 1973.

51. Hopkins, *Spending to Save*, p. 99; Edith Abbott, *Public Assistance; New York Times*, Feb. 15, 1936, p. 17.

52. Edwin E. Witte to G. Abbott, Aug. 17, 1934, Abbott Papers,

Box 54, Folder 1; Katharine Lenroot to G. Abbott, Aug. 17, 1934, ibid.; Witte to G. Abbott, Aug. 22 and Aug. 25, 1934, ibid.

53. G. Abbott to Edwin E. Witte, Sept. 6, 1934, Abbott Papers, Box 61, Folder 3; Witte to G. Abbott, Sept. 11, 1934, ibid., Box 54, Folder 1.

54. Correspondence between Marguerite M. Wells and Grace Abbott, Abbott Papers, Box 76, Folders 4–10.

55. Abbott's interest in crippled children began earlier. See Children's Bureau, *Annual Report*, 1925, pp. 5–6, in which she records the launching of an inquiry into public and private provisions for such children in eight states.

56. Edwin E. Witte, *The Development of the Social Security Act* (Madison: University of Wisconsin Press, 1962), p. 171.

57. Interview with Martha M. Eliot, M.D., July 6, 1973.

58. Appointment as consultant in July 1934, continued until 1938 on a yearly basis, and then extended without limitation. Abbott Papers, Box 37, Folder 3; interview with Martha M. Eliot, M.D., July 6, 1973.

59. Witte, *Development of Social Security Act*, pp. 162–71, quote on p. 167.

60. Katharine Lenroot to G. Abbott, Jan. 22, 1935, Abbott Papers, Box 54, Folder 2; Martha Eliot, M.D., to G. Abbott, Jan. 19, 1935, ibid.

61. Josephine C. Brown, *Public Relief 1929–1939* (New York: Henry Holt & Co., 1940), pp. 311–12.

62. Ibid., p. 308; Gertrude Springer, "In Predominantly Rural Areas," *Survey Midmonthly*, 77 (Feb. 1941), 39.

63. U.S., 74th Cong., 1st Sess., Senate, Committee on Finances, *Economic Security Act: Hearings on S. 1130*, Jan. 22 to Feb. 20, 1935, pp. 1080–91.

64. Edwin Witte to G. Abbott, Nov. 6, 1934, Abbott Papers, Box 54, Folder 1.

65. Martin, *Madame Secretary*, p. 351; Witte, *Development of Social Security Act*, p. 63.

66. Edwin E. Witte, to G. Abbott, Feb. 21, 1935, Abbott Papers, Box 54, Folder 2; G. Abbott to Marvin H. McIntyre, Mar. 17, 1935, ibid., Folder 4; Abbott to John B. Andrews, Mar. 17, 1935, ibid.

67. Witte, *Development of Social Security Act*, pp. 85–98; Witte to E. Abbott, Oct. 18, 1939, Abbott Papers, Box 51, Folder 1.

68. "Business, Labor, Welfare Leaders Sign Petition to President and Congress. Cite 'Solemn Covenant.' Representatives of the Catholic Protestant and Jewish Faiths Join in Plea," *New York Times*, Mar. 22, 1935, p. 9.

69. Witte, *Development of Social Security Act*, p. 97; Witte to E. Abbott, Oct. 18, 1939.

70. G. Abbott to Elisabeth Shirley Enochs, Jan. 19, 1935, letter supplied by Elisabeth Enochs.

71. G. Abbott to Frances Perkins, Aug. 1, 1935, Abbott Papers, Box 68, Folder 7.

CHAPTER 10: *Sisters and Comrades*

1. Quoted in Diogenes Laertius, *Lives and Opinions of Eminent Philosophers, 446–366 B.C.*, trans. R. D. Hicks (New York: G. P. Putnam's Sons, 1925), p. 7. The quotation actually reads "When brothers agree." Because it is so eminently applicable to sisters as well, I took the liberty of modifying it for the purposes of this book.

2. Edith Abbott, *Twenty-one Years of University Education for the Social Services, 1920–41* (Chicago: University of Chicago Press, 1943), pp. 8–14.

3. Ibid., p. 13.

4. Ibid., pp. 5–6.

5. Interview with Ethel Verry, Aug. 4, 1976; Clare L. McCausland, *Children of Circumstance. A History of the First 125 Years (1849–1974) of Chicago Child Care Society* (Chicago: Chicago Child Care Society, 1976).

6. Interview with Lilian Ripple and Mary Macdonald, Nov. 13, 1975.

7. Interview with Phyllis Osborn, May 16, 1977; Grace Abbott to Harry Hopkins, Oct. 27, 1934, Abbott Papers, Box 72, Folder 9.

8. Interviews with Ethel Verry, Aug. 4, 1976; Lilian Ripple and Mary Macdonald, Nov. 13, 1975; Phyllis Osborn, May 16, 1977.

9. For Pan-American Child Congress, Abbott Papers, Box 68, Folder 4; *New York Times*, Sept. 28, 1935, p. 15; for ILO, see telegram from Charles E. Wyzanski to Grace Abbott, May 16, 1935, Abbott Papers, C. A. Addenda; secretary of state to Grace Abbott, May 18, 1937, ibid.; International Labour Office, *Record of Proceedings*, Nineteenth Session, 1935; ibid., for Twenty-first Session, 1937; *New York Times*, May 20, 1937, p. 4; for Textile Committee appointment, telegram from Elmer F. Andrews to Grace Abbott, Sept. 13, 1938, Abbott Papers, Box 71, Folder 7; M. K. Wood to Grace Abbott, Sept. 30, 1938, ibid.

10. Interview with Wilma Walker, July 12, 1973; Grace Abbott to Agnes K. Hanna, Nov. 1, 1934, Abbott Papers, Box 37, Folder 3.

11. James Brown IV to Robert H. Bremner, Dec. 19, 1966, with copy of letter supplied by James Brown IV.

12. Helen Perlman and Bernece K. Simon, July 21, 1976.

13. E. Abbott received honorary degrees from Oberlin College in 1937, Beloit College in 1944, and Tulane University in 1944. G. Abbott received honorary degrees from the University of Nebraska in 1931, the University of Wisconsin in 1932, Wilson College in 1934, the University of New Hampshire in 1932, and Mount Holyoke College in 1935. In addition she was awarded the Gold Medal of the National Institute of Social Sciences in 1931 and termed "by far the most important social worker in public life today." In that same year she was named by *Good Housekeeping Magazine* as one of twelve most famous living women of America.

14. Gertrude Springer and Ruth A. Lerrigo, "Social Work in the Public Scene," *The Survey*, 72 (June 1936), 163–75.

15. E. Abbott to Gertrude Springer, Mar. 13, 1939, Survey Papers, editorial file, folder 903; Springer to Abbott, Mar. 17, 1939, ibid.

16. G. Abbott to C. Abbott, Aug. 6, 1935, Abbott Papers, C. A. Addenda; Grace Abbott to Elisabeth Shirley Enochs, Sept. 25, 1937, copy of letter supplied by E. Enochs.

17. Interview with Martha Eliot, July 6, 1973; Winifred A. Walsh, "Grace Abbott and Social Action, 1934–39" (Ph.D. dissertation, University of Chicago, 1965), p. v.

18. G. Abbott to Charlotte Abbott, June 13, July 14, Sept. 25, 1938, Abbott Papers, C. A. Addenda.

19. G. Abbott to C. Abbott, Aug. 22, 1938, Abbott Papers, C. A. Addenda; G. Abbott to S. P. Breckinridge, Sept. 2, 1938, Breckinridge Papers, Box 5; interview with Walter Friedlander, Feb. 26, 1973; "The German National Child Welfare Law," *Social Service Review*, 4 (1930), 608–28; Walter Friedlander and Earl Dewey Myers, *Child Welfare in Germany before and after Naziism* (Chicago: University of Chicago Press, 1940). This account was begun by Myers as a doctoral dissertation. He died unexpectedly before its completion. Friedlander later revised and extended it considerably. As Grace Abbott wrote, "Much more of it is Friedlander's than Myers'," G. Abbott to S. P. Breckinridge, Sept. 2, 1938.

20. G. Abbott to J. Addams, Sept. 20, 1933, Abbott Papers, Box 28, Folder 1; G. Abbott to Lillian Wald, Jan. 6, 1935, ibid., Box 72, Folder 1; J. Addams to G. Abbott, Mar. 10, 1935, ibid., Box 28, Folder 1, G. Abbott to Elisabeth Shirley Enochs, Aug. 12, 1936, copy supplied by E. Enochs; Jane Addams, *My Friend, Julia Lathrop* (New York: Macmillan Co., 1935).

21. G. Abbott to C. Abbott, Oct. 14, 1938, Nov. 26, 1938, Dec. 23, 1938, Jan. 3, 1939, Abbott Papers, C. A. Addenda.

22. G. Abbott to C. Abbott, Jan. 16 and Feb. 8, 1939, Abbott Papers, C. A. Addenda; Mary Zahrodsky to Charlotte Abbott, May 6, 1939, ibid.; Arthur Abbott to Othman Abbott, Jr., June 8, June 16, and June 17, 1939, ibid.; Charlotte Abbott to Othman A. Abbott, Jr., June 17, 1939, ibid.; Arthur G. Abbott to Othman A. Abbott, Jr., June 20, 1939, ibid.

23. Felix Frankfurter, "Grace Abbott: Social Inventor," *The Child*, 4 (Aug. 1939), 49.

24. Invitation to E. Abbott from Bethlehem Fairfield Shipyards, Inc. and the U.S. Maritime Commission to attend the launching of the S.S. *Grace Abbott*, on Oct. 10, at 11:30 a.m., Abbott Papers, C. A. Addenda.

25. Edith Abbott, in "Voice of the People," *Chicago Daily Tribune*, Feb. 6, 1941; Edith Abbott to Josephine Roche, Mar. 11, 1941, Josephine Roche Papers.

26. E. Abbott to Mrs. Joseph T. Bowen, Sept. 29, 1949, Abbott Papers, Box 2, Folder 9; E. Abbott to Josephine Roche, Jan. 4, 1950, Josephine Roche Papers.

27. Interview with Wilma Walker, July 12, 1973.

28. "A Report of the 78th National Conference of Social Work," *The Survey*, 87 (June 1951), 278.

29. E. Abbott, "A Sister's Memories," *Social Service Review*, 13 (Sept. 1939), 352–53.

30. Arthur G. Abbott to Charlotte Abbott, July 22 and July 28, 1957, Abbott Papers, C. A. Addenda.

31. Wayne McMillen to A. G. Abbott, Aug. 1, 1957, Abbott Papers, C. A. Addenda.

32. "1930—Twentieth Anniversary—1950, The Anniversary Dinner," *Public Welfare*, 9 (Jan. 1951), 4.

PUBLISHED WORKS OF
EDITH AND GRACE ABBOTT

PUBLISHED WORKS OF EDITH ABBOTT

"Wage Statistics in the Twelfth Census." *Journal of Political Economy*, 12 (June 1904), 339–61.
"Are Women Business Failures?" *Harper's Weekly*, 49 (Apr. 8, 1905), 496.
"Wages of Unskilled Labor in the United States." *Journal of Political Economy*, 13 (June 1905), 321–67.
The Wages of Unskilled Labor in the United States, 1850–1900. Chicago: University of Chicago Press, 1905.
"Harriett Martineau and the Employment of Women in 1836." *Journal of Political Economy*, 14 (Dec. 1906), 614–26.
"Employment of Women in Industries: Twelfth Census Statistics." *Journal of Political Economy*, 14 (Jan. 1906), 14–40 (with Breckinridge).
"Industrial Employment of Women in the United States." *Journal of Political Economy*, 14 (Oct. 1906), 461–501.
"Woman Suffrage Militant: The New Movement in England." *The Independent*, 61 (Nov. 29, 1906), 1276–78.
"Employment of Women in Industries: Cigar Making—Its History and Present Tendencies." *Journal of Political Economy*, 15 (Jan. 1907), 1–25.
"Municipal Employment of Unemployed Women in London." *Journal of Political Economy*, 15 (Nov. 1907), 513–30.
"Women in Manufactures," *Journal of Political Economy*, 15 (Dec. 1907), 619–24 (with Breckinridge and Anne S. Davis).
"A Study of the Early History of Child Labor in America." *American Journal of Sociology*, 14 (Nov. 1908), 15–37.
"English Working Women and the Franchise." *Atlantic*, 102 (Sept. 1908), 343–46.
"Employment of Women in Cotton Mills." *Journal of Political Economy*, 16 (Nov. 1908), 602–21, 680–92; 17 (Jan. 1909), 19–35.
"Women in Industry: The Manufacture of Boots and Shoes." *American Journal of Sociology*, 15 (Nov. 1909), 335–60.
"Child Labor Legislation." *Elementary School Teacher*, 9 (1909), 511–16 (with Breckinridge).

"Chicago's Housing Problem: Families in Furnished Rooms." *American Journal of Sociology*, 16 (Nov. 1910), 289–308 (with Breckinridge).

Woman in Industry. A Study of American Economic History. New York: Appleton and Co., 1910. Revised 1919.

The Housing Problem in Chicago. Chicago: University of Chicago Press, 1910–12 (with Breckinridge).

"English Poor-Law Reform." *Journal of Political Economy*, 19 (Jan. 1911), 47–59.

"Housing Conditions in Chicago, III: Back of the Yards." *American Journal of Sociology*, 16 (Jan. 1911), 433–68 (with Breckinridge).

"Chicago Housing Conditions, IV: The West Side Revisited." *American Journal of Sociology*, 17 (July 1911), 1–34 (with Breckinridge).

"South Chicago at the Gates of the Steel Mills." *American Journal of Sociology*, 17 (Sept. 1911), 145–76 (with Breckinridge).

Finding Employment for Children Who Leave the Grade Schools to Go to Work: Report to the Chicago Woman's Club, the Chicago Association of Collegiate Alumni, and the Womens City Club. Chicago: Hollister Press, 1911 (with Breckinridge and Anne S. Davis).

"Women in Industry: The Chicago Stockyards." *Journal of Political Economy*, 19 (Oct. 1911), 632–54 (with Breckinridge).

"The First Chief of the Children's Bureau." *Life and Labor*, 2 (Oct. 1912), 299–301.

Wage-earning Women and the State: A Reply to Miss Minnie Bronson. Boston: Equal Suffrage Association for Good Government, 1912 (with Breckinridge).

"Women's Wages in Chicago: Some Notes on Available Data." *Journal of Political Economy*, 21 (Feb. 1913), 143–58.

"Public Pensions to Widows and Children." *American Economic Review*, 3 (June 1913), 473–78.

"A Forgotten Minimum Wage Bill." *Life and Labor*, 5 (Jan. 1915), 13–16.

"Progress of the Minimum Wage in England." *Journal of Political Economy*, 23 (Mar. 1915), 268–77.

"Statistics Relating to Crime in Chicago." In *Report of the City Council Committee of Chicago on Crime in the City of Chicago*, pp. 19–88. Chicago: City Council Committee, 1915.

"The Copycat Vote." *New Republic*, 2 (Apr. 24, 1915), 304.

"Education for Social Work." In Department of Interior, Bureau of Education, *Report of the Commissioner of Education for the Year Ended June 30, 1915*, vol. 1 (Washington: Government Printing Office, 1915).

"Field-Work and the Training of the Social Workers." In *Proceedings of the National Conference of Charities and Correction at the Forty-Second An-*

nual Session held in Baltimore, Maryland, May 12–19, 1915, pp. 615–21. Chicago: Hildmann Printing Co., 1915.

"Statistics in Chicago Suffrage." *New Republic*, 3 (June 12, 1915), 151.

"Are Women a Force for Good Government?" *National Municipal Review*, 4 (July 1915), 435–47.

The Real Jail Problem. Chicago: Juvenile Protective Association of Chicago, 1915.

The One Hundred and One County Jails of Illinois and Why They Ought to Be Abolished. Chicago: Juvenile Protective Association of Chicago, 1916.

"Cheap Clothes and Nasty." *New Republic*, 4 (Jan. 1, 1916), 217–19.

"The Woman Voter and the Spoils System in Chicago." *National Municipal Review*, 5 (July 1916), 460–65.

"Administration of the Illinois Funds-to-Parents Law." United States Department of Labor Bulletin 212, pp. 805–10. Washington: Government Printing Office, 1917.

"The Experimental Period of Widows Pension Legislation." In *Proceedings of the National Conference of Social Work*, 1917, pp. 154–65.

"Charles Booth, 1840–1916." *Journal of Political Economy*, 25 (Feb. 1917), 195–200.

"The War and Women's Work in England." *Journal of Political Economy*, 15 (July 1917), 641–78.

"Field Work Training with Social Agencies." In *Report of the Association of Urban Universities*, November, 1917, pp. 92–103. Concord, N.H.: Rumford Press, 1917–18.

Truancy and Non-Attendance in the Chicago Schools: A Study of the Social Aspects of the Compulsory Education and Child Labor Legislation of Illinois. Chicago: University of Chicago Press, 1917 (with Breckinridge).

Democracy and Social Progress in England. University of Chicago War Papers, 8. Chicago: University of Chicago Press, 1918.

"The Social Case Worker and the Enforcement of Industrial Legislation." In *Proceedings of the National Conference of Social Work*, 1918, pp. 312–19.

"Pensions, Insurance and the State." In *Proceedings of the National Conference of Social Work*, 1918, pp. 388–89.

"Crime and the War." *Journal of the American Institute of Criminal Law and Criminology*, 9 (May 1918), 32–45.

"Health Insurance in Great Britain." In *Report of the Health Insurance Commission of the State of Illinois*, May 1, 1919, pp. 600–624. Springfield: Illinois State Journal Co., 1919. Also in *Report of the Ohio Health and Old Age Insurance Commission, February, 1919*, pp. 312–40. Columbus: F. J. Heer Printing Co., 1919.

"Probation and Suspended Sentence" (Report of Committee "B" of the

Institute). *Journal of the American Institute of Criminal Law and Criminology*, 10 (Nov. 1919), 341–50.

The Administration of the Aid-to-Mothers Law in Illinois. U.S. Children's Bureau. Washington: U.S. Government Printing Office, 1921 (with Breckinridge).

"The Promise and Practice of Social Legislation." *University Journal* (alumni edition, University of Nebraska), 17 (July 1921), 4–11.

The Delinquent Child and the Home. New York: Russell Sage Foundation, 1921 (with Breckinridge).

"Police Brutality in Chicago." *The Nation*, 114 (Mar. 8, 1922), 286–87.

"Tragedy of the Excess Quota." *New Republic*, 30 (Mar. 8, 1922), 52–53.

"The English Census of 1921." *Journal of Political Economy*, 30 (Dec. 1922), 827–40.

Discussion of "Immigration under the Percentum Limit Law," by W. W. Husband. In *Proceedings of the National Conference of Social Work*, 1922, pp. 463–66.

What the Women of Illinois Ought to Know and Ought to Do about the Questions of Social Hygiene: A Report Submitted to the Committee Appointed at the Request of the Joint Conference of the Women's Clubs of Chicago, 1922.

"Recent Statistics Relating to Crime in Chicago." *Journal of the American Institute of Criminal Law and Criminology*, 13 (Nov. 1922), 329–58.

"Training in Case Work and Special Administrative Problems in a University." In *The Social Service of the Courts: Proceedings of the Sixteenth Annual Conference of the National Probation Association*, 1922, pp. 59–68. New York: National Probation Association, 1923.

"The English Census of 1921." *Journal of Political Economy*, 30 (Dec. 1922), 827–40.

"Is One Per Cent Quarantine a Public Health Measure?" *Illinois League of Women Voters Bulletin*, 3 (1923), 7–9.

"Federal Immigration Policies, 1864–1924." *University Journal of Business*, 2 (1924), 133–56, 347–67, 455–80.

"Immigration Legislation and the Problems of Assimilation." In *Proceedings of the National Conference of Social Work*, 1924, pp. 82–91.

Immigration: Select Documents and Case Records. Chicago: University of Chicago Press, 1924.

"English Statistics of Pauperism during the War." *Journal of Political Economy*, 33 (Feb. 1925), 1–32.

Historical Aspects of the Immigration Problem. Chicago: University of Chicago Press, 1926.

"Training for the Policewoman's Job." *Woman Citizen*, 10 (Apr. 1926), 30.

"The Civil War and the Crime Wave of 1865–70." *Social Service Review*, 1 (June 1927), 212–34.

"The Webbs on the English Poor Law." *Social Service Review*, 3 (June 1929), 252–69.

Report on Crime and Criminal Justice in Relation to the Foreign Born, National Commission on Law Observance and Enforcement. Washington: Government Printing Office, 1931.

Social Welfare and Professional Education. Chicago: University of Chicago Press, 1931. 2nd ed. 1942.

"Poor People in Chicago." *New Republic*, 72 (Oct. 5, 1932), 209.

"The Fallacy of Local Relief." *New Republic*, 72 (Nov. 9, 1932), 348–50.

"The Crisis in Relief." *The Nation*, 137 (Oct. 11, 1933), 400–402.

"Abolish the Pauper Laws." *Social Service Review*, 8 (Mar. 1934), 1–16.

"Don't Do It, Mr. Hopkins!" *The Nation*, 140 (Jan. 9, 1935), 41–42.

"Evictions during the Chicago Rent Moratorium Established by the Relief Agencies, 1931–1932." *Social Service Review*, 9 (Mar. 1935), 34–57 (with Katherine Kiesling).

"The Pauper Laws Still Go On." *Social Service Review*, 9 (Dec. 1935), 731–56.

"Jane Addams Memorial Service." In *Proceedings of the National Conference of Social Work*, 1935, pp. 3–5.

The Tenements of Chicago, 1908–1935. Chicago: University of Chicago Press, 1936 (with Breckinridge).

"Federal Relief Sold down the River." *The Nation*, 142 (Mar. 18, 1936), 346.

"Training for the Public Welfare Services." *Public Welfare News*, 4 (Mar. 1936), 5.

"Public Welfare and Politics." In *Proceedings of the National Conference of Social Work*, 1936, pp. 27–45; also in *Social Service Review*, 10 (Sept. 1936), 395–412.

"Public Assistance—Whither Bound?" In *Proceedings of the National Conference of Social Work*, 1937, pp. 3–25.

Some American Pioneers in Social Welfare: Select Documents with Editorial Notes. Chicago: University of Chicago Press, 1937.

"Is There a Legal Right to Relief?" *Social Service Review*, 12 (June 1938), 260–75.

"Poor Law Provision for Family Responsibility." *Social Service Review*, 12 (Dec. 1938), 598–618.

"A Sister's Memories." *Social Service Review*, 13 (Sept. 1939), 351–408.

"The Children's Amendment Moves on to Victory: Federal Regulation of Child Labor." *Social Service Review*, 13 (Sept. 1939), 409–30.

"Unemployment Relief a Federal Responsibility." *Social Service Review*, 14 (Sept. 1940), 438–52.
"Relief, the No Man's Land, and How to Reclaim It." In *Proceedings of the National Conference of Social Work*, 1940, pp. 187–98.
Public Assistance. Chicago: University of Chicago Press, 1940.
United States, 76th Cong., 3rd Sess., House, Select Committee to Investigate the Interstate Migration of Destitute Citizens, Aug. 10, 20, and 21, 1940, pp. 1179–90.
"Work or Maintenance: A Federal Program for the Unemployed." In *Proceedings of the National Conference of Social Work*, 1941, pp. 332–43; revised in *Social Service Review*, 15 (Sept. 1941), 520–32.
"Twenty-one Years of University Education for the Social Services, 1920–41." A Report to the Alumni with a Register of Alumni Who Received Higher Degrees, 1920–1942, and Their Dissertation Subjects. *Social Service Review*, 15 (Dec. 1941), 670–705. Reprinted for private distribution by the School of Social Service Administration. Chicago: University of Chicago Press, 1943.
"Juvenile Delinquency during the First World War 1914–1918." *Social Service Review*, 17 (June 1943), 192–212.
"Some Charitable Bequests in Early English Wills (1284–1580) and Statutes (1414–1601) to Protect Charitable Gifts." *Social Service Review*, 20 (June 1946), 231–46.
"Three American Pioneers in International Social Welfare." *The Compass*, 28 (May 1947), 6.
"Work of Thomas H. Gallaudet and the Teaching of the Deaf." *Social Service Review*, 21 (Sept. 1947), 375–86.
"Sophonisba P. Breckinridge: Over the Years." *Social Service Review*, 22 (Dec. 1948), 417–23.
"Grace Abbott and Hull-House, 1908–21. Parts I and II." *Social Service Review* 24 (Sept., Dec. 1950), 374–94 and 493–518.
"The Survey Award: Acceptance Speech." In *Proceedings of the National Conference of Social Work*, 1951, pp. ix–x.
"The Hull-House of Jane Addams." *Social Service Review*, 26 (Sept. 1952), 334–38.

The library of the London School of Economics and Political Science contains two additional publications by Edith Abbott. They are as follows:

Co-operators and the Labour Party. Manchester, Eng.: Co-operative Wholesale Society's Works, 1906.
The Early Days of a Co-operative Society. Some Hints on Rules and Manage-

ment. Issued by the Co-operative Union as a Guide to Young Societies. Manchester, Eng.: Co-operative Wholesale Society's Printing Works, 1909 (with T. B. Butterworth).

These two pamphlets revealed no identifying information about the author (and in one case, of the co-author) other than name. A careful reading led me to believe that neither was written by the Edith Abbott of my study. The language did not clearly reflect her writing style and in some passages suggested that the author was English. Edith Abbott of Nebraska would not have presumed to speak as an English woman; she was highly conscious of her own national identity and of being a guest in another country. Furthermore, the content of the pamphlets is concerned mainly with domestic matters and details peculiar to a British cooperative society, rather than the broader developmental and philosophical matters that one would expect to interest Edith Abbott. I consulted with Mr. R. Garratt, Information Officer and Librarian of Co-operative Union Ltd. in Manchester. He was unable to identify the Edith Abbott who wrote the pamphlets. The *Dictionary of Labour Biography* makes no reference to either an English or an American Edith Abbott and the publishers of the *Dictionary* had nothing in their files about an Edith Abbott. Althought the second pamphlet carries a 1909 imprint, the *International Cooperative Bibliography*, published by the International Cooperative Alliance in 1906, lists this pamphlet as first published in 1904, a year earlier than Edith Abbott went to England. Mr. Garratt agreed that it is highly unlikely that the two pamphlets were written by the American Edith Abbott, but has been unable to bring any further information to light as to the identity of an English author.

PUBLISHED WORKS OF GRACE ABBOTT

"The Immigrant and Municipal Politics." *National Municipal League Review*, 2 (1905–9), 148–56.
"The Chicago Employment Agency and the Immigrant Worker." *American Journal of Sociology*, 14 (Nov. 1908), 289–305.
"A Study of the Greeks in Chicago." *American Journal of Sociology*, 15 (Oct. 1909), 379–93.
"The Bulgarians of Chicago." *Charities and the Commons*, 21 (1909), 653–60.
"Education of Foreigners in American Citizenship." In *Proceedings of the National Conference for Good City Government*, Philadelphia, 1910, pp. 375–84.

"Adjustment—Not Restriction." *The Survey*, 25 (Jan. 7, 1911), 527–29.

Report of the Commission on Immigration. The Problem of Immigration in Massachusetts. House Report 2300. Boston: Wright and Potter Printing Company, State Printers, 1914.

"The Midwife in Chicago." *American Journal of Sociology*, 20 (Mar. 1915), 684–99.

"The Democracy of Internationalism." *The Survey*, 36 (Aug. 5, 1916), 478–80.

The Immigrant and the Community. New York: Century Company, 1917.

"The Immigrant as a Problem in Community Planning." In *Twelfth Annual Meeting of the American Sociological Society Held in Philadelphia, Pa., December 27–29, 1917*, pp. 166–73. Chicago: University of Chicago Press, 1918.

"Enforcement of the U.S. Child Labor Law." In *Addresses and Proceedings, 56th Annual Meeting, National Education Association*, vol. 56, pp. 657–61. Washington: National Education Association of the United States, 1918.

"After Suffrage—Citizenship." *The Survey*, 44 (Sept. 1, 1920) 655–57.

Educational Needs of Immigrants in Illinois, and *The Immigrant and the Coalmining Communities in Illinois.* Springfield: Illinois State Immigrants' Commission, 1920.

"The Immigrant as a Miner." *The Survey*, 46 (June 4, 1921), 311–12.

Administration of the First Federal Child-Labor Law. C. B. Publication no. 78. Washington: Government Printing Office, 1921.

"Administration of the Sheppard-Towner Act: Plans for Maternal Care," *Transactions of the American Child Hygiene Association*, 130 (1922), 194–201.

"Federal Aid for the Protection of Maternity and Infancy." *American Journal of Sociology*, 12 (Aug. 1922), 734–42.

"Fundamental Questions Now before Us." In *Proceedings of the National Conference of Social Work*, 1922, pp. 21–24.

"Saving America's Children." *Current History Magazine of the New York Times*, 17 (Jan. 1923), 646–52.

"Ten Years Work for Children." *North American Magazine*, 218 (Aug. 1923), 189–200.

"Child Labor." In *Proceedings of the National Conference of Social Work*, 1923, pp. 109–10.

"Proposed Child Labor Amendment to the Constitution." *Homiletic Review*, 87 (Jan. 1924), 56–58.

"Child Labor Movement." *North American Magazine*, 220 (Dec. 1924), 223–37.

"History of Child Labor Laws." *Woman Citizen*, 9 (Dec. 27, 1924), 11.

"Public Protection of Children." In *Proceedings of the National Conference of Social Work*, 1924, pp. 3–14.

"What Have They Done?" *The Independent*, 115 (Oct. 24 1925), 475.

"Law's Protection of Children." *School and Society*, 24 (July 17, 1926), 64–68.

"Trend in Juvenile Delinquency Statistics." *Journal of the American Institute of Criminal Law and Criminology*, 17 (Aug. 1926), 167–72.

"What Is the Future of the Day Nursery?" *Child Health Bulletin*, 3 (Feb. 1927), 33–36.

"Developing Standards of Rural Child Welfare." In *Proceedings of the National Conference of Social Work*, 1927, pp. 26–37.

"Accomplishments and a Challenge." *Public Health Nurse*, 20 (Dec. 1928), 616–19.

"Casework Responsibility of Juvenile Courts." *Social Service Review*, 3 (Sept. 1929), 395–404.

"Casework Responsibility of Juvenile Courts." In *Proceedings of the National Conference of Social Work*, 1929, pp. 153–62.

"Looking Fore and Aft in Child Labor." *The Survey*, 63 (Dec. 15, 1929), 333–34.

"County vs. the Community as an Administrative Unit." *Social Service Review*, 4 (Mar. 1930), 11–16.

"The Federal Government in Relation to Maternity and Infancy." *Annals of the American Academy of Political and Social Science*, 151 (Sept. 1930), 92–101.

"What to Expect of the White House Conference." *Parent's Magazine*, 5 (Oct. 1930), 11.

"Safeguarding the Child in America." *Current History*, 33 (Mar. 1931), 820–40.

"Safeguarding the Rights of Childhood." *American Federationist*, 38 (May 1931), 537–44.

"Developing and Protecting Professional Standards in Public Welfare Work." *Social Service Review*, 5 (Sept. 1931), 384–94.

"Twenty Years of the Children's Bureau." *Social Service Review*, 6 (Mar. 1932), 140–44.

"The Child." *American Journal of Sociology*, 37 (May 1932), 949–55.

"A Ten Year Child Welfare Plan." *Parent's Magazine*, 7 (May 1932), 16–18.

"Improvement in Rural Public Relief: The Lessons of the Coal-Mining Communities." *Social Service Review*, 6 (June 1932), 183–222.

"Twentieth Anniversary of the Birth of the Federal Children's Bureau." In *Proceedings of the National Conference of Social Work*, 1932, pp. 45–51.

"Human Cost of Unemployment." *American Labor Legislation Review*, 23 (Mar. 1933), 29–35.

"The Child." *American Journal of Sociology*, 38 (May 1933), 880–88.

"May Day. Child Health Day, 1933." *Child Health Bulletin*, 9 (May 1933), 81–82.

"Child Health Recovery." *The Survey*, 69 (Aug. 1933), 349.

"The Government and Youth in a Troubled World." In *Proceedings of the National Conference of Social Work*, 1933, pp. 291–300.

"The Changing Position of Women." In Charles A. Beard, ed., *A Century of Progress*. Chicago: Harper & Bros., Publishers, 1933.

"New Measures of Values." Address in accepting the Gold Medal of the National Institute of Social Sciences, *Journal of the National Institute of Social Sciences*, 16–19 (May 1931–Dec. 1934).

"What about Mothers' Pensions Now?" *The Survey*, 70 (Mar. 1934), 80–81.

"Recent Trends in Mothers' Aid." *Social Service Review*, 8 (June 1934), 191–210.

"Toward Security in Health." *The Survey*, 71 (Feb. 1935), 42–43.

"Juvenile Courts." *The Survey*, 72 (May 1936), 131–33.

"The Juvenile Court and a Community Program for Treating and Preventing Delinquency." *Social Service Review*, 10 (June 1936), 227–42.

"O Tempora, O Mores." *The Survey*, 72 (July 1936), 199–200.

"How Secure Administrative Skills with Professional Competence for State and Local Public Welfare Service?" In *Proceedings of the National Conference of Social Work*, 1936, pp. 494–508.

"Time to Ratify." *Collier's*, 99 (Apr. 1937), 86.

The Child and the State. 2 vols. Chicago: University of Chicago Press, 1938.

Work Accidents to Minors in Illinois. Chicago: University of Chicago Press, 1938 (with Earl E. Klein).

"Federal Regulation of Child Labor 1906–38." *Social Service Review*, 13 (Sept. 1939), 409–30.

"War and Social Security." *Social Service Review*, 13 (Dec. 1939), 684–87.

From Relief to Social Security: The Development of the New Public Welfare Services and Their Administration. Edited by Edith Abbott. Chicago: University of Chicago Press, 1941.

TESTIMONY OF GRACE ABBOTT BEFORE VARIOUS CONGRESSIONAL COMMITTEES

Immigration

United States, 62nd Cong., 2nd Sess., House, Committee on Immigration and Naturalization, *Relative to the Further Restriction of Immigration: Hearings*, 1912, pp. 52–61.

Child Labor

United States, 67th Cong., 4th Sess., Senate, Committee on the Judiciary, *Child Labor Amendment to the Constitution: Hearings before a Subcommittee on S. J. Res. 200, S. J. Res. 224, S. J. Res. 232, S. J. Res. 256 and S. J. Res. 262*, Jan. 10, 1923, pp. 22–49. Ibid., Jan. 15, 1923, pp. 92–94; Jan. 18, 1923, pp. 113–20.

United States, 68th Cong., 1st Sess., House, Committee on the Judiciary, *Proposed Child Labor Amendments to the Constitution of the United States: Hearings*, 1924, pp. 17–28, 29–58, 257–86.

United States, 75th Cong., 1st Sess., Senate, Committee on Interstate Commerce, *To Regulate Products of Child Labor: Hearings on S. 592, S. 1976, S. 2068, S. 2226 and S. 2345*, May 12, 18, and 20, 1937, pp. 61–80.

Maternity and Infancy

United States, 70th Cong., 2nd Sess., House, Committee on Interstate and Foreign Commerce, *Child Welfare Extension Service: Hearing on H. R. 14070*, Jan. 24 and 25, 1929, pp. 238–45, 246–48.

United States, 71st Cong., 3rd Sess., House, Committee on Interstate and Foreign Commerce, *Child Welfare Extension Service: Hearings on S. 255 and H. R. 12995*, Jan. 20, 21, and 22, 1931, pp. 70–77.

Reorganization

United States, 68th Cong., 1st Sess., Joint Committee on the Reorganization of the Administrative Branch of the Government, *Reorganization of Executive Departments: Hearings on S. J. 282*, Jan. 7 to 31, 1924, pp. 634–35 (letter).

Relief

United States, 72nd Cong., 2nd Sess., Senate, Committee on

Manufactures, *Relief for Unemployed Transients: Hearings before a Subcommittee on S. 5121*, Jan. 13 to 25, 1933, pp. 23–35.

United States, 72nd Cong., 2nd Sess., Senate, Committee on Banking and Currency, *Further Unemployment Relief through the Reconstruction Finance Corporation: Hearings on S. 5336*, Feb. 2 and 3, 1933, pp. 77–97.

Social Security

United States, 74th Cong., 1st Sess., Senate, Committee on Finances, *Economic Security Act: Hearings on S. 1130*, Jan. 22 to Feb. 20, 1935, p. 1080–91.

United States, 74th Cong., 1st Sess., House, Committee on Ways and Means, *Economic Security Act: Hearings on H. R. 4120*, Jan. 21 to Feb. 12, 1935, pp. 493–99.

Appropriations for U.S. Children's Bureau

United States, 68th Cong., 1st Sess., House, Committee on Appropriations, *Second Deficiency Appropriation Bill, 1924: Hearing before Subcommittee*, 1924, pp. 244–45.

United States, 68th Cong., 1st Sess., House, Committee on Appropriations, *Dept. of Labor, Appropriation Bill, 1925: Hearing before Subcommittee*, 1924, pp. 46–52.

United States, 68th Cong., 2nd Sess., House, Committee on Appropriations, *Appropriations, Dept. of Labor, 1926: Hearing before Subcommittee*, 1925, pp. 46–55.

United States, 69th Cong., 1st Sess., House, Committee on Appropriations, *Appropriations, Dept. of Labor, 1927: Hearing before Subcommittee*, 1926, pp. 75–96.

United States, 69th Cong., 2nd Sess., House, Committee on Appropriations, *Appropriations, Dept. of Labor, 1928: Hearing before Subcommittee*, 1927, pp. 104–23.

United States, 70th Cong., 1st Sess., House, Committee on Appropriations, *Appropriations, Dept. of Labor, 1929: Hearing before Subcommittee*, 1928, pp. 68–80.

United States, 70th Cong., 2nd Sess., House, Committee on Appropriations, *Dept. of Labor, Appropriation Bill, 1930: Hearing before Subcommittee*, 1929, pp. 57–71.

United States, 71st Cong., 2nd Sess., House, Committee on Appropriations, *Dept. of Labor, Appropriation Bill for 1931: Hearing before Subcommittee*, 1930, pp. 63–80.

United States, 71st Cong., 3rd Sess., House, Committee on Appropriations, *Dept. of Labor, Appropriation Bill for 1932: Hearing before Subcommittee*, 1931, pp. 36–40.

United States, 73rd Cong., 2nd Sess., House, Committee on Appropriations, *Dept. of Labor, Appropriation Bill for 1935: Hearing before Subcommittee*, 1934, pp. 135–42.

INDEX

Abbott, Abiel, 5
Abbott, Arthur Griffin, 5, 14, 20, 38, 235, 238
Abbott, Charlotte, 119, 163–64, 165, 233, 234, 246*n*25
Abbott, Edith: childhood and adolescence, 3–14, 238, 247–48*n*11; Brownell Hall experiences, 11–12; early adulthood in Nebraska, 15–25; parental influences, x, 4–7, 20–23, 24, 53; support of parents, 16, 22, 39, 164; teacher in Grand Island, 14; characteristics, xi, 12, 16–17, 19, 22, 23–24, 37, 38, 39, 43–44, 45, 62, 66, 79, 82, 98–99, 119, 159, 160–64, 192, 196, 198–200, 232–33; partnership with sister, xi, 77, 80, 98–99, 159, 162–63, 181, 204, 236; Populist ideology: attitude toward, 15–16; western heritage concept, ix, 15, 24; University of Nebraska experiences, 16, 18–19, 24; teacher in Lincoln, Nebraska, 19; University of Chicago: graduate study, 19, 24, 26–28; coeducation: attitude toward, 26–27, 40, 58; Women's Trade Union League secretaryship, 28–29, 37–38; American Economic Association research assignment, 28–29, 30–31; Association of Collegiate Alumnae Foreign Fellowship, 31; London School of Economics: advanced study at, x, 31–32; and the Webbs, 26, 31–34, 36, 37; and Fabian concepts and strategies, x, 32–33; St. Hilda's settlement residence, 31, 34–35, 37; Wellesley College teaching, 38,

59; Hull-House residence, 35–36, 40, 41–50, 59, 98, 237; and Progressive movement, 16, 41, 46–47, 48–49; woman suffrage, x, 5–6, 36–37, 46–47, 49–51, 53; as pacifist, 237; trade-union movement, 80; relationship with Jane Addams, 97, 100–101; and Sophonisba P. Breckinridge, 26, 27, 28, 29, 40, 58, 60–61, 101, 184, 192, 193–94, 199, 203, 231, 236; interest in prison reform, 61–62, 77; study of crime and the foreign-born for Wickersham Commission, 202; immigration, xi, 68, 77, 193; European travel, 37, 81–82; research on women and children in industry, 28, 29–31, 101–2, 104, 118; Committee on Women in Industry of the Council of National Defense, 118; views on social work education, 63–64, 186, 187, 188–94, 201–2, 227–28; as dean and professor, 195–96, 197–203, 228–30, 236; and Robert Hutchins, 194–97, 236, 237; support for Herbert Hoover in 1928, 166; support for Franklin D. Roosevelt, 212; as advocate for the poor, viii, 204–5, 208–10, 212; honors, 237, 285*n*13; death, 238
Abbott, Elizabeth Griffin: birthdate and place, 4; attends Rockford Female Seminary, 4; teacher and high school principal, 4; courtship and marriage, 4–5; children born to, 5; influences on daughters, 4, 5, 8, 13, 45; characteristics and beliefs, 6, 8, 10–11, 15–16, 20–23;

301

A NOTE ON THE AUTHOR

LELA B. COSTIN *is a professor in the School of Social Work, University of Illinois at Urbana-Champaign. She is the author of* Child Welfare: Policies and Practice, *and a co-author of* Contemporary Social Work *and of* The Licensing of Homes in Child Welfare. *Her publications also include numerous scholarly articles in the areas of child welfare, school social work, and women's history. She is currently engaged in research into historical influences on the development of public policy with respect to child neglect and abuse.*